James Wilson

James Wilson

The Anxious Founder

Michael H. Taylor

LEXINGTON BOOKS
Lanham • Boulder • New York • London

Published by Lexington Books
An imprint of The Rowman & Littlefield Publishing Group, Inc.
4501 Forbes Boulevard, Suite 200, Lanham, Maryland 20706
www.rowman.com

86-90 Paul Street, London EC2A 4NE

Copyright © 2021 by The Rowman & Littlefield Publishing Group, Inc.

All rights reserved. No part of this book may be reproduced in any form or by any electronic or mechanical means, including information storage and retrieval systems, without written permission from the publisher, except by a reviewer who may quote passages in a review.

British Library Cataloguing in Publication Information Available

Library of Congress Cataloging-in-Publication Data
Names: Taylor, Michael H., author.
Title: James Wilson : the anxious founder / Michael H. Taylor.
Description: Lanham : Lexington Books, [2021] | Includes bibliographical references and index. | Summary: "This study includes James Wilson's intellectual, political, and legal contributions in American history. The author also analyzes Wilson's life as a transatlantic success story and looks at the impact of the Scottish Enlightenment on American society, discourse, and government"— Provided by publisher.
Identifiers: LCCN 2021025731 (print) | LCCN 2021025732 (ebook) | ISBN 9781498590792 (cloth) | ISBN 9781498590808 (ebook) | ISBN 9781498590815 (pbk)
Subjects: LCSH: Wilson, James, 1742-1798. | Wilson, James, 1742-1798—Influence. | Founding Fathers of the United States—Biography. | United States—Politics and government—1783-1789. | Constitutional history—United States. | United States. Constitution—Signers—Biography. | Lawyers—Pennsylvania—Biography.
Classification: LCC E302.6.W64 T39 2021 (print) | LCC E302.6.W64 (ebook) | DDC 973.3092 [B]—dc23
LC record available at https://lccn.loc.gov/2021025731
LC ebook record available at https://lccn.loc.gov/2021025732

I would like to dedicate this book to my wife, Dana Harbin. She has made me a better writer and has provided steadfast and unwavering support in the journey to produce this work. She also gave birth to our son, Kevin, who I hope one day will take the time to read the product that has taken so much time away from him and his mother.

Further, I would like to profoundly thank my maternal grandmother, Helen Sites. She encouraged an early love of reading that has carried through my life. Purchasing books, instead of toys, was the greatest lesson I could have learned from her.

Contents

Acknowledgments		ix
Introduction		xi
1	James Wilson Returns to Philadelphia	1
2	Leaving Scotland for America	35
3	Philadelphia 1768—James Wilson, William White, and The Visitant	45
4	Reading 1768—On the Edge of Empire	71
5	Philadelphia 1787—The Constitutional Convention	97
6	The State House Yard Speech—October 6, 1787	129
7	The Anti-Federalists Respond	153
8	Twilight	185
9	Lingering Effects—The Wilson-Roosevelt Doctrine	219
Concluding Thoughts—James Wilson's Contribution		241
References		245
Index		259
About the Author		267

Acknowledgments

First and foremost, I want to express my sincere appreciation for the guidance and mentorship of Professor Peter Hoffer. Shortly after arriving at the University of Georgia to begin work on my Ph.D., Professor Hoffer became my advisor. His wealth of knowledge, his prodigious literary output, and his sincere desire to create a positive experience during my work on what matured into this book helped me become a scholar, a better writer, and to think critically about my teaching.

I initially came to this project while working for the Center for the Constitution at James Madison's Montpelier. Professor Will Harris provided the initial spark which took more than a decade to culminate in this book. I will be forever grateful for his encouragement and introduction to the larger scholarly community.

While at Montpelier, I came to know Professor Ralph Ketchum. He was instrumental in my development as a scholar. The donation of his personal library to Montpelier for use by staff and participants in our programs brought my first encounter with the writings of James Wilson. Professor Ketchum provided guidance, support, and outstanding advice through all stages of this project, from master's thesis, to completed dissertation, and now book.

Among the circle of scholars which I became acquainted with while at Montpelier, Professor John Kaminski has been both a valuable resource and thoughtful critic of the project. Professor Tony Eksterowicz published my first scholarly article and has provided helpful critiques on every phase of my work. Professor Kevin Hardwick was my advisor at James Madison University and has continued to be both a friend and mentor.

My dissertation committee, Dr. Stephen Mihm, Dr. Jennifer Palmer, Dr. Keith Dougherty, and Dr. Iain McLean, have contributed in numerous ways during the various phases of this project. I was fortunate to have the benefit of having Dougherty and McLean on the committee as both are political scientists. In meetings of the American Founding Group, sponsored by Dr. Dougherty, I have been able to read, discuss, and write on a wide range of topics in the field during my active involvement with the group. It was through the AFG that I first met Dr. McLean on a visit to UGA from Oxford in the UK. We share a common interest in James Wilson, and he has provided a much-needed European, and more importantly Scottish, view of my work.

Dr. Mihm and Dr. Palmer have both made significant contributions. Dr. Mihm, first in his graduate course on American Capitalism and then working with me on the completion of my readings for comps on the first half of U.S. History and again with his insightful comments on draft chapters. Dr. Palmer exposed me to the European Enlightenment, particularly the Scottish, which is at the heart of James Wilson's writings. She was particularly central to the work found in chapter 3, but her influence was felt throughout the project.

In 2015, I was extremely fortunate to receive funding from several sources to conduct my primary research in Washington, D.C. and Philadelphia. The Graduate School at the University of Georgia and especially the funding available through the Department of History were vital to the completion of this project. Amanda and Greg Gregory are special people and their support of history graduate research at UGA allows graduate students to utilize resources outside of their means.

The support I have received from the University of Georgia main library and the Law Library were essential in obtaining research during my time at UGA. Wherever I have gone, archivists, librarians, and others were extremely helpful in locating and recommending sources. No search engine can ever replace such valuable people.

I must also thank the thousands of students that I have taught over the years, from my time as a social studies teacher at Turner Ashby High School in Bridgewater, VA, to my students at both Gwinnett Technical College and Kennesaw State University, who have pushed me to learn how to communicate complex ideas in ways they could understand. For me, they are the audience as I write and seek to explain the extraordinary life of James Wilson—a man of the eighteenth century introduced to an audience of the 21st.

In the Spring of 2009, my wife, Dana Harbin, encouraged me to pursue a Ph.D. At the time, I was working as an adjunct at James Madison University. She commented that when I came home from teaching it was the happiest that she had seen me after work during our marriage. That set us on the course to where we are today. This book's publication has been a partnership from the beginning. We did it!

Introduction

James Wilson has suffered from poor public relations; he didn't cut the dashing figure of Alexander Hamilton and George Washington, enjoy the longevity and accomplishment of James Madison, or practice a lively personal life, as did Gouverneur Morris and especially Benjamin Franklin. If Americans know Wilson, it most likely is from his portrayal in the stage play and movie *1776*. In *1776*, Wilson is portrayed as nothing more than a sycophant of his former law teacher, John Dickinson. When Wilson is first introduced, he arrives to the Second Continental Congress in a splendid carriage with Dickinson. The way Wilson is portrayed in the production is summed up by a statement from Delaware's Caesar Rodney: "How can anyone see you if you insist on standing in Mr. Dickinson's shadow?"

Wilson was a brilliant political theorist, engaging and forceful debater, and far-sighted visionary; however, he suffered a split personality. The political theorist was also an obsessive land speculator who was perpetually grasping for greater financial success. Having accomplished so much for his adopted country, Wilson spent his last days trying, unsuccessfully, to elude his creditors. He suffered the indignity of being jailed, first in New Jersey and finally in North Carolina, for his debts while riding circuit as an associate justice of the United States Supreme Court. Wilson died deep in debt in Edenton, North Carolina on August 21, 1798.

James Wilson grew up less than a dozen miles from the ancient University of St. Andrews in Scotland. His parents were determined that he would live the life of a man of the cloth, but he had other aspirations. He believed that his talents would be better utilized not in a pulpit, but as a member of the bar. After beginning his legal training in Scotland as a clerk, he looked to the west, across the Atlantic, to the vibrant city of Philadelphia.

Wilson immigrated to the colony of Pennsylvania from his native Scotland in the summer of 1765. Upon landing in New York City, he began a journey that saw him emerge as a well-regarded attorney, become a member of the Second Continental and Confederation Congresses, serve as a delegate to the 1787 Constitutional Convention, serve as the leader of the pro-ratification forces in Pennsylvania's convention, become a principal author of the 1790 Pennsylvania constitution, and serve as a founding member of the United States Supreme Court. Unfortunately for him this life filled with such accomplishments in the political arena was not complimented with financial success. James Wilson, as a sitting member of the Supreme Court, died with his young second wife in a rented room above a tavern in Edenton, NC on the run from his creditors. His heavily leveraged financial empire lay in ruins.

Table I.1. James Wilson Timeline

September 14, 1742	Born in Carskerdo, Scotland
Fall 1765	Emigrates to Philadelphia, PA
February 1, 1768	First appearance of *The Visitant* in print
July 2, 1776	Casts the deciding vote in favor of American Independence for the Pennsylvania Delegation to the Continental Congress
May 25 to September 17, 1787	James Wilson plays a pivotal role at the Constitutional Convention
October 6, 1787	Gives the first public defense of Constitutional Convention's proposal in his State House Yard Speech in Philadelphia
November 21 to December 12, 1787	Wilson is the leader of the pro-ratification forces in the Pennsylvania Ratification Convention
September 24, 1789	Appointed by President George Washington as an associate justice of the first United States Supreme Court
September 26, 1789	Confirmed by the U.S. Senate
October 5, 1789	Took the oath of office as an associate justice
September 19, 1793	Marries his second wife, Hannah Gray
August 21, 1798	Died at Edenton, NC
Burial	Johnston Family cemetery
March 7, 1904	Note in *The Washington Post* about the placing of a monument at Wilson's gravesite in Edenton
March 31, 1906	Article in *The Washington Post* about the plans of the James Wilson Memorial Committee to move Wilson's remains to Philadelphia
September 14, 1906	Letter from Lucien Alexander to Theodore Roosevelt
September 17, 1906	Theodore Roosevelt letter to Lucien Alexander
November 20, 1906	Disinterred in Edenton
November 21, 1906	*U.S.S. Dubuque* transits from Norfolk, VA to Philadelphia
November 22, 1906	Reburial in Philadelphia

Wilson's historical reputation has waxed and waned since his death. For nearly a century he was overlooked. But, beginning with praise he received from Max Farrand in 1913 to his prominent place in Clinton Rossiter's sweeping account of the Convention in 1966 and his reemergence as a central figure in discussion of the Constitutional Convention and the ratification process by Richard Beeman in 2009, Pauline Maier in 2010, and Michael J. Klarman in 2016, his reputation is once again on the rise. As previously unavailable or scarce materials on the work of the 1787 Constitutional Convention were published, interest in Wilson rose. Before and after Wilson's disinterment in 1906, there was a brief swell of scholarship published on Wilson, chiefly from the work of two men responsible for his reburial, Burton Alva Konkle and Lucien H. Alexander.

The first significant academic reappraisal of James Wilson came in 1913 in Max Farrand's account of the Constitutional Convention, *The Framing of the Constitution of the United States*, which served as a summary to his overseeing the publication of the three-volume *The Records of the Federal Convention*, which appeared in 1911.

In the final chapter of Farrand's book, he evaluated the contributions of select members at the convention. He gave primary importance to James Madison, but, "Second to Madison and almost on a par with him was James Wilson."[1] He concluded Wilson "[i]n some respects . . . was Madison's intellectual superior, but in the immediate work before them he was not as adaptable and not as practical."[2] Despite this, Wilson "was Madison's ablest supporter."[3] Wilson's principal contribution was his appreciation of the importance "of laying the foundations of the new government broad and deep, and he believed that this could only be done by basing it upon the people themselves."[4] In this pursuit, Farrand concluded that Wilson had experienced "a great measure of success."[5]

Clinton Rossiter's sweeping account of the Convention in 1966 also prominently featured James Wilson. In his evaluation of the delegates, Rossiter agreed with Farrand and rated Wilson: "Second only to Madison—and an honorable second—was the learned, inventive, painstaking lawyer from St. Andrews."[6] Wilson was Madison's trusted ally, as he "debated, drafted, bargained, and voted with unremitting zeal," and Rossiter acknowledged Wilson's contribution, "to give strength and independence to the executive," while quoting Ferrand's assessment of Wilson's efforts to found a government based on a broad popular consent.[7] In the present century, his significant contributions in the drafting and ratification of the Constitution of the United States have garnered new attention.[8]

James Wilson's life is an entry point into the events of the latter half of the eighteenth century and the impact of the Scottish Enlightenment on American society, discourse, and government. To date, there has only been one comprehensive biography published and this more than six decades ago.[9] Previous research on James Wilson has focused, primarily, on his tenure as a member of the first Supreme Court of the United States and his time teaching law at the University of Pennsylvania. This book is NOT a complete biography.

This book provides a new focus upon Wilson's first years in America, particularly his work with William White on *The Visitant*. The only work published on *The Visitant* had been the few pages that Wilson's biographer—Page Smith—devoted to the subject. However, Smith did not examine the series as a whole, nor did he place it within the larger framework of the Enlightenment and the literature culture of 1760s Philadelphia.

The Visitant appeared as a series of essays over a period of six months in the first half of 1768 in the *Pennsylvania Chronicle*. I view Wilson and White's work on *The Visitant* series as a virtual salon. Unlike the salons of Scotland—which were almost exclusively male, and the female-directed salons of France—the virtual salon, which Wilson and White created through their series, encouraged readers to submit comments on the observations of *The Visitant*, and to make contributions of their own. The subject of gender dominated discussion in the series. The proper deportment and role of men in society was an early and recurring subject. However, the dominant theme was that of women—their relationship to each other, to men, the conduct and appreciation of proper conversation, and the pursuit of a spouse. This participation of educated women in public discourse was unique for the time, especially in colonial America.

The virtual salon which Wilson and White created with their readers is a particularly useful avenue into the emerging social arrangements, beliefs, and practices of late 1760s Philadelphia. The authors and their readers have a lot to say about the role of men and women in a society in the early stages of the turbulent period leading up to the American Revolution.

Wilson's other significant literary work, "Considerations on the Nature and Extent of the Legislative Authority of the British Parliament," needs to be viewed in proper context. The pamphlet, written in the latter half of 1768, was not published at the time as it was deemed by friends with which he shared it as potentially damaging to his future prospects as a successful lawyer. The tract did appear but not for another six years.[10]

There exists a wealth of books covering the Constitutional Convention of 1787 in extreme detail—this is not one of them. Wilson's work at the Constitutional Convention is viewed from a new perspective. I will focus on the work of three delegates: James Wilson, Pierce Butler, and Alexander

Hamilton. All three men were born outside of what became the United States. Further, I will examine how these three interact with John Dickinson, Charles Cotesworth Pinckney, and John Rutledge—who were American born, but received extensive education in Europe. Debate on the creation of the Executive, the Senate, and citizenship qualifications for election will serve to frame the work of these delegates.

It was James Wilson who first stepped before the public, on October 6, 1787, to defend the plan put forth by the delegates of the Constitutional Convention. In what became known as the State House Yard Speech, Wilson became the public face of the Federalists, for good and bad. For good as the speech was reprinted throughout the country, reaching a larger audience at the time than those of the more well-known to posterity *Federalist Papers*. For many Americans, it was James Wilson's defense of the proposed constitution with which they were familiar. For bad as he became the figure—in part because of his Scottish heritage—to whom Anti-Federalist writers were drawn and with whose arguments they engaged in their writings.

In the first decade of the twentieth century, James Wilson was used by leaders, particularly President Theodore Roosevelt and industrialist Andrew Carnegie, to justify an expansion of federal powers and activities to address public issues of industrial America. The public ceremonies and attention garnered by the transportation of Wilson's remains from Edenton to Philadelphia in November of 1906 is singularly unique for a founding father and demands attention. Further, a new Wilson-Roosevelt Doctrine of interpretation of the Constitution appeared in legal and political science textbooks until the New Deal.

This book contains three distinct sections—Section One is comprised of chapter 1 and chapter 9, which explain what happened to James Wilson's earthly remains and legacy. In chapter 1, I detail the early twentieth century story of how James Wilson's remains were transported to Philadelphia in November 1906. Then, in chapter 9 I examine the efforts of Theodore Roosevelt and others to use Wilson's legacy as justification for Progressive policies in the early twentieth century. These chapters serve as bookends to Wilson's life in the eighteenth century.

Section Two encompasses chapters 3 and 4 on James Wilson's literary work of 1768. The year 1768 was significant in James Wilson's life. Not only was he a driving force behind *The Visitant*, but he also turned his intellectual attention to the looming imperial crisis. Wilson's pen brought forth "Considerations on the Nature and Extent of the Legislative Authority of the British Parliament." The pamphlet, when written, was far in advance of much colonial thinking, but on the advice of colleagues, he delayed publication until 1774.[11]

After Wilson left Philadelphia for Reading, established a law practice, moved to Carlisle, and embarked on married life, he increasingly turned his attention to politics. He was twice elected to the Pennsylvania Provincial Congress and subsequently selected to serve as a member of the Second Continental Congress and ultimately cast his support as the Philadelphia delegation voted to approve the Declaration of Independence. He served on numerous committees, including the committee on war with John Adams, during the American Revolution.

Section Three is comprised of chapters 5, 6, 7, and 8. I discuss Wilson's work at the Constitutional Convention of 1787—chapter 5; his defense of the proposed constitution on October 6, 1787—chapter 6; his prominence in the debate over ratification of the Constitution—chapter 7; and his tenure as an original justice of the United States Supreme Court—chapter 8. His relationship with fellow justice James Iredell will frame the treatment of Wilson's final years—particularly the difficult challenges of riding circuit.

Gender remained a theme through different facets of Wilson's life. In *The Visitant*, educated women are admired and encouraged; later when he gave his law lectures as the founding member of the law school of the University of Pennsylvania, he again turned to the subject of education and women before a gathering of President Washington, his cabinet, and many members of Congress. After his death in 1798, gender again became a component in the coverage of the transfer of his remains from Edenton to Philadelphia. Headlines across the nation celebrated the reunion of Wilson with his first wife who was buried on the grounds of Christ Church. Further, Theodore Roosevelt's administration used Wilson's political philosophy to argue for the expansion of federal power to include child welfare laws.

James Wilson was an American success story, coupled with a Greek tragedy. He hazarded the journey crossing the Atlantic to begin a new life, one he felt would be worthy of his ambition. However, James Wilson's story had no Hollywood ending. The higher he rose, the more he wanted to achieve. He launched an initiative to finance the building of entire communities and the transportation of immigrants from Europe, to land he owned, but his ambitious dreams outran his financial resources. While a sitting member of the United States Supreme Court, James Wilson was in jeopardy of being impeached for financial mismanagement of his affairs. He saved the Congress of the United States the trouble of impeaching him by dying from a stroke, brought on by contracting malaria, while on the run from his creditors in Edenton, North Carolina on August 21, 1798 at the age of 55.[12] James Wilson's life story is a testament to the success that tens of thousands of Scottish immigrants achieved after their trans-Atlantic voyage, but it also reminds us that not all had a happy ending.

Throughout his life, James Wilson was acutely aware of where his story had begun and where he wanted it to go. He swerved from the path his parents desired him to tread, leading to the pulpit, and chose a potentially more lucrative path far away in British North America. He reunited with his childhood friend in Philadelphia but was impatient to begin his new life. He worked as a college tutor, while quickly securing a law education under the tutelage of one of Pennsylvania's notable attorneys, John Dickinson.

Wilson, like many people eager to achieve success, worried about what the future would hold. Would he find a suitable wife? Have children? Achieve financial success? Become famous? All would come to him in one form or another, but he remained insecure and anxious. In his later years, his financial empire began to crumble, and attention was diverted from his job as a justice of the U.S. Supreme Court to putting out one financial brushfire after another. Despite the quantity of his success, he sought more, particularly schemes to earn more money to secure the vast tracts of land that he desperately worked to retain.

This book presents a more nuanced and complete picture of James Wilson's place within our history and historical memory. His contributions were far greater than just the attention paid to his legal lectures. His is a very human story of a Scottish immigrant who experienced success and acclaim for his activities on behalf of the American people during his public service, but in his personal affairs, and particularly financial life, he suffered the great heights and deep lows worthy of a Greek tragedy.

NOTES

1. Max Farrand, *The Framing of the Constitution of the United States*, (New Haven: Yale University Press, 1913), pp. 197.

2. Farrand, 197–98.

3. Ibid, 198.

4. Ibid, 198.

5. Ibid, 198.

6. Clinton Rossiter, *1787: The Grand Convention*, (New York, The Macmillan Company, 1966), pp. 247–48.

7. Rossiter, 248.

8. See *Collected Works of James Wilson*, eds. Kermit L. Hall and Mark David Hall, 2 vols., (Indianapolis: Liberty Fund, 2007); Richard Beeman, *Plain, Honest Men: The Making of the American Constitution*, (New York: Random House, 2009); Carol Berkin, *A Brilliant Solution: Inventing the American Constitution*, (New York: Harcourt, Inc., 2002); Christopher Collier and James Lincoln Collier, *Decision in*

Philadelphia: The Constitutional Convention of 1787, (New York: Ballantine Books, 2007); Michael J. Klarman, *The Framers' Coup: The Making of the United States Constitution*, (New York: Oxford University Press, 2016); Pauline Maier, *Ratification: The People Debate the Constitution, 1787–1788*, (New York: Simon and Schuster, 2010); James H. Read, *Power versus Liberty: Madison, Hamilton, Wilson, and Jefferson*, (Charlottesville: University Press of Virginia, 2000); and David Stewart, *The Summer of 1787: The Men Who Invented the Constitution*, (New York: Simon and Schuster, 2007).

9. Page Smith, *James Wilson: Founding Father, 1742–1798*, (Chapel Hill: University of North Carolina Press, 1956).

10. James Wilson, "Considerations on the Nature and Extent of the Legislative Authority of the British Parliament," in *Collected Works of James Wilson, Vol. I*, eds. Kermit L. Hall and Mark David Hall, 2 vols., (Indianapolis: Liberty Fund, 2007), pp. 3–31.

11. Ibid.

12. Smith, 388.

Chapter One

James Wilson Returns to Philadelphia

Today, visitors to Independence Hall, when taking the tour given by the Park Service, finish their tour by exiting through the rear of the building, facing north. Crossing Chestnut Street and walking north, up Independence Mall, visitors pass the museum housing the Liberty Bell on the left and at the corner of Market Street and 6th, they see the remains of the presidential residence of George Washington. Crossing Market and continuing north, in the middle of Independence Mall, is the visitor center. At the very northern tip of Independence Mall, across Arch Street, sits the National Constitution Center.

One of the most visited exhibits of the National Constitution Center is Signers' Hall. Here visitors interact with life-sized statues of delegates who were present at the close of the Constitutional Convention on September 17, 1787. Many take the time to shake hands with Ben Franklin (who was intentionally presented with an outstretched hand). Other delegates, such as Alexander Hamilton, James Madison, and especially George Washington, are placed in such a way as to allow patrons to take pictures. In this hall, the Center has turned the delegates of long ago into props for visitors' selfies.[1]

Even here, in a building dedicated to preserving the work of the Constitutional Convention, a particular version of history is presented. In the back corner, away from the rest of the delegates, representations of three particular delegates reside. The three—Elbridge Gerry, George Mason, and Edmund Randolph—refused to sign the final draft of the Constitution on September 17. These delegates have been not just metaphorically, but literally put in a corner. Despite their contributions both prior to, at, and after the Constitutional Convention, they are presented in a way that dims their historical reputation.

Walking into Signers' Hall, moving to the right of the glass sign designating the room as such, you first come to the members of the Pennsylvania delegation. Pennsylvania is at the front of the room, which is dominated by the statue of George Washington. To the left of the table (on Washington's right) stands the modest figure of James Madison. The Pennsylvania delegation consists of a representation of Gouverneur Morris, leaning over a seated Benjamin Franklin, on the right of the table—James Wilson stands to the left of the Pennsylvania delegation, alone. Wilson stands apart from the other Pennsylvania delegates seated at their table, and he is ignored by the public as they eagerly grasp Franklin's outstretched hand for a selfie and comment on Morris' peg leg. For a brief moment in 1906, James Wilson was brought back before the American public and celebrated for his contribution to the nation's founding. How did the effort to remove a Founder from his grave in Edenton, North Carolina and transport him to Philadelphia happen and more importantly, why?

On Wednesday, November 21, 1906, the *U.S.S. Dubuque*, a recently commissioned U.S. Navy patrol boat lay anchored in Delaware Bay enveloped by a heavy fog. The warship bore a distinguished cargo—a new casket containing the earthly remains of a Founding Father. The Philadelphia chapter of the St. Andrew's Society provided the casket; an organization he was president of from 1786–1796.[2] The casket rested on the afterdeck where it was watched over by an honor guard of U.S. Marines.[3] The *Dubuque* was due to arrive at 3pm at the League Island Navy Yard in Philadelphia, PA but, due to the fog, was delayed until early the next morning.[4] How did the remains of a man of the Revolutionary generation, who died in 1798, wind up on a Navy warship in 1906? This chapter tells the tale of how a Founding Father's remains were removed from an unmarked grave in Edenton, NC and transported to Philadelphia for reburial outside of Christ Church.

In a quiet family cemetery, the earthly remains of James Wilson lay undisturbed for more than a century. The cemetery, located on the Hayes Plantation in Edenton, NC, is only a short walk from the city's harbor on a low knoll. Enclosed by a six-foot-tall wrought-iron fence, it is surrounded by closely cropped grass and shaded by a small grove of trees on the side facing the bay. Upon entering the cemetery, one of the first graves encountered is that of Wilson's close friend and fellow member of the U.S. Supreme Court—James Iredell—on the right. Continuing another fifteen feet and on the left a visitor comes upon the plot that once held James Wilson. Due to Wilson's distressed financial situation at the time of his death, no monument, or even headstone, marked the grave.[5]

James Wilson's death in 1798 came at an inopportune time for his historical reputation. Federalists were being eclipsed by Thomas Jefferson's

Republican party and with the election of 1800, they became a minority party which subsequently fell apart after the War of 1812. During Jefferson's first presidential term, Wilson's son, Bird, collected and published some of his father's papers, particularly his law lectures at the University of Pennsylvania. A renewed interest in James Wilson did not arise until the turn of the twentieth century.

At the beginning of Theodore Roosevelt's second presidential term, several figures in Pennsylvania began to research Wilson and inquire as to why his grave was in Edenton, NC and not a place of prominence in Philadelphia. The previous year the American patriot John Paul Jones had been returned to America from a grave in Paris, France with much fanfare. The men seeking to do the same for Wilson wanted a similar high profile with President Roosevelt serving as master of ceremonies—this was not to be.

Roosevelt, and others like Andrew Carnegie, adopted particular writings of James Wilson to justify their drive to increase federal power in the first decade of the twentieth century. They didn't seek to resurrect the man, but his ideas, adapted to buttress their own agendas.

In an account of a visit to the cemetery in February 1904, a local resident, R. M. Lee, took several photographs of the cemetery and drafted an account of what he witnessed for S. Weir Mitchell—a noted physician and author from Philadelphia. Mitchell had secured Lee's services to locate and document the condition of James Wilson's grave. Lee gave some general information locating the graveyard in relation to the town's main street and who was the current owner. In his account, Lee relayed several incorrect facts regarding Wilson—most prominent among these was identifying Wilson as a "Senator of Pennsylvania."[6]

Lee noted, "There is no stone, save that of a rough rock, lying flat on the ground, that marks his resting place, upon which there is no inscription." He then described the other notable members of the cemetery: Justice Iredell; his son, James Iredell, Jr., who was also a judge and, in addition, Governor of North Carolina; and Samuel Johnston who had served as a member of Congress, Governor of North Carolina, U.S. Senator and judge of the Supreme Court of North Carolina. But it was in his description of James Wilson, the reason Lee was there, that local information was found wanting. He wrote, "Senator Wilson, a Northern Senator who came to visit his friend, Senator Johnston, and died on the visit . . . was a member of the Continental Congress from 1775 to 1778, so far as our information goes."[7]

The luster of Wilson's accomplishments as a Pennsylvania delegate to the Second Continental Congress, the casting of his vote in favor of the Declaration of Independence helping to move Pennsylvania into the "Aye" column, his work on various committees during the Revolutionary War, his active and vital participation in both the Constitutional Convention of 1787 and the subsequent Pennsylvania Ratification Convention, his role in drafting a new constitution for Pennsylvania in 1790, and work on the United States Supreme Court were forgotten. He was merely a "Senator of Pennsylvania" who was visiting his friend Senator Johnston when he died in Edenton—all of which was incorrect. His closest friend on the U.S. Supreme Court—James Iredell—was not remembered as such and Iredell's great comfort to Wilson's widow and family by taking care of the arrangements for Wilson's burial and his widow's journey back to Philadelphia were forgotten. How apt Lee's description of Wilson's grave turned out to be as a comment on his legacy for many Americans—including historians.

Shortly after, Mitchell received his first letter on the location and condition of James Wilson's grave, a little-noted blurb appeared in the March 7th edition of *The Washington Post*. The author, Helen DeBerniere H. Wills, identified herself as a genealogist, and member of the North Carolina Daughters of the Revolution and Raleigh Circle, Colonial Dames, lamented that "James Wilson, one of the signers of the Declaration of Independence, sleeps in an unmarked grave in the private lot of the Johnston family at 'Hayes' . . . , [h]is memory deserves better treatment."[8] She noted that for an appropriation of $1,000 by Pennsylvania's legislature, a monument could be erected over the gravesite to commemorate Wilson's service to both the state and nation.

Lee's initial account was accompanied on March 12th by a more detailed description of the cemetery with accompanying photos promised in the letter two weeks earlier. This description of Wilson's grave was more detailed, as it served as a caption for the images. The information related to the lack of a headstone remained, but new information was added. The grave "is bricked in and that is flat with the ground. A wide flat brick or rock is at the west end of the grave with the word 'Wilson' inscribed—there is no other inscription." In describing the condition of the cemetery, Lee noted "the grave, which is covered with weeds and straw, as the old grave yard is not looked after." He had erected a board at the foot of the brick outline of the grave and placed an "X" above the position to mark Wilson's grave in the photos.[9]

After receiving the two letters and photographs from Edenton, Mitchell immediately sat down and submitted a letter to a friend, William D. Lewis, Dean of the Law School at the University of Pennsylvania, on March 14th. Mitchell wanted to "send you two interesting letters from a very respectable colored man at Edentown [sic]"; the information provided by Lee "identify without doubt, the situation and present neglect of the tomb of one of the greatest men Pennsylvania can claim as her own." Mitchell urged Dean Lewis to submit the matter to his colleagues and get a project moving to bring Wilson's remains back to Philadelphia. This was the earliest proposal of what ultimately became the James Wilson Memorial. Mitchell even noted, "It might be made a very great state affair." Additionally, "It would be after all a very small cost, but no matter what it costs, it ought to be done." Mitchell wasn't a lawyer, he just had a number of friends who were, and this is why he had turned to Dean Lewis. "I have taken a good deal of pains to put the matter in shape and if it belonged to my profession, I would put it through, but as it is, I believe as the young ladies say, 'It is up to you.'" However, if Lewis was unsuccessful in initiating a project, Mitchell requested the letters and photos returned.[10]

At the next meeting of the Faculty of the Law Department, on April 4th, Dean Lewis submitted the correspondence and accompanying materials from Mitchell and that of Samuel Dickson, Chancellor of the Law Association of Philadelphia, on the condition of James Wilson's grave and proposals on what should be done. On a motion, the meeting resolved that "the Provost appoint a committee of two to confer with similar committees appointed by the Law Association, the Trustees of the University and other interested bodies in reference to the matter presented by Dr. Weir Mitchell."[11] Mitchell's proposal made little headway for more than a year, until the activities of Burton Alva Konkle and others rekindled interest in the project.

THE JAMES WILSON MEMORIAL COMMITTEE

The activities of the James Wilson Memorial revolve around the contributions of a relatively small group: Secretary of the James Wilson Memorial, Burton Alva Konkle; Lucien H. Alexander, a prominent Philadelphia attorney; industrialist Andrew Carnegie; U.S. Attorney General William H. Moody; and the President of the United States, Theodore Roosevelt. The two key actors were Konkle and Alexander who were the driving force behind the endeavour. However, what began as a collegial working relationship quickly dissolved into a bitter and ultimately public feud between the two men—almost immediately after Wilson was reburied at Christ Church on November 22, 1906.[12]

Burton Alva Konkle was a history professor at Swarthmore College southwest of Philadelphia. He became interested in the history of Pennsylvania while at Swarthmore and decided to write a series of biographies on Pennsylvanians who he felt needed further attention—one of which was James Wilson. Konkle had worked as the Director of the Historical Work for the Pennsylvania State Bar Association and in this capacity became familiar with Wilson.[13] Early in 1905, Konkle helped establish the Pennsylvania History Club, a group comprised of academics, politicians, librarians, archivists, and other like-minded members to "study and discuss the history of Pennsylvania and related subjects, and to aid in the collection, preservation and rendering accessible of historical material relating thereto."[14] The club held their meetings at the Historical Society of Pennsylvania, with the inaugural meeting on May 6th. Future meetings would be at 3pm on the last Saturday in September, November, January, March, and May. Konkle would come to rely upon a number of his fellow club members in the coming work.

While visiting the Valley Forge home of Pennsylvania U.S. Senator Philander C. Knox, a couple of months later on July 17th, Konkle and Knox pondered the idea of bringing Wilson's remains back to the state for reburial in Philadelphia at Christ Church beside his first wife, Rachel.[15] The two men began to plan what type of organization would be needed to bring the proposal to fruition. They would need to construct a memorial committee that would not only be able to speak on behalf of the people of Pennsylvania, but also have credibility in North Carolina to gain the necessary approval for the disinterment. Knox would lend his political support to the committee and Konkle would serve as the committee's secretary from 1905–07.[16] The James Wilson Memorial Committee was born.

According to Konkle's version of the birth of the committee, he reached out to the current owner on whose property the cemetery in Edenton lay, John G. Wood, and the president of the North Carolina Historical Society, William D. Pruden. After obtaining their consent to help in the work of the committee, Konkle turned his attention to his friends and acquaintances in Pennsylvania whose help would be crucial.[17]

Obtaining the necessary legal clearances for the movement of Wilson's remains and their reburial in Philadelphia required the cooperation of the executive branch of Pennsylvania's government. Konkle turned to fellow Pennsylvania History Club members, Attorney General Hampton L. Carson and Governor Samuel W. Pennypacker.[18] He then wrote to Pennsylvania's legislative branch by contacting President (*pro tem*) William C. Sproul and Speaker of the House Harry S. Walton. For the participation of Pennsylvania's judicial branch, he wrote Chief Justice James T. Mitchell. Konkle also reached out to Pennsylvania's junior U.S. Senator, Boies Penrose.[19]

James Wilson's stature as a lawyer, judge, and member of the Constitutional Convention of 1787 led Konkle to reach out to the wider legal community, both in Philadelphia and nationally. He dispatched letters to Francis Rawle, of the American Bar Association, and to Alexander Simpson, of the State Bar Association. Konkle remarked that they were "all personal friends, who authorized me to act in their names with full power to bring about the result in a wise way."[20] This is a telling comment in that Konkle was officially only the Secretary of the committee, not the chairman, but he proceeded to act as if he were. Konkle's interpretation of his importance to the success of the committee's efforts is what ultimately led to the feud with Lucien Alexander.

Late in January 1906, Konkle wrote a letter to Lucien Alexander thanking him for his positive review of Konkle's recently published book on Thomas Williams.[21] To express his thanks, Konkle offered to send Alexander copies of any pictures from his last two books and a picture of James Wilson. It is at this time that the offer to join the committee to bring Wilson's remains back to Philadelphia was made. Alexander would represent the younger members of the Philadelphia bar and all expenses associated with participation on the committee would be covered. Konkle requested a quick answer from Alexander. Earlier in the day, Konkle had received the consent of Judge George Shiras, Jr., former member of the Supreme Court of the United States, to join the committee. The letter closed with a note that a meeting of the committee would be held in the next few weeks.[22]

Alexander promptly replied on the 28th accepting Konkle's offer, and he also informed Konkle that he would avail himself of the opportunity to obtain a copy of the Wilson portrait and several others—the selections would follow in another letter on February 10th.[23] Three weeks later, Konkle wrote Alexander from the Lochiel Hotel in Harrisburg on February 20th. He asked Alexander to write a new letter of acceptance "dated 23rd January, 1906, as I wish to put it among the committee records, and your former one had in it certain personal matters that neither you nor I would want in a public collection."[24] The "personal matters" was the offer of pictures, including one of James Wilson, by Konkle to Alexander as a gift for his positive review of Konkle's book.

As the work of the committee began, Konkle extended invitations to Samuel Dickson, Chancellor of the Law Association of Philadelphia, who became the committee chairman; and to Francis Rawle, ex-President of the American Bar Association, who became the treasurer. William D. Lewis, Dean of the Law Department of the University of Pennsylvania (where James Wilson was the first law professor) and Charles C. Harrison, Provost of the University of Pennsylvania, also joined the committee.[25]

The membership of the committee continued to expand with the addition of physician and author, S. Weir Mitchell; former judge and Congressman, Harry White; ex-Justice of the Supreme Court of the United States George Shiras, Jr.; President of the St. Andrew's Society of Philadelphia Peter Boyd; and the mayor of Philadelphia John Weaver.[26] The net cast for new members, who could further the work of the committee, was wide and bountiful. However, the one catch most prized by everyone—President Theodore Roosevelt himself—remained elusive.

The first official act of the James Wilson Memorial Committee was to secure legal permission to remove Wilson's remains from their current resting place. A document was drawn up, after consultation with local attorneys in North Carolina, and signed by members of the committee—including the latest member, Lucien Alexander—for transmittal to the owner of the property, John Wood. There were no living direct descendants of James Wilson to make the request, and therefore the committee made it on behalf of the citizens of Pennsylvania.[27]

The work of the committee began to attract attention. In the morning edition of February 19th, Lucien Alexander "was startled to find this morning my picture in the Philadelphia Press, identifying me so conspicuously" as a member of the committee. He felt that having his picture accompanying the article "puts me out of proper perspective, and in the minds of those who happen to see it, out of proportion to the real workers in the cause." He remarked that he had good friends in the newspaper business, and they had used an old photo in their archive that he had forgotten about. He liked the attention, but only if it was deserved. It is very likely this was the time when Lucien Alexander began to think hard about his role on the committee and what they were trying to accomplish.[28]

The two most active members of the committee—Konkle and Alexander—began meeting outside of the formally called, and infrequent, meetings of the whole committee. When Konkle was in Philadelphia, at either a meeting of the Pennsylvania History Club or just researching at the Historical Society of Pennsylvania, he was less than a ten-minute walk from Alexander's office. On February 28th, Konkle dropped by Alexander's office on the 7th floor of the Arcade Building at Fifteenth and Market Streets, but found he was out on other business. When Alexander returned to his office, he learned of Konkle's visit and proceeded to send Konkle a telegram asking him to "drop me a line in advance, I will arrange to be in when it suits you to come again."[29] He set down his thoughts regarding the committee in a letter, which he then dispatched to Konkle.[30]

First, Alexander argued that, in light of Wilson's contribution to the adoption of the Declaration of Independence and the creation of the Constitution, it would be appropriate for his remains to "lie in state in Independence Hall for an appropriate period before interment, under guard by a detail of the National Guard of Pennsylvania." Second, given Wilson's work on behalf of the nation, "the national government should assign a warship to bring the remains from Norfolk, the nearest seaport to Edenton, to Philadelphia," preferably, as part of a convoy.[31]

With regard to the memorial service itself, Alexander proposed "it would add emphasis to the national character of Wilson's work if one of the justices of the Supreme Court of the United States—perhaps the Chief Justice—could be induced to be present and deliver a brief address." The committee needed to select a date for the memorial that would facilitate the acceptance of an invitation and ensure the subsequent participation of members of the Court.[32]

Then, turning his attention to participation of the U.S. Navy in bringing Wilson's remains to Philadelphia, Alexander suggested a detail of U.S. Marines "escort the remains to Independence Hall, where they would be received by the National Guard of Pennsylvania." It was important for Wilson to lie in state in the building which witnessed his most important contribution to the nation—service at the Constitutional Convention.

Pennsylvania troops would remain on duty as an honor guard. The next day the members of the delegation—members of the Philadelphia Bar, civil and military authorities, invited guests, and others—would then assemble in Independence Square and then enter the building to hear an oration in the largest room. At the end of the speech, the delegation "would escort the remains to Christ Church burial ground and be present at the interment."[33]

Alexander also suggested an alternative plan where the delegation would escort the remains to Christ Church and then "proceed elsewhere, say to Musical Fund Hall, for the ceremonies." The details would need to suit the number of official members of the delegation. For "[t]he more the proceedings do to throw into prominence Wilson's connection with our national life, the more easy it will be to achieve the monument project." Before sending the letter off, Alexander thought for a moment and added a handwritten note at the bottom: "Perhaps the memorial service could be held *in* Christ Church."[34] This letter, more than any other, established the outline of the form and scale of the James Wilson Memorial. Having only been an official member of the committee for little more than a month, Lucien Alexander put forth a vastly expanded vision of not only the memorial itself, but also placing it within a much larger national scope. This national scope is exactly the line of argument he would use in conversations with Theodore Roosevelt. Konkle and other members of the committee readily agreed to the expanded scope of the memorial, but having secured the adoption of his ideas, the work of seeing them come to pass was principally left to his efforts and perhaps more importantly, Alexander's political connections in Washington.

To secure the cooperation of the intended site for Wilson's reburial—Christ Church—the committee approached representatives of the church requesting their cooperation in the project. On March 7, the vestry minutes recorded that "Mr. William White, Jr. was 'appointed to represent Christ Church on the committee in charge of the internment of the remains of James Wilson in the Church 'Yard.'"[35] The fortunes of the Wilson and White families once again became intertwined. This William White was the great-great-grandson of the Bishop White who was James Wilson's closest friend and neighbor, who lived across the street.

It is unclear whether or not Lucien Alexander informed Burton Alva Konkle that he sought to enlist the aid of the President of the United States in furthering the work of the committee. Alexander corresponded with Roosevelt and his relationship with TR could not have gone unnoticed in Konkle's offer of January 22nd. The same week that the request was made to Christ Church seeking their involvement, Alexander wrote to Roosevelt. The President replied on March 12 in a letter marked "Personal." He had "read with great interest your letters and the accompanying documents." Roosevelt tackled Alexander's request for help with the committee's work first. He wrote: "Will you please get Senator Knox to take that up? I would have to have some initiative in one of the two houses in order to give me any kind of a free hand in the matter so that I could do effective work." [36] The President was willing to help, but he wanted the proper channels to be utilized and this meant a formal request from Pennsylvania's senior Republican senator, Philander C. Knox, who was a founding member of the James Wilson Memorial Committee and had also held the post of U.S. Attorney General when Roosevelt was sworn in as president in September 1901.

Konkle was once again in Philadelphia on March 20th to meet with Alexander on committee business. He visited Alexander's office to again find him not there—Alexander was at the Historical Society of Pennsylvania looking for Konkle. Alexander again wrote a brief letter to Konkle bringing him up to date on his activities. Both men had continued their research into Wilson, both with intentions of publication.[37] Alexander wanted to share news on Wilson he had discovered. "Wilson was at one time '*Director-General' of the Pennsylvania Militia*. This would make the presence of the National Guard of Pa. most appropriate, even imperative from standpoint of the reburial fitness of things." He closed, "Therefore everything is going OK."[38] Verification of Wilson's military status would permit another level of ceremony not available otherwise.

In continuation of his research on Wilson, Konkle dispatched letters to Scotland on March 29th. He wrote to the Universities of St. Andrews, Glasgow, and Edinburgh requesting any and all information on James Wilson as a student.[39] Konkle received a letter from the registrar at the University of Glasgow, W. Innes Addison. He found three different students with the name, but none from the correct birthplace or parents. Information concerning Wilson's early years in Scotland remains fragmentary and elusive, even today.

The first mention of the activities of the James Wilson Memorial Committee, outside of Philadelphia, even though it was not identified as such, came in an editorial published in *The Washington Post* on March 31st. With a headline of "Honor to a Forgotten Patriot," the editorial explained that the subject of the "belated honor" was a name "almost unknown to present-day Americans—James Wilson." The editorial read like a prospectus for the memorial. Through three paragraphs of biographical background and two explaining the agenda of the memorial, it ended with a plea for the participation of members of the United States Supreme Court and, in particular, the presence of President Theodore Roosevelt. The participation of the Court and the President would, it was hoped, "refute, on behalf of the nation, the old idea that republics are ungrateful." Further, an address from Roosevelt would "remov[e] the stigma of long neglect to the memory of such men as James Wilson, and reviv[e] the spirit of gratitude toward the builders of the nation, would be peculiarly appropriate and beneficial."[40] The editorial was orchestrated by Lucien Alexander.

At some point in the last half of March, Alexander had told Konkle that he planned on arranging for a favorable editorial to appear in *The Washington Post*. On April 3rd, four days after the editorial was published, Alexander enclosed a copy with a brief explanation for Konkle. Alexander explained that he knew for a fact "*The Post* is the one paper from which clippings are *not* made for President Roosevelt for the reason that he reads the editorial page each day for himself."[41] Alexander was preparing the ground for a face-to-face meeting with Roosevelt and Attorney General William H. Moody in the White House to formally request their help.

Shortly after the editorial appeared, Konkle and Alexander took the train down to Washington, D.C. for their appointment at the White House.[42] The two men explained the goals of the committee and why the participation of the federal government, especially that of the president, would be so valuable to the success of the memorial. Moody was very familiar with James Wilson's contributions and in a letter sent later that year, Roosevelt noted that Moody was "a great admirer of Wilson."[43] The meeting spurred Roosevelt's interest in Wilson, a feeling that was encouraged by Moody. The President remained non-committal regarding his attendance, but he did promise that if he could not come in person, the Attorney General would be his representative.

Konkle originally desired to hold the event on May 14, 1906, the 119th anniversary of the opening of the Constitutional Convention of 1787, which also happened to coincide with the annual meeting of the Historical Society of Pennsylvania where he was scheduled to give an address entitled "James Wilson and the Constitution," which was billed as the most comprehensive biography of Wilson yet published.[44] However, the date conflicted with the Benjamin Franklin Bi-Centenary and the members of the James Wilson

Memorial Committee decided to delay any further ceremonies until autumn when it was hoped that President Roosevelt and the members of the U.S. Supreme Court would be able to attend.

DIVERGENT INTERESTS

During the summer of 1906, Burton Alva Konkle and Lucien Alexander were pursuing independent avenues to publish their James Wilson research. Konkle envisioned a much larger project that encompassed the first attempt at a comprehensive biography, a collection of Wilson's correspondence, and collection of his writings. He shopped the proposed four-volume work to various publishers, with no success. Alexander worked on a project of his own, one that attracted the attention of the editor of the *North American Review*. He shared a draft of his work with Konkle and received a reply on May 17th.

Konkle reminded Alexander that he was also working on a Wilson project and was reluctant to endorse a publication that could possibly harm his own. He wrote: "Of course I welcome studies of Wilson, but you can readily see that should I get a publisher—*he* would measure values by exclusive proprietorship." One of his concerns was the lack of historical scholarship underpinning the article. "Then, too, I hate to see material go out, for the first time without foot-note credits; it cheapens it among real scholars in the historical field. Authorities are as necessary in that field as in a court." He cautioned Alexander to take this as constructive criticism. Again, Konkle urged him "to put in your foot-note authorities as you would in any argument. It will add to its power among all whose opinions are worthwhile."[45] Alexander continued with his work and the article appeared in print on November 16th, a few days before the events of the James Wilson Memorial.[46]

A few weeks after the meeting at the White House, Alexander began forwarding research on James Wilson to Attorney General Moody for his preparation of a proposed speech at the ceremonies in Philadelphia.[47] Konkle forwarded a copy of his May 14th speech to Moody as well.[48] Alexander willingly shared his research with anyone interested in the work of the committee. As he and Konkle wrote to potential participants in the memorial service, they often sent copies of Alexander's research. For example, when there was an effort to bring British academic and politician James Bryce onto the program, Alexander wrote Konkle, on August 24th, and suggested including the material as "it shows that he does not stand alone in his veneration of Wilson."[49] Bryce, who was then serving in the British cabinet as Chief Secretary for Ireland, would be named the new British Ambassador to the United States, a few months after the Wilson Memorial, in February 1907.

The ultimate prize for the members of the James Wilson Memorial Committee was to secure the active and very public participation of President Theodore Roosevelt. Lucien Alexander wrote the president on September 14th, again urging him to attend the November services in Philadelphia.[50] Roosevelt was vacationing at his home in Oyster Bay, NY and drafted a response to Alexander on September 17th. Roosevelt replied, "[y]ou may be quite right that I may not put James Wilson as high as I should, although I put him very high." He further explained that the role that Alexander wanted him to play at the services was incompatible with his job as President of the United States. Roosevelt noted that it was impossible for him to "do as you desire, which is to use himself and be used as an instrument for securing a different judgment of history on any man."[51]

Alexander proposed that Roosevelt use the memorial service as an opportunity to publicly disagree with recent rulings of the U. S. Supreme Court on corporations, which he and Roosevelt disagreed with. This would be highly inappropriate as a delegation from the court itself would be present and participating in the memorial. Roosevelt closed the letter to Alexander by stating, "My own view is that a public man while dealing with public questions should not be concerned with the proper place in history of either public men, who are dead, but with trying to draw from their lives lessons that will be of consequence to the living."[52] Roosevelt was scheduled to be in Panama inspecting the progress on the construction of the Panama Canal at the time of the memorial in Philadelphia.

A week later, on September 24th, Roosevelt again wrote Alexander from Oyster Bay. "In my speech at Harrisburg I shall make allusions to Wilson's services, of our debt to him, and what we can learn from him."[53] Roosevelt was to be the keynote speaker at the dedication of a new state capitol building on October 4th. This was Roosevelt's final "no" on the subject of attending the memorial services in November, but he did give Alexander the satisfaction of commenting on James Wilson in a very public way—six weeks before the memorial itself. The intent, from the very beginning of Alexander's involvement with the work of the committee, was to secure Theodore Roosevelt's public praise of James Wilson. That was going to happen, just not in Philadelphia, and not on a stage shared with other dignitaries.

In providing a preview of the Harrisburg speech, Roosevelt wrote, "Undoubtedly we can profit beyond measure by supplying to present day needs what Wilson, Hamilton, Marshall, Lincoln and many other great statesmen have said and done in the past; but for the President to attend memorial meetings of each of these statesmen does no good whatever." Instead, the proper role for the President would be "to point a lesson in present day affairs from their lives. The biographies of them and tributes to them should properly come from special students." In other words, tributes and biographies needed to come from trained academics able to examine historical figures and render judgments on their contributions to history.[54]

At the September 25th meeting of The St. Andrew's Society, Lucien Alexander moved that the society provide funds for the cost of preparing the grave at Christ Church to receive Wilson's remains and to provide a new casket. The society voted to approve the request with the stipulation that the cost not exceed $500.[55]

At the end of September, on the 28th, Lucien Alexander wrote to industrialist Andrew Carnegie at his retreat in Scotland—Skibo Castle. Alexander had discussed the work of the James Wilson Memorial Committee with Carnegie while on vacation in Hot Springs, Virginia, earlier in the year. He had promised to share the list of donors to the memorial with Carnegie and confided that "I have raised here all that is necessary for the expenses." Alexander quoted liberally from Roosevelt's most recent letter regarding his plans to pay tribute to Wilson in his Harrisburg speech. He shared with Carnegie Roosevelt's plan to visit Panama and send Attorney General Moody as his representative to the memorial. This also posed a problem as Moody would soon be elevated to the U.S. Supreme Court; he couldn't represent Roosevelt and the executive branch as a member of the Court, so plans were made to hold the memorial prior to Moody taking his judicial oath of office.[56]

Alexander then shared a very brief outline of the memorial services themselves and noted, "The exact date has not been determined upon and will not be until the Supreme Court of the United States has expressed a preference." He then shifted focus to the possible participation of James Bryce, who "seems to have been the first great historian or statesman to call public attention to Wilson's claim to public recognition." Alexander requested Carnegie to "induce Mr. Bryce to come to America for the Memorial Services and perhaps you may be inclined to do so, and as your guest." He explained that the expense of providing for Bryce's transportation for the memorial was "more than the committee could incur." He requested that Carnegie cable him with Bryce's answer to the invitation. To enhance the invitation, the time allotted to other speakers—5 minutes—would be enlarged to as much as an hour, if Bryce so desired, for his speech. Alexander had enclosed a copy of his Wilson memorandum for Carnegie's use. Carnegie dutifully discussed the invitation with Bryce, who was then vacationing with him at Skibo Castle, who declined due to his being a member of the British government as Chief Secretary for Ireland.[57]

ROOSEVELT'S SPEECH IN HARRISBURG

On October 4, President Roosevelt, accompanied by Pennsylvania's two U.S. Senators—Philander Knox and Boies Penrose, traveled on the Presidential train consisting of three coaches, with his observation car Mayflower at the end, to the events in Harrisburg dedicating the new Capitol Building.[58] Roosevelt was slated to give the keynote address—paying tribute to the new home of Pennsylvania's government, but also fulfilling his promise to Lucien Alexander to acknowledge the nation's debt to James Wilson. Festivities had begun the day before under brilliant fall sunshine, but on this day, a weather front had moved in after 2 a.m., obscuring the moon and unleashing a steady downpour.[59]

The dedication ceremonies, with the President in attendance, were expected to attract the "greatest crowd" ever assembled within the city.[60] In coverage of the event the next day, *The Philadelphia Inquirer* estimated that at least "[s]ixty thousand strangers were fellow guests of Harrisburg with the President today."[61] Including the city's own population in attendance, the paper determined that "at least 100,000 persons stood about Capitol Hill listening to the exercises."[62] The weather had kept some who had wanted to attend home, especially those who lived nearby and hadn't traveled to the city on the numerous special excursion trains, but the crowd was still impressive to welcome Roosevelt.

Prior to his arrival in the city, the President was apprised of the plight of two young patients in the city's hospital, which lay just outside of the city near the path of the Presidential train. The two boys were heartbroken that they were unable to see Roosevelt for themselves as they were recovering from broken limbs. Roosevelt sent a message to the hospital asking the staff to have the boys "near a window and I will see if they can't get a look at me." As the train pulled abreast of the hospital, Roosevelt made his way out onto "the rear platform in a driving rain to make a military salute" to the awestruck patients. Their nurse remarked that the President's kindness was "better than a week's treatment for both."[63]

The Presidential train was scheduled to arrive at 11am but was a little early and the twenty-one-gun salute, originating from the State Arsenal, commenced at 10:53. The booming of the guns dramatically spread the news to "the whole city and countryside within earshot . . . that Theodore Roosevelt had become a guest of Harrisburg."[64] A welcoming committee led by Pennsylvania Governor Samuel Pennypacker met him at the train station. The group made their way out of the station and climbed into waiting carriages for the trip to the Capitol Building.

Upon arrival, the group escorted the President on a quick tour of the new building as the official program had slated 11:30 as the time at which the formal dedication ceremonies were to begin with a parade to follow.[65] The group emerged from the building and made their way to the reviewing stand at 11:47.[66] The reviewing stand had been erected opposite the main entrance of the Capitol and accommodated reserved seating for three thousand, though they were unable to sit during the ceremonies due to the weather.[67] The rain continued throughout the scheduled events, lessening only for the forty minutes of Roosevelt's keynote address, and then intensifying once again.[68] Throwing off his raincoat and top hat, Roosevelt launched into his speech.[69]

In the early part of his speech, Roosevelt praised the people of Pennsylvania for their place in the founding of the nation and the magnificent building they were there to dedicate. But, turning from the past to the present, he noted: "The study of the great deeds of the past is of chief avail in so far as it incites us to grapple resolutely and effectively with the problems of the present."[70] The challenges of each generation were unique and he declared that "we of this generation have to struggle with evils springing from the very material success of which we are so proud, from the very growth and prosperity of which, with justice, we boast."[71] The difficulty was to identify how challenges were to be addressed: through efforts of individual citizens, collective actions through state governments, or action taken by the national government. Roosevelt forcefully argued for an increased scope of powers for the national government to address national problems that transcended state and local boundaries.

He placed the difficulty of expanding federal power directly on the efforts of lawyers who represented the interests of corporate America. These "astute lawyers strive to prevent the passage of efficient laws and strive to secure judicial determinations of those that pass which shall emasculate them."[72] Further, they "cry out that the Constitution is violated whenever any effort is made to invoke the aid of the National Government" in attempts to regulate any activity of their employers.[73] Their doctrine of constitutional interpretation "would make the Constitution merely the shield of incompetence and the excuse for government paralysis; they treat it as a justification for refusing to attempt the remedy of evil, instead of as the source of vital power necessary for the existence of a mighty and ever-growing nation."[74]

Roosevelt acknowledged that he was a strong supporter of increased powers for the national government, but that the bulk of regulatory action needed to be taken at the state level. However, if the states were unable or unwilling to take such action, then the national government must fill the void. It is at this point that Roosevelt turned to the thinking of James Wilson as worthy of emulation by Pennsylvania and the nation.

He declared, "So much for the State. Now for the Nation; and here I cannot do better than base my theory of government action upon the words and deeds of one of Pennsylvania's greatest sons, Justice James Wilson."[75] Roosevelt extended congratulations on the events of the James Wilson Memorial to take place the following month in Philadelphia—a fitting tribute and one long overdue. Despite Wilson's work in the Continental Congress during the Revolutionary War, Roosevelt identified his work in the "Constitutional Convention, and in securing the adoption of the Constitution and expounding what it meant," as Wilson's greatest and longest-lasting contribution to his adopted country.[76]

Roosevelt acknowledged Wilson's democratic beliefs and paid him this lofty tribute:

> He believed in the people with the faith of Abraham Lincoln; and coupled with his faith in the people he had what most of the men who in his generation believed in the people did not have; that is, the courage to recognize the fact that faith in the people amounted to nothing unless the representatives of the people assembled together in the National Government were given full and complete power to work on behalf of the people. He developed even before Marshall the doctrine (absolutely essential not merely to the efficiency but to the existence of this nation) that an inherent power rested in the nation, outside of the enumerated powers conferred upon it by the Constitution, in all cases where the object involved was beyond the power of the several States and was a power ordinarily exercised by sovereign nations.[77]

Alluding to recent decisions of the U.S. Supreme Court with which Roosevelt disagreed, he remarked that they "have done just what Wilson feared; they have, as a matter of fact, left vacancies, left blanks between the limits of possible State jurisdiction and the limits of actual national jurisdiction over the control of the great business corporations."[78] Adherence to a narrow construction of the Constitution was the principal shield used by "those great moneyed interests which oppose and dread any attempt to place them under efficient governmental control."[79] He was confident history and the federal courts would ultimately vindicate his position and comprehensive federal regulatory power would result. He thundered, "Only the nation can do this work. To relegate it to the States is a farce, and is simply another way of saying that it shall not be done at all."[80]

The key to Roosevelt's expansion of federal regulatory power resided in the Constitution's interstate commerce clause. "I maintain that the National Government should have complete power to deal with all of this wealth which in any way goes into the commerce between the States."[81] Federal regulations were the antidote for anarchy and socialism. Railroads were a particular target for regulation. Regulation was far preferable, for Roosevelt, than calls for government ownership of railroads, a policy "which would be evil in its results from every standpoint."[82] He declared, "The Government ought not to conduct the business of the country; but it ought to regulate it so that it shall be conducted in the interest of the public."[83] If there were to be a single impartial umpire of the national economy, Theodore Roosevelt firmly believed it should be the national government.

In closing his speech before the drenched, but enthusiastic crowd, Roosevelt told them, "It behooves us Americans to look ahead and plan out the right kind of a civilization, as that which we intend to develop from these wonderful new conditions of vast industrial growth."[84] Americans could effectively manage their transition into a modern, thriving, industrial economy if only a more expansive and progressive one replaced a narrow constitutional interpretation. Such an interpretation that relied upon the thinking of James Wilson would become known as the Wilson-Roosevelt Doctrine of Construction.[85]

Theodore Roosevelt delivered on his promise to Lucien Alexander to prominently feature James Wilson in the Harrisburg speech. The speech reverberated across the nation as a call for a "new nationalism," one based on the doctrine of inherent powers found in the writings of James Wilson. In 1946, political scientist Walter H. Bennett wrote, "At Harrisburg, Pennsylvania, in 1906, in a speech which was later to be both praised and condemned perhaps more than any other utterance of his entire career, Roosevelt called for an increase in the powers of the Federal Government through executive action, through legislation, and through judicial interpretation."[86]

This tribute increased interest in the coming activities in Philadelphia and numerous mentions of Roosevelt's esteem for Wilson would feature in media coverage of the event.

THE FINAL WEEKS

Two weeks after Roosevelt's tribute, on October 18th, the Committee received formal approval for Wilson's reburial at Christ Church. The vestry minutes record "that on motion of Mr. White it was resolved that if a request is made to inter the remains of the Hon. James Wilson in the church yard near those of his wife, that permission be and is hereby granted together with the erection of a proper memorial to be first approved by the vestry."[87]

At the October 31st meeting of The St. Andrew's Society, Lucien Alexander, who had joined the society the previous year, moved that a committee of five members be appointed to attend the memorial services at Christ Church on November 22nd. Four members, from among the leadership of the society, including Society President Peter Boyd, were selected.[88]

The James Wilson Memorial was a multi-faceted event, which took place over more than a week. The opening event was on Wednesday, November 14th, when the Law Academy of Philadelphia hosted an encore presentation of Burton Alva Konkle's address "James Wilson and the Constitution," which he had given on May 14th to the Historical Society of Pennsylvania.[89] Three days later, on the morning of Saturday the 17th, the *U.S.S. Dubuque* took aboard a coffin, provided by the chapter of the Philadelphia St. Andrew's Society—an organization for which James Wilson had once served as president.[90] After securing the coffin and taking aboard two U.S. Marines, one of whom was a trumpeter, who would participate in the military honors to Wilson, the crew spent the morning cleaning the ship.[91] The *Dubuque*'s participation was due in large part to the efforts of Lucien Alexander. His political connections in the Roosevelt administration arranged for the ship's participation. A previous request submitted by Konkle had been turned down.

That evening, Pennsylvania's much-reduced delegation to bring Wilson's body back from North Carolina, consisting of Konkle and Major General J. S. P. Gobin—commander of the Pennsylvania National Guard—who had been designated to represent Governor Pennypacker, boarded the *Dubuque* at Philadelphia's League Island Navy Yard. The original delegation was much larger and prestigious, consisting of Pennsylvania Governor Samuel Pennypacker; Israel W. Morris, Esq., who represented the last descendant of James Wilson; President William C. Sproul (pro tem) of the Pennsylvania State Senate, who represented the Legislature; and Dean William Draper Lewis, representing the University of Pennsylvania, but "owing to illness and other unavoidable causes" were unable to make the journey.[92]

Before dawn the next morning in a drizzling rain, Lucien Alexander joined the Pennsylvania delegation aboard ship as a representative of the Philadelphia chapter of The St. Andrew's Society, of which he was also a member. The *Dubuque* got underway, bound for Norfolk, Virginia, at 6:40am with Captain A. F. Fechteler manning the conn.[93] On the journey to and from Norfolk, the casket was draped in the American flag and under a U.S. Marine guard.[94] After being slowed by bad weather, the *Dubuque* anchored at the wharf owned by the Norfolk and Southern Railway at 8:15am on Monday, November 19th. The ship then fired a 13-gun salute to the Commandant of the Navy Yard. The casket and Pennsylvania delegation were taken ashore as another salute was fired to mark Major General Gobin's departure.[95]

On Tuesday morning, the Pennsylvania delegation, accompanied by the *Dubuque's* Captain Fechteler as a representative for the federal government, joined Major General Gobin and Konkle for the trip to Edenton. The group was met at Norfolk's Berkley station by North Carolina's Chief Justice Walter Clark as they boarded a special train, comprised of an official private car and a baggage car, provided by the railroad for the occasion. The train was manned by the railroad Vice-President M. K. King, General Superintendent M. W. Maguire, and Industrial Agent F. L. Merritt. With everyone on board, the train promptly left Norfolk at 7am for the 70-mile trip.[96]

After an uneventful journey, the special train pulled into the Edenton station a little before 9:30am. Waiting at the station were members of the North Carolina contingent of the James Wilson Memorial Committee. John G. Wood, the owner of the Hayes Plantation; was joined by the president of the North Carolina Historical Society, William D. Pruden, who served as the North Carolina chairman of the Memorial Committee; North Carolina's Lieutenant Governor Francis D. Winston; four representatives from the Society of the Cincinnati; two representatives from the Sons of the Revolution; and Rev. Dr. R. B. Drane. The assemblage was driven in a procession of carriages through Edenton to the Hayes Plantation and the private cemetery, which overlooked the head of Albemarle Sound.[97]

The evening prior to these events, the casket had been sent ahead to Edenton, accompanied by Robert R. Bringhurst, to Hayes.[98] There James Wilson's remains were disinterred and placed in the new coffin in the presence of the local undertaker and Mr. Wood. In Konkle's account of the disinterment, he wrote that "it is interesting to record that the results were so favorable that it is now known that Wilson's heavy hair, tied in the fashion of the day, was of a slightly sandy color, not unlike that of President Roosevelt, and his well-preserved teeth also rivalled those so well known at the White House." The cenotaph to mark Wilson's empty grave, which had previously been shipped to Hayes, was ready for use as well.[99]

Before the commencement of the ceremonies, which "were witnessed by a large number of citizens of Edenton and surrounding country," Rev. Dr. Drane, of the Edenton Episcopal Church, performed a short invocation.[100] William Pruden presided over the scheduled events. The new casket containing Wilson's remains rested on two wooden poles suspended over his grave of 108 years. On the ground next to the grave, also on two poles, lay the cenotaph to be placed over the empty grave to mark the occasion; a companion cenotaph would also be placed over Wilson's new grave in Philadelphia.[101]

After the invocation, Burton Alva Konkle read the formal request from the James Wilson Memorial Committee for the removal of Wilson's remains for transportation to and reburial in Philadelphia. Pruden then replied with Wood's written permission and then Lt. Governor Winston provided North Carolina's formal grant of permission. He then "delivered a short address touching upon the life and character of the eminent diplomat and jurist."[102]

On behalf of Pennsylvania Governor Pennypacker, Major General Gobin then received the casket and in brief remarks "emphasized particularly the sense of gratitude that the people of Pennsylvania felt toward the people of North Carolina for the courtesy extended on this occasion and the honor they had done the distinguished dead." He then unveiled the white cenotaph that now covered the empty grave.[103] After the services, Mr. Wood provided lunch at the Hayes mansion before departure for the train station.

After lunch, the assemblage climbed aboard waiting carriages, bound for the train station, to board the special train for the return journey to Norfolk. Accompanying the Pennsylvania delegation to Philadelphia were John Wood, William Pruden, and four members of the Society of Cincinnati, who served as honorary pallbearers.[104]

During the ceremonies in Edenton, back in Norfolk, the weather was overcast, misty, and warm with a gentle breeze from the southwest. In preparation for receiving the delegation and Wilson's casket, the *Dubuque* "lighted the fires in boiler 'A' at 10.00." The ship got underway at 1:00pm and pulled alongside Berkley wharf.[105]

In a cloud of steam, the special Norfolk and Southern train came to a stop at 2:00pm on the wharf to allow the delegation to board the *Dubuque* for the trip to Philadelphia. The flags of the harbor and of the Navy Yard were flown at half-mast.[106] At 2:10pm, with the ship's company at attention, a U.S. Marine trumpeter sounded two flourishes as the casket was brought aboard and the *Dubuque's* minute guns fired a 13-gun salute. After securing the casket and placing a Marine guard on the ship's afterdeck, the *Dubuque* got underway at 2:20pm. The ship made its way down to Hampton Roads and out to sea, with Captain Fechteler at the conn, sailing for Philadelphia.[107]

The party accompanying the casket was Major General Gobin, Konkle, and Mr. Wood who was the special guest of Pennsylvania. As the *Dubuque* pulled away from the wharf and sailed down the harbor towards the Chesapeake Bay, ships of all types and nations rendered appropriate honors.[108]

The voyage back to Philadelphia was even more troubled by weather than the previous journey to Norfolk. The *Dubuque* was scheduled to arrive at the Chestnut Street wharf at 3pm on Wednesday, November 21st. Shortly after midnight on the 21st, a thick fog began to envelop the ship. The ship slowed to a crawl as they began to pass other vessels that had already decided to drop anchor to await better weather. Making little progress, the ship dropped anchor at 4:40am as the fog cleared overhead but remained dense around the horizon. An attempt was made to get underway again at 8:58am, but after only a half-hour, the anchor was again dropped on account of heavy fog. The fog lifted at 10:50am and within ten minutes the *Dubuque* got underway and took aboard a pilot to guide the journey up the Delaware River.[109]

An overcast sky and thick fog hounded the *Dubuque's* course up the Delaware. Even with an experienced pilot aboard, the ship was again forced to drop anchor at 4:10pm. Throughout the night and into the early morning hours of Thursday, November 22nd, clouds remained overhead and fog shrouded the ship. The weather began to clear before dawn and the *Dubuque* got underway at 6:35am with the Captain and the pilot on the bridge. By 8am, the ship was off of Wilmington, Delaware with the colors at half-mast.[110]

As the weather cleared, the *Dubuque* made good progress and by 9:50am passed the League Island Navy Yard. There a small convoy, comprised of U.S. Navy, city, and government craft, joined the *Dubuque* as she made her way to Philadelphia to drop anchor at 10:23am at the foot of Market Street. The U.S. Navy tug *Modoc* came alongside to transfer the casket and delegation to the wharf. At 11:00am the delegation and river pilot disembarked and five minutes later Wilson's casket was transferred with appropriate honors and another salute of thirteen minute guns. After the casket reached the wharf, the *Dubuque* again full masted her colors and got underway at 11:40am to return to the Navy Yard. After dropping anchor, the crew of the *U.S.S. Dubuque* was given liberty and Captain Fechteler left on a ten-day leave, after attending the memorial ceremonies.[111]

As Wilson's casket and the delegation came ashore to the salute from the *Dubuque*, the bell at Independence Hall tolled. Governor Pennypacker led the Pennsylvania delegation, which met the casket as it came ashore. The group, including a contingent of U.S. Marines, followed the procession of the casket, which was borne on the shoulders of sailors from the *Dubuque*. A Marine band played the funeral march and the procession made its way down the waterfront to Walnut Street where it turned onto Third Street. This path took them past the location where James Wilson's home of "Fort Wilson" notoriety once stood.[112] At Fifth Street the procession turned onto the Chestnut Street front of Independence Hall.[113]

Upon reaching Independence Hall, the casket was placed on a catafalque, in the room where Wilson participated in the adoption of the Declaration of Independence and drafting of the Constitution of the United States. The casket was under a guard of the First City Troop, with a life-sized portrait of Wilson by Albert Rosenthal, painted in 1899, overlooking it. Major General Gobin formally delivered the casket to Governor Pennypacker. The doors were then opened, and the public was allowed to view the casket draped in the colors and adorned with a laurel wreath from the President of the United States.[114]

At 1:30pm the procession reformed, headed by Major General Gobin, serving as Grand Marshall, and the First City Troop with members of the U. S. Supreme Court in attendance serving as honorary pallbearers: Chief Justice

Fuller and Justices Day, Holmes, Peckham, and White. The casket was borne on the shoulders of law students from the University of Pennsylvania, where Wilson had taught as the first Professor of Law.[115] The color guard of the Philadelphia Sons of the Revolution joined the procession as it moved down Fifth Street to Arch, where they stopped for a moment before the tomb of Benjamin Franklin.[116]

Upon arrival at Christ Church, as the procession entered through the tower room, the organ began playing "My Country, 'Tis of Thee," which was sung as a processional.[117] Members of the U.S. Supreme Court were escorted to and seated in the highest place of honor—President George Washington's pew. The religious component of the memorial was conducted according to the rights of Christ Church, where Wilson had been a member and his close friend William White served as Bishop. Bishop-Coadjutor Mackay-Smith conducted the service with the flag-draped casket before the assembled quests.

Governor Pennypacker served as the presiding officer for the scheduled tributes and spoke on behalf of Wilson's adopted state of Pennsylvania. Pennypacker set the tone for the memorial noting: "Nations that fail to give due recognition to the achievements and the characters of the able men among them who have aided in the upbuilding of their institutions, either still linger within the trammels of barbarism or are moving on the downward path toward decadence."[118] James Wilson deserved the thanks and recognition of not only his adopted state, but of the nation as a whole. "Of no other man could it be written with truth that he signed the American Declaration of Independence, the Constitution of the United States, and the decrees of its Supreme Court."[119]

The Governor closed his tribute to Wilson with a ringing endorsement of Theodore Roosevelt's speech in Harrisburg the prior month. He quoted Wilson's belief: "That the Supreme Power therefore should be vested in the people, is in my judgment the great panacea of human politics. It is a power paramount to every constitution, inalienable in its nature and indefinite in its extent."[120] The power inherent in the body politic encompassed any area and topic that the American people saw fit to exercise. Pennypacker concluded, "If the development and extension of the national authority can be legally supported it must be by the acceptance of his doctrine that the government possesses not only the powers specifically conferred by the Constitution but in addition those which inhere in every nation and which the States were not capable of granting."[121] Each tribute was allocated five minutes, except for the keynote oration by Pennsylvania Attorney General Hampton Carson.

Samuel Dickson, Chancellor of the Law Association of Philadelphia for the Bar of Pennsylvania, next rose to speak. He discussed Wilson's training as a lawyer and his contribution to Pennsylvania in her courts and political sphere. He declared that the American Revolution was a revolution of lawyers, with Wilson and his colleagues at the forefront. They waged a "conservative revolution, which, while severing the connection with the mother country, held on to all that was best in its institutions—down to that time the best the world had known."[122]

Wilson's legal training served him best as a member of the Constitutional Convention of 1787, the Pennsylvania Constitutional Convention of 1790, and his "accepting a professorship in the University of Pennsylvania, and undertaking to teach those who were to become the lawyers and judges of the future." Wilson's service, as a lawyer, reached from the classroom, to the courtroom, to the statehouse. Dickson urged the assemblage to view Wilson's life through the prism of his legal career.[123]

Dean William Draper Lewis of the Law School then rose to speak on behalf of the University of Pennsylvania. He provided an overview of Wilson's relationship with the school, from his time as a tutor of Latin; to being elected a member of the Board of Trustees; and finally the first professor of law at the university. Lewis proudly noted that Wilson "became the second person in the United States to hold such a position, Chancellor George Wythe of the College of William and Mary being the first."[124] He paid tribute to Wilson's oldest son, Bird Wilson, who first collected and published James Wilson's law lectures in 1804. Though incomplete and unrevised, "they are to-day and will continue to be an enduring monument to his memory." He urged, "No student of our legal or political institutes should fail to master the conceptions of law and sovereignty which he here states, explains, and defends."[125]

In Lewis's reading of Wilson's thinking, no "government, state or national, did not, as such, possess sovereignty." "Sovereignty resides and can only reside in the people; not the people collectively but separately—each individual is sovereign."[126] Here again, we find Lewis joining previous speakers in his praise of Wilson's interpretation of the Constitution, one consistent with the views of Theodore Roosevelt. Wilson's law lectures were a path to enlarging the scope of federal powers and their utilization for the benefit of the American people.

Noted author and medical doctor S. Weir Mitchell then paid tribute to Wilson on behalf of American literature. It was Mitchell, after all, who set in motion the train of events that had culminated in the day's activities. He expanded his subject to include all those who, though not born a native of Pennsylvania, chose to make their home in the colony and then helped guide the transition to that of a state in a continental republic. He declared, "Most fitting it is of all that these who came to us of their own will and helped to make us, should have the hospitality of memory and lasting record in bronze or marble of what they have done."[127]

One of the most prominent men of the day, Andrew Carnegie, rose to pay tribute to Wilson as a fellow native of Fife and in his capacity as Lord Rector of St. Andrew's University, where Wilson had earned his undergraduate degree. Like Mitchell's expanded focus, Carnegie sought to draw attention to all of the children of Scotland who contributed to the establishment of the United States. To understand Wilson, you had to understand that he "was democratic and republican, and an intense advocate of independence by virtue of his Scottish birth and education."[128]

The former Democratic Presidential candidate Alton B. Parker spoke in his capacity as the President of the American Bar Association. He paid tribute to Wilson's tenure on the U.S. Supreme Court, particularly his written opinion in the case of *Chisholm v. Georgia* (1793). He noted that during Wilson's nine years on the bench, this was the only strictly constitutional case to come before the body. Parker praised Wilson's "prescience in foreseeing the result of a controversy between the Federal and State governments must, in the light of a century's history, be pronounced remarkable."[129]

Representing the U.S. Supreme Court and the federal judiciary, Justice Edward D. White's tribute was quite different from those given before. He talked of the Civil War and urged that it was the obligation of the living to preserve the Union that those on both sides had died for. He hoped that the memorial "may enkindle in all our hearts a keener purpose to preserve and perpetuate the government which our fathers gave us." Even this Democrat from Louisiana, paraphrasing Lincoln at Gettysburg, sought a "government of the Constitution, a government of liberty protected by law, which affords the substantial hope that civil liberty may not pass away from the face of the earth."[130]

President Roosevelt's personal representative, U.S. Attorney General William Moody, spoke for him and the nation. Moody was a fan of Wilson and was extremely pleased to be at the memorial and in a short time would himself become a member of the U.S. Supreme Court. "We are joining to-day in an act of long-delayed justice," he began.[131] He believed the memorial "is full of interest for every lover of liberty, for every believer in a strong and efficient government, capable of protecting the rights of its citizens, of compelling obedience to its lawful decrees, and of fulfilling its obligations to the other nations of the earth."[132] Moody continued the theme developed during the memorial of praising Wilson's belief in a strong, active national government, a belief that buttressed similar efforts by the Roosevelt administration.

Moody first became acquainted with Wilson while he was in law school. He encountered him in the pages of Madison's report of the debates of the

Constitutional Convention and liked what he read. He shared, "It is one of the mysteries of history, which I have not been able to solve, why his fame has not kept pace with his service."[133] Moody had been a driving force, within the federal government, to facilitate the events of which he was a prominent part. His support had been crucial at key moments during the previous year.

He proceeded to provide a detailed summary of James Wilson's contributions at the Constitutional Convention, paying particular attention to his desire for a popularly elected president and U.S. Senators. In less than seven years from Wilson's reburial, the U.S. Constitution would be amended on April 8, 1913, providing for the direct election of Senators by the electorate. He lauded Wilson's very modern view of where the nation was headed. "He was a believer in Democracy and Nationalism—the first man, I believe, in all our history who united the two opinions." Further, Moody emphasized that Wilson "had no fears of a strong national government, if it were a government of the people."[134] Wilson also did not fear, but welcomed, the expansion of the nation westward to the far horizon—unlike his colleague Gouverneur Morris. Moody quoted Wilson's view: "If the interior countries should acquire the majority, it will not only have the right to govern, but will avail itself of it whether we will or not."[135] Wilson's commitment to democracy, even to the detriment of his adopted state, and a faith in a strong national government acting on behalf of all Americans was, for Moody, a founder whose beliefs were long overdue to again come before the public to garner their attention.

The final speaker, and the keynote, was reserved for Pennsylvania Attorney General Hampton L. Carson.[136] Not only was he a lawyer and a politician, but also a published historian. Carson saw great value in civic remembrances like the James Wilson Memorial. He reminded those assembled of the tribute paid to men who had made great contributions to the Roman Republic by erecting statues and monuments along the Via Appia and the Via Sacra. As for the Wilson Memorial, "it is well that we should pause in these busy days to glance at our historic past and exhume the noble proportions of a great character who did so much to shape our institutions while they were still in the mould."[137] Without a similar method of recognition used by the Romans, Carson noted, "It is by recalling to the youth of the present, as well as to middle and venerable age, the language and deeds of the builders of our nation, that we can best insure the perpetuity of our institutions, for American Liberty is a golden chain binding generation to generation and stretching link by link from the receding past to the opening future."[138]

Carson's address provided a more biographical approach than previous tributes, but he expanded upon several areas commented on by Parker and Moody. The heart of his oration dealt with Wilson's role at the Constitutional

Convention and subsequent time on the U.S. Supreme Court, especially the *Chisholm v. Georgia* opinion. Carson agreed with previous speakers that the crowning moment of Wilson's career was his work at the Constitutional Convention, but he viewed the *Chisholm* opinion as solidifying Wilson's thinking on American government. "This opinion, in its essence and in its potentiality, must be regarded as the climax of Federalism."[139]

According to Carson, "Wilson viewed the Constitution, not as an instrument fashioned to meet the needs of the hour, nor as a weapon to be retempered or reshaped from time to time, but as an organism, a political being."[140] This political being is what we now consider the living Constitution. The Constitution was comprised of many parts—the three branches of government, the states, and the electorate—with each having individual functions and roles, which were "essential to the existence of the whole." If the American Constitution was a political being, it was a being capable of both growth and change. Carson argued, "Wilson viewed the Constitution of the United States as a political *intelligence* served by organs."[141] The keynote address carried through with the theme established by prior speakers of James Wilson's belief in a strong national government serving the interests of the American people.

The ceremony then heard the organ playing "Lest We Forget" for the recessional. The casket was again taken upon the shoulders of the pallbearers and carried through the doors of Christ Church for the last time. The participants followed and gathered beside the southern wall of the church and received the invocation. Then, Wilson's remains were lowered into the crypt beside those of his first wife, Rachel. A cenotaph, a duplicate of the one in Edenton, rested on top of the grave.[142]

In the evening, the leading participants in the day's events and invited guests gathered at the Historical Society of Pennsylvania for a reception where items related to James Wilson were on display from the Society's archives. The Historical Society had also served as the home of the James Wilson Memorial Committee and the Pennsylvania History Club—both groups shared a large number of common members. During the week, portraits of the members of the first U.S. Supreme Court were on display in their original room in the old City Hall located at Fifth and Chestnut Streets.[143]

The events of the James Wilson Memorial were at an end, but the ramifications of these events would be felt for the remainder of Theodore Roosevelt's term and beyond. Several of the members of the committee who brought the memorial off soon fell into a bitter dispute that marred not only the work they had done, but also their reputations. Before that story is told in chapter 9, we turn our attention to the man himself—James Wilson.

NOTES

1. On the National Constitution Center's website they encourage visitors to "Walk alongside 42 LIFE-SIZE, bronze statues of the FOUNDING FATHERS and relive the moment that launched a government ruled by 'We the People.' Further they exclaim, "Pose beside your favorite Founding Father for a great photo op!" http://constitutioncenter.org/experience/exhibitions/main-exhibition/signers-hall. Accessed 10:04am, March 7, 2016.

2. St. Andrew's Society of Philadelphia, *An Historical Catalogue of The St. Andrew's Society of Philadelphia: With Biographical Sketches of Deceased Members 1749–1907*, Philadelphia: Printed for the Society, 1907, 65.

3. Burton Alva Konkle, "The James Wilson Memorial." *The American Law Register* (1898–1907), Vol. 55, No. 1, Volume 46 New Series. (Jan 1907), 6.

4. _____, "Never Such a Tie-Up, Mariners Declare," *Public Ledger* (Philadelphia, PA), Nov. 22, 1906, 9.

5. Eventually, a small brick bearing only the name "Wilson" was placed at the foot of the grave, flush with the ground.

6. Letter from R. M. Lee to S. Weir Mitchell, February 24, 1904, in the *Lucien H. Alexander Papers*, Historical Society of Pennsylvania.

7. Ibid.

8. Helen DeBerniere H. Wills, "Grave of a Signer Unmarked," *The Washington Post* (1877–1954), Mar. 7, 1904, 9. There had been an earlier effort by Judge Harry White of the Pennsylvania State Bar Association to establish a statue of James Wilson, but nothing came of it.

9. Letter from R. M. Lee to S. Weir Mitchell, March 12, 1904, in the *Lucien H. Alexander Papers*, Historical Society of Pennsylvania.

10. Letter from S. Weir Mitchell to William D. Lewis, March 14, 1904, in the *Lucien H. Alexander Papers*, Historical Society of Pennsylvania.

11. Minutes from the April 4, 1904 meeting of the Faculty of the Law Department at the University of Pennsylvania, in the *Lucien H. Alexander Papers*, Historical Society of Pennsylvania.

12. For the only published account of the conflict, see David W. Maxey, "The Translation of James Wilson," in *Supreme Court Historical Society 1990 Yearbook*, (Washington, D.C.: Supreme Court Historical Society, 1990), 29–43.

13. Pennsylvania History Club, *Publications of the Pennsylvania History Club. Vol. I.: A Contribution of Pennsylvania Historical Bibliography*, (Philadelphia: Pennsylvania History Club, 1909), 41.

14. Ibid., p. ii.

15. Konkle, "The James Wilson Memorial," 3.

16. Pennsylvania History Club, 41.

17. Konkle, "The James Wilson Memorial," 3.

18. Carson had previously published an article on James Wilson. Hampton L. Carson, "The Works of James Wilson," *The American Law Register and Review*, Vol. 44, No. 10, Volume 35 New Series (Oct 1896), 633–641. Later, he examined Wilson's time on the U.S. Supreme Court. Hampton L. Carson, "James Wilson and James

Iredell: A Parallel and a Contrast," *Pennsylvania Magazine of History and Biography*, Vol. 45, No. 1 (Jan 1921), 1–33.

19. Ibid., 3.

20. Ibid., 3.

21. Burton Alva Konkle, *The Life and Speeches of Thomas Williams: Orator, Statesman and Jurist, 1806–1872, a Founder of the Whig and Republican Parties*, (Philadelphia: Campion and Company, 1905).

22. Letter from Burton Alva Konkle to Lucien H. Alexander, January 22, 1906, *Papers of Lucien H. Alexander*, Historical Society of Pennsylvania.

23. Letter from Lucien H. Alexander to Burton Alva Konkle, January 28, 1906, *Papers of Lucien H. Alexander*, Historical Society of Pennsylvania.

24. Letter from Burton Alva Konkle to Lucien H. Alexander, February 20, 1906, *Papers of Lucien H. Alexander*, Historical Society of Pennsylvania. Alexander duly sent another letter to Konkle along the lines of the request.

25. Konkle, "The James Wilson Memorial," 3–4.

26. Ibid., 4.

27. Burton Alva Konkle, *James Wilson and the Constitution*, (Philadelphia: Published by Order of the Law Academy, 1907), 1.

28. Letter from Lucien H. Alexander to Burton Alva Konkle, February 19, 1906, *Papers of Lucien H. Alexander*, Historical Society of Pennsylvania.

29. Telegram from Lucien H. Alexander to Burton Alva Konkle, February 28, 1906, *Papers of Lucien H. Alexander*, Historical Society of Pennsylvania.

30. Letter from Lucien H. Alexander to Burton Alva Konkle, February 28, 1906, *Papers of Lucien H. Alexander*, Historical Society of Pennsylvania.

31. Ibid. There had been precedent set, the year before, with the reburial of John Paul Jones. His grave had been located in France and the remains were brought back to the Naval Academy for reburial aboard a U.S. battleship and escorted by a sizable portion of the U.S. fleet. President Theodore Roosevelt had served as master of ceremonies, a similar role that was envisioned for him in the reburial of James Wilson. For further information see: Michael Kamen, *Digging Up the Dead: A History of Notable American Reburials*, (Chicago: University of Chicago Press, 2010), 117–24.

32. Ibid.

33. Ibid.

34. Ibid.

35. Email from Carol Smith to Michael Taylor, June 29, 2015. Information from the vestry minutes of Christ Church, Philadelphia, PA.

36. Letter from Theodore Roosevelt to Lucien H. Alexander, March 12, 1906, in *The Papers of Theodore Roosevelt*.

37. Lucien Alexander published three articles on the subject of James Wilson: "James Wilson and the Wilson Doctrine," *North American Review*, Vol. 183, No. 8 (Nov. 16, 1906), 971–89; "The James Wilson Memorial," *The Albany Law Journal: A Weekly Record of the Law and the Lawyers* (1870–1908), (Dec. 1906), 380–82; and "Memorandum *in re Corpus Juris*," *The Green Bag*, Vol. 22, No. 2 (Feb. 1910), 59–90. Burton Alva Konkle was working on a multi-volume set containing a biography of Wilson, correspondence, and other materials.

38. Letter from Lucien H. Alexander to Burton Alva Konkle, March 20, 1906, *Papers of Lucien H. Alexander*, Historical Society of Pennsylvania.

39. Letter from W. Innes Addison to Burton Alva Konkle, April 10, 1906; Letter from I. Waitland Anderson to Burton Alva Konkle, April 12, 1906; and Letter from Thomas F. Harley to Burton Alva Konkle, April 24, 1906, in the *Lucien H. Alexander Papers*, Historical Society of Pennsylvania.

40. _____, "Honor to a Forgotten Patriot," *The Washington Post* (1877–1954), Mar. 31, 1906, 6.

41. Letter from Lucien H. Alexander to Burton Alva Konkle, April 3, 1906, in the *Lucien H. Alexander Papers*, Historical Society of Pennsylvania.

42. Konkle was a last-minute addition to the trip. In correspondence in 1907, Alexander related that he had to pay for Konkle's expenses to go to Washington and Konkle was extremely reluctant to go to the White House meeting.

43. Letter from Theodore Roosevelt to James Andrews, December 26, 1906, in *The Papers of Theodore Roosevelt*.

44. Konkle, "The James Wilson Memorial," 5.

45. Letter from Burton Alva Konkle to Lucien H. Alexander, May 17, 1906, *Papers of Lucien H. Alexander*, Historical Society of Pennsylvania.

46. Lucien H. Alexander, "James Wilson, Patriot, and the Wilson Doctrine," *North American Review*, Vol. 183, No. 8 (Nov. 16, 1906), 971–89.

47. Alexander had prepared a lengthy, eight-legal-page-sized, memorandum for the Attorney General to use. It was extensive, including new research that Alexander had gleaned from a research trip to archives in Washington. This memorandum would be shared with many of the members of the committee and others involved in the project. Letter from Lucien H. Alexander to Burton Alva Konkle, August 6, 1906, *Papers of Lucien H. Alexander*, Historical Society of Pennsylvania.

48. Letter from Lucien H. Alexander to William H. Moody, July 14, 1906, in Volume 15 of the *William H. Moody Papers*, Library of Congress. Among the research that Alexander forwarded was his own lengthy memoranda on Wilson, an article from Frank Gaylord Cook in the September 1889 *Atlantic Monthly*, and Andrew C. McLaughlin, *James Wilson in the Philadelphia Convention*, Boston: Ginn and Co., 1897.

49. Letter from Lucien H. Alexander to Burton Alva Konkle, August 24, 1906, *Papers of Lucien H. Alexander*, Historical Society of Pennsylvania.

50. I have been unable to obtain a copy of this letter, either in Alexander's or Roosevelt's papers, but I do have Roosevelt's response. Alexander loaned a copy of the letter to Hampton Carson and requested it back, early in 1907, but appears to have not received it.

51. Letter from Theodore Roosevelt to Lucien H. Alexander on September 17, 1906 in *The Papers of Theodore Roosevelt*.

52. Ibid.

53. Letter from Theodore Roosevelt to Lucien H. Alexander on September 24, 1906 in *The Papers of Theodore Roosevelt*.

54. Ibid.

55. Minutes of The St. Andrew's Society for 1906, 89.

56. Letter from Lucien H. Alexander to Andrew Carnegie, September 28, 1906, in *Papers of Andrew Carnegie*, #133, Library of Congress. As we will see later in the story, Alexander was incorrect regarding the finances of the committee, something that would give him much concern and trouble.

57. Ibid.

58. _____, "Ovation for President Throughout His Visit," *Patriot* (Harrisburg, PA), (Oct. 5, 1906), 1.

59. Ibid.

60. _____, "Thousands Flock to the Dedication," *Patriot* (Harrisburg, PA), (Oct. 4, 1906), 1.

61. _____, "Roosevelt, Rain-Soaked and Exposed to Storm, Gets Splendid Ovation at Capitol's Dedication," *The Philadelphia Inquirer* (Philadelphia, PA), (Oct. 5, 1906), 1.

62. Ibid.

63. Ibid.

64. _____, "Ovation for President Throughout His Visit," 1.

65. _____, "The Program," *Patriot* (Harrisburg, PA), (Oct. 4, 1906), 1.

66. _____, "Ovation for President Throughout His Visit," 2.

67. _____, "Roosevelt, Rain-Soaked and Exposed to Storm, Gets Splendid Ovation at Capitol's Dedication," 1.

68. _____, "Ovation for President Throughout His Visit," 2.

69. The speech would be published in pamphlet form. Theodore Roosevelt, "Address of President Roosevelt at the Dedication Ceremonies of the New State Capitol Building at Harrisburg, Pennsylvania, October 4, 1906," (Washington, D.C.: Government Printing Office, 1906).

70. Roosevelt, "Address," 5–6.

71. Ibid, 6.

72. Ibid, 10.

73. Ibid, 11.

74. Ibid, 11–12.

75. Ibid, 20.

76. Ibid, 21.

77. Ibid, 22–3.

78. Ibid, 26.

79. Ibid, 27.

80. Ibid, 32.

81. Ibid, 32.

82. Ibid, 37.

83. Ibid, 39.

84. Ibid, 45.

85. See chapter 9 for a discussion of this doctrine.

86. Walter H. Bennett, "Twentieth-Century Theories of the Nature of the Union," *The Journal of Politics*, Vol. 8, No. 2 (May 1946), 162.

87. Email from Carol Smith to Michael Taylor, June 29, 2015. Information from the vestry minutes of Christ Church, Philadelphia, PA.

88. Minutes of The St. Andrew's Society for 1906, 105.
89. Konkle, "The James Wilson Memorial," 5.
90. Konkle, "The James Wilson Memorial," 5.
91. Logbook entry for *U.S.S. Dubuque*, November 17, 1906.
92. Konkle, "The James Wilson Memorial," 5.
93. Logbook entry for *U.S.S. Dubuque*, November 18, 1906.
94. Konkle, "The James Wilson Memorial," 6.
95. Logbook entry for *U.S.S. Dubuque*, November 19, 1906.
96. _____, "James Wilson's Remains Pass Through Norfolk Enroute to Philadelphia," *Virginian Pilot* (Norfolk, VA), November 21, 1906, 4.
97. For the Society of the Cincinnati there were present General Bennehan Cameron, NC; Colonel Wilson G. Lamb, Williamston, NC; General Julian S. Carr, Durham, NC; and William E. Bush, Augusta, GA; for the Sons of the Revolution Wm. B. Shepard, Dr. Richard Dillard. _____, "James Wilson's Remains Pass Through Norfolk Enroute to Philadelphia," 4.
98. A new casket and Bringhurst's services had been acquired by The St. Andrew's Society for the cost of $250.00. Treasurer's Book of The St. Andrew's Society for 1906, 285.
99. Konkle, "The James Wilson Memorial," 6.
100. _____, "James Wilson's Remains Pass Through Norfolk Enroute to Philadelphia," 4.
101. Ibid.
102. Ibid.
103. Ibid.
104. Ibid.
105. Logbook entry for *U.S.S. Dubuque*, November 20, 1906.
106. Konkle, "The James Wilson Memorial," 7.
107. Logbook entry for *U.S.S. Dubuque*, November 20, 1906.
108. Konkle, "The James Wilson Memorial," 7.
109. Logbook entry for *U.S.S. Dubuque*, November 21, 1906.
110. Logbook entry for *U.S.S. Dubuque*, November 21 and 22, 1906.
111. Logbook entry for *U.S.S. Dubuque*, November 22, 1906.
112. For a detailed examination of the Fort Wilson incident, see John K. Alexander, "The Fort Wilson Incident of 1779: A Case Study of the Revolutionary Crowd," *The William and Mary Quarterly*, (3rd Ser.), Vol. 31, No. 4. (Oct 1974), 589–612; and Smith, 1956: 133–36.
113. Konkle, "The James Wilson Memorial," 8.
114. Ibid, 8.
115. Ibid, 8.
116. Ibid, 9.
117. St. Andrew's Society of Philadelphia, *An Historical Catalogue of The St. Andrew's Society of Philadelphia: With Biographical Sketches of Deceased Members 1749–1907*, Philadelphia: Printed for the Society, 1907, 66.

118. Samuel W. Pennypacker, et al., "Tributes Delivered at the Memorial Services," *The American Law Register* (1898–1907), Vol. 55, No. 1, Volume 46 New Series, (Jan 1907), 12.
119. Pennypacker, "Tributes," 12.
120. Ibid, 13.
121. Ibid, 13.
122. Samuel Dickson in Samuel W. Pennypacker, et al., "Tributes Delivered at the Memorial Services," *The American Law Register* (1898–1907), Vol. 55, No. 1, Volume 46 New Series, (Jan 1907), 15.
123. Dickson, "Tributes," 19.
124. William Draper Lewis in Samuel W. Pennypacker, et al., "Tributes Delivered at the Memorial Services," *The American Law Register* (1898–1907), Vol. 55, No. 1, Volume 46 New Series, (Jan 1907), 20.
125. Lewis, "Tributes," 21.
126. Ibid, 21.
127. S. Weir Mitchell in Samuel W. Pennypacker, et al., "Tributes Delivered at the Memorial Services," *The American Law Register* (1898–1907), Vol. 55, No. 1, Volume 46 New Series, (Jan 1907), 23.
128. Andrew Carnegie in Samuel W. Pennypacker, et al., "Tributes Delivered at the Memorial Services," *The American Law Register* (1898–1907), Vol. 55, No. 1, Volume 46 New Series, (Jan 1907), 25.
129. Alton B. Parker in Samuel W. Pennypacker, et al., "Tributes Delivered at the Memorial Services," *The American Law Register* (1898–1907), Vol. 55, No. 1, Volume 46 New Series, (Jan 1907), 27.
130. Edward D. White in Samuel W. Pennypacker, et al., "Tributes Delivered at the Memorial Services," *The American Law Register* (1898–1907), Vol. 55, No. 1, Volume 46 New Series, (Jan 1907), 31.
131. William H. Moody in Samuel W. Pennypacker, et al., "Tributes Delivered at the Memorial Services," *The American Law Register* (1898–1907), Vol. 55, No. 1, Volume 46 New Series, (Jan 1907), 31.
132. Moody, "Tributes," 32.
133. Ibid, 32.
134. Ibid, 33.
135. Ibid, 34.
136. Carson was a distant relation to James Wilson. The brother of his maternal grandfather married Wilson's daughter. Hampton L. Carson, "James Wilson and James Iredell: A Parallel and a Contrast," *Pennsylvania Magazine of History and Biography*, Vol. 45, No. 1 (Jan 1921), 3.
137. Hampton L. Carson, "Oration," *The American Law Register* (1898–1907), Vol. 55, No. 1, Volume 46 New Series, (Jan 1907), 35.
138. Carson, "Oration," 45.
139. Ibid, 45.
140. Ibid, 45.
141. Ibid, 45.

142. Konkle, "The James Wilson Memorial," 10.
143. Ibid, 10.

Chapter Two

Leaving Scotland for America

Like many of his Scottish countrymen, James Wilson sought a better life in the British colonies of North America. However, he was a rare exception. Wilson was a product of the Scottish Enlightenment, studying at the leading Scottish universities before embarking for America. He was typical of the Scots of the period who were predominately from the Lowlands but was atypical in his level of education and training in Scottish law. He was also typical in that he already had a relative in America. Wilson was pushed by his ambition to leave Scotland and his family ties pulled him to America's center of the Enlightenment—Philadelphia.

Wilson quickly became a member of the city's literate society as he first served as a tutor at the College of Philadelphia, then studied law under John Dickinson, and began his career as a lawyer. Shortly after arriving in the city, Wilson became a member of The St. Andrew's Society. This membership allowed him to nourish relationships with fellow Scots, many of whom would nurture his future endeavors as a lawyer, politician, and land speculator.

The young Scotsman stood on the pitching deck as the ship slowly made its way out of Glasgow's harbor, down the River Clyde and into the Firth of Clyde, late in the summer of 1765. At 23, James Wilson was like many of his fellow Scots who had determined that the journey to America was worth the risk. Opportunities to succeed in life—outside of the church, or service in the British Army—were few and difficult to acquire. Wilson, like many sons and daughters of Scotland, sought to make his fortune by migrating to the burgeoning British colonies of North America. As the hills of Scotland slipped from view and Wilson's attention shifted from his past, to his future, he had to have wondered if he had made the correct decision to leave. How typical was James Wilson's experience and what did he find when he arrived in Philadelphia in the autumn of 1765?

James Wilson was born a few miles southwest of St. Andrews, Scotland, on a farm called Carskerdo on September 14, 1742.[1] He was the first son born to his parents, William and Alison, after three daughters. When Wilson's parents were married in 1734, his father was nearly twice as old as his wife. In subsequent years, the family would grow to include three younger brothers and another sister as well.[2] Wilson's parents were pious members of the Scottish Presbyterian Church and desired that he one day join the ranks of the clergy.

Wilson began his education, like other children at the time, at the age of eight, when he enrolled at Cupar Grammar School in 1750.[3] In 1757, at the age of fifteen, he travelled east to the University of St. Andrews where he competed for and was awarded a scholarship to begin his university studies. Due to financial concerns, however, Wilson had to leave St. Andrews after two years and return to Cupar Grammar School, which he attended from May 1759 through January 1761.[4] To supplement the family income, according to a cousin's account, Wilson "became for some time a tutor in a gentleman's family. His genius being too sublime for such drudgery he formed a resolution to try his fortune in America."[5] With a possible journey to America in his future, James Wilson began preparing himself.

In addition to working as a tutor, Wilson became an apprentice to lawyer William Robertson. While working for Robertson, his signature first appeared in the Cupar Town Record Book on April 16, 1762.[6] According to the custom of the time, apprentices served a term of two to three years before being promoted to the status of clerk. It is unclear if James Wilson completed his apprenticeship with William Robertson. His university experience resumed when he attended the University of Glasgow from the fall of 1763 through the spring of 1765.[7] Wilson spent the summer break of 1764 back in Cupar working with Robertson, who was then the town clerk.[8]

COMING TO AMERICA

James Wilson sought to blaze a path different from the one which his parents had charted for him. His ambition drove him to look across the Atlantic, to the British colonies of North America. Wilson's childhood companion and cousin, Robert Annan, attended the University of St. Andrews several years before his own arrival. Annan withdrew from St. Andrews to study theology. While Wilson was still attending the university, Annan completed his training and was licensed as a minister in the Associate Presbyterian Church.[9] He left Scotland for America in 1761 and settled on a farm outside of Philadelphia.[10] Annan would be on hand to help get Wilson started in the New World.

His mother begged him not to go, as she was certain that she would never see him again. Wilson's effort to persuade his mother to give her blessing for his departure eventually bore fruit—reluctantly, she helped him prepare for the journey. The endeavor to send James Wilson to America became a family enterprise as they pooled their resources to help him pay for the crossing.

The voyage from Scotland to America in 1765 was not inexpensive. On a ship leaving from Scotland's west coast port of Glasgow, a fee of £15 or £20 was required.[11] The cost of passage plus additional funds for clothing, baggage, and living expenses for use upon arrival in North America added to the necessary sum. In that day, "a skilled plowman made £16 or £18 a year, and a hired hand got as little as £3 or £4 . . . it took most of the liquid capital of the little community" to fund Wilson's trans-Atlantic journey.[12]

In the late summer of 1765, bidding his family and friends goodbye, James Wilson climbed aboard a farmer's wagon for the first leg of the journey northwest to Perth. Once there, he took the ferry to Edinburgh and continued on his way west to Glasgow. The vessel conveying Wilson to America was not a first-class affair. The ship that carried him across the Atlantic to a landing in New York was filthy and uncomfortable with a rough crossing. James Wilson spent "much of his time over the lee rail," and before he made landfall, vowed he would never, ever go to sea again.[13]

How typical was James Wilson's journey when compared to the experience of fellow Scottish immigrants to North America of the time? In the twelve years before the outbreak of the American Revolution, from 1763 to 1775, immigration to British North America saw more than 130,000 souls make the journey from Europe; this did not include the additional 50–75,000 enslaved Africans who arrived as well.[14] To place this number in perspective, this surge of immigrants equaled "about one quarter of the white population's increase during those years, and it accounted for at least one third of the rise in the number of slaves."[15] During the same period, 1763 to 1775, the nationality of these immigrants consisted of 30,000 English, Welsh; 40,000 Scots; 55,000 Irish; and 12,000 Germans, Swiss, and Dutch.[16] Nearly 30 percent of all immigrants from this period were from Scotland.

During this period, English immigrants traveling to North America were drawn to Pennsylvania and the Chesapeake colonies of Maryland and Virginia. Unlike Wilson, 70 percent of Scots settled in New York and North Carolina—destinations of Scottish colonial settlement since the 1730s.[17] The best estimates are that, from the end of the French and Indian War in 1763, until the outbreak of the American Revolution in 1775, "25,000 Scots settled in America."[18]

Where Scots came from within Scotland was important. Lowland Scots were more educated, more comfortable reading and writing English, and could more easily assimilate into the colonies of British North America.[19] Around 80 percent of those immigrating to America, prior to the American Revolution, were from the Lowlands.[20] After the war, the ratio reversed as Highlanders headed "for the Maritime Provinces or eastern Upper Canada."[21]

Lowland Scots were present in significant numbers in several key professions of colonial life: higher education, medicine, religion, colonial administration, and particularly in commerce—especially the trade in tobacco, which generated "envy and worse on both sides of the ocean."[22] James Wilson was a prime example of a Lowland Scot who was well-educated, young, and pursued success far from home.

His Scottish Enlightenment university education and legal training under William Robertson marked James Wilson as a rare exception. Scottish immigrants to British North America fell into the following categories: craftsmen, artisans (37.7 percent); laborers, servants (31.9 percent); agriculture (24.0 percent); merchandising (5.2 percent); gentleman, gentlewoman (1.0 percent); and the smallest category of learned profession (law, etc.), which included Wilson, at .2 percent.[23] New York, the destination of Wilson's ship, was the primary point of debarkation for 43 percent of European immigrants of the period, with North Carolina (27.8 percent) and Pennsylvania (13.4 percent) ranking next.[24]

Wilson was representative of 60 percent of all Scottish immigrants who traveled to America, who were men; more than 19 percent of these male Scottish immigrants were in Wilson's age group of 20–25.[25] Like Wilson, a little more than half of Scottish immigrants travelled alone and nearly 82 percent financed their own passage. In comparison, 31 percent of English-Welsh immigrants financed their own passage, with the remainder arriving in North America as indentured servants.[26]

The 1707 Act of Union gave Scots full access to both England itself and the Atlantic empire. In some sense, Scots left Europe to retain a society that was slipping away with increased interaction with England. "The very fear of provincialization, the danger of cultural assimilation, may have been the goad that generated Scotland's extraordinary vigorous response. It was expressed most favorably in the development of Scottish trade and industry, in the northern version of the Enlightenment, and in the preservation of the Scottish identity, attenuated and redefined though it was."[27] One area in which Scots excelled was the fur trade, deep in the interior of North America.[28] Scottish immigrants "displayed a compulsion to adapt, to change, to improve."[29]

In the major North American ports of New York, Philadelphia, Charleston, and around the Chesapeake, Scottish merchants formed powerful and extensive commercial networks. The Scottish influence upon the medical profession was profound as "more than 150 Scottish doctors emigrated to America during the eighteenth century, and almost the whole of the colonial medical profession was Scottish émigré or Scottish trained."[30] In the middle colonies, Scots and Scottish-trained ministers "dominated both the Presbyterian and Episcopal Churches in America."[31]

Arguably, the area of colonial life in North America where Scots exerted the most influence was in the field of education. Educators such as John Witherspoon at the College of New Jersey (now Princeton) and William Smith at the College of Philadelphia (now the University of Pennsylvania) exerted significant influence over curriculum. It is not a coincidence that Wilson's first job in America was working as a Latin tutor. Outside of higher education, many Scots taught in Presbyterian academies in the middle and southern colonies and served as tutors in the Carolinas and throughout the Chesapeake.[32]

With the Act of Union, ambitious Scots could not secure positions in the Scottish Parliament, which had joined with the British. London, not Edinburgh or Glasgow, became the center of the political world. Looking outward, into the British Atlantic empire, ambitious Scots were well prepared to succeed. "Having failed to carve an independent Scottish empire, they elbowed their way into England's."[33] The sons and daughters of Scotland experienced success on distant shores that was impossible if they had remained home.[34]

Upon regaining his land legs, James Wilson took the first available stage to Philadelphia. To secure a job, he carried with him a letter of introduction to Dr. Richard Peters, an Anglican minister and trustee of the College of Philadelphia.[35] Like many well-educated and ambitious Scots before him, James Wilson journeyed to where he could utilize his talents to the fullest. "The exodus of the able has been a constant theme in Scottish history, even in the most dynamic phases of the nation's development."[36] Wilson's university education in Scotland easily secured him a job as a tutor of Latin, where he began building a network of acquaintances among Philadelphia's elite—relationships that would further the career of the ambitious Scot.

After working at the College of Philadelphia for a year, he studied law with the renowned lawyer John Dickinson, who, during the course of his legal studies, became a friend and political mentor until their political break over the Declaration of Independence in July 1776, even though they remained friends. Through personal acquaintances Wilson became the principal lawyer for the Bank of North America and became its largest debtor as he engaged in land speculation.

After arriving in America, James Wilson was determined to make his way in life. His mother's fear that he may never return to her and stray from her religion came to pass. His mother was unable to write to him directly, as she was unable to write; she relied upon relatives, principally her sons to whom she dictated letters. Throughout his life, friends and relatives chastised Wilson for his neglect of writing home. One of the earliest surviving letters from Rachel Wilson to her son is filled with concern for his eternal soul at the expense of earthly pleasures. She desired him "to be mending your journey to the other Country and that it would give her more pleasure to see evidences of your being bound in the way to Zion and set out for the Celestial Country." Instead, she received word "of your purchasing the greatest fortunes." Despite this, the grateful mother had "reason to bless God for his countenancing you in your secular affairs."[37]

In a letter dated July 6th, 1770, Wilson's mother included a letter with one sent by his brother-in-law, James Balfour. "Dear Jamie the last letter I hade from you gives no account of any you have got from us and we have sent a good many since your last as above."[38] She chastised him to include the date of the last letter that he received from Scotland. "[I]t gives me great trouble that we get so Seldom word from you and it seems you get as Seldom word from us, but it is not for want of writing."[39] Given Wilson's track record of neglecting personal correspondence, it is likely that letters were not being lost in transit, just going unanswered.

Rachel Wilson concluded her portion of the letter with a short summary of her lengthy period of ill health. Her recovery provided her an opportunity to: "Exort you above all things to make Sure an interest in Crist as your all and only trust for time and Eternity. for I'll assure you you will find the best things ever you did will yealld you no Comfort in a Deying hour none but Crist none but Crist."[40] She concluded with several recommendations on religious readings and urged him to do them, "which is the Ernest desire of your affectionate Mother in her Distress."[41]

As James Wilson completed his legal training with John Dickinson and began his legal career in Carlisle, his contact with friends and family remaining in Scotland was put aside. Professional interests dominated his time and initial forays into land speculation consumed more and more of his time. Wilson did remain in touch with his Scottish heritage as he became an active member of The St. Andrew's Society of Philadelphia. He became a member in 1767, a little over a year after arriving in Philadelphia. To be accepted as a member, an applicant must be sponsored by an active member. According to the minutes, the Vice President in 1767 was William Smith, the president of the College of Philadelphia.[42] It is likely that Smith served as Wilson's sponsor. After the American Revolution, James Wilson served as the organization's president from 1786–1796.[43]

In Philadelphia, James Wilson's Scottish Enlightenment education gained him entry into the city's literate and legal world. While a tutor of Latin at the College of Philadelphia, he first met William White who quickly became his closest friend and future minister. The two men would collaborate in early 1768 on a newspaper series, *The Visitant*, which garnered significant attention.

After finishing his legal studies with prominent attorney John Dickinson, Wilson decided to move west to Carlisle, for Philadelphia already had too many lawyers to provide space for a newly minted attorney. Carlisle provided distance from which to ponder the plight of young, ambitious men and the empire in which they lived.

Through his membership in The St. Andrew's Society, Wilson celebrated his ties to Scotland, but, despite urgent pleas from his mother, he never again embarked for home. Pennsylvania, and more broadly Britain's North American colonies and the future United States, would witness his future of great success and failure.

NOTES

1. Martin Clagett, "James Wilson—His Scottish Background: Corrections and Additions," *Pennsylvania History: A Journal of Mid-Atlantic Studies*, Vol. 79, No. 2 (Spring 2012), 158.

2. Ibid, 158.

3. Ibid, 159. The school is now known as Bell-Baxter High School. Iain McLean, "Adam Smith, James Wilson, and the US Constitution," in *The Adam Smith Review*, Vol. 8, (London: Routledge, 2014), 20 pages.

4. Ibid, 163.

5. Robert Annan to Bird Wilson, May 16, 1805, quoted in Clagett, 163. Robert Annan, who was James Wilson's cousin and childhood companion, wrote to James Wilson's son, Bird Wilson, in response to a letter seeking information on James Wilson as Bird was preparing the publication of his father's papers.

6. Ibid, 163.

7. Ibid, 164.

8. Ibid, 167.

9. Page Smith, *James Wilson: Founding Father, 1742–1798*, (Chapel Hill: University of North Carolina Press, 1956), 16.

10. David Dobson, *The Original Scots Colonists of Early America 1612–1783*, (Baltimore: Genealogical Publishing Co., Inc., 1989), 10. Dobson's book lists every

Scottish colonist, by name, found in the surviving documentary history. Unfortunately, no record exists for James Wilson's trip across the Atlantic in 1765.

11. Smith, 20.

12. Smith, 20.

13. Smith, 20. Wilson never did cross the Atlantic again. In his final years, he planned on visiting Europe in an effort to attract financing for his plan to settle thousands of European immigrants on land in the Northwest Territory. His final slide into bankruptcy forever sidelined this plan.

14. Thomas L. Purvis, *Almanacs of American Life: Revolutionary America 1763 to 1800*, (New York: Facts on File, Inc., 1995), 180.

15. Purvis, *Almanacs of American Life*, 180.

16. Purvis, 180.

17. Tanja Bueltmann, Andrew Hinson, and Graeme Morton, *The Scottish Diaspora*, (Edinburgh: Edinburgh University Press, 2013), 175.

18. Bueltmann, 183.

19. Eric Richards in Bailyn, Bernard and Philip D. Morgan, eds., "Scotland and the Uses of the Atlantic Empire," in *Strangers within the Realm: Cultural Margins of the First British Empire*, (Chapel Hill: The University of North Carolina Press, 1991), 95.

20. David Allan, *Scotland in the Eighteenth Century: Union and Enlightenment*, (London: Pearson Education, 2002), 176.

21. Allan, 176.

22. Richards, 95.

23. Purvis, 181.

24. Ibid, 181.

25. Ibid, 180.

26. Ibid, 181.

27. Richards, 69.

28. Colin G. Calloway, *White People, Indians, and Highlanders: Tribal Peoples and Colonial Encounters in Scotland and America*, (New York: Oxford University Press, 2008).

29. Richards, 84.

30. Ned Landsman, quoted in T. M. Devine, *Scottish Emigration and Scottish Society*, (Edinburgh: John Donald Publishers, LTD, 1992), 5.

31. Ibid., 5.

32. Ibid., 5.

33. Richards, 112.

34. To examine the role of Scots within the empire, see: Emma Rothschild, *The Inner Life of Empires: An Eighteenth-Century History*, (Princeton: Princeton University Press, 2011).

35. Smith, 21.

36. T. M. Devine, *Scottish Emigration and Scottish Society*, (Edinburgh: John Donald Publishers, LTD, 1992), 5.

37. Andrew Wilson to James Wilson, 1769, in the James Wilson Papers, Historical Society of Pennsylvania.

38. James Balfour to James Wilson, 6 July 1770, in the James Wilson Papers, Historical Society of Pennsylvania.
39. Ibid.
40. Ibid.
41. Ibid.
42. Minutes of The St. Andrew's Society of Philadelphia for 1767.
43. St. Andrew's Society of Philadelphia, *An Historical Catalogue of The St. Andrew's Society of Philadelphia: With Biographical Sketches of Deceased Members 1749–1907*, Philadelphia: Printed for the Society, 1907, 357.

Chapter Three

Philadelphia 1768
James Wilson, William White, and The Visitant

Upon leaving Scotland in 1765 and docking in New York that fall, James Wilson's life revolved around the city of Philadelphia. His childhood friend and cousin, Robert Annan, was a familiar face who greeted him upon his arrival. The two men had left Scotland for the opportunity to become successful in America—Annan as a minister and Wilson as a lawyer.

James Wilson quickly obtained a job at the College of Philadelphia and it was here that he first encountered William White, a man who would become a close, life-long friend. Wilson worked as a tutor at the college for only a year before securing a position as a law student of influential John Dickinson. Wilson became acquainted with Dickinson's writings on the imperial crisis and chafed to make his own mark in literate society. In early 1768, Wilson and White began publishing a commentary on society entitled *The Visitant*. The series was a success and led to widespread speculation on the identity of the author(s). After the series ended, Wilson decided that he needed to put forth his analysis of the imperial crisis. This time, his name would be prominently featured as the author. The year 1768 was a pivotal one for Wilson as he took his first steps to secure a place in literary circles, separate from his legal mentor, John Dickinson.

Among all the cities of British North America in 1765, Philadelphia was the best fit for James Wilson. In his native Scotland, opportunities to succeed in life—outside of the church, or service in the British Army—were few and difficult to acquire. At 23, the Scotsman, like many of his fellow countrymen, sought to make his fortune in life by migrating to the burgeoning British colonies of North America; his childhood friend and cousin, Robert Annan, had already preceded him and worked a nearby farm.

At the time, Philadelphia was the American center of the Enlightenment, due in large part to the efforts of its most famous citizen—Benjamin Franklin. The city was the hub of the colonial publishing industry. As a man of letters, ready access to books and a literate society was essential for James Wilson. However, even a bustling, growing city like Philadelphia could be a cold and impersonal place without friends. Upon his arrival in the city, in the fall of 1765, he quickly secured a job as a tutor of Latin at the College of Philadelphia. He was further fortunate that within a short period of time he forged the most important friendship of his life with William White, a recent graduate of his new employer.

Wilson was raised in the Scottish Presbyterian Church, but theological differences did not hinder his friendship with White, who would one day rise to the post of bishop in the Protestant Episcopal Church.[1] Once begun, their friendship endured beyond their lifetimes. White, along with Wilson's son, Bird, and Thomas Fitzsimons were appointed administrators of Wilson's estate in 1799. Bird Wilson would publish the first collection of his father's papers in 1804. He would also subsequently publish a biography of Bishop White in 1839, after a request from the bishop's family and the Episcopal clergy of Philadelphia.[2]

Wilson's relationship with White introduced him into a much wider and influential set of Philadelphia's elite—among them Robert Morris, who married White's younger sister Mary.[3] Wilson's friendship with White brought with it a religious reorientation as well—Wilson became a member of White's church and a devout Episcopalian. The influence of religion on James Wilson may have been more significant than has been acknowledged by scholars as his first wife, Rachel Bird, was the daughter of an Episcopal minister, and his son Bird became an Episcopal priest late in life, after a career as a lawyer.[4] In a letter dated October 25th, 1822, Bishop White wrote to the then Reverend Bird Wilson, responding to inquiries from Bird regarding his father. White wrote: "It is probable, that I was ye first Person in America, with whom your Father formed any considerable Degree of Acquaintance." He explained that their friendship "began in the year 1766, and continued throughout his Life: our Intercourse being also promoted by his subsequent Marriage to your Mother; between whom and my Mrs. White, there had been a still earlier Friendship."[5] When James Wilson moved back to Philadelphia in July 1778, after nearly a decade in Carlisle establishing himself with a wife, children, and a burgeoning law practice, he acquired a house across the street from William White.[6]

WILLIAM WHITE—BACKGROUND

Unlike Wilson, White had been born and educated in Philadelphia. His father, Colonel Thomas White, was a native of the imperial capital—London. After the death of his father, at the age of sixteen, Thomas White set out from London for the colony of Maryland. He was the second youngest of six children, a family that had been left in strained circumstances due to the meager resources left by their patriarch. In Maryland, he was apprenticed to a Mr. Stokes, who was the clerk of Baltimore County. At the end of his apprenticeship, Thomas White became Stokes' deputy and embarked on an intensive self-study of the law. Upon being admitted to the bar, White gained the favor of Governor Samuel Ogle who bestowed the job of county surveyor upon him. In this post, White began his acquisition of large tracts of land. Further, he was also installed as one of the two militia colonels for the county.[7]

After the death of his first wife, who was the daughter of the other militia colonel in Baltimore county, Thomas White moved to Philadelphia and married a widow, Esther Newman. The only children of the second marriage were William, born on April 4, 1748, six years younger and an ocean away from his future co-author Wilson, and a younger sister Mary, who was a year younger.[8] Later, Mary would become the wife of Robert Morris, dubbed the financier of the American Revolution. Morris would also work with James Wilson in the Second Continental Congress, Bank of North America, and Constitutional Convention of 1787.

Thomas White was enlisted as a trustee for the new College of Philadelphia. He became a trustee while the institution was still just an academy, and young William began attending when he was seven and remained a student for the next decade. William completed his studies on his birthday in 1765, a few months before James Wilson arrived in Philadelphia.[9]

Before his graduation, William White pondered what path his life would take. In 1764, he was heavily influenced by a visit to Philadelphia by the revivalist Rev. George Whitfield and the recent death of a friend of his younger sister. White wrote: "His coming, at this time, caused religion to be more than commonly a subject of conversation; and this added to the existing tendency of my mind."[10] He was particularly taken with Whitfield's oratorical style, noting, "I heard him with great delight, in his wonderful elocution . . . his force of emphasis, and the melodies of his tones and cadences, exceeded what I have ever witnessed in any other person."[11]

White's interest in the ministry attracted the attention and support of Rev. Dr. Richard Peters and Rev. Jacob Duché, who were the rector and one of the assistant ministers of Christ Church and St. Peter's. White's family were members of Christ Church.[12] In October 1770, he boarded a ship bound for

England, carrying with him recommendations for holy orders.[13] He remained in England until his ordination as a priest by the Bishop of London in June 1772; the delay was due to the need for him to reach the required age.[14] Later, that month, White embarked a ship for the return voyage to Philadelphia, where he arrived on September 13.[15] His ministerial career began in the same church that facilitated his training as he became an assistant minister.[16]

THE VISITANT

However James Wilson and William White first came to meet, their friendship was an enduring and meaningful one for both men. They were educated men who exemplified the ideals of the Enlightenment—thinking and writing about the world around them. During the winter of 1767–68, Wilson and White decided to share their observations of life in Philadelphia with the readers of the recently established *Pennsylvania Chronicle*. The paper had a liberal policy with regard to content, especially when it came from authors who could write well. The *Pennsylvania Chronicle* first made its appearance on Monday, January 26, 1767, with subsequent editions appearing each Monday until ceasing publication on February 8, 1774.[17] The *Chronicle* joined the *Pennsylvania Gazette*, the *Pennsylvania Journal,* and the German-language *Der Wöchentliche pennsylvanische Staatsbote* as weekly newspapers published in Philadelphia that year.[18] Wilson and White wrote under a pseudonym, *The Visitant*.

Why use a pseudonym? A popular convention of authors of the time was to mask their true identity and not sign with their given name.[19] The principal reason for using this tactic was explained by Herbert J. Storing: "But a pseudonym was used not merely or even mainly to enable the author to conceal or to protect himself; it was a convention aimed at directing attention at the arguments rather than at personalities."[20] Authors remained anonymous to ensure that their arguments were considered on their merit, not summarily dismissed if the reader disliked the author. A pseudonym was essential for the two young authors—Wilson sought to launch a successful law practice and White to become an ordained minister. Remaining anonymous allowed the authors to delve into issues that could have been politically ill-advised and career damaging.

Their first essay as *The Visitant* appeared in the *Pennsylvania Chronicle* on February 1, 1768, on the front page, right below the masthead, a place of prominence which it held throughout the run.[21] Only about half of the articles carried a title—usually those written by Wilson—but each installment ended with *The Visitant* as a signature. The series continued uninterrupted for the next sixteen weeks.[22] The two authors divided the writing of the series by alternating contributions.[23] Wilson wrote the odd-numbered pieces, only breaking the sequence by also writing No. XIV on the subject of the usefulness of the study of history, while White wrote the even-numbered installments.

Wilson and White used *The Visitant* as a means to "communicate to the public my observations on the common incidents of life in a loose unconnected manner, as my humour shall prompt me, or as the subjects themselves shall direct."[24] Masquerading as a visitor—a mere observer—in Philadelphia's society would permit the authors to comment on any topic or facet of society that drew their attention. A well-tested and effective Enlightenment strategy of exploring topics dealing with politics, history, social customs, and even dating all fell within the purview of the series. In the debut installment, Wilson wrote: "My readers will judge of my remarks. If they are thought sensible or entertaining, I expect they will be received with applause; if they are thought to have the opposite qualities, I shall be obliged to the first pen that will give me a friendly admonition to discontinue them."[25] *The Visitant*—No. I, served as an introduction to the series as a whole. Wilson identified "happiness, which is the final end of our existence, and the mark at which we aim," as the rationale for the series.[26]

To examine happiness, all the components, the object of the happiness as well as the person desiring happiness required observation and a relationship established between the two. This method of scientific inquiry served as a foundation upon which discussion of topics rested in the series. Wilson argued that neither a purely scientific, nor a purely observational approach would suffice—the two approaches "should be joined."[27]

The pursuit of knowledge "is delightful to the mind; and every new idea brings along with it a new pleasure: the pleasure is increased if the idea is important as well as new."[28] Wilson urged readers to participate in what I have labeled a virtual salon, an intellectual exercise to examine Philadelphia society in minute detail and share their observations with each other and fellow readers of the column. This give-and-take between author and reader created an expanded public sphere for enlightened discussion. The traditional European salon of the Enlightenment was one that could only be accessed through invitation.[29] From the very beginning of the series, Wilson extended an open invitation to each and every reader, creating something new—something uniquely American and more inclusive than its European counterparts.

The examination of human nature was the first and foremost use of our powers of reason. Wilson wrote that "every thing becomes important in proportion as it is connected with us: nothing has a stricter connection with us than reflections on human nature."[30] The full and complete nature of human endeavour was the study of the human condition. "Logic considers us as men of sense; ethics, as men of virtue; criticism, as men of taste; jurisprudence, as members of society."[31] Even disciplines such as mathematics and natural philosophy were, in their own way, of use in the study of humanity as "they derive all their value either from improving our judgments, from enlarging our conceptions, or from ministering to our conveniency."[32] The sum total of all human learning was an attempt to evaluate, assess, and improve humanity itself.

In a later installment, No. XIV, Wilson explained the value of the study of history for informing our decisions in the present, grounded in lessons of the past. Here, in No. I, he remarked, "If we would study human nature with success, . . . [w]e must have experience, in order to correct our reasoning in order to profit by our experience."[33] Wilson put forth an eloquent summation of the Enlightenment itself: "Formed for society, and fond of it, I experience, from my observations on the usual occurrences of life, not only the intellectual delight of having the number of my ideas increased, but the moral one of participating in the joys and differences of those I converse with."[34] Here was the definition and character of *The Visitant* himself.

Wilson provided an example of the proper way to conduct such observations. "I conform myself to the temper of my company . . . I talk of state affairs with the politician; of commerce with the merchant; of trifles with the coquette; of divinity with the parson."[35] He confessed that he was "happiest in small companies; and those I think are best, when they are composed of near an equal number of both sexes. The conversation has then an agreeable mixture of sense and delicacy."[36] Wilson closed the series' first installment and set the tone for the future by acknowledging, "I prefer the conversation of a fine woman to that of a philosopher."[37]

Shortly after the first appearance of *The Visitant*, speculation as to the identity of the author(s) became a topic of conversation in Philadelphia gatherings. At the same time that the series was attracting attention, the final installments of John Dickinson's *Letters of a Pennsylvania Farmer* were appearing in the *Pennsylvania Chronicle*. Dickinson was Wilson's law teacher and political mentor. The authorial identity of both series was touched upon in a letter from John Macpherson to William Patterson on March 11; though Dickinson was mentioned as a possible author for *Letters*, the public's attention never fell upon the young authors of Wilson and White for *The Visitant*, but more prominent Philadelphia men.[38]

The Visitant struck a chord with Philadelphia's reading public as readers took the authors up on their offer and submitted letters to the *Pennsylvania Chronicle*, which Wilson and White reprinted in subsequent installments and commented upon.[39] This give-and-take between author and reader, what I have labeled a virtual salon, created an expanded public sphere for enlightened discussion.

The virtual salon was an American adaptation of the formal salon seen in Europe. In France, the salon took the form of a gathering of intellectuals at the home of a lady of stature who had received training on the proper form and manner of hosting a salon.[40] Salons exchanged letters with groups in other French cities to facilitate the circulation of information among French intellectuals. However, once a letter left the possession of the author, the information contained therein could enter the public sphere and became a concern for public discussion and judgment. In Wilson's Scotland, gatherings of Enlightenment thinkers were almost exclusively male. The innovation in Philadelphia was the deliberate incorporation of the public from the very outset of *The Visitant*. In 1768, the virtual salon found in the pages of the *Pennsylvania Chronicle* was a salon where participants interacted in print, not in person, and which embraced the reading public of Philadelphia—both male *and* female.

When the series, as a whole, is examined, topics revolving around, dealing with, and of interest to women is the overarching thread that dominates the virtual salon of *The Visitant*. In early installments, *The Visitant* commented on proper behavior and responsibilities of men, but once women began contributing to the series, the role of women in society, particularly unmarried

Table 3.1. The Visitant in Print: *Pennsylvania Chronicle*, Philadelphia, PA

Date	Author	No.	Topic
February 1, 1768	James Wilson	1	Introduction to Series*
February 8	William White	2	Remarks on Conversation.
February 15	Wilson	3	Remarks on the fair sex—on female conversation and accomplishments
February 22	White	4	Politeness*
February 29	Wilson	5	Pleasures*
March 7	White	6	Modesty*
March 14	Wilson	7	Remarks on the fair sex.
March 21	White	8	Remarks on the dress of the ladies.
March 28	Wilson	9	Remarks on the fair sex.
April 4	White	10	Remarks on Sex
April 11	Wilson	11	The Turn of the Ladies*
April 18	White	12	Courage*
April 25	Wilson	13	Morality and Math*
May 2	Wilson	14	History*
May 9	Wilson	15	Usefulness of History for Virtue*
May 16	White	16	Ladies*

* Denotes a topic that I have given the column.

women, filled the series' columns and it is the contribution made by readers—who took the time and effort to compose pieces for submission—to which our attention now turns.

THE VISITANT, NO. II

William White's first contribution to the series investigated the topic of proper conversation. Building upon themes present in Wilson's No. I, White desired that "conversation would always turn upon agreeable and important subjects. Every subject is agreeable and important, in proportion as it is connected with human nature, and has an influence upon the happiness of ourselves or others."[41] White believed there was benefit in such conversation as "it enriches me with the sentiments of other men; and by raising in my mind a series of useful reflections, call forth new ones of my own."[42] The vital component of good, stimulating conversation was "associating with men of different tempers and dispositions."[43] This was the key for obtaining an education in the "science of human nature"—adoption of the role of *The Visitant* facilitated contact with members of Philadelphia society of all professions, education, social standing, and background.

White directed his attention to what he labeled "men of pleasure," men who "may be said to act without thinking."[44] In future installments of the series, *The Visitant* challenged historical female stereotypes. Unlike stereotypes of emotional, uninformed women, White took aim at contemporaries he was acquainted with. These men were found deficient in the very attributes that White exalted as desirable—an open, inquiring mind capable of sustained discussion and examination of a wide variety of topics, leading ultimately to informed and judicious determinations. Their lack of focus and disinterest in learning was off-putting and he determined to "avoid these impertinent triflers, as often as it may be done consistent with the rules of good-breeding."[45] However, avoiding these men was difficult as "they are usually found in the most frequent places, and politest companies."[46] But, in the interest of an examination of human nature, they were useful as practical examples of conduct and lifestyles to be avoided.

Good conversation was a give-and-take, not a one-sided lecture. He believed that "[n]o regard should be paid to the particular circumstances of any one; the lawyer, the merchant, and the politician, should each lay aside what distinguishes him from the rest, and appear in no other character, than as a man of sense."[47] However, for those who were incapable of this type of behavior, White declared: "How tiresome is it, when any single person undertakes to entertain others with matters that concern none but himself, and with which no one else can be affected?"[48] How could anyone so wrapped up in themselves and their personal affairs ever learn something new, if they didn't take the time to observe the world around them and listen to others? At the very least, this behavior was an affront to those in attendance.

The affront was compounded when the offending party possessed a "loud voice and voluble pronunciation."[49] When White found himself in these situations, he determined to remain in the background, an observer to the proceedings going on around him. This tactic served his research interests as "[t]his power of abstracting myself from the company, I esteem a considerable advantage, because I thereby receive improvement from what displeases many, and make other men's faults serviceable to my enquiries into human nature."[50] Once again, virtually any social situation could be useful in the interest of research.

In a discussion of what constituted proper conversation, White closed with comments on the propensity of people to gossip. He considered gossip as "diverting ourselves at the expence of others" and no less an offense than dominating a conversation with talk of yourself and ignoring the interests of those present.[51] Such conduct wasted valuable time that could be put to better use. When conversation turned to gossip, White used the opportunity "to observe the different motives which influence the several persons present—but without relying upon the truth of what they advance, for those who are actuated by an uncharitable principle, seldom fail to aggravate a bad action, if not entirely misrepresent a good one."[52] The *motivations* of those gossiping were the most valuable part of the conversation, not the content of the gossip itself.

White offered readers a few concluding comments on how to effectively deal with men of pleasure, men who were conceited, and those consumed by gossip. He urged readers to "cultivate good humour and politeness; let a man be pleased himself, and he will of course be pleased with others: let a man be desirous of entertaining others, and he will avoid every thing that may be disagreeable to them."[53] *How* conversation was conducted was, in some ways, just as important as *what* was discussed.

Wilson's No. III was the first installment of the series on the subject of women, constraining itself to "female conversation and accomplishments," appearing the day after Valentine's Day.[54] He noted that in the role of *The Visitant*, he had frequent opportunities to be in the company of women, "and I must acknowledge, that I receive great improvement, as well as pleasure, from their society."[55] Reminding readers that he had concluded No. I with an observation that he preferred the company of a fine woman to that of a philosopher, he proceeded to explain his reasoning. "The reflections of the philosopher are deduced in a chain of abstract reasoning," while "the sentiments of a sensible woman, arise in an easy and natural way from matters of common observation, without the intervention of many intermediate ideas—hence your fair companion will entertain you with more plain, agreeable and just reflections than the profound philosopher."[56]

To allay any concerns, on the part of the reader, that he was only siding with a woman because of her beauty, Wilson explained, "I *admire* the beauties of her person, though I am *enslaved* by the virtues of her mind."[57] Further, the expense of her wardrobe had no effect on him, as he wrote, "I prefer simplicity to finery, because simplicity in dress seems to adorn the lady, whereas finery engages the attention to itself."[58] Wilson identified what he called principal qualities—wit, sense, and delicacy—as those components comprising good female conversation.

Addressing a common stereotype, Wilson noted, "How often is it pretended that women have little minds, that they are naturally vain, and disposed to be pleased with trifles!"[59] This belief, he argued, was due more to the person making the statement, because they were men, than from direct experience through observation. He also took issue with the assertion "that the cultivation of the mind is of less importance than the external accomplishments of person and behaviour."[60] He identified this sentiment with the insecurities of men and the constrained opportunities for female education, than from any deficiency on the part of women to acquire knowledge. Wilson realized that the social convention of his day discouraged women from overtly displaying their learning. He praised the condition where "good sense, improved by reading, is united with the amiable virtues of modesty and submission, with a desire of being, rather than appearing to be, wiser than others . . . a character that exposes their own, without assuming the privilege of doing so."[61] It would be his duty, as *The Visitant*, to seek out such women.

Before continuing with his discussion of admirable women, Wilson took two types of men to task—the fop and the debauchee. These men were deficient in their dealings with women as "[t]he life of the debauchee makes him undervalue a virtuous woman; and the respects of the fop can be no compliment to her understanding."[62] He further identified a third type of deficient man—the gossip who seeks to tarnish the reputations and good name of women, deriving pleasure from doing so. Even though No. III was titled "Remarks on the fair sex—on female conversation and accomplishments," Wilson felt it necessary to chastise the actions of men as a factor in the relative reputations of his subject—the single women of Philadelphia.

Why should readers—especially his female readers—place any credence in his observations of women? Wilson reassured them by explaining: "My diligent application to those things that employ their attention, has made me more learned upon subjects that lie within the province of a lady, than the generality of my sex. This makes me a competent judge in matters that lie beyond the reach of other men's capacities."[63] In other words, he had observed and paid attention to what women had told him of their interests, views on various topics, which qualified him to speak as he did. Further, he confided that "I always avoid those arts of flattery which many of our sex have employed to insinuate themselves into your good graces; these I utterly disclaim; not only because flattery is in itself contemptible, but because I do not observe . . . that it meets in general with the expected success."[64] One has to wonder how much of this belief was due to his own inadequacy when pursuing romantic relationships and how much came from observations of others.

During the next three installments of *The Visitant*, White examined the topic of politeness on February 22 and modesty on March 7; Wilson delved into a discussion of pleasure on February 29. With the appearance of No. VII on March 14, written by Wilson, through No. XI on April 11, again written by Wilson, *The Visitant* dealt almost exclusively with the topic of women.

Readers of *The Visitant* were concerned with issues other than just how to act in polite society and how to hold an intelligent and mutually enjoyable conversation in mixed company. Just like the young, eligible bachelor authors, readers wrote letters to the editor wanting to gain tips on how to successfully find a spouse. In a letter to John Alleyne in the year that *The Visitant* appeared, 1768, Benjamin Franklin commented on the importance of marriage in the colonies:

> With us in America, marriages are generally in the morning of life—our children are therefore educated, and settled in the world, by noon; we have an afternoon and evening of chearful leizure to ourselves — . . . By these early marriages, we are blest with more children; and, from the mode among us—founded in nature—of every mother suckling and nursing her own child, more of them are raised. Thence the swift progress of population, among us—unparalleled in Europe![65]

In the period of 1771–1800 in nearby Lancaster County, the median age at first marriage for men was 25.8 and for women 21.9; these marriages produced a median of 8 children per family, with a median of 6.4 children surviving to the age of 20.[66] The mortality rates for children living in Philadelphia were not as favorable. From 1765–1770, children under the age of 5 suffered a mortality rate in excess of 46 percent.[67]

As James Wilson began his law career in 1768, he eagerly sought a spouse with whom to start a family. The stakes were high; divorce was virtually unknown, for in the period 1766–1774, only 6 divorce petitions in the entire colony were filed and only 2 granted.[68] The careful selection of a spouse would be exceedingly beneficial for the future careers of Wilson and White.

THE VIRTUAL SALON

The March 14 publication of No. VII marked the initiation of the virtual salon phase of *The Visitant*. At the very end of the installment, a response from a reader was included. Identified as being "from a circle of ladies" who, responding to Wilson's No. III on February 15, decided to compose a poem.[69]

The poem began by praising the author,

> HAIL, candid, gen'rous man, whoe'er thou art;
> Thy sentiments bespeak a noble heart.

the ladies then agree to recognize the series as a legitimate commentator on the subject of women,

> With joy we stile thee censor of the fair—
> To rectify their foibles by thy care.
>
> Thee, who canst give to virtue praises due,
> We safely trust—to lash our errors too.

weighty issues and informed discussion would shape this virtual salon,

> No keen reproach from satire's pen we fear,
> Of little minds, or painted toys to hear.

they concurred with the assessment from No. III that any deficiency in learning was from lack of education, not a physical defect,

> You, sir, with better sense, will justly fix
> Our faults on education, not our sex;
> Will shew the source, which makes the female mind
> So oft appear but puerile and blind.

by submitting their poem for publication, this circle of ladies, had become part of a larger, more public conversation,

> How many would surmount stern custom's laws,
> And prove the want of genius not the cause;
> But that the odium of a bookish fair,

> Or female pedant, or "they quit their sphere,"
> Damps all their views, and they must drag the chain,
> And sigh for sweet instruction's page in vain.

they closed by urging *The Visitant* on, to lead the conversation where he would and they would gladly follow,

> But we commit our injur'd cause to you—
> Point out the medium which we should pursue;
> So may each scene of soft domestic peace
> Heighten your joys, and animate your bliss.[70]

During the remainder of the series, a number of letters were submitted to the paper and published with comments from Wilson and White.

The next letter was published with No. IX on March 28. Signed with just the initials T.S.B., the letter took *The Visitant* to task with previous characterizations of women. T.S.B., after reading previous numbers of the series, "discovered you were rather velvet mouthed; and that instead of lashing the foibles of those delightful objects, at the same time that you praise their virtues, you seem much inclined to think they have no foibles at all."[71] To place the comments of T.S.B. in context, Wilson had attached a brief introduction to the letter by determining the author "appears to be out of humour with the fair sex; whether his reflexions are just or not, I leave to be considered by the accused party."[72] In the true spirit of a virtual salon, Wilson did not censor the piece, but allowed readers to determine the value of the submission.

The principle point T.S.B. wanted dealt with was female gossip. He charged that when ladies gathered for conversation, "the voice of slander is often too predominant."[73] Unlike the polite, constructive conversation *The Visitant* had championed, too often the ladies "confine themselves too much to raillery, and throwing out severe sarcasms against those of their coevals whom they think handsomer, or who dress finer than themselves."[74] T.S.B. advised *The Visitant* to "enlarge not only upon these, but upon every other of their faults that comes within your knowledge."[75] If the authors would heed his advice, "then you will act up to your character; and without that, I think you cannot properly take upon yourself the title of a Visitant."[76]

T.S.B. believed that it was the proper role of men in society to criticize the behavior of women and to guide them onto a path of improvement. He noted that virtually all women needed some form of correction and those "who are all perfection" were "Something seldom to be found."[77] This established an interesting dynamic between T.S.B. and *The Visitant*—the former sought to retain the traditional prerogatives of men, while the latter advocated a more equivalent partnership.

T.S.B. felt compelled to submit another letter, this time in response to the publication of his first, which appeared at the beginning of No. XI on April 11. He did not take kindly the insinuation that Wilson had included in the introduction where he posited that T.S.B. "was out of humour with the Ladies."[78] He alleged this was not the case, but that the purpose of his letter "was to give you a little jog, to put you in mind of your duty; and as your style is very delicate, and your address much admired by the lovely creatures in general, you might, at the same time that you delight, give them a few lines of instruction."[79] This appears to be a slap at Wilson as he emasculates his style as "very delicate" and then urges him to use his forum to give "the lovely creatures . . . a few lines of instruction."[80] T.S.B. then explained what type of "instruction" he had in mind.

He "would have you paint their virtues in the most glaring light."[81] The observations conducted of female behavior would garner the evidence needed to "represent their vices in the grossest deformity."[82] Summarizing his advice: "In short, my only meaning was, that you should permit them to behold themselves in an impartial mirror, that they may avoid those follies that make beauty disgustful, and even good sense disagreeable."[83]

Wilson felt it necessary to respond to these criticisms and planned to comment "on the love of dominion in the fair sex," but stopped when he "received the following excellent letter, which wholly diverted me from executing my design."[84] A noteworthy feature of No. XI is that it not only contained a letter from T.S.B., but also a remarkable contribution from a Philadelphian who signed using the name Aspasia. In previous installments of the series and in both letters from T.S.B., authors had included quotes from authorities both ancient and modern. It was a sign of her breadth of education that Aspasia took the name of a figure from Greek history. The historical Aspasia, through her relationship with Pericles, established a salon in her home in Athens, according to Plutarch. Prominent writers, philosophers, and thinkers frequented her home, including Socrates.[85] Aspasia was the prototype of a model for the hostesses of the French Enlightenment. By adopting this pseudonym, the 1768 version both exhibited her own learning and validated her inclusion in the virtual salon.[86]

Wilson agreed with Aspasia's "observations upon the ungenerous conduct of us men are but too well founded," which forced him to admit that "an immoderate attachment to power in us is one reason why we complain so much of it in the women."[87] The collection and use of power would dominate his thinking later in the year as he considered the state of the imperial crisis, but here, the use of power within a relationship between two people, not nations or continents, held his attention. Foreshadowing future arguments in the political realm, Wilson determined that "we would see fewer *rebels*, were there fewer *tyrants*, who provoke them to rebellion."[88]

The exercise of power, not the sex of the individual, was the topic of discussion. Wilson agreed with the belief "that many a Lady is content to take a fool for her husband, in order to govern with absolute sway"; however, this was no less true for many men as well.[89] No. XI is a fascinating artifact of the time. Here, in a public forum, men and women of colonial Philadelphia, part of the periphery of the British Empire, but a rising city with a vibrant intellectual community, debated the very foundations and central questions of the Enlightenment. T.S.B. represented the segment of society committed to the established order, Aspasia stepped forth to argue on behalf of unmarried women, and *The Visitant* moderated the debate, but lent support to Aspasia's side of the discussion.

At the outset of her contribution, Aspasia addressed an issue, which readers of the series had to ask themselves: Who was *The Visitant*? What type of person were they? Did they really support what they were arguing (i.e., support for increased appreciation of women's ideas and their contribution to society) or were they just playing a role to spark debate? She professed she was "totally ignorant" of *The Visitant*'s true nature but was determined to give the author the benefit of the doubt. "I hope the kind advocate of our cause is as agreeable in private life, as in public; and in this he is truly amiable."[90]

Aspasia examined *The Visitant* series as a whole—a wide-ranging commentary on society—to which she would respond. Commenting on White's No. IV concerning the topic of politeness, and Wilson's No. VII and No. IX on the fair sex, she acknowledged, "Among many good things you say, you endeavour to shew what are the steps to attain esteem, and what to attain admiration." However, she responded by remarking, "Sir, you must correct some faults in your own sex, before you can brighten the shades of ours."[91]

The social dance of acquiring a spouse dominated the balance of Aspasia's letter. She disparaged the attention paid to beautiful women of limited education, something that *The Visitant* himself had dealt with in Nos. VII and IX. After the time and effort of acquiring an education, a young woman "enters upon life, and mixes in a polite circle of both sexes; must it not give her a sensible mortification to see a girl of sprightly levity, whose understanding, if she is pretty, is thought brilliant; whose tartness is styled elegant repartee."[92] According to Aspasia, this attention to beauty and not intellect damaged the prospects of a woman of learning. "[M]ust it not mortify her to see such an one singled out and draw the attention of men of merit, while *she* is passed by without notice?"[93] Men, like moths, are drawn to the appearance of beauty, not the merits of the mind.

Aspasia admonished men's taste in women as possessing "extremely confined" notions of what constituted a desirable spouse. She acknowledged that not all men subscribed to the "coarse, inelegant, trite saying, 'Give me a wife that can make a shirt and a pudding.'"[94] However, she urged *The Visitant*, if he was consistent, he would need to agree with her that "this sentiment runs through the major part of the lordly race."[95]

The core of Aspasia's argument is quite simple: men needed to recognize that an educated, thinking, *partner* constituted a valuable asset to a marriage, not a hindrance. She ridiculed the belief that "the more a woman's understanding is improved, the more apt she will be to despise her husband—That the strengthening of her reason will weaken her affection—That the duties of tenderness and attention, and all the social train will be disregarded in proportion as her knowledge is increased."[96] This argument is not as radical as it might sound. Aspasia believed that as women became more educated, they would come to understand their role in society. She asked, "Does not the enlargement of the understanding point out the relative duties? And is not subordination to a husband one of them?"[97] Further, the notion that as women became more educated they were less affectionate was also false. "Does not knowledge dilate and expand the finer feelings of the mind, and make it thrill in a thousand vibrations, unknown to the savage and untutored soul?"[98] For a marriage to be fruitful for both parties, Aspasia argued for a reimagining of the institution, toward the now-familiar companionate ideal.

Aspasia explained her ideals versus those of social expectation. She remarked, "Steadiness to a degree of perseverance is absolutely requisite in us."[99] Expectations for women were to secure the best husband possible and then be the best wife and mother possible. "Before marriage, it is necessary in the important point of dismissing or accepting lovers: For you know, Sir, that is all a single woman has to do."[100] After agreeing to become a wife, she then became responsible for the education of children and overseeing matters concerning the household, including subordinate members of the family. A wife's role, in relation to her husband, "is a virtue never to peep out, where his lordly prerogative is concerned."[101] Her role changed again, after the death of her husband, in the "widowed state, where we have to act in so many different capacities."[102] Throughout her life, the value of a wife was determined by her relationship with those around her.

At the end of William White's No. XII, another letter appeared, this time from a man who identified himself as A.B. A.B. identified himself as an "old man," marking a new participant to the series and the final public contribution to the virtual salon.[103] His contribution is unique in that it is offered by one who has lived the life of excess—a lifestyle the series warned against. A.B. brings the time-worn wisdom of life experience to the salon. He applauded the appearance of *The Visitant*, a voice that needed to be heard. "For my part I only mean in this letter to cast in the small mite which my own experience furnishes, against the prevailing corruption of the age."[104]

Early in life, A.B. noted, he had fallen in with a peer group for which "pleasure was the object of our wishes, and dissipation its constant attendant: Scarcely did we ever deny ourselves the gratification of our desires, however criminal in their nature." Their driving force was to find new and interesting ways to fulfill these desires. Further, they "derided those who, from our rectitude of heart, and a generous concern for our welfare, could not but pity and lament our ill conduct."[105] For A.B. and his friends, life was a grand banquet from which they liberally partook to the detriment of all around them. The story of A.B. and his peers stood as a warning to readers who did not heed the advice found in *The Visitant*. This frank discussion of masculinity broadened the reach of the virtual salon to encompass the roles and responsibilities of *both* genders.

One member of his company contracted a fatal disease from their activities. A.B. did not spell out what type of malady befell his friend, but instead, he quoted a few lines from the "Dying Rake's Soliloquy."[106] After the death of his friend, the lesson imparted to the rest of the group quickly faded, who quickly returned to their life of pleasure. Their revelries continued unabated, only curbed by lack of financial means. When the time came to seek a living, many found it difficult, if not impossible, to change direction as a "long mischievous habit of indolence had rendered very difficult."[107] A few were diligent in their work only until they had amassed funds for another round of pleasure seeking.

Others sought refuge in the institution of marriage, much to the detriment of their wives. These men quickly turned their backs on any responsibility to family and returned to their previous lifestyle. They quickly squandered their "patrimonal inheritance, but even suffered their families to want the common necessaries of life."[108] Wives were neglected, humiliated, and ridiculed, while their children were "unnaturally neglected and suffered to run loose in the world," and thus another generation was created who "often become a scandal to their friends, and a reproach to their country."[109] The cycle of dysfunctional male behavior continued into a new generation.

A.B.'s contribution to the virtual salon cast a shadow over previous discussions; issues of courtship, marriage, and responsibility to family took on a new shape as the story of a group of pleasure-seeking men unfolded. He lamented, "Such, Sir, has been the unhappy fate of my companions, which I think an instructive lesson to the world, because it is the natural effect of a similar course of life."[110] He hoped that his observations would be useful to readers. For "it will afford me matter of real pleasure."[111] However, "if it should not, at least, an old man, may comfort himself with having attempted to cast in his mite against that growing and dangerous evil, of giving in our youth an ungoverned rein to our passions."[112] The wisdom of age and experience complimented the observations of others in the virtual salon and served as a potent warning to others from the end of a life lived in the pursuit of pleasure.

The series ended with White's publication of No. XVI, on May 16, which also dealt with the topic of women. White addressed the perception that a single woman was "too fond of displaying her charms upon every occasion."[113] This fed into a belief among "the silly part of our sex (who) imagines the Ladies are continually employed in studying how to take them in, as it is called."[114] This turned the entire process of finding a spouse into a game.

To change the perception of a game of entrapment, White offered this advice: "Dress serves to adorn the person; to dress too much, shews that you give too much attention to your person."[115] If dress became the standard by which to judge the quality of a woman, then it lent credence to the determination that single women were fierce rivals for the affection of men and relationships between these women would be grounded in hate for one another. White concluded the series with an observation that "these reflections against the fair sex are frequently unjust, but that the Ladies have it in their power to inspire more favourable sentiments."[116]

The issue that had dominated the attention of *The Visitant*—women, their worldview and relationships between men and women—also dominated the attention of both of the series' authors. Just as they had offered commentary on courtship, the two men consulted and confided in each other as they sought spouses. Mary Harrison and Rachel Bird were friends before the two women became recipients of attention from William White and James Wilson. James and Rachel were married on November 5, 1771.[117] William and Mary were married in February 1773, after his return from England.[118]

Looking at the virtual salon of *The Visitant*, several observations need to be made. William White, a future bishop in the Protestant Episcopal Church, functioned as the more conservative voice of the two authors. Conservative in the sense that his contributions to the series concerning women were more traditional critiques of their subject, much like those forwarded by outside contributor A.B. James Wilson's contributions were much more willing to address the current role of women in society and how that might evolve, especially through the expansion of education for women.

The men's writing style differed as well. White's style, much like that of many ministers, was more critical toward the topics under discussion and Wilson's was more vibrant and argumentative, much like that of a defense attorney whose client was the group of young single women in Philadelphia polite society. Despite these differing styles, *The Visitant* was a very public space where the thinking men and women of Philadelphia gathered and felt free to discuss issues that concerned everyone as members of the Enlightenment.

ASPASIA UNMASKED

The disguised identities of contributors to *The Visitant*, besides the principal authors themselves, ensured anonymity but raised questions as to who they actually were. In the case of Aspasia, she can be identified.

James Wilson arrived in Philadelphia in the fall of 1765. He quickly became immersed in the literate culture of the city and sought out contacts among the Scottish community. A prominent figure in that community was Elizabeth Graeme Fergusson.[119]

While James Wilson was preparing for his journey to North America, Miss Elizabeth Graeme of Philadelphia traveled to England for a year's stay in 1764, chaperoned by Rev. Dr. Richard Peters, the rector of Christ Church. Peters introduced Graeme to notable figures throughout the British Isles, many of whom Graeme continued to correspond with upon her return to Philadelphia. She was even introduced to King George III himself. The pair then traveled to Scotland to visit her father's relatives. While there she was given the family coat-of-arms.[120]

During their stay in London, Miss Graeme began a friendship with Thomas Penn and his wife Juliana, who had previously donated books to the circulating library in Lancaster.[121] The relationship with Pennsylvania's proprietor family aligned Elizabeth Graeme firmly with the establishment in colonial and imperial society. She kept a travel journal of her time in the heart of the British Empire.

Her time in the British Isles introduced Graeme to the salon society of the literary elite. Upon her return to Philadelphia, she determined to recreate an American version of what she had participated in abroad. After the death of her mother, Miss Graeme lived with her father in a large house on the north side of Chestnut Street above Sixth, which had once served as the home of Governor Thomas from 1738 to 1747.[122] It was here that Miss Graeme established a Philadelphia salon.

Invitations were extended to interesting individuals, a frequent guest being Dr. Benjamin Rush, to gather at her home. According to Rush, "all strangers of note who visited Philadelphia were introduced to it. Saturday evenings were appropriated, for many years during Miss Graeme's winter residence in the city, for the entertainment, not only of strangers, but of such of her friends of both sexes as were considered the most suitable company for them."[123] One of the many attendees was a young gentleman, Mr. Henry Hugh Fergusson, recently arrived from Scotland. The two were soon inseparable, despite Fergusson being ten years junior to Miss Graeme, and after a brief courtship the two were married.[124]

James Wilson would naturally have attracted the attention of Elizabeth Graeme Fergusson as a Scotsman and a man of letters. Her father helped found the Philadelphia chapter of the St. Andrew's Society in 1749 and served as its president until his death.[125] Wilson joined the group in 1767 and also served as president during the last decade of his life.

Wilson was a natural fit to receive invitations to Fergusson's Philadelphia salon and as such it is entirely possible that she knew that one of the authors of *The Visitant* was James Wilson. Submitting contributions to the series as Aspasia was completely in character as the two moved Saturday evening sessions from a physical location to a weekly virtual one.

The Visitant allowed James Wilson to try out his ideas and writing style in a public forum and was favorably received by readers. Working with William White had been a positive experience, but with an eye towards their future careers in the law and clergy, the use of a pseudonym was deemed necessary. Wilson desired to see his own ideas in print, like those of his mentor John Dickinson.

James Wilson remained anxious of the future. He had experienced a small taste of notoriety and wanted more. He was single, ambitious, and looking to make a name for himself. He had taken his first steps on his American journey, but wanted much, much more.

The year 1768 was significant in James Wilson's life. Not only was he a driving force behind *The Visitant*, but he also turned his intellectual attention to the looming imperial crisis. Wilson's pen brought forth *Considerations on the Nature and Extent of the Legislative Authority of the British Parliament*. The pamphlet, when written, was far in advance of much colonial thinking, but on the advice of colleagues, he delayed publication until 1774.

NOTES

1. Bird Wilson, *Memoir of the Life of the Right Reverend William White, D.D., Bishop of the Protestant Episcopal Church in the State of Pennsylvania*, (Philadelphia: James Kay, Jun. and Brother, 1839), 12.

2. Bird Wilson began the biography for Bishop White shortly after White's funeral on July 21, 1836. The manuscript was delivered for publication in September 1837

and was published in 1839. B. Wilson, iii. The only mention of James Wilson in the biography of William White is in a footnote on page 69 relating to the Fort Wilson incident.

3. B. Wilson, 15.

4. Martin Clagett, "James Wilson—His Scottish Background: Corrections and Additions," *Pennsylvania History: A Journal of Mid-Atlantic Studies*, Vol. 79, No. 2 (Spring 2012), 172.

5. Letter from William White to Bird Wilson, October 25, 1822, James Wilson Papers (Collection 721), The Historical Society of Pennsylvania.

6. This would be the home where James Wilson and his friends came under siege during the Fort Wilson incident of October 4, 1779. He would live there until forced to move, due to constrained finances, to a rental property in the last years of his life.

7. This account is constructed from B. Wilson, 12–13.

8. Ibid., 15.

9. Ibid., 18.

10. Ibid., 22.

11. Ibid., 22–23.

12. Ibid., 26.

13. Ibid., 31.

14. Ibid., 41.

15. Ibid., 42.

16. Ibid., 42.

17. John J. Zimmerman, "Benjamin Franklin and the Pennsylvania Chronicle," *The Pennsylvania Magazine of History and Biography*, Vol. 81, No. 4 (Oct 1957), 354.

18. Clarence S. Brigham, *History and Bibliography of American Newspapers 1690–1820 Volume Two*, (Worcester, MA: American Antiquarian Society, 1947), 929–37.

19. See Eran Shalev, "Ancient Masks, American Fathers: Classical Pseudonyms during the American Revolution and Early Republic," *Journal of the Early Republic*, 23, No. 2. (Summer, 2003), 151–72. Also useful is Eric Burns, *Infamous Scribblers: The Founding Fathers and the Rowdy Beginnings of American Journalism*. New York: PublicAffairs, 2006.

20. Herbert J. Storing, ed., *The Complete Anti-Federalist: Vol. 2–Objections of Non-Signers of the Constitution and Major Series of Essays at the Outset*, (Chicago: The University of Chicago Press, 1981), 222.

21. See **Table 3.1** for a complete publishing and authorial history of *The Visitant*'s initial run. Only one installment of the series, No. VI, on March 7, 1768, appeared on an inside page. The front page was reserved for the prospectus of a new organization, the American Society. It received similar place of honor in the week's edition of the *Pennsylvania Gazette*.

22. The series came to an end as Wilson prepared to begin his legal career by moving to Carlisle, PA and White embarked on his divinity training.

23. After studying the series, Burton Alva Konkle determined that the odd-numbered pieces "have the unmistakable peculiarities of this young lawyer's

expression, tone, and dignity, and are of much more marked virility than those of his colleague." Burton Alva Konkle, "The Life and Writings of James Wilson, 1742–1798," page 42 of the manuscript for "Volume I—Life of Times."

24. James Wilson, "The Visitant—No. I," *Pennsylvania Chronicle*, 1 February 1768.

25. Wilson, "The Visitant—No. I."

26. Ibid.

27. Ibid.

28. Ibid.

29. For discussion of how salons worked in France see: Dena Goodman, *The Republic of Letters: A Cultural History of the French Enlightenment*, Ithaca, NY: Cornell University Press, 1994. For discussion of the Scottish Enlightenment see: James Buchan, *Crowded with Genius: Edinburgh, 1745–1789*, New York: Harper-Collins, 2003.

30. Wilson, "The Visitant—No. I."

31. Ibid.

32. Ibid.

33. Ibid.

34. Ibid.

35. Ibid.

36. Ibid.

37. Ibid.

38. John Macpherson to William Patterson, March 11, 1768.

39. Authorship of the letters from readers appears to be from both men and women, unless Wilson and White resorted to a tactic utilized by Benjamin Franklin of impersonating readers, especially women.

40. See Dena Goodman, *The Republic of Letters: A Cultural History of the French Enlightenment*, Ithaca, NY: Cornell University Press, 1994, 6–10, 76, and chapter 3.

41. William White, "The Visitant—No. II," *Pennsylvania Chronicle*, 8 February 1768.

42. White, "The Visitant–No. II."

43. Ibid.

44. Ibid.

45. Ibid.

46. Ibid.

47. Ibid.

48. Ibid.

49. Ibid.

50. Ibid.

51. Ibid.

52. Ibid.

53. Ibid.

54. James Wilson, "The Visitant—No. III," *Pennsylvania Chronicle*, 15 February 1768.

55. Wilson, "The Visitant—No. III."

56. Ibid.
57. Ibid.
58. Ibid.
59. Ibid.
60. Ibid.
61. Ibid.
62. Ibid.
63. Ibid.
64. Ibid.
65. Susan E. Klepp, *"The Swift Progress of Population": A Documentary and Bibliographic Study of Philadelphia's Growth, 1642–1859*. (Philadelphia: American Philosophical Society, 1991), 1.
66. Thomas L. Purvis, *Almanacs of American Life: Revolutionary America 1763 to 1800,* (New York: Facts on File, Inc., 1995), 179.
67. Purvis, 179.
68. Purvis, 310. Of the 6, 5 were filed by the husband and only 1 by the wife.
69. James Wilson, "The Visitant—No. VII," *Pennsylvania Chronicle*, 14 March 1768.
70. Wilson, "The Visitant—No. VII."
71. James Wilson, "The Visitant—No. IX," *Pennsylvania Chronicle*, 28 March 1768.
72. Wilson, "The Visitant—No. IX."
73. Ibid.
74. Ibid.
75. Ibid.
76. Ibid.
77. Ibid.
78. James Wilson, "The Visitant—No. XI," *Pennsylvania Chronicle*, 11 April 1768.
79. Wilson, "The Visitant—No. XI."
80. Ibid.
81. Ibid.
82. Ibid.
83. Ibid.
84. Ibid.
85. Plutarch, "Pericles," *The Internet Classics Archive*. http://classics.mit.edu/Plutarch/pericles.html. Accessed May 16, 2015 at 1:15pm. These are the relevant passages from Plutarch: "Aspasia, this may be a fit point for inquiry about the woman, what art or charming faculty she had that enabled her to captivate, as she did, the greatest statesmen, and to give the philosophers occasion to speak so much about her, and that, too, not to her disparagement. . . . Aspasia, some say, was courted and caressed by Pericles upon account of her knowledge and skill in politics. Socrates himself would sometimes go to visit her, and some of his acquaintance with him; and those who frequented her company would carry their wives with them to listen

to her. . . . Still thus much seems to be historical, that she had the repute of being resorted to by many of the Athenians for instruction in the art of speaking."

86. In the collection of the *Pennsylvania Chronicle* at the Library Company of Philadelphia, someone has written, in pencil, underneath Aspasia's name at the end of the letter "Mrs. Ferguson."

87. Wilson, "The Visitant—No. XI."
88. Ibid.
89. Ibid.
90. Ibid.
91. Ibid.
92. Ibid.
93. Ibid.
94. Ibid.
95. Ibid.
96. Ibid.
97. Ibid.
98. Ibid.
99. Ibid.
100. Ibid.
101. Ibid.
102. Ibid.
103. William White, "The Visitant—No. XII," *Pennsylvania Chronicle*, 18 April 1768.
104. White, "The Visitant—No. XII."
105. Ibid.
106. The first known publication of this poem is found in the magazine *Universal Visitor* in 1759, No. 3, p. 40 by Dr. Bartholomew. It was revised for inclusion in an anthology the next year, *The Annual Register, Or, A View of the History, Politicks, and Literature of the Year 1759*, 2nd Ed. (London, 1760), pp. 455–56. It was included in later anthologies in the eighteenth century on the subject of temperance and moderation, including "Useful Hints to Single Gentlemen Respecting Marriage, Concubinance, and Adultery." The stock character of "the dying rake" appeared frequently in English folk song, and even earlier in medieval literature.
107. White, "The Visitant—No. XII."
108. Ibid.
109. Ibid.
110. Ibid.
111. Ibid.
112. Ibid.
113. William White, "The Visitant—No. XVI," *Pennsylvania Chronicle*, 16 May 1768.
114. Ibid.
115. Ibid.
116. Ibid.

117. Page Smith, *James Wilson: Founding Father, 1742–1798*, (Chapel Hill: University of North Carolina Press, 1956), 42.

118. B. Wilson, 45.

119. For a complete biography on Elizabeth Graeme Fergusson see Anne M. Ousterhout, *The Most Learned Woman in America: A Life of Elizabeth Graeme Fergusson*, (University Park, PA: The Pennsylvania State University Press, 2004).

120. Anne Hollingsworth Wharton, *Salons Colonial and Republican*, 1st pub. 1900, (New York: Benjamin Blom, Inc., 1971), 17.

121. Ibid., 17.

122. Ibid., 19.

123. Ibid., 21.

124. Ibid., 21.

125. Anne M. Ousterhout, *The Most Learned Woman in America: A Life of Elizabeth Graeme Fergusson*, (University Park, PA: The Pennsylvania State University Press, 2004), 35.

Chapter Four

Reading 1768
On the Edge of Empire

When James Wilson's *Considerations on the Nature and Extent of the Legislative Authority of the British Parliament* is examined as a component of the body of literature dealing with the role of British North America and its place within the British Empire, it is invariably discussed as relating to the year in which it was published—1774.

After finishing work on *The Visitant*, Wilson set himself a task of examining the history of the imperial crisis and then making recommendations based on his findings. As his legal career was at an early stage—meaning few clients—he had time to conduct research and to write. His conclusions were truly revolutionary for the world of 1768, particularly when compared to those of his mentor and friend, John Dickinson. However, when it came time to publish, he hesitated. He acceded to advice of friends and colleagues who urged caution and delayed publication until a time in which it would not be seen as revolutionary and potentially damaging to his young career.

The year 1768 was a significant one for James Wilson. Early the previous year, he completed his training with John Dickinson and embarked upon his legal career. Due to the abundance of lawyers in Philadelphia, Wilson decided in mid-1767 to move fifty miles northwest of the city to Reading, the county seat of Berks County.[1] As his practice struggled to gain clients, Wilson maintained a firm correspondence with William White. The two friends collaborated on *The Visitant* with notable success. After the end of the series on May 16, 1768, Wilson turned his attention to a new writing project.

Reading, when Wilson moved there, was a small outpost of the empire with fewer than a thousand souls, with a majority of the residents of German descent. The principal economic activity of the town revolved around the production of felt hats—the production of which left a distinct odor that marked the town and provided a product destined for sale within the wider Atlantic world. Though small in size, Reading was home to thirty-one taverns.² It was from this perspective, on the periphery of Philadelphia's economic and cultural influence, which itself was on the periphery of the larger British Atlantic world, that James Wilson contemplated the role of how Britain's North American colonies fit within that larger world.

A little over two years before Wilson embarked for America, on February 10, 1763, representatives of the warring powers signed the Treaty of Paris. The treaty ended the lengthy war for empire between the British and the French, but it planted the seeds for the next great battle over North America—a civil war within the British Empire itself.

As James Wilson prepared to come to America in 1765, he must have given attention to newspaper coverage of passage of the Sugar Act of 1764, on April 5th, and the resolve adopted by Parliament to enact a Stamp Act in 1765. News of this legislation broke upon America's shores as a rogue wave, washing away the euphoria of victory in the French and Indian War.³ Americans had been gazing covetously at the seemingly open territory, in the west, brought within their view with the removal of the French. Instead, America's attention turned eastward, to the Houses of Parliament in London. Authors—principally lawyers—took to their writing desks to wage a battle for public opinion, sending forth pamphlets arguing the merits or ominous portents of Parliament's legislative maneuvers.

FRAMING THE DEBATE

The first to attract widepread attention were the writings of James Otis, Jr. of Massachusetts. Otis' *The Rights of the British Colonies Asserted and Proved*, was the opening shot aimed at the Stamp Act to appear in America after news of the proposed act arrived.⁴ Parliament's actions were an attempt to come to terms with the ramifications of the enlarged British Empire in North America acquired through the Treaty of Paris. Vital issues of how to address the massive national debt incurred during the war; relations between North American colonists and Native Americans; governance of French colonists left behind in Canada; and the proper relationship between the British Isles and her colonies in the Western Hemisphere all vied for attention. The Ministry of George Grenville sought to bring order, while preserving prosperity, to the Empire. A crucial component for this enlarged and improved British Empire was to be new taxes levied in America. These taxes would help defray expenses of protecting His Majesty's North American possessions and contribute to lowering the tax burden in the British Isles, while also addressing the national debt. James Otis celebrated the victory of the British Empire over the French, but he openly challenged the authority of Parliament to extract taxes directly from His Majesty's American subjects.

In laying the groundwork for his assault on the Stamp Act's constitutionality, Otis inquired into the very nature and foundation of English government and the Glorious Revolution of 1688. He argued that during the events of the Glorious Revolution, the North American colonies were not consulted during the settlement bringing William and Mary of Orange to the English throne. The relationship between the charters—granted by the crown—of the colonies and what became the British Empire, existed between the colonies and the throne. Ultimate sovereignty, Otis named this "*earthly* power," must be "[s]overeign, absolute, and uncontroulable," a power, "from whose final decisions there can be no appeal but directly to Heaven."[5] Where did such power reside? Otis proclaimed, "It is therefore *originally* and *ultimately* in the people."[6]

He argued that the people can allocate portions of their sovereignty to governments, but never completely relinquish it. These governments exist to further the interests of the people from whom the power was bestowed. If the government failed to rule in the interests of the people, the government was no longer legitimate, and the sovereign power of the people could be withdrawn.

With the reality of slow travel and communication between the disparate components of the British Empire, it was only natural that colonists may enjoy more "rights, liberties and priviledges" than those enjoyed by British subjects in the home islands.[7] However, Otis carried this one step further: "The Colonists are by the law of nature free born, as indeed all men are, white or black."[8] Not a sentiment entertained by large numbers of his fellow colonists in North America, particularly in the British colonies of the South and the Caribbean.

Otis acknowledged that the colonies were "subject to, and dependent on Great Britain; and that therefore as over subordinate governments, the parliament of Great Britain has an undoubted power and lawful authority to make acts for the general good."[9] This was the crucial point—the "general good," legislation that existed to regulate the activities of the Empire as a whole, principally through navigation acts. Parliament existed as the final umpire within the Empire for the component parts, but Otis believed that it fell outside of their power to enact legislation, such as the Stamp Act, that only existed to raise revenue within the North American colonies. This was a power reserved exclusively for the elected assemblies of the colonies themselves.

American representation in Parliament was one possible solution, but not necessarily the most desirable. "No representation of the Colonies in parliament alone, would however be equivalent to a subordinate legislative among themselves."[10] Given the slow communication between the colonies and Britain, Otis advocated an American parliament. This parliament, subordinate to the British parliament in matters of concern for the Empire as a whole, would concern itself with areas where a parliament on the far side of the Atlantic lacked experience and information of American conditions, such as "their abilities to bear taxes, impositions on trade, and other duties and burthens, or of the local laws that might be really needful."[11]

One of the justifications for new taxes found in the Stamp Act was to defray costs incurred by the Empire to defend new territories in North America. Otis questioned the logic of stationing a standing army in North America—a dangerous new precedent—to defend against whom? Particularly in the case of New England, these colonies "were not only settled without the least expence to the mother country, but they have all along defended themselves against the frequent incursions of the most inhuman Salvages, perhaps on the face of the whole earth, at *their own* cost."[12] With the French gone, why did the ministry feel it necessary to choose the extremely costly and taxing path of stationing regiments permanently on America's borders? Was their mission to protect the colonies *or* to restrain them? Many of these arguments put forth by Otis were picked up by other authors.

Until the Stamp Act was repealed, and even after, American authors took up many of Otis' arguments and expanded them. By the close of 1764, the Rhode Island governor and friend of Otis, Stephen Hopkins, published his views. Hopkins' *The Rights of Colonies Examined*, written in November, appeared in print on December 22, 1764.[13] He echoed many of the arguments put forth by Otis.

Whereas Otis called for full American representation in Parliament, Hopkins went a step further; he sought an American parliament, subservient in matters only of imperial policy. Hopkins also sought representation, but in a different form, "some way or other, in parliament; at least whilst these general matters are under consideration."[14] How this would function in practice was not clear, but Hopkins believed, "They ought to have such notice, that they may appear and be heard by their agents, by council, or written representation, or by some other equitable and effectual way."[15]

This conditional representation raised many questions. Hopkins sought representation in Parliament, but did his proposal only provide an avenue for colonies to be heard on proposed legislation? Could they vote? If not, how would this differ from the current system of colonial access to Parliament? How Hopkins' proposal would safeguard American rights is unclear. Such an unwieldy apparatus is hard to imagine being successfully implemented with components of the empire spread all over world.

Unlike James Otis' plan for an American parliament sovereign in domestic affairs, Stephen Hopkins defended the colonial assemblies by decrying the expansion of parliamentary power into areas that had traditionally been reserved for them. Even if Hopkins' ideas on representation were implemented, it is hard to conceive how legislation, like the proposed Stamp Act, could be stopped. American representation in Parliament—presumably based on the same principles as the Scottish delegation—would never constitute a voting bloc that could ensure defeat of legislation harmful to North America. Only the prospect of representation, based on population, which would accommodate America's future numerical growth could address such an imbalance—this could benefit their posterity, but would not address pressing contemporary political disagreements.

Following the publication of Hopkins' pamphlet at the close of 1764, a vigorous battle in print broke out between those opposing Parliament's acts and those supporting them. A political opponent of Stephen Hopkins in Rhode Island, Martin Howard, Jr., was the first to take the field. His *A Letter from a Gentleman at Halifax to his Friend in Rhode Island* appeared two months later, in February 1765.[16] Hopkins replied to the pamphlet in the pages of the *Providence Gazette* on four occasions.[17] James Otis leapt to the defense of his friend with a pointed rebuttal of Howard.[18] The next phase of the pamphlet wars appeared after news of the passage of the Stamp Act arrived from London—it came from the Chesapeake colony of Maryland.

Daniel Dulany was a member of a prominent Maryland family who had been educated in England, first at Cambridge and then at the Middle Temple in London to study law. During the first half of 1765, Dulany collected various writings from supporters of Parliament. This coincided with the time when James Wilson prepared to leave Scotland and sail to America. While Wilson was at sea, in August 1765, Daniel Dulany's *Considerations on the Propriety of Imposing Taxes in the British Colonies, For the Purpose of Raising a Revenue, by Act of Parliament* was published.[19] The pamphlet would be reprinted throughout America, with a London edition appearing in 1766.[20]

Considerations addressed front and center the issue of representation. Dulany pointedly asked, "But who are the Representatives of the Colonies? To whom shall THEY send their Instructions, when desirous to obtain the Repeal of a Law."[21] The subject of *virtual* versus *actual* presentation drove Dulany's analysis of the political divide existing between the North American colonies and Parliament. The questioning of Parliament's authority "might be dangerous," but he did not feel "bound to acknowledge it's Inerrability, nor precluded from examining the Principles and Consequences of Laws, or from pointing out their Improprieties, and Defects."[22] Unlike the pamphlet wars in

New England, which had degenerated into personal attacks, Dulany chose an academic—a lawyerly—discourse.

Where did Parliament believe they had acquired the authority to directly tax the colonies? "To give Property, not belonging to the Giver, and without the Consent of the Owner, is such evident and flagrant Injustice."[23] Responding to supporters of Parliament's authority, Dulany noted, "But it is alledged that there is a *Virtual*, or *implied Representation* of the Colonies springing out of the Constitution of the *British* government. . . . the Representation is not actual, it is virtual, or it doth not exist at all."[24] For British subjects in North America, virtual representation was alien; lower houses of colonial assemblies were filled through elections of candidates residing in the colony.

Relying upon his interpretation of the colonial charters, Dulany brazenly declared, "The Inhabitants of the Colonies claim an Exemption from *all* Taxes not imposed by their own Consent, and to infer from their Objection to a Taxation, to which their Consent is not, nor can be given."[25] But it is at this point that Dulany backs off from the logical outcome of this statement. He retreated into a discussion of parliamentary acts that impose taxes "for *the single Purpose of Revenue*," and those "made for the Regulation of Trade, and have produced some Revenue in *Consequence of their Effect* and Operation as *Regulations of Trade*."[26] This line of argument rendered a conclusion where "A Right to impose an internal Tax on the Colonies, without their Consent *for the single Purpose of Revenue*, is denied, a Right to regulate their Trade without their Consent is admitted."[27]

As Dulany's *Considerations* made its way around the colonies in the fall of 1765, James Wilson disembarked in New York City and made his way to Philadelphia, where he would soon meet noted Pennsylvania lawyer John Dickinson. Dickinson himself was thinking about the stresses appearing in the British empire and what should be done about it. On December 7, his pamphlet *The Late Regulations Respecting the British Colonies on the Continent of America Considered, in a letter from a gentleman in Philadelphia to his friend in London* was published.[28]

Using the fiction of a letter, which was common during this era, allowed Dickinson to answer questions he wanted to examine in a conversational manner. The letter was intended to support his belief "that the late measures respecting America, would not only be extremely injurious to the *Colonies*, but also to *Great Britain*."[29] He relied principally upon an economic argument. The colonies needed to trade with the French islands in the Caribbean and other European colonies to earn hard currency needed to purchase goods desired from British manufacturers. Trade between the colonies and Great Britain alone would be insufficient as the British market was incapable of absorbing all that America produced. Further, the demand of the American domestic market for British goods would only grow with the rapid population growth in the colonies.

Dickinson criticized Parliament's restrictions upon the emission of paper money in the colonies, citing "their emissions were of vast benefit both to the provinces and to Great Britain."[30] The scarcity of hard currency in the colonies constrained trade and hurt the economies on both sides of the Atlantic. Where would the specie required by the Stamp Act come from?

One possible solution, Dickinson put forward, was the establishment of "a currency throughout the colonies," which, perhaps, may generate great benefits for everyone, but first it must be tried.[31] If Parliament was unwilling to sanction emissions of paper money from individual colonies, the creation of a continental currency with the backing of Parliament was one way forward. Liquidity of credit and a reliable circulating medium would alleviate the shortage of money and allow all segments of the colonial economy, from merchants; to creditors and debtors; and taxpayers to meet their obligations. Dickinson shared a story that sheriffs in Virginia, when collecting taxes due, were forced to bring back, not hard currency, but "effects which they have taken in execution, but could not sell, as there were no bidders for ready money."[32] Estates were being seized and sold at auction for a fraction of their true worth to satisfy slight debts, due to lack of money.

If the Stamp Act and restrictions on American trade were not addressed, then action must be taken. Dickinson joined Dulany in warning of an economic boycott and import substitution for British goods. "We have our choice of these two things—to continue our present limited and disadvantageous commerce—or to promote manufactures among ourselves, with a habit of œconomy, and thereby remove the necessity we are now under of being supplied by *Great Britain*."[33]

Dickinson argued, "May not the mother country more justly be called *expensive* to her colonies, than they can be called *expensive* to her?"[34] Wasn't the very idea of establishing colonies to acquire raw materials to enrich the mother country? If this was the case, what difference did it make "if the colonies enable *her* to pay taxes, is it not as useful to her, as if *they* paid them?"[35] The shortage of specie was a problem that did not exist in Britain, but it was an acute problem in America.

If the colonies curtailed their purchases of British goods and substituted domestic ones, the decline in sales of goods by British manufacturers would necessitate a decline in employment in Great Britain. Dickinson argued that whatever the amount raised by the Stamp Act, the decline in "demand will be as much less for British manufactures, as the amount of the sums raised by the taxes."[36] The damage would be greater and longer lasting in Britain than in the colonies, where the economic hardship would be "so much the more distressed at first, and afterwards so much the more frugal, ingenious, laborious and independent will the colonists become."[37] In short, in an economic war between the colonies and Great Britain, Dickinson argued that the colonies would emerge stronger for it.

Dickinson addressed a fear, one he did not share, of which he had been informed, "that many persons at home affect to speak of the colonists, as of a people designing and endeavoring to render themselves independent, and therefore it may be said to be proper as much as possible to depress them."[38] He reassured his readers that no plans for withdrawal from the empire had been formulated. However, he did warn that pursuing a course of harsh and unjust treatment of colonial aspirations might very well lead to that undesirable condition. "In short, we never can be made an independent people, except it be by *Great Britain* herself; and the only way for her to do it, is to make us frugal, ingenious, united and discontented."[39]

In the closing paragraphs of his pamphlet, Dickinson spoke to the spurned affection that Americans felt towards Great Britain. He, like other authors, believed that Great Britain had not sufficiently appreciated the sacrifices the colonies undertook to assist in the successful outcome of the late war. He questioned the value of the territory gained from France, if the end result was an estrangement between colonies and mother country. The obedience of the colonists to the empire was "secured by the best and strongest ties, *those of affection*, which alone can, and I hope *will* form an everlasting union."[40] If Parliament took the correct steps, colonial membership in the empire could continue for the foreseeable future; however, if Parliament acted unwisely, then colonials may come "to fear her victories or to repine at her glories."[41] The choice was up to Parliament.

After the turn of the new year, Parliament began debating repeal of the Stamp Act. In a speech on January 14, 1766, William Pitt rose in the House of Commons and forcefully demanded the repeal, earning him adoring adulation from Americans, when they read newspaper accounts later that spring. Pitt had read Daniel Dulaney's *Considerations* and agreed with much of it.[42] However, while acknowledging the wisdom of repeal, Pitt also urged the adoption of an assertion of Parliament's legislative authority over the colonies—what became known as the Declaratory Act.

Three days after Pitt's speech, a meeting of leading cabinet ministers gathered at the home of the Marquis of Rockingham, who had assumed the post of prime minister from Grenville the previous July. They agreed that the way forward was to adopt what Pitt had proposed in his speech. In early February, the 3rd, Rockingham introduced a resolution that would become the

Declaratory Act. It was not until two weeks later, on the 21st, that the resolution for complete repeal of the Stamp Act was submitted to Parliament.[43] Repeal passed a crucial vote early the next morning at 2am.[44] Americans and their British allies had achieved their goal, but at what cost? The Stamp Act was repealed, but the Declaratory Act would emerge as the key point of contention between America and Parliament, eventually sparking Lexington and Concord nine years later.

As events unfolded in London, Americans continued to think, write, and argue for the Stamp Act's repeal. Virginia's Richard Bland published *An Inquiry into the Rights of the British Colonies* a few weeks after repeal and nearly two months before word reached America, in March 1766.[45] Bland took a slightly different line of reasoning from his predecessors; the thesis of his work was "whether the Ministry, by imposing Taxes upon the Colonies by Authority of Parliament, have pursued a wise and salutary Plan of Government, or whether they have exerted pernicious and destructive Acts of Power."[46]

Bland first addressed representation in a manner similar to that of Daniel Dulany. Colonial legislatures were elected by a broader representation of the white male population than that found in Great Britain. Responding to advocates of virtual representation, Bland wrote, "If what you say is a real Fact, that nine Tenths of the People of *Britain* are deprived of the high Privilege of being Electors, it shows a great Defect in the present Constitution, which has departed so much from its original Purity; but never can prove that those People are even *virtually* represented in Parliament."[47] This reasoning cannot be applied to the British subjects of North America, "who are considered by the *British* Government itself, in every Instance of Parliamentary Legislation, as a distinct People."[48] Precedent held that the acts of Parliament only applied to the American colonies if they were explicitly named in them.

Expanding upon arguments first put forward by Otis in the pamphlet debate, Bland argued that America was not a conquered land, like Ireland, and thus had a different relationship to the empire, through settlement sanctioned with charters bestowed by the English crown. Englishmen who settled the colonies conducted their affairs by adhering to the provisions of each colony's charter, whether it be royal or proprietary. The colonial relationship ran through the crown, not through Parliament.

The great flaw in this argument is that the events of the English Civil War in the mid-seventeenth century and especially the settlement, between crown and Parliament, concluded during the Glorious Revolution of 1688, fundamentally altered the relationship between the two. Bland and others may argue that the original relationship was still in force and that America never consented to a revised constitutional framework, but the reality was that the structure of empire had changed. Sovereignty, post-1688, resided in Parliament and it could be argued that future colonial charters would be issued by the king, serving as the executive, on behalf of Parliament.

Even prior to 1688, the constitutional reality of the empire had changed; Bland "admitted that after the Restoration the Colonies lost that Liberty of Commerce with foreign Nations they had enjoyed before that Time."[49] The navigation acts adopted by Parliament restricted colonial trade to the benefit of the mother country, this well-established precedent validated the authority of Parliament—at least in the area of trade regulation for the empire as a whole. Bland decried regulations preferential to Britain and detrimental to the colonies but remained unconvinced that Parliament had any authority to extract taxes from within the mainland colonies.

As Richard Bland's *Inquiry* garnered notice around the colonies, James Wilson was completing the college term at the College of Philadelphia as a tutor of Latin. His horizon extended far beyond the walls of the school and he took steps to secure the services of John Dickinson to qualify him for a career as a lawyer. Before he began work with Dickinson in the summer of 1766, Wilson took part in the graduation ceremonies at the college held on May 20. He was awarded an honorary master's degree for his work at the school. This very week of commencement was also the week when first word of the Stamp Act's repeal reached Philadelphia.

During the winter of 1767–68, as James Wilson and William White began work on their newspaper series, *The Visitant*, a series of essays appeared in Philadelphia's newspapers. Written by John Dickinson, *Letters from a Farmer in Pennsylvania to the Inhabitants of the British Colonies*, first appeared on the front page of the *Pennsylvania Chronicle* on December 2, 1767.[50] Dickinson's work was republished throughout the colonies as first, individual installments, and then as a collection. The series appeared in every colonial newspaper in the thirteen colonies, except for three.[51] *Letters from a Farmer* went through eight editions in America, two editions in London, one in Ireland, and another, in French, in Amsterdam.[52] "Almost overnight, they made him the most popular patriot in America."[53] John Dickinson was one of the rare colonists who had earned advanced legal training at the heart of the British Empire. He possessed a personal understanding of Great Britain, her laws, and empire few of his peers enjoyed.

Dickinson's *Letters from a Farmer* series is an examination of the history of disputes between the colonies and Great Britain since the repeal of the Stamp Act and the passage of the Declaratory Act in early 1766. As a published series, *Letters* was comprised of twelve installments. The very first letter focused on the importance of legislatures, particularly the suspension of the New York legislature for alleged non-compliance with an order from Parliament to provide enumerated supplies for imperial troops stationed in the colony.

Dickinson disagreed with the "conduct in that instance" of the New York legislature, but this had "not blinded me so much, that I cannot plainly perceive, that they have been punished in a manner pernicious to *American* freedom, and justly alarming to all the colonies."[54] If the legislature of one colony could be suspended, by Parliament, what might lead to further suspensions and for what offenses?

The Declaratory Act provided justification for Parliament's action, but it was a legal authority with which John Dickinson, one of the most prominent lawyers in Pennsylvania, wholeheartedly disagreed. He first queried whether there existed any limit to the possible demands of Parliament—upon colonial legislatures and ultimately their citizens. He declared, "An act of parliament, commanding us to do a certain thing, if it has any validity, is a tax upon us for the expence that accrues in complying with it."[55] The incomplete submission to parliamentary direction was "regarded as an act of 'disobedience to the authority of the BRITISH LEGISLATURE.' This gives the suspension a consequence vastly more affecting."[56] Here were the real-world consequences of the Declaratory Act. "It is a parliamentary assertion of the *supreme authority* of the *British* legislature over these colonies, in *the point of taxation*, and it is intended to COMPEL *New York* into a submission to that authority." Parliament's authority would be backed by a commitment to the use of military force to ensure compliance.

The plight of New York was the plight of all the colonies. "If the parliament may lawfully deprive *New York* of any of *her* rights, it may deprive any, or all the other colonies of *their* rights; and nothing can possibly so much encourage such attempts, as a mutual inattention to the interests of each other."[57] Dickinson argued that the true design of the British ministry was: "*To divide, and thus to destroy*, is the first political maxim in attacking those, who are powerful by their union."[58] Previous success in safeguarding American rights required the cooperation of all the colonies, just as in the successful fight against the Stamp Act, and the colonies needed to stay united in their defense against parliamentary encroachment. Failing to remain united would bring devastating consequences.

In Letter II, Dickinson turned to the extent of Parliament's authority. Parliamentary supporters believed there were no limits upon the body's sphere within which it could legislate. Dickinson, like many other authors, acknowledged "a legal authority to regulate the trade of *Great Britain*, and all her colonies."[59] As all constitutional authorities of the time agreed, there needed to "exist a power somewhere, to preside, and preserve the connection in due order."⁶⁰ Parliament held the power to regulate the constituent parts of the empire for the benefit of the whole. Dickinson wrote he had "looked over *every statute* relating to these colonies," from their individual founding until the present; and until the events surrounding the Stamp Act, all previous statutes were "calculated to regulate trade, and preserve or promote a mutually beneficial intercourse between the several constituent parts of the empire."⁶¹

He acknowledged that many of the duties enacted raised revenue, "yet those duties were always imposed *with design* to restrain the commerce of one part, that was injurious to another, and thus to promote the general welfare."⁶² Any revenue generated was inconsequential. This was the heart of Dickinson's argument; the *intent* of Parliament, until the Stamp Act, was never "FOR THE PURPOSE OF RAISING A REVENUE," only for the regulation of trade.⁶³ He summarized this new expansion of Parliament's authority in America: "This I call an innovation; and a most dangerous innovation."⁶⁴

Concluding Letter II with a summarizing thought on the actions of Parliament, beginning with the Stamp Act, Dickinson identified the vital question vexing the colonies' relationship with Great Britain: "[W]hether the parliament can legally impose duties to be paid *by the people of these colonies only*, FOR THE SOLE PURPOSE OF RAISING A REVENUE, *on commodities which she obliges us to take from her alone*, or, in other words, whether the parliament can legally take money out of our pockets, without our consent."⁶⁵ If this new authority could be enforced, in the thirteen colonies, then "our boasted liberty is but, *Vox et pratera nihil*, A sound and nothing else."⁶⁶

The subject of Letter III was "whether 'our rights *are* invaded.'"⁶⁷ He dismissed previous authors who inclined towards armed resistance: "To talk of 'defending' them, as if they could be no otherwise 'defended' than by arms, is as much out of the way, as if a man having a choice of several roads to reach his journey's end, should prefer the worst, for no other reason, but because it *is* the worst."⁶⁸ Throughout the series, Dickinson was very clear in his abhorrence of any resort to armed resistance. The conservative he was sought to defend American rights with every means at his disposal, short of armed force or mob resistance. The overriding goal of *Letters from a Farmer* was "to convince the people of these colonies, that they are at this moment exposed to the most imminent dangers; and to persuade them immediately, vigorously, and unanimously, to exert themselves, in the most firm, but most peaceable manner, for obtaining relief."⁶⁹

Dickinson, in educating his readers, explained, "Every government at some time or other falls into wrong measures"; however, "every such measure does not dissolve the obligation between the governors and the governed."⁷⁰ "It is the duty of the governed to endeavor to rectify the mistake," for "they have not at first any other right, than to represent their grievances, and to pray for redress."[71] The only exception to this lesson, for Dickinson, was in the eventuality in which a situation arose where there was not "time for receiving an answer to their applications, which rarely happens."[72] If a situation again arose, like that during the passage of the Stamp Act when petitions from the colonies were not even read before Parliament, then, and only then, "that kind of *opposition* becomes justifiable, which can be made without breaking the laws, or disturbing the public peace."[73] Dickinson was referring to the use of economic boycotts of British goods. "For experience may teach them, what reason did not; and harsh methods cannot be proper, till milder ones have failed."[74]

He did acknowledge that after a lengthy period of peaceful petitions, economic boycotts, and domestic substitutions, if Parliament still failed to redress colonial objections, armed resistance may become justified. However, Dickinson set a very high threshold for armed resistance. "[I]t never can be justifiable, until the people are FULLY CONVINCED, that any further submission will be destructive to their happiness."[75] In the course of his research and thinking on the imperial relationship, Dickinson became convinced that "the prosperity of these provinces is founded in their dependance on Great Britain."[76] Americans must be of one mind if force was resorted to, for the fortunes and futures of all would be at risk.

Early in Letter IV, which he devoted to the subject of taxation, Dickinson boldly declared his "total denial of the power of parliament to lay upon these colonies any 'tax' whatever."[77] He then defined the word: "I annex that meaning which the constitution and history of England require to be annexed to it; that is—that it is *an imposition on the subject, for the sole purpose of levying money.*"[78] Here again, Dickinson's focus remains on the *intent* of parliamentary legislation. After a discussion of the history of taxation in English history, he closed with the quote: "*Habemus quidem senatus consultum,—tanquam gladium in vagina repositum.* We have a statute, laid up for future use, like a sword in the scabbard."[79] The warning reminded Americans that any precedent established conceding Parliament's taxing authority in the colonies was intolerable and likely to be relied upon in the future with increased frequency.

Returning to the issue of parliamentary intent in enacting legislation, Dickinson, in Letter VII, focused on *whom* laws were applied. "Where these laws are to bind *themselves*, it may be expected that the house of commons will very carefully consider them: But when they are making laws that are not designed to bind *themselves*, we cannot imagine that their deliberations will be as cautious and scrupulous, as in their own case."[80] Drawing attention to a recent parliamentary act imposing taxes on the importation of glass and paper from Britain to America, Dickinson declared, "For I am convinced, that the authors of this law would never have obtained an act to raise so trifling a sum as it must do, had they not intended by *it* to establish a *precedent* for future use."[81] Americans couldn't risk acquiescing in even the most trivial of taxes enacted by Parliament, for to do so would establish the precedent that Dickinson and other authors feared. Once the precedent was accepted then there would exist no limit to demands for revenue. "In short, if they have a right *to* levy a tax of *one penny* upon us, they have a right to levy a *million* upon us: For where does their right stop?"[82] Once accepted, the parliamentary power to tax would result in a chilling result—"whether *our own money* shall continue in *our own pockets* or not, depends no longer on *us*, but on *them*."[83]

In the remaining installments of the series, Dickinson returned again and again to arguments put forth in those published in the first half. In Letter X, he paused for a moment to consider what he believed a future historian—looking back on the present day—would write about the imminent future. In the eighth year of George III's reign "*a very memorable event*" occurred, for the "American colonies" acquiesced, "for the *FIRST* time, to be *taxed* by the *British* parliament."[84] The historian praised the conduct of the colonies in successfully achieving repeal of the Stamp Act, but repeal heralded the moment of their downfall. "This affair rendered the SUBMISSIVE CONDUCT of the colonies so soon after, the more extraordinary; there being no difference between the mode of taxation which they opposed, and that to which they submitted."[85] Their acceptance of parliamentary taxation was the last and most crucial act. "From thence the decline of their freedom began, and its decay was extremely rapid; for as *money* was always raised upon them by the parliament, their *assemblies* grew immediately useless, and in a short time *contemptible*: And in less than one hundred years, the people sunk down into that *tameness* and *supineness* of spirit, by which they still continue to be distinguished."[86]

Dickinson's account of a possible future was bleak, but he offered an alternative. Relying upon the experience of previous successful colonial protest, he closed his final contribution, Letter XII, and the series as a whole with the following admonition: "Is there not the strongest probability, that if the universal sense of these colonies is immediately expressed by RESOLVES of the assemblies, in support of their rights, by INSTRUCTIONS to their agents on the subject, and by PETITIONS to the crown and parliament for redress, these measures will have the same success now, that they had in the time of the *Stamp Act*."[87]

Dickinson's *Letters from a Farmer* held a prominent position, appearing just below the masthead, in the pages of the *Pennsylvania Chronicle*, until the initial appearance of his former law student's *The Visitant* on February 1, 1768. *Letters* remained a component of the paper, for two more weeks, until Letter XII was published on February 15.

JAMES WILSON'S VIEW OF EMPIRE

James Wilson drew upon his broad Scottish Enlightenment education to write what he titled *Considerations on the Nature and Extent of the Legislative Authority of the British Parliament*.[88] This research project, which he began after completing his last installment of *The Visitant*, was envisioned as an attempt to make a name for himself within Philadelphia's literary community. The success of *The Visitant* demonstrated his writing ability to the reading public, but since he and William White used a pseudonym, readers were left to ponder the identity of the author. The authorship of *Considerations* would be prominent on the title page.

Wilson began his pamphlet with a simple question that would form the thesis of the whole: "No question can be more important to Great Britain, and to the colonies, than this—does the legislative authority of the British parliament extend over them?"[89] In Letter II, John Dickinson examined the authority of Parliament and concluded that it held "a legal authority to regulate the trade of *Great Britain*, and all her colonies."[90] Wilson wasn't ready to concede that the regulation of trade—virtually all of the authors since James Otis, Jr. conceded this authority—came within the sphere of the powers of the British Parliament. "Oppression is not a plant of the British soil; and the late severe proceedings against the colonies must have arisen from the detestable schemes of interested ministers, who have misinformed and misled the people."[91] In other words, the British public had been misled by ministers, pushing taxation on America to lighten the burden of taxation upon British taxpayers, into believing they held a power which Wilson argued they didn't possess.

Joining with authors who had written before him, James Wilson agreed what Americans were fighting for was to be "reinstated in the enjoyment of those rights, to which we are entitled by the supreme and uncontrollable laws of nature, and the fundamental principles of the British constitution."[92] Relying upon the laws of nature, as he understood them, "All men are, by nature, equal and free: no one has a right to any authority over another without his consent."[93] This was the crucial point; if Americans were unable to bestow their consent, then legislation enacted designed to apply to them was null and void. "All lawful government is founded on the consent of those who are subject to it: such consent was given with a view to ensure and to increase the happiness of the governed, above what they could enjoy in an independent and unconnected state of nature."[94] Wilson had read and thoroughly understood John Locke. For him, this justification for government held a consequence—"that the happiness of the society is the *first* law of every government."[95]

By placing the "happiness of the society" as the foundation upon which all governmental authority rested, James Wilson applied a new standard to the relationship of the North American colonies to the parliament of Great Britain and to the wider British Empire. "The people have a right to insist that this rule be observed; and are entitled to demand a moral security that the legislature will observe it."[96] From this demand, he concluded, "If they have not the first, they are slaves; if they have not the second, they are, every moment, exposed to slavery."[97] He then rhetorically asked if placing a "supreme, irresistible, uncontrolled authority over" America, in the British parliament, was conducive to the happiness of Americans.[98] He answered in the negative, for "parliaments are not infallible: they are not always just. The members, of whom they are composed, are human; and, therefore, they may err; they are influenced by interest; and, therefore, they may deviate from their duty."[99]

In the heated debate between supporters of actual or virtual representation, Wilson fully supported actual. "[T]he colonies are entitled to all the privileges of Britons," and this required actual representation in Parliament.[100] Since Americans elected no members to Parliament, any laws, irrespective of their design, were inoperative on them. On the retention of the rights of Britons, "We have committed no crimes to forfeit them: we have too much spirit to resign them. We will leave our posterity as free as our ancestors left us."[101]

In Letter VII, John Dickinson explained why it was important legislation enacted by Parliament that was evaluated by who it applied to. James Wilson noted the importance of elected representatives coming from the body that put them in office. It was essential that "the interest of the representatives is the same with that of their constituents. Every measure, that is prejudicial to the nation, must be prejudicial to them and their posterity. They cannot betray their electors, without, at the same time, injuring themselves."[102] The resort to frequent elections was necessary as "the first maxims of jurisprudence are ever kept in view—that all power is derived from the people—that their happiness is the end of government."[103] If members of Parliament never, or even very infrequently, faced voters, then constitutional restraints would be broken and the interests of government would become selfish, to the detriment of the people. "A regard for the publick was now no longer the spring of their actions: their only view was to aggrandize themselves, and to establish their grandeur on the ruins of their country."[104]

If legislators were immune from accountability, then it mattered not how many of them there were. Wilson declared, "Kings are not the only tyrants: the conduct of the long parliament will justify me in adding, that kings are not the severest tyrants."[105] If the primary objective of any government was the happiness of the people, how could the happiness of Americans reside in a body—Parliament—comprised of legislators who were unfamiliar with the land, interests, and desires of those for whom they enacted laws?

James Wilson—along with every pro-American author since James Otis—agreed, "One of the most ancient maxims of the English law is, that no freeman can be taxed at pleasure."[106] He acknowledged there existed classifications of subjects who were ineligible to vote, but he argued that these distinctions did not apply to America. First, he asked where the power to pass laws binding Americans came from. Were Americans not fellow British subjects? If so, when did this relationship change? "By what title do they claim to be our master? What act of ours has rendered us subject to those, to whom we were formerly equal?"[107] Could it be that "British freedom [is] denominated from the *soil*, or from the *people* of Britain?"[108] If freedom is held in the soil of the British Isles, "do they lose it by quitting the soil? Do those, who embark, freemen, in Great Britain, disembark, slaves, in America?"[109] Logically, if this were true, why would any British subject—other than those ordered to do so, such as soldiers and convicts—ever leave home? The establishment of another class of citizenship, consisting of a constrained set of rights, was not conducive to the flourishing of trade or the expansion of the empire.

In a footnote, Wilson argued that the supporters of parliamentary authority over America grounded their position "upon the very absurd principle of their being *virtually* represented in the house of commons."[110] Returning to the subject of the legislators themselves, Wilson argued that it was impossible for the British parliament to hold authority over America. "Can members, whom the Americans do not elect; with whom the Americans are not connected in interest; whom the Americans cannot remove; over whom the Americans have no influence—can such members be styled, with any propriety, the magistrates of the Americans?"[111] In elections in Britain, where Americans could not participate, "a member of the house of commons may plume himself upon his ingenuity in inventing schemes to serve the mother country at the expense of the colonies; and may boast of their impotent resentment against him on that account."[112] This situation "is repugnant to the essential maxims of jurisprudence, to the ultimate end of all governments, to the genius of the British constitution, and to the liberty and happiness of the colonies, that they have no share in the British legislature."[113]

After dismissing the authority of Parliament over America with a survey of English history and case law, Wilson put forth the foundations of the relationship between Great Britain and her North American colonies. The relationship did not rest upon conquest, as that between Britain and Ireland. America's place, within the British Empire, existed in a relationship between the colonies and the crown. "They took possession of the country in the *king's* name: they treated, or made war with the Indians by *his* authority: they held the lands under *his* grants, and paid *him* the rents reserved upon them: they established governments under the sanction of *his* prerogative, or by virtue of *his* charters."[114] Parliament did not exercise a role in this relationship, for "no application for those purposes was made to the parliament: no ratification of the charters or letters patent was solicited from that assembly, as is usual in England with regard to grants and franchises of much less importance."[115]

In an extended footnote at the end of the pamphlet, Wilson noted, "After considering, with all the attention of which I am capable, the foregoing opinion—that all the different members of the British empire are distinct states, independent of each other, but connected together under the same sovereign in right of the same crown."[116] Here was where James Wilson departed from the writings of previous authors. He not only denied all parliamentary authority over America, but for all colonies in the British Empire. The empire existed through the person of the king, but all local governance, including trade, resided in colonial assemblies elected by the colonists themselves.

When James Wilson's *Considerations* appeared in August 1774, inside the front cover there was a section labeled "Advertisement." The publisher included a paragraph from Wilson explaining why and when the pamphlet was written. He explained that it had been written during "the late Non-Importation Agreement," but that the situation was resolved before the pamphlet was ready for publication.[117] When he began his research, "he entered upon them with a view and expectation of being able to trace some constitutional Line between those cases, in which we ought, and those in which we ought not, to acknowledge the power of Parliament over us."[118] However, by the end of the work, "he became fully convinced, that such a Line does not exist; and that there can be no medium between *acknowledging* and *denying* that power in *all* cases."[119] *Considerations* appeared nearly six years after it was written and long after James Wilson desired it to reach the public.

In a letter from his close friend William White, sent from Philadelphia to Wilson in Reading, on November 27, 1768, Wilson was advised to delay publication.[120] Not only had White received a copy of *Considerations*, but so had Dr. Francis Alison, rector of the Academy and professor in the College of Philadelphia. Wilson had attached a note to Alison's copy saying he would soon be visiting Philadelphia. Dr. Alison had sent a letter to Wilson urging him to delay publication of the pamphlet until they could talk in person. His objection rested on two parts: First, Alison felt that the pamphlet was too long; and second, John Dickinson was envious that the last two installments of his *Farmer's Letters* had been relegated to the interior pages of the *Pennsylvania Chronicle* by the appearance of Wilson and White's *The Visitant*.

White had a private conversation with Alison before sending his letter to Wilson. He explained that the authorship of *The Visitant* among the reading public was unknown, but Alison believed it soon would be. In Alison's opinion, being the author of both *The Visitant* and *Considerations* "might be a disadvantage to you."[121] White included a postscript at the end of the letter. He was "surprised you did not submit your piece to Mr. Ewing rather than Dr. Alison."[122] White referred to Mr. John Ewing, later Rev. Dr. John Ewing, who subsequently served as Provost of the University of Pennsylvania. White believed that Ewing might "have been as good a Judge of ye Merit of it, and I think a better Judge as to ye Propriety of publishing it."[123]

James Wilson listened to the advice he received from friends in Philadelphia and shelved plans for immediate publication of *Considerations*. Not until a more favorable climate arose in 1774 did Wilson dust off the work and arrange for publication. In the latest published collection of pamphlets of the era, Gordon Wood declared Wilson's pamphlet "as radical as Jefferson's."[124] Thomas Jefferson's *A Summary View of the Rights of British America* also appeared in 1774 and became better known among the general public.

1768 was an important year when examining James Wilson's life. His acceptance, by the reading public, of his contributions to *The Visitant* nourished his innate ambition to make a name in Philadelphia's polite society. *Considerations* was to be his solo debut upon the very same stage, but this time without the cloak of a pseudonym.

Wilson had taken a position far in advance of other colonial authors of the day, including John Dickinson. His argument that the parliament of Great Britain had no power, whatsoever, over the North American colonies was so revolutionary in the fall of 1768 that he heeded the urging of his friends to shelve the pamphlet until a more favorable political climate arrived.

In *The Visitant*, Wilson examined the society of colonial America from the perspective of one who was part of it; with *Considerations*, he stepped back and examined colonial America within the context of the British Empire and found that a new path was necessary. In advocating his conclusions in *Considerations*, what one day would become known as the British Commonwealth, James Wilson prepared his thinking for his vote on July 2, 1776 in the Pennsylvania State House declaring independence from the British Empire. Further, it equipped him for battle with John Dickinson over the drafting of a new national constitution at the Constitutional Convention of 1787.

The young lawyer, living among a predominately German population in Reading, needed to think of his fledgling career. If his work had appeared in late 1768, it would have set him apart as a new voice proclaiming a more radical stance on American rights, but when it did appear in 1774, it was one of several arguments treading the same ground.

IN TEMPORE INTER

In the nearly two decades between the summer of 1768 and the convening of the Constitutional Convention in May 1787, James Wilson's law practice prospered, his legal abilities attracted attention, and his personal life took a more domestic turn. His outlook on life became more conservative as he acquired status, financial success, and a family. The young lawyer who heeded the advice of his friends not to publish his treatise in 1768 matured into a prominent member of the Pennsylvania delegation to the Continental Congress and a forceful presence in his state's delegation to the Constitutional Convention.

At the Court of Common Pleas session for August 1768, held in Reading, Wilson represented clients in fourteen cases.[125] Early the next year, during the February 1769 term of the same court, Wilson's name appeared on the docket as attorney representing twenty-eight cases.[126] His name also began to appear in Carlisle as an attorney during the same term. In April, he traveled to Philadelphia, to be admitted as an attorney before the Supreme Court of Pennsylvania—sponsored by his legal mentor and friend, John Dickinson.[127]

As a result of his friendship with William White, Wilson became acquainted with Rachel Bird. She was the stepdaughter of Colonel Patton, a prominent citizen of Carlisle, whose family estate was named Birdsboro.[128] In May 1769, Wilson was retained by a client in a case brought against Rachel's brother Mark Bird and his business partner, her stepfather Colonel Patton.[129] With such a delicate situation—being the legal representative of a client suing his prospective in-laws—James Wilson apparently presented himself well as the Colonel agreed to his request to begin courting Rachel. Nearly a year into their relationship, Wilson moved from Reading to Carlisle, ostensibly in the belief that he would secure a more lucrative practice, but also to be closer to Rachel.[130] James and Rachel were married on November 5, 1771, at St. Gabriel's Episcopal Church, across the river from Birdsboro.[131] The couple moved into a home that Wilson had recently purchased, a block from the courthouse in Carlisle, on the corner of Penn and Hanover Streets.[132]

The first of six children, Mary, but called Polly by her parents, was born in September 1772.[133] As the relationship between Britain and her North

American colonies deteriorated, Wilson's family and legal practice continued to grow. His legal reputation garnered attention in Philadelphia, where his services were secured by Robert Morris and Thomas Willing, who were partners in one of the largest trading companies in North America, to represent their interests in a land case.[134]

On July 12th, 1774, James Wilson was an active participant in a meeting held at the First Presbyterian Church in Carlisle, where he was elected one of three deputies to represent Cumberland County (in which Carlisle was located) in Philadelphia at the opening of the Provincial Convention, meeting in Carpenters' Hall, to discuss the passage of the British Parliament's Intolerable Acts.[135] The Convention adopted a document, principally written by John Dickinson, which served as instructions to the Pennsylvania Assembly and recommendations to the delegates selected to represent the colony in the Continental Congress.[136]

James Wilson had become comfortable in his own beliefs and judgment. It was at this moment, after working with his peers in Philadelphia at the Provincial Convention, that he dusted off his treatise of 1768 and sought a publisher. He found one in the firm of William and Thomas Bradford, Printers, at the London Coffee House.[137] "Considerations on the Nature and Extent of the Legislative Authority of the British Parliament" appeared in late August 1774.[138]

He was elected, once again, to serve as a delegate from Cumberland County at the Provincial Convention which convened on January 23, 1775.[139] The purpose of the body was to assess the work of the First Continental Congress and to implement new resolves to carry into effect enhanced resistance to the policies of Great Britain. Here, before a hall filled with his peers from around Pennsylvania, James Wilson was chosen to address the delegates on the imperial crisis and the virtue of colonial resistance.[140]

When the Second Continental Congress convened in Philadelphia in May 1775, James Wilson was included as a member of the Pennsylvania delegation. In just a few months, Wilson had moved from the stage of working with his peers from around the colony, to one where he stepped forth upon a much larger, continental, stage. He arrived in Philadelphia and first appeared in the Congress on May 15th.[141]

Over the next eight years, James Wilson would serve Pennsylvania, on and off, in the Congress as the political balance-of-power in the state's legislature shifted. His first opportunity to work with John Adams came when he was appointed to a committee, after the Battle of Bunker Hill, to arrange for the printing of money to support the army around Boston.[142] He also served as the Pennsylvania delegate on the permanent Committee on Indian Affairs, a committee on which he served until September 1777.[143] In November 1775,

Wilson was selected to serve on the maritime prize committee. It was in this capacity that he served on the Committee on Appeals to hear appeals in prize cases, until a permanent standing committee was formed in January 1777.[144]

Just prior to the formal conclusion of the American Revolution, James Wilson was once again elected to serve Pennsylvania, this time as a delegate to the Confederation Congress. He took his seat on January 2nd, 1783.[145] He worked with James Madison and Alexander Hamilton, unsuccessfully, to secure taxing authority in order to address financial obligations of the Confederation government. His frustration with the Articles of Confederation led to his strong support of and active participation in the Constitutional Convention of 1787.

NOTES

1. Page Smith, *James Wilson: Founding Father, 1742–1798*, (Chapel Hill: University of North Carolina Press, 1956), 29.
2. Smith, 29.
3. For a British perspective of these events, see: I. R. Christie, *Crisis of Empire: Great Britain and the American Colonies 1754–1783*, (New York: W.W. Norton and Company, 1966).
4. Merrill Jensen, ed., *Tracts of the American Revolution, 1763–1776*, (New York: The Bobbs-Merrill Company, Inc., 1967), xxi.
5. Ibid., 50.
6. Ibid., 50.
7. In a contemporary setting, aerospace entrepreneur Elon Musk has argued that any colony established on Mars must be governed through a direct democracy, a right that his employees in the United States do not enjoy.
8. James Otis, *The Rights of of the British Colonies Asserted and Proved*, in Gordon Wood, ed., *The American Revolution: Writings from the Pamphlet Debate 1764–1772*, (New York: Library of America, 2015), 69.
9. Ibid., 73.
10. Ibid., 77.
11. Ibid., 77.
12. Ibid., 97.
13. Stephen Hopkins, *The Rights of Colonies Examined*, in Gordon Wood, ed., *The American Revolution: Writings from the Pamphlet Debate 1764–1772*, (New York: Library of America, 2015), 123–42.
14. Ibid., 131.
15. Ibid., 131.
16. Martin Howard, Jr., *A Letter from a Gentleman at Halifax to his Friend in Rhode Island*, in Gordon Wood, ed., *The American Revolution: Writings from the Pamphlet Debate 1764–1772*, (New York: Library of America, 2015), 147–61.

17. Edmund S. Morgan and Helen M. Morgan, *The Stamp Act Crisis: Prologue to Revolution*, 1st ed. 1953, (Chapel Hill: The University of North Carolina Press, 1995), 52.

18. James Otis, *A Vindication of the British Colonies against the Aspersions of the Halifax Gentleman in his Letter to a Rhode Island Friend*, in Bernard Bailyn, ed., *Pamphlets of the American Revolution 1750–1776*. (Cambridge: Harvard University Press, 1965), 553–79.

19. Daniel Dulany, *Consideration on the Propriety of Imposing Taxes in the British Colonies, For the Purpose of Raising a Revenue, by Act of Parliament*, in Gordon Wood, ed., *The American Revolution: Writings from the Pamphlet Debate 1764–1772*, (New York: Library of America, 2015), 243–304.

20. Gordon Wood, ed., *The American Revolution: Writings from the Pamphlet Debate 1764–1772*, (New York: Library of America, 2015), 241.

21. Dulany, 245.

22. Ibid., 246.

23. Ibid., 247.

24. Ibid., 247.

25. Ibid., 275.

26. Ibid., 279.

27. Ibid., 280.

28. John Dickinson, *The Late Regulations Respecting the British Colonies*, in Paul Leicester Ford, ed., *The Political Writings of John Dickinson 1764–1774*, 1st pub. 1895, (New York: Da Capo Press, 1970), 208–44.

29. Dickinson, 213.

30. Ibid., 218.

31. Ibid., 221.

32. Ibid., 227.

33. Ibid., 234.

34. Ibid., 239.

35. Ibid., 238.

36. Ibid., 240.

37. Ibid., 240.

38. Ibid., 241.

39. Ibid., 241–42.

40. Ibid., 244.

41. Ibid., 244.

42. Morgan, 283.

43. Ibid., 279.

44. Ibid., 291.

45. Jensen, xxxiv.

46. Richard Bland, *An Inquiry into the Rights of the British Colonies*, in Gordon Wood, ed., *The American Revolution: Writings from the Pamphlet Debate 1764–1772*, (New York: Library of America, 2015), 309–29.

47. Ibid., 315.

48. Ibid., 315.

49. Ibid., 323.
50. Wood, 405. John Dickinson, *Letters from a Farmer in Pennsylvania to the Inhabitants of the British Colonies*, in Gordon Wood, ed., *The American Revolution: Writings from the Pamphlet Debate 1764–1772*, (New York: Library of America, 2015), 407–89.
51. Philip Davidson, *Propaganda and the American Revolution 1763–1783*, 1st pub. 1941, (New York: W.W. Norton and Company, 1973), 102.
52. Wood, 405.
53. Wood, 405.
54. Dickinson, *Letters*, 410.
55. Ibid., 410.
56. Ibid., 411.
57. Ibid., 412.
58. Ibid., 412.
59. Ibid., 413.
60. Ibid., 413.
61. Ibid., 413–14.
62. Ibid., 414.
63. Ibid., 415.
64. Ibid., 416.
65. Ibid., 421.
66. Ibid., 421.
67. Ibid., 422.
68. Ibid., 422.
69. Ibid., 422.
70. Ibid., 423.
71. Ibid., 423.
72. Ibid., 424.
73. Ibid., 424.
74. Ibid., 424.
75. Ibid., 424.
76. Ibid., 425.
77. Ibid., 426.
78. Ibid., 427.
79. Ibid., 432.
80. Ibid., 445.
81. Ibid., 449.
82. Ibid., 449.
83. Ibid., 450.
84. Ibid., 472.
85. Ibid., 472.
86. Ibid., 473.
87. Ibid., 489.

88. James Wilson, *Considerations on the Nature and Extent of the Legislative Authority of the British Parliament*, in *Collected Works of James Wilson*, Eds. Kermit L. Hall and Mark David Hall, 2 vols., (Indianapolis: Liberty Fund, 2007), 3–31.
89. Wilson, 3.
90. Dickinson, *Letters*, 413.
91. Wilson, 3.
92. Ibid., 4.
93. Ibid., 4.
94. Ibid., 5.
95. Ibid., 5.
96. Ibid., 5.
97. Ibid., 5.
98. Ibid., 5.
99. Ibid., 5.
100. Ibid., 6.
101. Ibid., 6.
102. Ibid., 8.
103. Ibid., 9.
104. Wilson gave a lengthy discourse on the history of the Long parliament, begun under Charles I and resurrected under Charles II. Ibid., 10.
105. Ibid., 10.
106. Ibid., 13.
107. Ibid., 16.
108. Ibid., 16.
109. Ibid., 16.
110. Ibid., 15.
111. Ibid., 15.
112. Ibid., 17.
113. Ibid., 18.
114. Ibid., 27.
115. Ibid., 27.
116. Ibid., 30.
117. James Wilson, *Considerations on the Nature and Extent of the Legislative Authority of the British Parliament*, in Gordon Wood, ed., *The American Revolution: Writings from the Pamphlet Debate 1773–1776*, (New York: Library of America, 2015), 113.
118. Ibid., 113.
119. Ibid., 113.
120. Letter from William White to James Wilson, November 27, 1768, Case 8, Box 35, Gratz Miscellaneous Collection, Historical Society of Pennsylvania.
121. Ibid.
122. Ibid. This was Mr. John Ewing, later Rev. Dr. John Ewing, Provost of the University of Pennsylvania, into which the College of Philadelphia was transformed in 1779.
123. Ibid.

124. Wood, 109.
125. Smith, 37.
126. Ibid., 37.
127. Ibid., 37.
128. Ibid., 38.
129. Ibid., 38.
130. Ibid., 41.
131. Ibid., 42.
132. Ibid., 41.
133. Ibid., 49.
134. Ibid., 46.
135. Ibid., 52.
136. Ibid., 53.
137. Ibid., 54.
138. James Wilson, *Considerations on the Nature and Extent of the Legislative Authority of the British Parliament*, in *Collected Works of James Wilson*, Eds. Kermit L. Hall and Mark David Hall, 2 vols., (Indianapolis: Liberty Fund, 2007), 3–31.
139. Smith, 59.
140. James Wilson, *Speech Delivered in the Convention for the Province of Pennsylvania, Held at Philadelphia, in January 1775*, in *Collected Works of James Wilson*, Eds. Kermit L. Hall and Mark David Hall, 2 vols., (Indianapolis: Liberty Fund, 2007), 32–45.
141. Smith, 62.
142. Ibid., 67.
143. Ibid., 67.
144. Ibid., 125.
145. Ibid., 177.

Chapter Five

Philadelphia 1787

The Constitutional Convention

As delegates worked to finish a draft of a new national constitution, a brief commentary appeared in the *Pennsylvania Gazette* on September 5 placing their work in context.

1776 VS. 1787

The year 1776 is celebrated for a revolution in favor of *Liberty*. The year 1787, it is expected, will be celebrated with equal joy, for a revolution in favor of *Government*. The impatience with which all classes of people wait to receive the new federal constitution, can only be equaled by their zealous determination to support it.

Every state has its SHAYS, who, either with their pens—or tongues—or offices—are endeavouring to effect what *Shays* attempted in vain with his sword. . . . The spirit and wickedness of SHAYS is in each of these principles and measures. Let Americans be wise. Toryism and Shayism are nearly allied. They both lead to slavery, poverty, and misery.[1]

The Constitutional Convention of 1787 received significant scholarly attention during the commemoration of the 200th anniversary.[2] In this chapter, I will examine the work of the Convention through a different lens—that of the delegates who were not natural-born Americans.[3] Of the eight delegates who meet this criteria, it was three men—Pierce Butler, Alexander Hamilton, and James Wilson—who were the most active at the Constitutional Convention.

This lens will examine the positions which they took during debates on the presidency, composition of the U.S. Senate, and issues of citizenship. All three men were born outside of what became the United States—Butler,

Table 5.1. Delegates to the Constitutional Convention of 1787

New Hampshire	**Delaware**
Nicholas Gilman	Richard Bassett
John Langdon	Gunning Bedord, Jr.
	Jacob Broom
Massachusetts	*John Dickinson*
Elbridge Gerry	George Read
Nathaniel Gorham	
Rufus King	**Maryland**
Caleb Strong	Daniel Carroll
	Luther Martin
Connecticut	**James McHenry**
Oliver Ellsworth	John Francis Mercer
William Samuel Johnson	Daniel of St. Thomas Jenifer
Roger Sherman	
	Virginia
Rhode Island	John Blair
[Did not send a delegation.]	James Madison
	George Mason
New York	James McClung
Alexander Hamilton	Edmund Randolph
John Lansing	George Washington
Robert Yates	George Wythe
New Jersey	**North Carolina**
David Brearly	William Blount
Jonathan Dayton	**William R. Davie**
William Churchill Houston	Alexander Martin
William Livingston	*Richard Dobbs Spaight*
William Patterson	Hugh Williamson
Pennsylvania	**South Carolina**
George Clymer	**Pierce Butler**
Thomas Fitzsimons	Charles Pinckney
Benjamin Franklin	*Charles Cotesworth Pinckney*
Jared Ingersoll	*John Rutledge*
Thomas Mifflin	
Gouverneur Morris	**Georgia**
Robert Morris	Abraham Baldwin
James Wilson	William Few
	William Houston
	William Pierce

* Bolded delegates were born outside of what became the United States.
\# Italicized delegates were born in North America but received higher education in England.

though English, was born in Ireland; Hamilton was born in the West Indies; and Wilson was born in Scotland. They were born on the periphery, not at the heart, of the British Empire. I contend that their place of birth and subsequent education, outside of North America, shaped positions they advocated at the Constitutional Convention.

Those delegates who received an advanced education in England, though born in America, will also receive attention. They journeyed to the seat of empire for legal training: John Blair, John Dickinson, William Houston, Charles Cotesworth Pinckney, and John Rutledge.[4]

Pierce Butler was a military man, a son of an English baronet, who fought to wrest control of Canada away from the French for the British Empire. A son of the English aristocracy, Butler, at the age of 29, became enamored with America and married the daughter of a prominent South Carolina planter and politician in 1763.

James Wilson, like many of his fellow Scots, concluded that the uncertain journey to America was worth the risk. He sought to make his fortune by migrating to the burgeoning British colonies of North America. At the age of 23, he journeyed west, across the North Atlantic, in the summer of 1765.

Alexander Hamilton, born on the island of Nevis, in the British West Indies, attracted the attention of influential men when his account of a hurricane strike on the island group was published. His development was encouraged when they sponsored his university education in New York City. Hamilton left for America, at the age of 17, in 1772.

These three were but a few of the tens of thousands of subjects of the British Empire who journeyed to America to better themselves and their families. The distinction for these three men was their ability to take an active role in shaping the new nation that became the United States. These three, born on the periphery of the British Empire, were present when an unprecedented event unfolded—the creation of a new plan of government drafted by delegates at the Constitutional Convention of 1787.

Delegates were appointed by their respective state legislatures to represent *state* interests at the convention, but on the first full day after beginning their business, on Tuesday, May 29th, the delegates voted to abolish the operating constitution of the United States, the Articles of Confederation, in order to construct a new frame of government. Delegates did indeed represent their respective states, but as the convention began working on the proposal put forth by Virginia Governor Edmund Randolph—what became known as the Virginia Plan—they sometimes took positions unfriendly to their states. Traditionally, accounts of the Constitutional Convention revolve around a chronological framework focusing on positions taken by delegates within

Table 5.2. Place of Birth for Delegates Born Outside of the Future United States[1]

Delegation	Delegate	Place of Birth	Age*
SC	Pierce Butler	County Carlow, Ireland	29
NC	William R. Davie	Egremont, Cumberlandshire, England	7
PA	Thomas Fitzsimons	County Wicklow, Ireland	19
NY	Alexander Hamilton	Nevis, British West Indies	17**
MD	James McHenry	Ballymena, County Antrim, Ireland	25
PA	Robert Morris	Liverpool, England	14
NJ	William Patterson	County Antrim, Ireland	2
PA	James Wilson	Near St. Andrews, Scotland	23

* This is the age at which they arrived in North America.

** Hamilton's year of birth is uncertain, either 1755 or 1757; he arrived in North America in the autumn of 1772. This figure is the oldest that he would have been at the time.

1. Information for this table is derived from biographies contained in: John R. Vile, *The Constitutional Convention of 1787: A Comprehensive Encyclopedia of America's Founding*, 2 vols., (Santa Barbara: ABC-CLIO, 2005) and Clinton Rossiter, *1787: The Grand Convention*, (New York: The Macmillan Company, 1966). The latest biographical treatment of the delegates is to be found in: John R. Vile, *The Men Who Made the Constitution: Lives of the Delegates to the Constitutional Convention of 1787*, (Lanham, MD: Scarecrow Press, 2013).

state delegations. A feature missing from this framework requires delving into the delegates' upbringing.

Scholars, such as Charles Beard, attempted to use an economic analysis to explain why certain delegates argued and voted the way they did.[5] Others, such as Forrest McDonald, saw a much more complex and nuanced economic rationale for some delegates.[6] The work of Gordon Wood and Pauline Maier, building on the emphasis upon ideology advocated by their mentor Bernard Bailyn, brought renewed attention to the intellectual foundations of convention delegates.[7] One aspect of the delegates themselves has received little attention—their place of birth and subsequent education.

The story of the work of the delegates has been told many times and in many different ways. This chapter will, most certainly, *not reconstruct* the intricate workings of the convention and the work it produced—the Constitution of the United States. Instead, it will focus on the arguments of Butler, Hamilton, and Wilson during the creation of the presidency and the Senate and issues concerning citizenship.

Prior to their productive collaboration during the summer of 1787, James Wilson and James Madison developed a working relationship while tackling a host of national issues from January 2 until October 25, 1783. Central to their work, and ally Alexander Hamilton's, was to provide a source of revenue for the Confederation Congress. The failure of states to implement the Impost of 1783 led to Wilson's vigorous support for a stronger federal government. The partnership between Madison and Wilson experienced a lull when Madison was required to return to Virginia due to term limits. Their collaboration in the Confederation Congress foreshadowed their efforts at the Constitutional Convention four years later.[8]

Madison and Wilson dominated the attention of the convention like no other combination of speakers. Wilson spoke 168 times and Madison 161; only Wilson's fellow delegate from Pennsylvania, Gouverneur Morris, eclipsed these efforts at 173. Irving Brant, one of the most prolific of James Madison's biographers, wrote: "James Madison and James Wilson stand out as constructive statesmen among the fifty-five men who participated in the framing of the Constitution. Madison had the better historical grasp of public law and displayed superior talent in applying the lessons of history to American experience. Wilson excelled in fitting the structure of government to Madison's balanced federalism."[9] After the conclusion of the Convention the battle moved into the states to secure ratification of the Constitution, the subject of the next two chapters.

The delegations attending the Constitutional Convention brought together an impressive array of talent from their respective states.[10] Six of the twelve delegations participating in the convention—Rhode Island never saw fit to send delegates—were comprised entirely of men who were all born in what became the United States. Pennsylvania's delegation was the most diverse: Thomas Fitzsimons was from Ireland, Robert Morris was from Liverpool, England, and James Wilson was from near St. Andrews, Scotland.

Delegates born abroad were clustered among the members of the middle states; only two were from the South—Pierce Butler from South Carolina, born in Ireland, and William R. Davie from North Carolina, born in Egremont, Cumberlandshire, England. Not a single delegate who served among the New England delegations was born abroad.[11]

BIOGRAPHICAL VIGNETTES

Pierce Butler

In 1744, Pierce Butler[12] was the third son born into the family of Sir Richard Butler,[13] the fifth Baronet of Cloughgrenan in County Carlow, Ireland, and a member of the Irish Parliament.[14] His father bought him a commission in the 22d Regiment of Foot and he was subsequently deployed to North America in 1758 as part of the French and Indian War.[15] He served in campaigns resulting in the capture of French Canada, before returning to Ireland in 1762.[16] Butler transferred to the 29th Foot and was ordered back to Nova Scotia to garrison the newly acquired territory. In 1768, his unit was assigned to Boston and was present during the events of the Boston Massacre in 1770. In 1771, Butler, now a major, married Mary Middleton, the daughter of a wealthy South Carolina planter and colonial leader. After the marriage, Butler sold his commission and bought a plantation in South Carolina, eventually joining the Patriot cause.[17]

During the Revolutionary War, Butler was elected to and served in the South Carolina legislature for nearly a decade. He also served in 1779 as the state's adjutant general.[18] Butler was the only member of the South Carolina delegation at the Constitutional Convention who did not possess formal legal training. He was the oldest member of those delegates at the Convention who had been born and educated abroad.

Alexander Hamilton

Born in either 1755 or 1757, on the island of Nevis, in the British West Indies, Alexander Hamilton[19] was impatient to make a mark on the world.[20] He had a proclivity for attaching himself to influential and powerful patrons. First, he served as a merchant's apprentice which exposed him to the wide-ranging trading network of the British North Atlantic, then after catching the eye of several notable figures on the island after the publication of his account of a hurricane strike on the island, a minister's family sponsored Hamilton's journey to New York City and enrollment in King's College, today's Columbia University.[21]

With the imperial crisis escalating around him, Hamilton joined the fray by writing pamphlets for local newspapers. His talent soon attracted the attention of local patriots, who were surprised by his youth. After the outbreak of war, he became a captain of artillery and ultimately served as an aide on General Washington's personal staff. As much as any delegate at the Constitutional Convention, Alexander Hamilton possessed a national outlook that was not beholden to the interests of New York, which was merely his state of residence.

What became known as the Constitutional Convention of 1787 was slated to begin work on the second Monday in May, according to the resolutions passed by the individual state legislatures appointing delegates.[22] However, due to the difficulty of travel from various states to Philadelphia, the Convention did not begin its work with a quorum until Friday, May 25. The first order of business was to select a presiding officer and Virginia's George Washington was unanimously elected. Another of Virginia's delegates, James Madison, had worked with colleagues from his delegation and those of Pennsylvania to draft a plan for the new government seeking to replace the Articles of Confederation.[23]

After dealing with procedural details on the morning of Tuesday, May 29, Governor Edmund Randolph was recognized by the presiding officer, George Washington, and presented what came to be known as the Virginia Plan. The convention then convened as a committee of the whole house to allow for free-ranging discussion—debate began in earnest.

During the first full week of debate, on May 30th, General Charles Cotesworth Pinckney, of South Carolina, rose to address his colleagues for the first time. He "expressed doubt whether the act of Congress recommending the Convention" authorized the delegates to consider "a System founded on different principles from the federal Constitution."[24] The delegate who had accumulated the lengthiest period of formalized education—sixteen years—questioned whether delegates could even discuss the components of the Virginia Plan.[25]

The convention proceeded through the Virginia Plan on a resolution-by-resolution basis. It was not until Friday, June 1, when attention turned to resolutions seven and eight of the Virginia Plan, dealing with a national executive.

THE EXECUTIVE

Unlike James Madison, who arrived at the Philadelphia Convention having given little explicit prior thought to the proper allocation of executive authority,[26] Pennsylvania delegate James Wilson's views were well developed. Thus, while Wilson was closely allied to Madison during the convention and spoke frequently in support of Madison's overall agenda, Wilson's role in shaping what ultimately became the second article of the United States Constitution was more profound.[27]

As Carol Berkin has noted, debate in the Philadelphia Convention "seemed to circle back upon itself, as arguments were fashioned and refashioned, sometimes into incoherence.[28] This recursive character to the deliberations added a certain layered quality to the discussion, as new proposals or topics provided opportunity for older issues to be reopened. During the Convention debates, discussion of the executive clustered in three bursts of deliberation. Starting on June 1 and continuing for the next several days, the delegates opened discussion of the Virginia Plan's seventh and eighth resolutions, which provided for a national executive. A second extended discussion of the national executive began on July 17 continuing until July 26. Late in the Convention, the delegates returned to the executive a third time, in early September. Throughout, delegates focused on a number of concrete and contentious issues. What was the proper number of persons in whom executive authority should be vested? What was the proper method for selecting the executive? For what term of office should the executive serve? Should the executive be eligible for more than one term? Should the executive possess the power to veto congressional legislation? What was the proper means for removing an ineffective or malicious executive?[29]

After the convention gaveled into session on Friday, June 1st, Resolution 7 of the Virginia Plan was read. South Carolina's Charles Pinckney was the first to rise to express his support for a "vigorous Executive," but was concerned by potentially placing too much power in the office, "which would render the Executive a monarchy, of the worst kind, to wit an elective one."[30] James Wilson then put forth a motion that silenced the convention—the executive should reside in a single person. With memories of the American Revolution and the rejection of British monarchy fresh, delegates were faced with establishing an *American* executive. Would it reside in one person, as Wilson proposed, or a number of people, such as Governor Randolph's proposal of a three-person executive consisting of a representative from each section—east, central, and south—to carry out the executive's duties?[31]

South Carolina's John Rutledge supported Wilson's motion, but he "was not for giving him the power of war and peace." Further, he believed, "a single man would feel the greatest responsibility and administer the public affairs best."[32] Over the course of the debates, positions taken by Wilson, Hamilton, and Butler reinforced the plan of a strong executive. In defending his proposal of executive powers residing in a single person, Wilson supported Rutledge's argument, as he "preferred a single magistrate, as giving most energy, dispatch, and responsibility to the office." Further, "he did not consider the Prerogatives of the British Monarch as a proper guide in defining the Executive powers."[33] Wilson advocated something completely unprecedented in political experience—a republican executive with extensive powers—nothing like it had been contemplated since the days of the Roman Republic. Why vest such powers in a single person? Wilson argued, "Unity in the Executive instead of being the fetus of monarchy" (responding to criticisms put forth by Randolph) "would be the best safeguard against tyranny."[34] For Wilson, the key would be accountability for the actions of the Executive, he would be unable to pass responsibility for his actions to other parts of the government—voters would know who to blame if they were unsatisfied with the Executive's job performance and be able to remove them from office at the next election.

How would the Executive be elected? Wilson proposed a radical mode of election—only the governors of Massachusetts and New York were similarly elected in 1787, and he was for a direct "election by the people."[35] Further, he proposed that the Executive should fill a term of three years, which would allow the people recourse to regular judgment on the Executive's effectiveness and allow re-election of those found competent. During the second round of debate on the Executive on Thursday, July 19, Pierce Butler supported longer terms for office. He "was against the frequency of the election," as "Georgia and South Carolina were too distant to send electors often."[36] The geographic reality of both the size of the United States and the woeful condition of inter-state transportation shaped what was physically possible.

James Wilson stood alone, receiving no support from among the convention's delegates over the issue of the Executive's direct election by the public. At the close of the first day of debate on the Executive, John Rutledge shared with fellow delegates his belief that the office should be elected by "the second branch" of the new Congress—what became the Senate.[37] Wilson would continue to forcefully argue for his plan for the remainder of the convention, but the most he could accomplish was to propose what became the Electoral College, which was adopted in the closing days of the convention in September. His support for direct election was fueled by a desire to bypass any possible role for state legislatures in selecting a national executive.[38] Both Alexander Hamilton and Pierce Butler were silent on the first day of debate on the Executive.

On June 2, the first of many Saturday sessions during the convention, debate on the Executive resumed. Wilson rose and proposed a plan of election, what became known as the Electoral College, which found not a single supporter, other than himself. After the rejection of his plan, he joined with James Madison in urging the delegates to reject the proposal, put forth by Delaware's John Dickinson, to give "the National Legislature on the request of a majority of the Legislatures of individual States" the power to remove the Executive.[39] This power would give an undue influence to state legislatures over the Executive that both Madison and Wilson believed unwise.

Dickinson defended his motion against Madison and Wilson's attacks. He believed "that such an Executive as some seemed to have in contemplation was not consistent with a republic: that a firm Executive could only exist in a limited monarchy."[40] He considered a limited monarchy "as *one* of the best Governments in the world."[41] However, this form was "out of the question. The spirit of the times—the state of our affairs, forbade the experiment, if it was desireable."[42] Dickinson's motion received support only from his own delegation.

At the end of the second day of debate on the Executive, South Carolina's Pierce Butler rose to support Wilson's unitary executive. He "contended strongly for a single magistrate as most likely to answer the purpose of the remote parts."[43] Drawing upon his military background, Butler recognized the benefits of unity of command and agreed with Wilson's argument that only a single person, not Randolph's triumvirate, would be able to represent all Americans. Directing his comments at Randolph, he believed that in a multi-headed Executive, "there would be a constant struggle for local advantages."[44] He then provided a historical example where such an arrangement had been tried in Holland, and when the leaders issued orders to deal with an invasion, their orders were prejudicial to their respective regions, to the detriment of a unified defense for the whole.[45]

Alexander Hamilton entered the debate on Monday, June 4, when he joined with James Wilson urging the convention to grant the power of an absolute veto over congressional acts to the Executive. He commented that the experience in England was such that even though the King had the power, he "had not exerted his negative since the Revolution."[46] The mere threat of a veto would modify congressional legislation to conform to what the Executive would be willing to sign.

An absolute veto found favor with Hamilton and Wilson, but not Butler. He continued to support a unitary Executive, but if a "compleat negative on the laws was to be given him he certainly should have acted very differently."[47] Butler reminded the delegates that "in all countries the Executive power is in a constant course of increase."[48] Why did some delegates believe that an American Cataline or Cromwell wouldn't arise here as well? The convention continued to wrestle with these issues and others; with agreement on the composition of the Executive elusive, they moved on to other matters to return to the same concerns more than a month later.

Alexander Hamilton was the focus of attention during the convention session held on Monday, June 18. This was an opportunity for him to put forth his own plan, distinct from the Virginia Plan and its rival New Jersey Plan. He was particularly opposed to the New Jersey Plan, which relied upon amending the existing Articles of Confederation, since this would leave "the States in possession of their Sovereignty," leaving unfixed issues at the heart of the weakness of the Articles.[49]

During the course of his speech, Hamilton compared and contrasted the two plans before the convention and proposed remedies to their flaws, particularly the Virginia Plan, which he found more useful. He fundamentally disagreed with the attempt, by the convention, to craft a constitution that would share sovereignty between a new national government and the states. He remarked: "The general power whatever be its form if it preserves itself, must swallow up the State powers. Otherwise it will be swallowed up by them."[50] In other words, there could only be one sovereign, and in Hamilton's opinion this had to be a new national government. His views on the Executive were equally strong.

"As to the Executive, it seemed to be admitted that no good one could be established on Republican principles."[51] The inability of delegates to arrive at a satisfactory arrangement over the composition of the Executive led Hamilton to believe that it was fruitless to continue. He argued, "The English model was the only good one on this subject."[52] Here, a delegate from the state of New York was advocating the recreation of a British style of government for the United States less than five years after the Treaty of Paris formally ended the American Revolution! A monarch would be free from foreign influence as his interests and the nation's would be inseparable. Hamilton placed more faith in a monarch than an elected president, who would most likely originate from "men of little character," who after "acquiring great power become easily the tools of intermedling Neibours."[53]

As to term limits, Hamilton believed that the Executive should serve for life. He argued for an elective monarch, who would "serve during good behavior" and be elected by a version of the Electoral College.[54] Among the powers he enumerated for what he called a Governour, instead of President, were provisions for an absolute veto over legislative acts; to serve as commander in chief after war has been declared or military action authorized; the power to make treaties with the advice and consent of the Senate; the sole ability to appoint heads of the departments of Finance, War, and Foreign Affairs; to nominate all other officers with the Senate's approval; and to have an unrestricted ability to pardon, except in the case of treason, which required the approval of the Senate.[55] Further, the national government would select a governor or president for each state. Alexander Hamilton presented a constitution that was so outside of the realm of possibility that the delegates heard him out, but then promptly ignored the speech as if it never happened.

During the second, sustained, discussion of the Executive, John Rutledge reaffirmed his opposition to any method of election deviating from one relying upon appointment by Congress. Appointment, he argued, would make the president "sufficiently independent, if he be not re-eligible."[56] William Houston was concerned with the possible cost of an electoral arrangement "drawing together men from all the States for the single purpose of electing the Chief Magistrate."[57] This concern led Houston to offer a motion, on July 24th, to once again return to appointment of the Executive by Congress—the delegates approved the motion. The recursive nature of the debate over the Executive meant that no vote was the end of the matter and the final contours of a workable arrangement remained elusive.

Pierce Butler on Wednesday, July 25, presented his most extended discussion of the composition of the Executive. Surveying the variety of proposals pertaining to different aspects of the Executive, Butler noted: "The two great evils to be avoided are cabal at home and influence from abroad."[58] How to safeguard the republic from foreign influence, through financial rewards such as those extended to members of the Confederation Congress by the French ambassador to further French interests, and from an Executive favoring one section of the nation over another? If the proposal to provide for the election of the Executive by the national legislature was adopted, "it will be difficult to avoid either" alternative.[59] For Butler, the solution would not be to adopt Wilson's proposal of a direct election by the people, as "the government should not be made so complex and unwieldy as to disgust the states," which would be the result of such an election.[60] He was also against the possibility of re-election in all cases. Any method of selecting the national Executive should see equality among the states, something that he did not favor for apportionment of seats in the National Legislature.

John Dickinson evaluated the state of the debate over the Executive, paying particular attention to the dissatisfaction with the numerous methods of election proposed. "He had long leaned towards an election by the people which he regarded as the best and purest source."[61] This was a strong endorsement of Wilson's initial proposal for a direct election of the chief executive by the people. However, Dickinson acknowledged the objections raised by this method, but he thought they were "not so great . . . as against the other modes."[62] He then put forth his plan: voters, in their respective states, were to select the "most eminent characters," which would form a list of potential presidents—a final selection would be made either by Congress "or by Electors appointed by it."[63]

In the waning days of the convention, the proposal for the Electoral College again came before the delegates. On Tuesday, September 4, Pierce Butler concluded that "the mode not free from objections, but much more so than an election by the legislature, where as in elective monarchies, cabal, faction, and violence would be sure to prevail."[64] Butler, like many of his fellow delegates had grown weary of debate over the Executive and sought a path that led to the end of the convention.

James Wilson, who initially proposed what became the Electoral College, acknowledged that the method of electing a president "is in truth the most difficult of all on which we have had to decide."[65] Turning away from an electoral scheme that relied upon exclusive selection by Congress cleared "the way also for a discussion of the question of re-eligibility on its own merits, which the former mode of election seems to forbid."[66] If Congress was to have a role in the process, Wilson preferred the body as a whole have a role, as "the House of Rep[resentatives] will be so often changed as to be free from the influence and faction to which the permanence of the Senate may subject that branch."[67] The Electoral College wasn't perfect, but it was the best that the delegates could agree to.

In debate the next day, John Rutledge rose to object to the emerging plan of relying upon an Electoral College. He sought to return to a previous method where a joint ballot of Congress selected the president, who would serve a single, seven-year term. The only delegation supporting Rutledge was his own.[68] Returning to the proposal before them, John Dickinson supported James Wilson's attempt to modify the plan to utilize all of Congress, not just the Senate, to determine a final choice if no candidate received a majority of electoral votes—an occurrence that many delegates believed would be the norm.

On Thursday, September 6, James Wilson shared his displeasure with the plan before them—it still relied upon the Senate for a final choice of president. "[H]e was obliged to consider the whole as having a dangerous tendency to aristocracy; as throwing a dangerous power into the hands of the Senate."[69] He reminded his colleagues that they had already placed powers of appointment, treaty making, and impeachment in the Senate, allocating the body a final say over the Executive was a step too far.

Alexander Hamilton presented his view of the constitution, his most extensive remarks since Monday, June 18, when he dominated discussion with a plan much more monarchical than anything the delegates had considered.[70] Hamilton believed the Senate, upon whom the office would likely owe election, would dominate the proposed Executive under the Electoral College. He believed it was likely that the Senate would decide most presidential elections. Later this same day, the delegates accepted a proposal from Roger Sherman of Connecticut that placed the election of the Executive in the House of Representatives, and not the Senate, if there was no clear winner in the Electoral College.

Pierce Butler rejoined discussion on the Executive on Friday, September 7, when he seconded a motion put forth by James Madison that provided power to the Senate to "make treaties of peace, without the concurrence of the President," if two-thirds of its members concurred.[71] Butler was "strenuous for the motion, as a necessary security against ambitious and corrupt Presidents."[72] Here, again, he provided a historical example from Holland where the Stadtholder prolonged a conflict to his personal benefit. The delegates rejected Madison's motion and it was not included in the Constitution.

THE LEGISLATIVE BRANCH

Before the convention moved on to engage in the first debate on the creation of what became known as the Senate, Pierce Butler shared with his colleagues that he "thought an election by the people an impracticable mode" for selecting members for the first branch of the new legislature.[73] Not only was he unhappy with allowing the people to elect representatives, he "apprehended that the taking so many powers out of the hands of the States as was proposed, tended to destroy all that balance and security of interests among the States which it was necessary to preserve"; he therefore urged Edmund Randolph to "explain the extent of his ideas, and particularly the number of members he meant to assign to this second branch."[74]

James Wilson argued "strenuously for drawing the most numerous branch of the Legislature immediately from the people."[75] The widest possible base of popular support was necessary: "He was for raising the federal pyramid to a considerable altitude."[76] This broad popular support would serve a secondary—and in Wilson's view essential—objective; the power of state legislatures, relative to the federal government, would be curbed. This consideration appeared again as Wilson "opposed both a nomination by the State Legislatures, and an election by the first branch of the national Legislature."[77] He "thought both branches of the National Legislature ought to be chosen by the people."[78]

Here, Wilson proposed another method of grounding the legitimacy of a body of the federal legislature on the consent of the American people. Unlike election of members of the House of Representatives, which were derived from voters within states, Wilson advocated special senatorial districts that, very likely, would cross state boundaries. This plan would have given a unique sampling of public opinions, one transcending state borders and resting upon voters as members of the American polity, not as citizens of a particular state.

John Dickinson disagreed with his former law student. Instead of allowing voters to select representatives to both houses of Congress, he "considered it as essential that one branch of the Legislature should be drawn immediately from the people; and as expedient that the other should be chosen by the Legislatures of the States."[79] This comingling of the state legislatures with the federal government "was as politic as it was unavoidable."[80] In creating a Senate and providing for the election of members, Dickinson believed that the goal would be to "carry it through such a refining process as will assimilate it as near as may be to the House of Lords in England."[81] He joined Wilson in advocating an energetic national government, "but for leaving the States a considerable agency in the System."[82] He proposed senatorial terms of "three, five or seven years."[83]

General Pinckney "wished to have a good National Government and at the same time to leave a considerable share of power in the States."[84] He opposed placing any election for members of Congress, either in the House or the Senate, in the hands of the people. "An election of either branch by the people scattered as they are in many States, particularly in South Carolina was totally impracticable."[85] He doubted not only the ability to hold elections, but the wisdom of doing so. "He differed from gentlemen who thought that a choice by the people would be a better guard against bad measures, than by the Legislatures."[86] He declared that state legislatures would make better decisions than voters, and that adoption of the proposed constitution would rest upon making those state legislatures play a role in the new government.

James Wilson followed Pinckney and shared his view: "He saw no incompatibility between the National and State Governments provided the latter were restrained to certain local purposes; nor any probability of their being devoured by the former."[87] As long as the two levels of government remained in their respective spheres of influence, Wilson envisioned no problem arising from two legislatures holding power over Americans.

At the start of the next day's debate, John Dickinson put forth a motion calling for the selection of senators by state legislatures. He explained his two reasons underpinning the motion. First, he believed the "sense of the States would be better collected through their Governments; than immediately from the people at large;" and second, "he wished the Senate to consist of the most distinguished characters."[88] Again, Dickinson wanted a Senate as closely modeled upon the House of Lords as possible.

James Wilson rose to challenge Dickinson's thinking. He argued that a national government "ought to flow from the people at large."[89] By electing the lower house from the people, and the upper by the state legislatures, "the two branches will rest on different foundations, and dissensions will naturally arise between them."[90] He reiterated his support for giving voters the ability to elect both houses, through special districts.

Dickinson responded to Wilson with an analogy. "He compared the proposed National System to the Solar System, in which the States were the planets, and ought to be left to move freely in their proper orbits."[91] By placing the election of both houses of Congress with the people, Dickinson alleged,

Wilson "wished to extinguish these planets."[92] He warned that this led to an unbalanced system, where the legislative power of Congress would "unite the 13 small streams into one great current pursuing the same course without any opposition whatever."[93] The central issue of the American Revolution—the unchecked sovereignty of the British parliament—would be recreated in the constitution under debate.

Wilson immediately responded to Dickinson. He declared, "The British Government cannot be our model."[94] Dickinson's reliance upon Great Britain as a guide for America was mistaken. "Our manners, our laws, the abolition of entails and of primogeniture, the whole genius of the people, are opposed to it."[95] He was more concerned with providing sufficient powers to the national government to allow it to withstand encroachments from state legislatures. Commenting on Dickinson's analogy, he responded that he was not for eliminating the states, but acknowledged the necessity of keeping the states "[w]ithin their proper orbits," "for their existence is made essential by the great extent of our Country."[96] He could not "comprehend in what manner the landed interest would be rendered less predominant in the Senate, by an election through the medium of the Legislatures than by the people themselves."[97] The rationale being that in large senatorial election districts, it would be the notable "men of intelligence and uprightness" who would win election.[98]

On this day, June 7th, John Dickinson's arguments won. His fellow delegates voted—unanimously—to allow state legislatures to select Senators. This was an argument that James Wilson would lose time and again.

Connecticut's Roger Sherman opened debate on Monday, June 11th, with a proposal that would initially divide, but ultimately unite, the delegations behind a workable compromise on representation in the new Congress. He "proposed that the proportion of suffrage in the 1st branch should be according to the respective numbers of free inhabitants; and that in the second branch or Senate, each State should have one vote and no more."[99] He explained that the proposal would provide individual states, through the Senate, the ability to influence legislation coming from the lower house—an arrangement similar to the House of Lords' relationship with the House of Commons.

John Rutledge proposed an amendment, which based representation in the lower house "according to the quotas of contribution."[100] Pierce Butler seconded the motion, remarking that "money was power; and that the States ought to have weight in the Government in proportion to their wealth."[101] James Wilson joined Rufus King in opposing this motion, by making one of their own. They wanted the convention to adopt the principle that the method of representation used in the Articles of Confederation would not be used but provided "according to some equitable ratio of representation."[102]

Dickinson responded that his motion would "connect the interest of the States with their duty, the latter would be sure to be performed."[103] This connection, based on the "*actual* contributions of the States," would help correct a defect from the Articles of Confederation where states often ignored, or only minimally complied with, requisition requests from Congress—if a state failed to contribute their share to the national treasury, they would lose representation in Congress.[104]

Wilson and King won the vote on their motion—Dickinson and Butler attempted to amend it by attaching the words "according to the quotas of contribution," but Wilson blocked the motion with one of his own.[105] Instead of Dickinson's wording, he substituted "in proportion to the whole number of white and other free Citizens and inhabitants of every age, sex, and condition including those bound to servitude for a term of years and three-fifths of all other persons not comprehended in the foregoing description, except Indians not paying taxes, in each State."[106] This was the accepted language used by the Confederation Congress "for apportioning quotas of revenue on the States, and requiring a Census only every 5–7, or 10 years."[107] The motion carried without the support of New Jersey or Delaware.

Roger Sherman then called a vote on the second component of his plan—a Senate comprised of a single member from each state. By one state, Sherman's motion failed. James Wilson and Alexander Hamilton immediately moved that the convention adopt the same suffrage provision in the Senate as for the House. This was adopted, again by one vote. The next weeks of the convention were filled with energized debate over representation. Not until July 16th, would the delegates finally adopt Sherman's plan for the Senate. However, this was not to be its final form as it was amended to provide two Senators from each state who would not vote as a bloc, but independently.

Moving their attention to other components of the new Congress, the next day, Pierce Butler and John Rutledge proposed a motion precluding Senators from receiving "a salary or compensation for their services."[108] This would restrict membership to those wealthy enough to donate their time, while supporting themselves, presumably only the wealthiest candidates. The motion was defeated.

Resuming debate the next morning, Pierce Butler objected to a motion that would restrict origination of money bills to the House of Representatives. He "saw no reason for such a discrimination." "There was no analogy between the House of Lords and the body proposed to be established."[109] In his opinion, this would deter "the best men" from serving in the Senate as they may seek election to the House instead.[110]

On Wednesday, June 20th, delegates were forced to consider objections to the draft constitution raised by New York's Robert Lansing. He proposed a motion that would do away with a two-house Congress and return to the model used under the Articles of Confederation. Lansing challenged James Wilson's argument that the convention was empowered to recommend anything. "He differed much from him. Any act whatever of so respectable a body must have a great effect, and if it does not succeed, will be a source of great dissentions."[111] Foreshadowing the events of the ratification process of the following year, the esteem, held by the public, for the members of the convention—especially George Washington and Benjamin Franklin—did indeed incline them to supporting any plan the body produced.

Maryland's Luther Martin supported Lansing's motion to return to a single-chamber Congress and, surprisingly, so did Roger Sherman, who seconded the motion—the delegate who proposed the compromise on representation, which resided in a two-chamber Congress. Sherman explained, "He admitted two branches to be necessary in the State Legislatures, but saw no necessity for them in a Confederacy of States."[112] He believed that placing election of one of the houses of Congress in the hands of the people was unwise. "The people would not much interest themselves in the election, a few designing men in the large districts would carry their points, and the people would have no more confidence in their new representatives than in Cong[ress]."[113] However, if it was necessary to adopt a two-house Congress to settle the issue of representation, once and for all—as long as one house rested upon an equality of the states—then he would support it.

James Wilson rose and "urged the necessity of two branches," and he "observed that if a proper model was not to be found in other Confederacies it was not to be wondered at."[114] He then provided the delegates—some would say subjected them to—a survey of world history to emphasize the lack of adequate precedent. Pointing to his own experience of service—first in the Second Continental Congress and then in the Confederation Congress—in six of the past twelve years, he urged his colleagues to remember their experience under the Articles. "He appealed to the recollection of others whether on many important occasions, the public interest had not been obstructed by the small members of the Union. The success of the Revolution was owing to other causes, than the Constitution of Congress."[115] Indeed, in some cases the Revolution was won in spite of the work of Congress.

Returning to debate on the composition of Congress, General Pinckney put forth a motion allowing state legislatures to determine the method of election to the lower house. He explained that "[t]his liberty would give more satisfaction, as the Legislatures could then accommodate the mode to the convenience and opinions of the people."[116] Luther Martin quickly seconded the motion.

Alexander Hamilton "considered the motion as intended manifestly to transfer the election from the people to the State Legislatures, which would essentially vitiate the plan."[117] Hamilton, along with Wilson and other nationalists, was concerned "it would increase that State influence which could not be too watchfully guarded ag[ainst]."[118] Roger Sherman "would like an election by the Legislatures best, but is content with the plan as it stands."[119] John Rutledge believed, "An election by the Legislature would be more refined than an election immediately by the people: and would be more likely to correspond with the sense of the whole community."[120]

James Wilson "considered the election of the 1st branch by the people not only as the corner Stone, but as the foundation of the fabric: and that the difference between a mediate and immediate election was immense."[121] He was very much for expanding the power and influence of the national government, but this needed to be grounded on the direct consent of the people with respect to a direct election of the lower house. Further, he reminded his colleagues that members of state legislatures were "actuated not merely by the sentiment of the people; but have an official sentiment opposed to that of the Gen[eral] Gov[ernment] and perhaps to that of the people themselves."[122] Wilson continued to support election by the people as a method of checking the powers of state legislatures.

This concern appeared again, the next day, as discussion moved to compensation for members of Congress. Wilson was "ag[ain]st fixing the compensation as circumstances would change and call for a change of the amount." Further, he thought "it of great moment that the members of the Nat[iona]l Gov[ernmen]t should be left as independent as possible of the State Gov[ernmen]ts in all respects."[123] Alexander Hamilton echoed Wilson's arguments: "He was strenuous ag[ain]st making the National Council dependent on the Legislative rewards of the States." With this in mind, he reminded his colleagues, "Those who pay are the masters of those who are paid."[124]

To support his own beliefs and those of Hamilton, Wilson made a motion allocating power to the lower house to control their own compensation and such compensation to be "paid out of the Nat[iona]l Treasury."[125] Wilson's proposal, at this time, was defeated, only receiving the support of his own delegation and that of New Jersey.

Debate moved to qualifications for office. George Mason argued that candidates for the lower house must be at least twenty-five years of age. James Wilson "was ag[ain]st abridging the rights of election in any shape."[126] He then gave several historical examples of where men of a young age provided great service to their countries. Wilson lost the argument.

Delegates then addressed whether to bar members of Congress from holding other offices, either in the national or state governments, and for one year after the end of their term of office. Citing the history of the British parliament, Pierce Butler and George Mason believed the provision was necessary to preclude corruption. Mason considered the disqualification "as a corner stone in the fabric."[127]

James Wilson and Alexander Hamilton opposed the motion. Wilson was "ag[ain]st fettering elections, and discouraging merit."[128] He alluded to the service of George Washington during the American Revolution—Washington had been elected commander of the Continental Army as a member of the Second Continental Congress. Hamilton acknowledged, "There are inconvenience on both sides." However, "we must take man as we find him, and if we expect him to serve the public must interest his passions in doing so."[129] Wilson and Hamilton sought to entice the most qualified candidates to stand for election to the national government.

At the beginning of the next session, General Pinckney sought to delete the ineligibility of members of the lower house from holding offices established by the states. He argued that limiting states from availing themselves of citizens of ability was an "inconveniency" that was unwise.[130] Roger Sherman concurred by noting the ineligibility seemed to create "a Kingdom at war with itself. The Legislature ought not to be fettered in such a case."[131] The convention agreed.

Returning to debate, after a Sunday of rest, delegates returned to issues related to the organization of the Senate. James Wilson continued to hammer away at his opposition to the selection of Senators by state legislatures. Explaining his stance, he remarked, "When he considered the amazing extent of Country—the immense population which is to fill it, the influence of the Gov[ernmen]t we are to form will have, not only on the present generation of our people and their multiplied posterity, but on the whole Globe, he was lost in the magnitude of it."[132] Despite these awesome prospects before them, they had to create a workable government. "The Gen[era]l Gov[ernmen]t is not an assemblage of States, but of individuals for certain political purposes—it is not meant for the States, but for the individuals composing them; the *individuals* therefore not the *States*, ought to be represented in it."[133] Wilson was losing the argument of a popularly elected Senate, and Pierce Butler shared his frustration that it was difficult to foresee a final vote on the election of the Senate, either by the public or state legislatures; he moved to go on to other business and the convention so voted.

Setting the length of a Senator's term also proved elusive. General Pinckney suggested 4 years. "A longer term w[oul]d fix them at the seat of Gov[ernmen]t. They w[oul]d acquire an interest there, perhaps transfer their property and lose sight of the States they represent."[134] James Wilson supported Nathaniel Gorham's motion, which provided for a term of six years, with one-third of the members up for election every two years.[135] General Pinckney opposed the length as it would lead to Senators losing touch with the state that elected them. "[T]hey w[oul]d settle in the State where they exercised their functions; and would in a little time be rather the representatives of that than of the State appoint[in]g them."[136]

Alexander Hamilton supported James Madison's contention that the convention was to "decide for ever the fate of Republican Government; and that if we did not give to that form the due stability and wisdom, it would be disgraced and lost among ourselves, disgraced and lost to mankind for ever."[137] He also reminded his colleagues that the lower house was "to render it particularly the guardians of the poorer order of Citizens."[138] The Senate was to be the check, on behalf of property, to the popular House. With this in mind, James Wilson reiterated his support, and the convention so adopted, for Senators to be elected for six-year terms, with one-third to be elected every two years.

After the adoption of a six-year term, General Pinckney proposed that Senators should serve without compensation. If the Senate was to safeguard wealth, then "it ought to be composed of persons of wealth; and if no allowance was to be made the wealthy alone would undertake the service."[139] Benjamin Franklin supported this motion, just as he had proposed the president serve without compensation. The delegates narrowly disapproved.

For the rest of the week, debate meandered from topic to topic concerning the composition and powers of Congress. On Saturday, June 30th, James Wilson sallied forth with another impassioned speech against a lower house elected by the people and an upper house selected by state legislatures. He just couldn't move on from what he perceived to be a fatal flaw. "Can we forget for whom we are forming a Government? Is it for *men*, or for the imaginary beings called *States*?"[140] Once again he argued, "The rule of suffrage ought on every principle to be the same in the 2nd as in the 1st branch. If the Government be not laid on this foundation, it can be neither solid nor lasting."[141]

Wilson, joined by James Madison, opposed a committee created to forge a compromise over the composition and election of a new Congress. On July 5th, the delegates began debate on the report—a report that Wilson and Madison remained forcefully opposed to. Pierce Butler praised the report's provision of equal state representation in the Senate. John Rutledge reminded his colleagues, "Property was certainly the principal object of Society. If numbers should be made the rule of representation, the Atlantic States would be subjected to the Western."[142] He proposed an amendment that modified representation in Congress to be based on tax payments to the national treasury. The delegations overwhelmingly defeated the amendment, with only his own voting in the affirmative.

The next day, debate returned to Rutledge's motion to retain an advantage for the original states in the new government. Pierce Butler "concurred with those who thought some balance was necessary between the old and new states. He contended strenuously that property was the only just measure of representation. This was the great object of Governm[en]t: the great cause of war; the great means of carrying it on."[143] Delegates from South Carolina tried again and again to base representation in Congress on wealth. James Wilson consistently opposed the use of wealth, in any form, as a basis of representation, as "impracticable."[144]

In debate in mid-July, Wilson explained, "If equality in the 2nd branch was an error that time would correct, he should be less anxious to exclude it being sensible that perfection was unattainable in any plan; but being a fundamental and a perpetual error, it ought by all means to be avoided."[145]

In late July, John Dickinson and James Wilson found themselves allies on the issue of qualifications for members of Congress—they were opposed to them. Dickinson "was against any recital of qualifications in the Constitution."[146] In part, because it was impossible to draft a complete list, best to leave such matters to the Congress to determine for themselves. He argued, "The best defense lay in the freeholders who were to elect the Legislature. Whilst this Source should remain pure, the public interest would be safe. If it ever should be corrupt, no little expedients would repel the danger."[147] Further, "he doubted the policy of interweaving into a Republican constitution a veneration for wealth. He had always understood that a veneration for poverty and virtue, were the objects of republican encouragement."[148]

As to restrictions on who could hold office, Wilson "was for striking them out."[149] As one of several delegates who were engaged in land speculation, he was particularly sensitive to any obstacles that would prevent him from both participating in the new government which they were framing and continuing his business activities. He urged his colleagues to "consider that we are providing a Constitution for future generations, and not merely for the peculiar circumstances of the moment."[150] The time may come again when individuals and their services—either leadership in government, the military, or financial—would be needed in a moment of crisis, "when the public safety may depend on the voluntary aids of individuals which will necessarily open acc[oun]ts with the public, and when such acc[oun]ts will be a characteristic of patriotism."[151]

As the Convention moved into the early days of August, John Dickinson continued to urge provisions for suffrage to be based on voters free from debt. "He considered them as the best guardians of liberty; And the restriction of the right to them as a necessary defence ag[ain]st the dangerous influence of those multitudes without property and without principle with which our Country like all others, will in time abound."[152] Interestingly, South Carolina's John Rutledge disagreed with Dickinson. He "thought the idea of restraining the right of suffrage to the freeholders a very unadvised one. It would create division among the people and make enemies of all those who should be excluded."[153]

CITIZENSHIP

It is valuable to examine what Wilson, Butler, and Hamilton, all born outside of the United States, thought on the issue of citizenship—not only as it applies to becoming a citizen of the nation, but also the requirements each advocated as the convention crafted new positions of authority in the Executive and Legislative branches.

On August 8th, debate turned to the residency qualifications for potential members of the House of Representatives. Virginia's George Mason "was for opening a wide door for emigrants; but did not chuse to let foreigners and adventurers make laws for us and govern us."[154] He objected to only requiring three years' residency before being able to stand for election to the lower house. Instead, he moved that it be raised to seven. John Rutledge concurred with Mason, but for a different reason. He was thinking of internal, not external emigration. "An emigrant from N. England to S. C. or Georgia would know little of its affairs and could not be supposed to acquire a thorough knowledge in less time."[155]

Delaware's George Read reminded Rutledge and his colleagues that the Convention was "not forming a Nati[ona]l Gov[ernmen]t and such a regulation would correspond little with the idea that we were one people,"[156] a sentiment that James Wilson wholeheartedly agreed with. In response, Dickinson proposed a change where the provision read, "inhabitant actually resident for ___ year."[157] Wilson objected on the grounds that this could be read to exclude members of the national government who lived at the national capital while performing their duties.

When debate turned to residency qualifications for the Senate, Gouverneur Morris urged raising it from four to fourteen years. This would parry "the danger of admitting strangers into our public Councils."[158] Pierce Butler, "was decidedly opposed to the admission of foreigners without a long residency in the Country. They bring with them, not only attachments to other Countries; but ideas of Gov[ernmen]t so distinct from ours that in every point of view they are dangerous."[159] Acknowledging his own experience of emigrating to America, he believed "his foreign habits, opinions and attachments would have rendered him an improper agent in public affairs."[160]

James Wilson followed heartfelt pleas for a short residency qualification by Benjamin Franklin and Edmund Randolph. He "rose with feelings which were perhaps peculiar; mentioned the circumstance of his not being a native, and the possibility, if the ideas of some gentlemen should be pursued, of his being incapacitated from holding a place under the very Constitution, which he had shared in the trust of making."[161] In some way, he felt an obligation to serve as an advocate for those desiring to come to America and align their future with the new nation. A short residency qualification would encourage "meritorious foreigners" to emigrate, but a lengthy one would discourage many as "they must feel from the degrading discrimination."[162] New citizens should be brought within the American polity as quickly and painlessly as possible.

With the Convention having already voted to require at least a seven-year residency for candidates to the House of Representatives, John Rutledge argued, "Surely a longer term is requisite for the Senate, which will have more power."[163] Debate meandered between qualifications for both the House and Senate. Delegates agreed that there should be differing residency qualification for the two bodies but couldn't settle upon terms which could garner majority support. Wilson again urged lowering the residency requirement, in the House, from seven to three years.[164]

A week later, joined by Edmund Randolph, James Wilson attempted to lower the length of residency, for election to the House, to four years.[165] Elbridge Gerry sought to restrict eligibility to native-born citizens.[166] Hugh Williamson sought nine years.[167] Alexander Hamilton and James Madison both urged lenient requirements, which would "invite foreigners of merit and republican principles among us."[168] Wilson reminded his colleagues of his adopted state's experience, "as a proof of the advantage of encouraging emigrations."[169] He remarked "almost all the Gen[era]l officers of the Pen[nsylvani]a line of the late army were foreigners. And no complaint had ever been made against their fidelity or merit."[170] A further example was provided by the very delegates from Pennsylvania at the Convention. "Three of her deputies . . . [Mr. R. Morris, Mr. Fitzsimons and himself] were also not natives."[171] Despite an appearance of hypocrisy, Pierce Butler was "strenuous ag[ain]st admitting foreigners into our public Councils."[172]

A problem facing the delegates was that the thirteen states each had different terms of naturalization. If the new Constitution did not address this problem, how could residency qualifications be defined? James Wilson read the relevant clause from the Pennsylvania constitution of 1776, which provided full citizenship to foreigners after only two years of residence.[173] He then combined this clause with Article IV from the Articles of Confederation, which made "the Citizens of one State Citizens of all," to argue that Pennsylvania was obligated to safeguard and maintain "the faith thus pledged to her citizens of foreign birth."[174] Despite his eloquent and well-reasoned arguments, Wilson's fellow delegates repeatedly voted against him to lower residency requirements—instead they voted to raise them. Naturalized citizens could stand for election to the House of Representatives after attaining the age of twenty-five and being a citizen of the United States for seven years. The Senate required an age of thirty and a residency of nine years. The Convention adopted longer terms than Wilson wanted, but not nearly as restrictive as those advocated by Gouverneur Morris and Elbridge Gerry.

James Wilson, Alexander Hamilton, and Pierce Butler each argued for a strong Executive who would serve as a representative of all Americans. They differed to the degree in which power would be allocated to this unitary Executive. Hamilton was the most expansive in power of the three, with Butler the most restrained. However, they all agreed on the need for a president who would provide energy through executive actions to a national government superior to the individual states, unlike the situation existing under the Articles of Confederation.

The American Presidency is unlike any comparable position around the world. Butler, Hamilton, and especially Wilson nudged the delegates at the Constitutional Convention to consider a truly republican office, but one that wielded significant powers within a framework that shared sovereignty, not only between the individual states and the national government, but within the national government itself among the three branches—executive, legislative, and judicial.

It was when debate turned to requirements for those to serve in Congress that a split became apparent between the three men. Wilson and Hamilton were consistent in the support for limited qualifications, especially for a short term of residency. Butler was wary of foreign influence in government and supported the stance of Elbridge Gerry—restricting election to natural-born citizens—a requirement Butler himself failed to meet.

To what degree did the fact that all three were foreign-born contribute to their positions? All three drew from both life experience outside of America and their extensive educations to advocate for a strong national government with a strong executive branch only a few short years after the conclusion of the American Revolution. Some scholars have called this a revolution *in favor* of government.[175] The experience of becoming Americans, for Wilson, Hamilton, and Butler, may not completely qualify for the traditional definition of ethnogenesis, but all three willingly, unlike enslaved Africans, left their land of birth and traveled to America to become Americans.[176] They were present at the birth of a new nation where a structure of an entirely new society was born, with their help. The process known as the Great American Melting Pot was very much a part of the deliberations of the Constitutional Convention of 1787.

The months from May to September 1787 were moments of James Wilson's life where he shined the brightest. His adopted city, where he had arrived twenty-two years previously, hosted the greatest American political salon in history. His extensive Scottish education supremely prepared him for the role which he played. Of those delegates born and educated outside of the future United States, James Wilson's contributions were of the first rank. It is to him that we look for the creation of a unified executive with the qualified power of veto over legislation. He is also the delegate who first proposed what became the method of presidential selection—the Electoral College.

Wilson was also the first delegate to publicly defend the Convention's work at a public meeting held on the grounds of the Pennsylvania State House (now known as Independence Hall), on October 6th. He led the pro-ratification forces at the Pennsylvania Ratification Convention and helped draft a new constitution for Pennsylvania in 1789–90, based in large part on the federal constitution of 1787. In helping launch the new federal government, James Wilson accepted an appointment from President Washington as an associate justice of the first Supreme Court of the United States in September 1789. Before all of this could happen, the American people would have to give their consent to the new plan, a prospect that faced significant obstacles.

NOTES

1. Untitled, *Pennsylvania Gazette*, 5 September 1787, in John P. Kaminski and Gaspare J. Saladino, eds., *The Documentary History of the Ratification of the Constitution, Vol. XIII Commentaries on the Constitution: Public and Private, Vol. 1, 21 February to 7 November 1787*. (Madison: State Historical Society of Wisconsin, 1981), 192.

2. See: Max Farrand, *The Framing of the Constitution of the United States*, (New Haven: Yale University Press, 1913); Charles Warren, *The Making of the Constitution*, (Boston: Little, Brown, and Company, 1928); Carl Van Doren, *The Great Rehearsal*, (New York: The Viking Press: 1948); Catherine Drinker Bowen, *Miracle at Philadelphia: The Story of the Constitutional Convention May to September 1787*, (Boston: Little, Brown and Company, 1966); Clinton Rossiter, *1787: The Grand Convention*, (New York: The Macmillan Company, 1966); Christopher Collier and James Lincoln Collier, *Decision in Philadelphia: The Constitutional Convention of 1787*, 1st Pub. 1987, (New York: Ballantine Books, 2007); Carol Berkin, *A Brilliant Solution: Inventing the American Constitution*, (New York: Harcourt, Inc., 2002); David O. Stewart, *The Summer of 1787: The Men Who Invented the Constitution*, (New York: Simon & Schuster, 2007); Richard Beeman, *Plain, Honest Men: The Making of the American Constitution*, (New York: Random House, 2009); and John R. Vile, *The Writing and Ratification of the U.S. Constitution*, (New York: Rowman & Littlefield Publishers, Inc., 2012).

3. See Table 5.2 for a complete list.

4. John Blair of Virginia does not appear in the record as having spoken at the Constitutional Convention. His legal background and training in London prepared him for a substantial role, but he did not seize the opportunity.

5. Charles Beard, *An Economic Interpretation of the Constitution of the United States*, 1st pub. 1913, (New York: Macmillan Company, 1941).

6. Forrest McDonald, *We the People: The Economic Origins of the Constitution*, (Chicago: University of Chicago Press, 1958).

7. Gordon S. Wood, *The Creation of the American Republic 1776–1787*, (Chapel Hill, NC: The University of North Carolina Press, 1998); Pauline Maier, *Ratification: The People Debate the Constitution, 1787–1788*, (New York: Simon and Schuster, 2010); and Bernard Bailyn, *The Ideological Origins of the American Revolution*, enlarged ed., (Cambridge: Harvard University Press, 1992).

8. For a discussion of the period where Madison and Wilson served in the Confederation Congress, consult the following: Geoffrey Seed, *James Wilson*, (Millwood, NY: KTO Press, 1978); Page Smith, *James Wilson: Founding Father, 1742–1798*, (Chapel Hill: University of North Carolina Press, 1956); Ralph Ketcham, *James Madison: A Biography*, (Charlottesville: University Press of Virginia, 1971); Irving Brant, *James Madison: The Nationalist 1780–1787*, New York: The Bobbs-Merrill Company, 1948); Merrill Jensen, *The New Nation: A History of the United States during the Confederation, 1781–1789*, (New York: Alfred A. Knopf, 1967); H. James Henderson, *Party Politics in the Continental Congress*, (New York: McGraw-Hill, 1974); Jack N. Rakove, *The Beginnings of National Politics*, (New York: Alfred A. Knopf, 1979); and Edmund Cody Burnett, *The Continental Congress*, (New York: W.W. Norton & Company, Inc., 1941).

9. Irving Brant, *The Fourth President: A Life of James Madison*, (New York: The Bobbs-Merrill Company, 1970), 195.

10. For a complete list of the delegations and their members, see Table 5.1.

11. For a complete breakdown of the foreign-born delegates, see Table 5.2.

12. For the only published biography on Pierce Butler see: Lewright B. Sikes, *The Public Life of Pierce Butler*, (Washington, D.C.: University Press of America, 1979). Also see biographical entries in John R. Vile, *The Constitutional Convention of 1787: A Comprehensive Encyclopedia of America's Founding*, 2 vols., (Santa Barbara: ABC-CLIO, 2005), 70–76; Clinton Rossiter, *1787: The Grand Convention*, (New York: The Macmillan Company, 1966), 133; and a brief, but useful sketch: U.S. Army Center of Military History, *Pierce Butler*, (Washington, D.C.: U.S. Army Center of Military History, 1986).

13. A vignette for James Wilson is not given; this was the subject of chapter 2.

14. U.S. Army Center of Military History, *Pierce Butler*, (Washington, D.C.: U.S. Army Center of Military History, 1986), 2.

15. Ibid., 2.

16. Ibid., 2.

17. Ibid., 3.

18. Vile, *The Constitutional Convention of 1787*, 71.

19. For recent biographies of Alexander Hamilton see: Richard Brookhiser, *Alexander Hamilton: American*, (New York: The Free Press, 1999) and especially Ron Chernow, *Alexander Hamilton*, (New York: Penguin Press, 2004).

20. Hamilton's year of birth is uncertain, either 1755 or 1757; he arrived in North America in the autumn of 1772. Vile, *The Constitutional Convention of 1787*, 340.

21. Ibid., 340.

22. Rhode Island did not deem it proper to appoint a delegation, and as a consequence they had no input in the drafting of the Constitution.

23. Two delegations, Pennsylvania and Virginia, were both present when the convention first convened, but lacked a quorum to conduct business. To effectively use their time, while they waited for other state delegations to arrive, the members met for dinner each evening and crafted a joint proposal for the convention to consider — the Virginia Plan. The plan was based on extensive research that James Madison had conducted on both the history of governments in America and around the world.

24. James Madison, *Notes on Debates in the Federal Convention of 1787*, (New York: W.W. Norton & Company, 1987), 35.

25. Pinckney's European education included tenures at Christ Church College at Oxford, where he took classes with William Blackstone; the Temple in London for study of law; and at the Royal Military Academy in Caen, France. (John R. Vile, *The Men Who Made the Constitution*, 258.)

26. Madison wrote George Washington on April 16, 1787, to convey what he described as "some outlines of a new system," pertinent to "the subject which is to undergo the discussion of the Convention." As Madison went on to confess, "A national Executive must also be provided," but "I have scarcely ventured as yet to form my own opinion either of the manner in which it ought to be constituted or of the authorities with which it ought to be cloathed." Jack Rakove, ed., *Madison: Writings* (New York: Library of America: 1999), 80, 82–83.

27. Wilson's influence may have been more significant than previously thought; see: William Ewald, "James Wilson and the Drafting of the Constitution," *Journal of Constitutional Law*, Vol. 10, No. 5 (June 2008), 901–1009.

28. Carol Berkin, *A Brilliant Solution: Inventing the American Constitution*, (New York: Harcourt, Inc., 2002), 78.

29. Wilson's thought regarding the creation of the executive has been the subject of a number of studies: see especially Richard Beeman, *Plain, Honest Men: The Making of the American Constitution*, (New York: Random House, 2009), 127–37; Robert E. DiClerico, "James Wilson's Presidency," *Presidential Studies Quarterly*, Vol. 17, No. 2 (1987), 301–17; Daniel J. McCarthy, "James Wilson and the Creation of the Presidency," *Presidential Studies Quarterly*, Vol. 17, No. 4 (1987), 689–96; and Michael H. Taylor and Kevin Hardwick, "The Presidency of James Wilson," *White House Studies*, Vol. 9, No. 4, (Winter 2010), 331–346.

30. Madison, *Notes* . . . , 45.

31. At the time, the states of New England were called the "east."

32. Madison, *Notes* . . . , 46.

33. Ibid., 46.

34. Ibid., 47.

35. Ibid., 48.
36. Ibid., 329.
37. Ibid., 50.
38. Ibid., 49.
39. Ibid., 55.
40. Ibid., 56.
41. Ibid., 57.
42. Ibid., 57.
43. Ibid., 58.
44. Ibid., 58.
45. Ibid., 59.
46. Ibid., 62.
47. Ibid., 63.
48. Ibid., 63.
49. Ibid., 129.
50. Ibid., 133.
51. Ibid., 135.
52. Ibid., 135.
53. Ibid., 136.
54. Ibid., 138.
55. Ibid., 138.
56. Ibid., 328.
57. Ibid., 355.
58. Ibid., 366.
59. Ibid., 366.
60. Ibid., 366.
61. Ibid., 369
62. Ibid., 369.
63. Ibid., 369.
64. Ibid., 577.
65. Ibid., 578.
66. Ibid., 578.
67. Ibid., 578.
68. Ibid., 583.
69. Ibid., 587.
70. Delegates continued debate the next day without taking any action upon Hamilton's proposals. Hamilton had only recently returned to the Convention.
71. Madison, *Notes* . . . , 599.
72. Ibid., 600.
73. Ibid., 41.
74. Ibid., 41–42.
75. Ibid., 40.
76. Ibid., 40.
77. Ibid., 42.
78. Ibid., 42.

79. Ibid., 77.
80. Ibid., 77.
81. Ibid., 77.
82. Ibid., 77.
83. Ibid., 78.
84. Ibid., 78.
85. Ibid., 78.
86. Ibid., 78.
87. Ibid., 78–79.
88. Ibid., 82.
89. Ibid., 82.
90. Ibid., 82.
91. Ibid., 84.
92. Ibid., 84.
93. Ibid., 85.
94. Ibid., 85.
95. Ibid., 85.
96. Ibid., 85.
97. Ibid., 85.
98. Ibid., 85.
99. Ibid., 98.
100. Ibid., 98.
101. Ibid., 98.
102. Ibid., 99.
103. Ibid., 99.
104. Ibid., 99.
105. Ibid., 103.
106. Ibid., 103.
107. Ibid., 103.
108. Ibid., 111.
109. Ibid., 113.
110. Ibid., 113.
111. Ibid., 155.
112. Ibid., 160.
113. Ibid., 161.
114. Ibid., 161.
115. Ibid., 162.
116. Ibid., 166.
117. Ibid., 166–67.
118. Ibid., 167.
119. Ibid., 167.
120. Ibid., 167.
121. Ibid., 167.
122. Ibid., 167.
123. Ibid., 172.

124. Ibid., 172.
125. Ibid., 172.
126. Ibid., 174.
127. Ibid., 175.
128. Ibid., 175.
129. Ibid., 175.
130. Ibid., 176.
131. Ibid., 176.
132. Ibid., 188.
133. Ibid., 189.
134. Ibid., 192.
135. Ibid., 193.
136. Ibid., 193.
137. Ibid., 196.
138. Ibid., 196.
139. Ibid., 198.
140. Ibid., 221. Wilson would return to this argument during his written opinion in the U.S. Supreme Court case of *Chisholm v. Georgia* (1793), where he set forth his view of American citizenship.
141. Ibid., 221.
142. Ibid., 245.
143. Ibid., 247.
144. Ibid., 270.
145. Ibid., 295.
146. Ibid., 374.
147. Ibid., 374.
148. Ibid., 374.
149. Ibid., 376.
150. Ibid., 376.
151. Ibid., 376–77.
152. Ibid., 402.
153. Ibid., 405.
154. Ibid., 406.
155. Ibid., 407.
156. Ibid., 407.
157. Ibid., 407.
158. Ibid., 418.
159. Ibid., 419.
160. Ibid., 419.
161. Ibid., 420.
162. Ibid., 420.
163. Ibid., 422.
164. Ibid., 428.
165. Ibid., 437.
166. Ibid., 437.

167. Ibid., 438.
168. Ibid., 438.
169. Ibid., 438.
170. Ibid., 439.
171. Ibid., 439.
172. Ibid., 439.

173. Section 42 reads: "Every foreigner of good character who comes to settle in this state, having first taken an oath or affirmation of allegiance to the same, may purchase, or by other just means acquire, hold, and transfer land or other real estate; and after one year's residence, shall be deemed a free denizen thereof, and entitled to all the rights of a natural born subject of this state, except that he shall not be capable of being elected a representative until after two years residence."

174. Madison, *Notes . . .*, 441.

175. See Max M. Edling, *A Revolution in Favor of Government: Origins of the U.S. Constitution and the Making of the American State*, (New York: Oxford University Press, 2003).

176. James Sidbury and Jorge Cañizares-Esguerra, "Mapping Ethnogenesis in the Early Modern Atlantic," *The William and Mary Quarterly* Vol. 68, No. 2 (April 1, 2011), 181–208.

Chapter Six

The State House Yard Speech
October 6, 1787

The debate over ratification of what became the United States Constitution was fought state-by-state, vote-by-vote. The first steps in the battle were taken on September 18, the day after the Constitutional Convention adjourned in Philadelphia. Pennsylvania's delegates took advantage of the state legislature being in session by presenting them the Convention's constitutional blueprint. The body had graciously offered the use of their normal chamber for the Convention and had been displaced to a room directly above where the Convention had deliberated. Pennsylvania's government was comprised of two factions: the Constitutionalists[1] who supported the 1776 Pennsylvania Constitution and the Republicans who advocated the adoption of a new constitution. James Wilson was a prominent member of the Republicans and Benjamin Franklin was a member of the Constitutionalists.

Support or opposition to the work of the Constitutional Convention came from all walks of life as the proposal was read, commented on, and evaluated by Americans. A short piece appearing in the *Pennsylvania Herald* on the day after Christmas 1787, "An Overheard Conversation," shared different views of the Constitution.

> A gentleman was passing by the place where a group of convicts was at work, and overheard the following conversation:
>
> 1st. Man. I can never agree to it—for I am confident, it will destroy the liberties of the people.
>
> 2d. Man. My great motive for supporting it, is that it will enable us to be honest, and pay our debts.

3d. Man. Ay, but I will oppose it pell mell; for it takes away that laudanum of our liberties, a free press.

4th. Man. Peace! I say it ought to be adopted, and it shall too, for it will give strength and energy to public officers.

On enquiry, the gentleman found the subject of conversation to be the proposed constitution, that the first man was a convict in chains, the second a debtor just released by the Insolvent act, the third a printer's devil, and the fourth a constable, who superintended the convicts.[2]

Proponents of the Constitution wasted no time launching the drive for ratification. Only hours after the Convention's secretary, Major Jackson, left on the stage for New York to present the proposed constitution to Congress, the Constitution was read at the State House to the Pennsylvania Assembly at the urging of Benjamin Franklin.[3] Once the reading was finished, Franklin suggested "it would be advisable to pass a law, granting jurisdiction over any place in Pennsylvania, not exceeding ten miles square, which . . . the Congress might choose for their residence."[4] By placing their offer on the table, Pennsylvania was making the first bid to host the new national capital. Philadelphia was already the largest and most influential city in America; if it were to be the home of the new capital its importance would be secured for generations to come.

The first step in a concerted effort to secure speedy ratification of the Constitution by Pennsylvania was taken on September 18 with its reading by Speaker Thomas Mifflin.[5] Events over the next two weeks cast a shadow of suspicion on the motives of Federalists for the remainder of the ratification struggle. The confrontation between Constitutionalists and Republicans in the Pennsylvania Assembly over the matter of when to convene a ratification convention would make James Wilson's task much harder than necessary. Wilson was not a member of the Assembly, but as a prominent leader of the Republican Party he was tainted by their behavior.

The Assembly's legislative session was scheduled to adjourn on September 29, with elections on October 9 to select members for the new session scheduled to convene October 22. Pro-ratification forces in Pennsylvania were determined their state would be the first to ratify. In a move designed to fulfill the requirements of Article VII of the proposed constitution that called for "Ratification of the Conventions of nine States," the Republican-controlled Assembly was determined to enact legislation necessary to convene a ratification convention as quickly as possible.

The Confederation Congress, sitting in New York, received Major Jackson's documents and proceeded to debate for nearly three days, from

September 26 to 28, over what to do. In Philadelphia, the scheduled adjournment of the legislative session was fast approaching, which forced the legislature's leadership to schedule debate on establishing a ratification convention before the action taken by the Confederation Congress was known. This course of action brought howls of protest from members of the Constitutional party who urged postponing action until a new Assembly was elected, which also brought the benefit of learning what action Congress had taken.

On the morning of Friday, September 28, a member of Pennsylvania's delegation to the Philadelphia Convention, George Clymer, submitted resolutions authorizing a state ratification convention. The resolution establishing a convention was adopted on a party-line vote, but the body adjourned until 4:00pm without providing for the election of delegates and the time and location for the convention. Upon reconvening, the leaders of the Assembly found that they lacked a quorum because nineteen members of the opposition had left.[6] The Constitutional Party had used the tactic of a session boycott before, in September of 1784. Constitutionalists remained vigilant against any modifications to the Pennsylvania Constitution of 1776. In legislative sessions where Republicans held the majority, Constitutionalists fought any attempts by Republicans to change the basic structure of Pennsylvania government, particularly the one chamber legislature and weak executive. Having been stung once by such a maneuver, the Speaker dispatched the sergeant-at-arms to search for missing members, but he returned empty-handed. By necessity, an adjournment was called until 9:30 the morning of the 29th—the final day of the session.[7]

A special courier was dispatched from New York to Philadelphia conveying the transmission of the Constitution to the states and was received by Clymer sometime before 7:00am. When the Assembly gaveled back into session at 9:30, the resolution from Congress was read before the body, which still lacked a quorum. With the reading completed, the sergeant-at-arms and the assistant clerk were detailed to once again contact boycotters and inform them that one of their chief objections had been met. Again, the two men were unsuccessful in convincing any of the members to return to the chamber.

The Assembly then voted to "require" the attendance of the missing members. A mob accompanied the two men to carry out their task. Two members, James McCalmont and Jacob Miley, were found in their lodgings and forcibly returned to the State House.[8] Having achieved a quorum, the assembly quickly passed the remaining resolutions to establish the Pennsylvania Ratification Convention. The convention, over the objections of McCalmont and Miley, would be held in Philadelphia, open its session on November 20, consist of a number of delegates equal to the assembly itself, and their election would be held on the first Tuesday in November.

Constitutionalists were defeated in their attempt to delay the convening of a ratification convention but were successful in launching the first public volley against ratification. On the very day of the vote to authorize a convention, the boycotting members[9] of the Pennsylvania Assembly wrote a treatise for publication detailing their opposition to the actions of the assembly and to the proposed Constitution. On October 2, the treatise entitled *An Address of the Subscribers Members of the late House of Representatives of the Commonwealth of Pennsylvania to their Constituents* was published by Eleazer Oswald in the *Independent Gazetteer*.[10] Oswald was pressured by a number of Republicans to withhold the document, but he published the treatise again on October 3 and within a month it was reprinted in Pennsylvania twelve times, including once as a German broadside, and by November 8 it was reprinted sixteen times outside of the state.[11]

The seceding Assembly members took this opportunity to speak directly to the citizens of Pennsylvania about their misgivings of the actions taken by Republicans and warned of dangerous consequences of adopting the proposed Constitution. They urged their readers to: "Provide yourselves with the new constitution offered to you by the Convention, look it over with attention that you be enabled to think for yourselves."[12] They explained that "[w]e are persuaded that a free and candid discussion of any subject tends greatly to the improvement of knowledge, and that a matter in which the public are so deeply interested cannot be too well understood."[13] The seceding members rationalized their actions by explaining that they were trying to slow down the drive for ratification in order to educate the public.

The *Address* was an attempt by seceding members[14] to put forth a systematic critique of the Constitution before the public and to justify their action of withdrawing from the Assembly. The treatise focused attention on the following topics: (1) the Pennsylvania delegation to the Constitutional Convention had no authority to "annihilate the present confederation and form a constitution entirely new";[15] (2) the cost of running the new government; (3) the likelihood that state governments would be "annihilated"; (4) internal taxes would be established and collected by a "continental collector assisted by a few faithful soldiers";[16] (5) no protection for the liberty of the press; (6) no declaration of rights; (7) no provision against a standing army in time of peace; and (8) judicial supremacy of federal courts which would "absorb and destroy the judiciaries of the several states."[17] Anti-Federalist writers used each of these objections during the ratification period. Critics of the Constitution drew upon the *Address* to mount a cohesive theoretical attack against the document. It is interesting to note that their objection relating to a missing declaration of rights was mentioned far down the list—the issue that history most closely associates

Table 6.1. Ratification Timeline

Constitutional Convention	May 25–Sept. 17, 1787
Constitution read to Pennsylvania Assembly	September 18
Pennsylvania Assembly debates the creation of Ratification Convention	September 28–29
Address of the seceding Assemblymen published in Philadelphia	October 2
George Mason's *Objections* begins to circulate in Philadelphia	October 4
"Centinel" I published in Philadelphia	October 5
Wilson's *State House Yard Speech*	October 6
Response to the *Address* published in Philadelphia	October 8
Wilson speech first published in Philadelphia	October 9
Pennsylvania Assembly elections	October 9
"A Citizen of Pennsylvania" published in Philadelphia	October 12
"A Democratic Federalist" published in Philadelphia	October 17
"An Old Whig" II published in Philadelphia	October 17
"An Old Whig" III published in Philadelphia	October 20
"Centinel" II published in Philadelphia	October 24
"A Citizen" published in Carlisle	October 24
"Cincinnatus" I published in New York	November 1
"An Officer of the Late Continental Army" published in Philadelphia	November 6
Pennsylvania voters elect delegates to Ratification Convention	November 6
Pennsylvania Ratification Convention	Nov. 20–Dec. 15
"Cincinnatus" V published in New York	November 29
Delaware Ratifies Constitution Vote: (30–0)	December 7
Pennsylvania Ratifies Constitution Vote: (46–23)	December 12
New Jersey Ratifies Constitution Vote: (38–0)	December 18
Jefferson letter written to Madison	December 20
Georgia Ratifies Constitution Vote: (26–0)	December 31
Connecticut Ratifies Constitution Vote: (128–40)	January 9, 1788

with Anti-Federalists. A response was written by six Federalists from the Assembly, refuting the *Address*, but it was not published until October 8 in the *Pennsylvania Packet*.[18]

In the three weeks following the close of the Constitutional Convention, the press was increasingly filled with attacks on the proposed plan from detractors who were labeled, by their opponents, Anti-Federalists. Leadership of the Constitutional Party quickly realized the dangers of the proposed Constitution to the Pennsylvania Constitution of 1776. Once adopted, the federal Constitution would provide for the very structural changes in government which Republicans in Pennsylvania had been advocating since the adoption of the 1776 Constitution. Pennsylvania's Anti-Federalists gathered their forces and used every weapon at their disposal to defeat a quick ratification without substantial amendments.

A week after the dramatic events in the Pennsylvania Assembly establishing a ratification convention and providing for the election of delegates, Republicans took a second step—they needed to respond to negative coverage appearing in local newspapers. In the weeks following the adjournment of the Constitutional Convention, the plan had been published in papers throughout the country and first reactions, many negative, began to appear in print. In Pennsylvania, battle lines were drawn: Republicans (Federalists) supported the Constitution and the Constitutionalists (Anti-Federalists) opposed it. Federalists felt an urgency to mount a vigorous defense, in print and publicly.

JAMES WILSON TAKES CENTER STAGE

On the evening of October 6, 1787, a large public meeting was held on the grounds of the Pennsylvania State House (now known as Independence Hall). Originally, the meeting was called to nominate delegates to stand for election, on October 9, to the next Pennsylvania Assembly, but it quickly became a public forum for debate on the Constitution. Prior to the meeting, James Wilson was approached by friends and urged to mount a public defense of the Constitution. He quickly agreed and prepared a spirited defense addressing criticisms of the plan from opponents—especially those of George Mason,[19] one of three convention delegates who refused to sign the final version of the Constitution.

In what became known as the "State House Yard Speech," James Wilson put forth arguments that echoed throughout the nation in every ratification convention.[20] The importance of this speech should not be underestimated. Alexander J. Dallas, the editor of the *Herald*, rated the speech as *"excellent"* and wrote that "it is the first authoritative explanation of the principles of the NEW FEDERAL CONSTITUTION, and as it may serve to obviate some objections, which have been raised to that system, we consider it sufficiently interesting for publication in the present form." Dallas immediately reprinted the speech in his edition of the *Herald* on the 10th.[21] After publication as an "extra" issue of the *Pennsylvania Herald*[22] on October 9, the speech was reprinted thirty-four times, in every state except North Carolina, in twenty-seven towns, over the following twelve weeks.[23] The speech was reprinted from Portland, District of Maine, in the north, to Augusta, Georgia, in the south. October 21 saw the publication of the speech in a collection of Federalist writings by the publishers of the influential *Pennsylvania Gazette*[24] in a four-page broadside anthology.²⁵ In Virginia in mid-December, Augustine Davis of the *Virginia Independent Chronicle* included the speech in a collection of both Federalist and Anti-Federalist writings as a sixty-four-page pamphlet entitled *Various Extracts on the Federal Government.*²⁶

Wilson's speech marked the beginning of a period of intense activity in the press in every state over which course America should chart. Would Americans follow the plan formulated by the delegates in Philadelphia, or heed the warnings of Anti-Federalists, which warned of dangerous currents and shoals over the horizon? Herbert J. Storing, editor of *The Complete Anti-Federalist*, wrote: "it is hardly too much to say that among the "front-line" debaters, the Anti-Federalists criticized the Constitution and the Federalists criticized the Anti-Federalists."²⁷ In the ensuing weeks and months, however, Anti-Federalists not only criticized features of the Constitution, but also took great delight in criticizing James Wilson personally. Wilson would be attacked, by name, more than any other prominent Federalist.

For many Americans, it was the arguments put forth by James Wilson in the *State House Yard Speech* that framed the Federalist rationale for ratification. The *State House Yard Speech* was distributed to a far wider audience than the more detailed arguments made by "Publius" in *The Federalist.*²⁸ The essays of Hamilton, Madison, and Jay were aimed at influencing the people of New York but served—like Wilson's speech—to arm the supporters of the Constitution, in states that had not yet ratified, with rhetorical ammunition. Wilson delivered what can be considered as a preface for *The Federalist.* Historical attention, which has lavished attention upon *The Federalist*, has perpetuated a misleading image of Federalists as a whole.²⁹

The day-to-day business of "moving the ball" on the drive towards ratification was carried out by a host of Federalist writers neglected by history. According to Storing, "those 'other' Federalist writings carried the main burden of the public defense of the proposed Constitution in 1787 and 1788; many are quite substantial; several were vastly more influential than *The Federalist.*"³⁰ Bernard Bailyn concurred in the enlarged edition of his influential book, *The Ideological Origins of the American Revolution*. He wrote that "the mass of federalist writings reveals the great range and variety of thinking on that side of the struggle, by no means all represented in the Federalist Papers."³¹ He concluded his assessment by observing that "in the full context of the political writings of 1787–88 the importance of the Federalist Papers seems diminished."³²

James Wilson was one of the men who gladly shouldered the burden of defending the work of the delegates at the Constitutional Convention. Bernard Bailyn places the State House Yard Speech in context:

But in the "transient circumstances" of the time it was not so much the Federalist Papers that captured most people's imaginations as James Wilson's speech of October 6, 1787, the most famous, to some the most notorious, federalist statement of the time. To this early, brief, and luminous pronouncement there were floods of refutations, confirmations, and miscellaneous responses. Comments on the Federalist Papers, on the other hand, were few, usually scholarly and technical, and politically unremarkable.[33]

One week before Wilson's speech, on September 29, the Pennsylvania Assembly had created the mechanisms necessary for the convening of a Ratification Convention; on October 2, the *Address* of the seceding Assemblymen had been published denouncing the Assembly and the proposed Constitution; on October 4, the *Objections* of George Mason began to circulate in Philadelphia; and just the day after, on October 5, the first of eighteen essays by "Centinel"[34] had appeared in the *Independent Gazetteer*. Over the course of his essays "Centinel" was more than willing to take on the illustrious names supporting the Constitution, especially George Washington and Benjamin Franklin.

In *Centinel I*, groundwork was laid for future attacks and support given to efforts first initiated in the *Address* to educate the public, writing, "It behooves you well to consider, uninfluenced by the authority of names."[35] He argued that the Constitution "ought to be dispassionately and deliberately examined, and its own intrinsic merit the only criterion of your patronage."[36] "Centinel" explained the gravity of what he was asking the public to do: "If ever free and unbiased discussion was proper or necessary, it is on such an occasion.—All the blessings of liberty and the dearest privileges of freemen, are now at stake and dependent on your present conduct."[37] The drumbeat of negativity emanating from those opposed to the Constitution required a response.

Before James Wilson was introduced to begin his speech before the friendly crowd gathered on the grounds of the Pennsylvania State House, he may have thought how important it was for a member of the Constitutional Convention to take a positive stand on what they had labored so long to produce. Focusing on the task at hand, Wilson began his defense of the Constitution by discussing the origin of authority for the new government. He first described the powers given by the people to their state governments: "When the people established the powers of legislation under their separate governments, they invested their representatives with every right and authority which they did not in explicit terms *reserve*; and therefore upon every question respecting the jurisdiction of the House of Assembly, if the frame of government is *silent*, the jurisdiction is efficient and *complete*."[38]

Separation from the British Empire had left the former colonists of North America in a state of nature, and so the people of the states held complete sovereignty of their polity in their hands; they allocated their sovereignty through the act of establishing state constitutions. The grant of power was all-encompassing, except for those limitations that were placed in the constitution of the state when the people ratified the document.[39] Wilson turned his attention to the work of establishing a national government; he said, "in delegating federal powers, another criterion was necessarily introduced, and the *congressional power is to be collected* . . . from the positive grant expressed *in the instrument of union*."[40] When he compared the two grants of power—to the states and to the national government—he found that in the case of the states "*everything which is not reserved is given*" and in the case of the national government "*everything which is not given is reserved*."[41]

An argument lodged against the framers of the Constitution was that they exceeded the bounds of their mandate, granted by the states to suggest amendments for the Articles of Confederation. Yes, the federal government had the potential to be vastly stronger than the individual states, but it would still be a government of limited powers. James Wilson's task was as difficult as it was simple—to allay the fears of the public of an all-encompassing consolidated leviathan that would abolish the states and hold sway over each American. If the new national government was to be granted expanded powers, the *limit* of those powers needed to be defined for all to see.

Wilson then addressed the most damaging Anti-Federalist argument, the omission of a bill of rights, head-on. He declared that "it would have been *superfluous and absurd* to have stipulated with a federal body of our own creation, that we should *enjoy those privileges of which we are not divested*, either by the intention or the act that has brought the body into existence."[42] To put it simply, why would the public need protection from a body that didn't have the power to infringe on their rights in the first place? The lack of authority to curb personal rights within the text of the Constitution gave no opportunity for their infringement, according to Wilson's thinking.

Opponents of the Constitution were quick to focus their attacks against a perceived lack of protection for the press. Anti-Federalists feared that Congress would restrict speech and forbid criticism of the new government and its officials. A decade later, after the passage of the Sedition Act, Anti-Federalists' fears were proven to have been well-founded. Four days prior to Wilson's speech, the seceding members of the Assembly, in their *Address*, charged that there was no protection in the Constitution for the freedom of the press. Just the day before, "Centinel" wrote that now was the time to "use my pen with the boldness of a freeman, it is because I know that *the liberty of the press yet remains unviolated,* and *juries yet are judges.*"⁴³ The implication was that the current Pennsylvania constitution protected his freedom to publish, but that the adoption of the proposed national constitution would restrict free speech and access to courts containing juries of his peers. Later in *Centinel I,* the author damned the work of the Constitutional Convention for having "made no provision for the *liberty of the press,* that grand *palladium of freedom,* and *scourge of tyrants*; but observed a total silence on that head."⁴⁴

To counter these arguments, Wilson rhetorically asked, "What control can proceed from the Federal government to shackle or destroy that sacred palladium of national freedom?"⁴⁵ He returned to his argument that he put forth at the very beginning of the address, that in the case of the national government *"everything which is not given is* reserved.*"*⁴⁶ Therefore, the Constitution allocates no power to Congress to restrict the freedom of the press, unlike the powers given to regulate commerce, which are explicitly given. Wilson contrasts the lack of power to regulate the press with the expressed power found in Article I, Section 3, Clause 3, "To regulate Commerce with foreign Nations, and among the several States, and with the Indian Tribes," and Clause 1 of the same section which states that all taxes, duties, imposts, and excises "shall be uniform throughout the United States."

It was important that the Convention had taken great care in detailing the commerce power. For Wilson, the care shown with the commerce power and the lack of any delegated authority to regulate the press meant that a specific prohibition of such a power—written into the Constitution—was superfluous. He explained to the crowd, *"That very declaration* might have been construed to imply that *some degree of power* was given, since we undertook to define its extent."⁴⁷ Wilson argued the Constitution was a positive grant of power; therefore, restrictions were unnecessary and even potentially dangerous.

Virtually every Anti-Federalist commentary on the Constitution decried the lack of an explicit protection of the press. In his *Objections to this Constitution of Government,* George Mason wrote: "There is no declaration of any kind, for preserving the liberty of the press, or the trial by jury in civil cases; nor against the danger of standing armies in time of peace."⁴⁸ After addressing freedom of the press, James Wilson turned his attention to the next two items from Mason's objections—trial by jury in civil cases and standing armies.

For many Anti-Federalists, lack of formal protections regarding the use of juries in civil cases was alarming. They saw a potential for the rise of tyrannical judges and the creation of a judicial system hostile to the interests of most citizens. The *Address* of October 2 asked Pennsylvanians "whether the trial by jury in civil cases is become dangerous and ought to be abolished."⁴⁹

Wilson objected to the "disingenuous form, 'The trial by jury is abolished in civil cases,'" in which the issue had been presented.[50] Wilson told the assembled crowd that *the business of the Federal Convention was not local, but general*—not limited to the views and establishments of a single State, but co-extensive with the continent, and comprehending the views and establishments of thirteen independent sovereignties."[51] Wilson found it necessary to remind listeners that the Constitutional Convention was composed of representatives from throughout the country (except Rhode Island, which refused to send delegates). The composition of the delegations and the myriad state constitutions that they represented could not be effectively condensed into a common set of rules for jury trials in civil cases without negating the state criteria and substituting a uniform national one. Despite reserving this sphere for the states, the opponents of the Constitution detected a threat in the omission.

Anti-Federalists attacked the provision for an independent federal judiciary. The *Address* asked "whether the judiciary of the United States is not so constructed as to absorb and destroy the judiciaries of the several states."[52] Two days later, George Mason warned that "[t]he Judiciary of the United States is so constructed and extended, as to absorb and destroy the judiciaries of the several States,"[53] yet with the issue of civil cases, the Constitutional Convention had decided to leave the matter with the states. The day before Wilson's speech, *Centinel I* argued that the stakes were thus: "Whether the *trial by jury* is to continue as your birth-right, the freemen of Pennsylvania, nay, of all America, are now called upon to declare."[54] "Centinel," ruminating upon the proposed Constitution, decided that "it is more than probable that the state judicatories would be wholly superceded,"[55] and that all Americans would suffer from the closure of access to justice available through state courts.

Wilson parried these attacks on the federal judiciary. He simply explained that it was too difficult to reach consensus among the Convention delegates. He shared instances where jury trials were not appropriate. "Besides, it is not in all cases that the trial by jury is adopted in civil questions; for cases depending in courts of admiralty, such as relate to maritime captures, and such as are agitated in courts of equity, do not require the intervention of that tribunal. How, then was the line of discrimination to be drawn?"[56]

Another argument employed by the forces arrayed against the new plan of government was that it threatened the sovereignty of the states, that the object of the document was the establishment of a consolidated government. Wilson explained that the uniqueness of the states had to be taken into account and that the people's branch—Congress—would protect their right of trial by jury. He knew that Article III, Section 2, Clause 2 had given Congress authority to proscribe the jurisdiction of the Supreme Court. He alluded to this when he said, "The proceedings of the Supreme Court are to be regulated by the Congress, which is a faithful representation of the people; and the oppression of government is effectually barred, by declaring that in all criminal cases the trial by jury shall be preserved."[57]

Another point which Anti-Federalists hammered away at was the ability of the proposed national government to maintain standing armies. The *Address* from October 2 declared that it was up to the public "to determine, whether in a free government there ought or ought not to be any provision against a standing army in time of peace."[58] Two days later, George Mason warned that the Constitution did not provide safeguards "against the danger of standing armies in time of peace."[59] On the previous day, "Centinel" bluntly warned that peacetime standing armies were the vital component of "that grand engine of oppression."[60]

The fight over ratification was a very public affair. Charges put forth by Anti-Federalists had to be answered by Federalists, such as James Wilson. Literary volleys of rhetoric were fired at opponents and the ultimate judge of their effectiveness was the public. In essence, the reading public resembled spectators gathered in a great public forum comprised of the newspapers of the day.

Many of the states had explicit written provisions in their state Bill of Rights that prohibited maintaining standing armies in peacetime. Wilson could have used the example of Pennsylvania's own Bill of Rights but did not. Alexander Hamilton, however, used it in *Federalist* #25, which appeared in the New York newspaper *The Independent Journal* on December 21, 1787. He wrote, "Pennsylvania, at this instant, affords an example of the truth of this remark. The Bill of Rights of that State declares that standing armies are dangerous to liberty, and ought not to be kept up in time of peace. Pennsylvania, nevertheless, in a time of profound peace, from the existence of partial disorders in one or two of her counties, has resolved to raise a body of troops; and in all probability will keep them up as long as there is any appearance of danger to the public peace."[61] It must be remembered that there were no established police forces as exist today. If a state government desired to keep the peace it was forced to call out the militia.

James Wilson refocused attention to this issue by taking a broader view of how the United States should conduct itself as a member of the "family of nations." "This constitution, it has been further urged, is of a pernicious tendency, because it tolerates a standing army in the time of peace. This has always been a topic of popular declamation; and yet *I do not know a nation in the world which has not found it necessary and useful to maintain the appearance of strength in a season of the most profound tranquility.*"[62] If the United

States were to take its place among the nations of the world, it would have to adopt some of the trappings of other nations and for Wilson that included the creation and maintenance of a permanent military establishment.

Many opponents took Wilson to task as they reminded readers of the special status enjoyed by America—due to geographical distance from potential foes—by explaining why it would be dangerous to follow examples established by the nations of Europe and of antiquity. The day before Wilson's speech, "Centinel" had written that "the present distracted state of Europe secures us from injury on that quarter."[63] For "Centinel" the threat wasn't from over the horizon, but closer to home: "As to domestic dissentions, we have not so much to fear from them, as to precipitate us into this form of government, without it is a safe and a proper one. For remember, of all *possible* evils, that of *despotism* is the *worst* and the most to be *dreaded*."[64]

Ever the lawyer, James Wilson turned his attention to contemporary practice and the precedent established by the Confederation Congress. The ability to maintain a standing army was not an "innovation," he explained, but an action consistent with accepted precedent. "Nor is it a novelty with us; for under the present articles of confederation, Congress certainly possesses this reprobated power, and the exercise of that power is proved at this moment by her cantonments along the banks of the Ohio."[65] Congress maintained forces in the West to guard against Indian attacks and deter action by the residual British forces who remained within the recognized boundaries of the United States. After dismissing the "novelty" of a standing army, Wilson put before his audience a scenario that detailed the danger that would follow from a lack of vigilance:

> But what would be our national situation were it otherwise? Every principle of policy must be subverted, and the government must declare war, before they are prepared to carry it on. Whatever may be the provocation, however important the object in view, and however necessary dispatch and secrecy may be, still the declaration must precede the preparation, and the enemy will be informed of your intention, not only before you are equipped for an attack, but even before you are fortified for a defence. The consequence is too obvious to require any further delineation, and *no man who regards the dignity and safety of his country can deny the necessity of a military force*, under the control and with the restrictions which the new constitution provides.[66]

To garner the respect and influence that Americans expected, they needed to create instruments of power through which respect and influence would be *earned*. Wilson wanted to establish the United States as a world power, which required a permanent military establishment. He was a realist who believed America's existence, as a sovereign state, could only be guaranteed by *American* arms.

Provisions for an upper body in the new Congress, the United States Senate, drew considerable attention from Anti-Federalists. In their *Address*, the seceding Assemblymen asked Pennsylvanians to consider whether "the Senate, the most powerful [branch], the members of which are for six years, are likely to lessen your burthens or increase your taxes."[67] Anti-Federalists warned that senators, who enjoyed six-year terms, would lose touch with their fellow citizens and would find it easy to infringe upon their rights and property once they were safely ensconced in the federal capital. Mason echoed this sentiment when he wrote that senators "are not the representatives of the people or amenable to them."[68] Wilson had advocated the direct election of senators but had been defeated at the Constitutional Convention when delegates voted to have state legislatures select senators. One of those who voted against Wilson was George Mason.

George Mason's thinking on the role of the Senate changed during the course of the Constitutional Convention. On June 7, Mason took the floor and asserted that "whatever power may be necessary for the Nat[ional] Gov[ernment] a certain portion must necessarily be left in the States. . . . The State Legislatures also ought to have some means of defending themselves ag[ain]st encroachments of the Nat[ional] Gov[ernment]. . . . And what better means can we provide than the giving them some share in, or rather to make them a constituent part of, the Nat[ional] Establishment."[69] By September, when he wrote his *Objections*, Mason had changed his mind and now criticized the Senate: "Their duration of office and their being a constantly existing body . . . will destroy any balance in the government, and enable them to accomplish what usurpations they please upon the rights and liberties of the people."[70]

Anti-Federalist opposition on the subject of the proposed Senate came from virtually every writer, especially "Centinel." On October 5, "Centinel" expressed his displeasure with the Senate this way: "The senate, the great efficient body in this plan of government, is constituted on the most unequal principles."[71] He detailed the deficiencies of the Senate and concluded: "From this investigation into the organization of this government, it appears that it is devoid of all responsibility or accountability to the great body of the people, and that so far from being a regular balanced government, it would be in practice a *permanent* ARISTOCRACY."[72] The charge that the United States Senate would become the bastion of aristocracy in the nation became a much-used component of nearly every Anti-Federalist essay. The Pennsylvania Constitutional Party believed that their 1776 Constitution had broken the hold of aristocracy on the state. If the federal Constitution was adopted, they feared that the Senate would provide a natural home from which the aristocracy could regain power on a national stage.

James Wilson was disappointed in the final form that the Senate took. Nevertheless, he explained to the crowd on October 6 that the dangers put forth by the *Address*, the *Objections*, and *Centinel I* were illusory for "[i]n its legislative character it [the Senate] can effect no purpose, without the co-operation of the House of Representatives, and in its executive character it can accomplish no object without the concurrence of the President."[73] "Centinel" disparaged the "mixing" of the powers between the Executive and Legislative branches, especially the powers of confirming presidential appointments. Wilson focused the crowd's attention on the work of Constitutional Convention delegates and the diverse interests which they represented and urged them to evaluate the compromise over the Senate's composition from the perspective of the delegates themselves. "[T]his evidence of mutual concession and accommodation ought rather to command a generous applause, than to excite jealously and reproach. For my part, my admiration can only be equaled by my astonishment in beholding so perfect a system formed from such heterogeneous materials."[74]

An issue attracting the attention of virtually every Anti-Federalist writer was the prospect of the dissolution of state governments. The authors of the *Address* asked the people of Pennsylvania to consider which level of government would be more attentive to their needs; "or whether in case your state government should be annihilated, which will probably be the case, or dwindle into a mere corporation, the continental government will be competent to attend to your local concerns."[75] George Mason wrote, "In the House of Representatives there is not the substance but the shadow only of representation."[76] "Centinel" asked, on what basis was there a rush to adopt a new government? "But our situation is represented to be so *critically* dreadful, that, however reprehensible and exceptionable the proposed plan of government may be, there is no alternative, between the adoption of it and absolute ruin.—My fellow citizens, things are not at that crisis, it is the argument of tyrants."[77]

James Wilson needed to quiet fears generated by the authors of the *Address*, Mason, and "Centinel" over the consolidating character of the Constitution. He drew attention to the mechanisms of the Constitution that required action by state governments to function. He first pointed to the office of the President of the United States. "The President is to be chosen by electors, nominated in such manner as the legislature of each State may direct; so that if there is no legislature there can be no electors, and consequently the office of President cannot be supplied."[78] He next turned to the component that garnered the most negative attention from Anti-Federalists—the Senate. "The Senate is to be composed of two Senators from each State, chosen by the Legislature."[79] Wilson concluded by emphasizing the democratic qualities of the House of Representatives. Of the two branches, the House of Representatives most closely adhered to Wilson's vision. He had advocated popular election for both the Senate and Presidency but was rejected by his fellow delegates. "The House of Representatives is to be composed of members chosen every second year by the people of the several States, and the electors in each State shall have the qualifications requisite for electors of the most numerous branch of the State Legislature."[80] The authority of the House would be drawn from the people themselves, something that the Confederation Congress—a creature of the state governments—could not claim. "[T]he people at large will acquire an additional privilege in returning members to the House of Representatives; whereas, by the present confederation, it is the Legislature alone that appoints the delegates to Congress."[81]

For the people gathered to listen to Wilson, to those who read the speech when it was printed, and to his opponents, Wilson advocated an unfamiliar form of government. The Pennsylvania Constitution of 1776 had only one branch—the Assembly—that held the legislative powers of government. Members of the Assembly were elected for a term of only one year; the new U.S. House of Representatives would be filled with members who served two-year terms. This was certainly an "innovation" to those who heard Wilson's words. Further, there had only existed a single-chamber legislature as far back as the 1701 *Charter of Privileges*.[82] Among political theorists it had been an accepted maxim that a two-chamber legislature was best, but that had never been the case in Pennsylvania, so the arguments for a United States Senate were foreign to Pennsylvanians. The executive power, what little there was in Pennsylvania's Constitution, rested with a Supreme Executive Council elected by the voters for three-year terms. A President and Vice President who were elected "by the joint ballot of the general assembly and council" headed it.[83]

James Wilson was able to highlight the move towards a more direct democracy found in the Federal Constitution's method of election for the House of Representatives. The voters themselves would elect the members of the House, unlike the members of the Pennsylvania delegation to the Confederation Congress who were selected by the Assembly. Further, the President and Vice President of the United States would be elected by electors who were selected by the people, similar to the indirect method of electing the President and Vice President for Pennsylvania's Supreme Executive Council.

If there is one fact that schoolchildren from across America remember about the Revolution, it is that the war started over the issue of taxes. This was also a favorite topic of discussion for Anti-Federalists. After repudiating the arguments put forth by his adversaries regarding the structure of the proposed Federal government, Wilson turned his attention to their stance on taxes.

The fear spread by Anti-Federalists over the issue of new and burdensome taxes, which could potentially be enacted by the new government, was a staple of their writings. The tax issue had been one of the factors sparking the American Revolution and Anti-Federalists pressed the issue whenever possible. The seceding Assemblymen in their *Address* put it simply before their fellow Pennsylvanians: "You can also best determine whether the power of levying and imposing internal taxes at pleasure, will be of real use to you or not? or whether a continental collector assisted by a few faithful soldiers will be more eligible than your present collectors of taxes?"[84] One of the frequent images used by Anti-Federalist writers was the ravenous federal tax collector, backed by the dreaded standing army, who would suck the lifeblood from all hard-working Americans, if the Constitution were ratified.

Taxation was a favorite topic of Anti-Federalist authors, but especially "Centinel." The day before Wilson stood to address the crowd gathered in the State House Yard, "Centinel" warned that the new Federal Congress would "be vested with every species of *internal* taxation;—whatever taxes, duties and excises that they may deem requisite for the *general welfare*, may be imposed on the citizens of these states."[85] These taxes would be "levied by the officers of Congress, distributed through every district in America; and the collection would be enforced by the standing army,"[86] regardless of the damage such taxes would cause to the public. "The Congress may construe every purpose for which the state legislatures now lay taxes, to be for the *general welfare*, and thereby seize upon every object of revenue."[87] This line of argument was used to show that the ultimate aim of the Constitution was to weaken the states and lead to their dissolution. How could state governments function if Congress decided to take all available revenue sources for its use?

Wilson had to walk a fine line with a public that was ill-disposed towards the imposition of new taxes from yet another level of government. He appealed to the public's reason when he said that "it must be acknowledged that those upon whom such important obligations are imposed, ought in justice and in policy to possess every means requisite for a faithful performance of their trust."[88] It became a standard argument of Anti-Federalists that the requisition system employed by the Confederation Congress should be retained, but augmented, not replaced with federal tax collectors. Wilson persisted: "Still, however, the objects of direct taxation should be within reach in all cases of emergency."[89] If America was to become a powerful and respected nation, then its government must be able to gather the financial resources necessary from the public to meet any contingency; there should be no limits upon their capacity to directly tax Americans. He reminded his audience that "it was the imbecility of the present confederation which gave rise to the funding law."[90] Wilson worked with Alexander Hamilton, James Madison, and other nationalists in the Confederation Congress in 1783 to put the nation's financial house in order, but they were unsuccessful. The authority to tax Americans directly by the new Congress would correct the most blatant flaw of the Articles of Confederation.

James Wilson's style of argument intended to place the Constitution within a larger framework of documents with which the public had experience—their own state constitutions. Americans had lived under state constitutions since independence and many of them contained components used to construct the federal Constitution. His task was to show the innovations (which had a negative connotation in Wilson's era) in a positive and beneficial light. Wilson cast the motives of the opponents of the Constitution in an ominous light. "After all, my fellow-citizens, it is neither extraordinary or unexpected that the constitution offered to your consideration should meet with opposition. *It is the nature of man to pursue his own interest in preference to the public good*, and I do not mean to make any personal reflection when I add that it is the interest of a very numerous, powerful and respectable body to counteract and destroy the excellent work produced by the late convention."[91]

He then launched an attack upon the motives of opponents arrayed against the proposed plan, those who currently held offices in the state governments. "All the offices of government and all the appointments for the administration of justice and the collection of the public revenue which are transferred from the individual to the aggregate sovereignty of the States, will necessarily turn the stream of influence and emolument into a new channel. Every person, therefore, who enjoys or expects to enjoy a place of profit under the present establishment, will object to the proposed innovation; not, in truth, because it is injurious to the liberties of his country, but because it affects his schemes of wealth and consequence."[92] It is true that the power of officeholders in the governments of each state would be curtailed by ratification of the Constitution. This was an example of negative campaigning, 1787 style. The motives of all those holding a position in state government who opposed the Constitution should not have been tarred with such a broad brush.

Wilson shared with his audience that the Constitution did not assume a form that garnered his full approval: "I will confess, indeed, that I am not a blind admirer of this plan of government, and that there are some parts of it which, if my wish had prevailed, would certainly have been altered."[93]

He then discussed the difficulties of crafting a plan that the delegates to the Convention would approve and reminded his audience that the delegates' work was far from perfect, but within itself contained the seeds for its own improvement. Wilson concluded by placing the Constitution of the United States within the broader context of the world community.

> But when I reflect how widely men differ in their opinions, and that every man (and the observation applies likewise to every State) has an equal pretension to assert his own, I am satisfied that anything nearer to perfection could not have been accomplished. *If there are errors, it should be remembered that the seeds of reformation are sown in the work itself and the concurrence of two-thirds of the Congress may at any time introduce alterations and amendments.* Regarding it, then, in every point of view, with a candid and disinterested mind, I am bold to assert that it is the *best form of government* which has ever been offered to the world.[94]

It was indeed a bold assertion to say that an untested plan devised in Philadelphia during the summer of 1787 was "the best form of government which has ever been offered to the world." This was a direct shot at the Anti-Federalists who had been quick to tear down the work of the Constitutional Convention, but who found it difficult to agree among themselves on a plan to replace it. The Anti-Federalists never stepped forward with an alternative constitution, which represented their philosophy of government; most authors seemed content with modifications to the existing Articles of Confederation.

James Wilson's speech received an enthusiastic reception from those in the crowd and favorable reviews from members of the press. A member of the crowd, Erkuries Beatty, wrote in his diary the evening of October 6: "A Great meeting at the State house this evening to form a ticket for Assembly men . . . Mr. Wilson spoke very well."[95] In the introduction which accompanied the speech when published in the *Pennsylvania Herald* on October 9: "Mr. Wilson then rose, and delivered a long and eloquent speech upon the principles of the Foederal Constitution proposed by the late convention. The outlines of this speech we shall endeavour to lay before the public, as tending to reflect great light upon the interesting subject now in general discussion."[96] Alexander J. Dallas, the editor of the *Herald*, closed coverage of the speech by writing: "Mr. Wilson's speech was frequently interrupted with loud and unanimous testimonies of approbation, and the applause which was reiterated at the conclusion evinced the general sense of its excellence, and the conviction which it had impressed upon every mind.[97]

James Wilson sent a copy of his speech, published in Philadelphia's *General Advertiser,* to George Washington at Mount Vernon. A little over a week after Wilson's speech, on October 17, Washington wrote his friend David Stuart and enclosed the copy of the speech and said that it "contains a speech of Mr. Wilson's (as able, candid, and honest a Member as any in the Convention) which will place most of Col. Mason's objections in their true point of light. . . . The re-publications (if you can get it done) will be of service at this juncture."[98] Washington considered Wilson to be the foremost jurist of his time and would later select Wilson to train Bushrod Washington in the practice of law.[99]

James Wilson quickly became the most prominent figure among those who supported ratification—the Federalists. His stature would only grow as he quickly arrayed his forces for the convening of the Pennsylvania Ratification Convention. His increased visibility was a double-edged sword; he also became the man Anti-Federalists loved to hate.

NOTES

1. Some works use the name Radicals for the Constitutionalists, but for this work Constitutionalists will be used because of their support for the Pennsylvania Constitution of 1776. For a discussion of this period: Robert L. Brunhouse, *The Counter-Revolution in Pennsylvania: 1776–1790*, 1st ed. 1942. (Harrisburg: The Pennsylvania Historical and Museum Commission, 1971).

2. Untitled, *Pennsylvania Herald*, 26 December 1787, in Jensen, *Pennsylvania*, text-fiche, page 1398, (Card #23, Row #1, #12).

3. Clinton Rossiter, *1787: The Grand Convention*, (New York: The Macmillan Company, 1966), 257.

4. Merrill Jensen, ed. *The Documentary History of the Ratification of the Constitution, Vol. II Ratification of the Constitution by the States: Pennsylvania*, (Madison: State Historical Society of Wisconsin, 1976), 60. Hereafter cited as Jensen, *Pennsylvania*.

5. Speaker Thomas Mifflin had also served as a member of the Pennsylvania delegation to the Constitutional Convention.

6. In Section 10 of the 1776 Pennsylvania Constitution, "A quorum of the house of representatives shall consist of two-thirds of the whole number of members elected."

7. For an account: Robert L. Brunhouse, *The Counter-Revolution in Pennsylvania: 1776–1790*, 1st ed. 1942, (Harrisburg: The Pennsylvania Historical and Museum Commission, 1971), 200–2. Hereafter cited as Brunhouse; Jensen, *Pennsylvania*, 54–56.

8. Brunhouse, 201.

9. The members of the Constitutionalist Party who withdrew from the Pennsylvania Assembly on September 28, 1787 were quickly dubbed the "seceding members" for their actions. I shall use that term to identify them.

10. "An Address of the Subscribers Members of the late House of Representatives of the Commonwealth of Pennsylvania to their Constituents," 2 October, 1787, in Jensen, *Pennsylvania*, 112–17. Hereafter cited as "Address."

11. Jensen, *Pennsylvania*, 294.

12. "Address," 115.

13. Ibid., 114.

14. There is evidence to suggest that the authors of the "Address" had a copy of George Mason's then unpublished *Objections* in hand when they wrote their treatise.

15. Ibid., 115.

16. Ibid., 116.

17. Ibid., 116.

18. Jensen, *Pennsylvania*, 117–20. By November 26, this treatise was republished seven times in Pennsylvania and nine times outside of the state.

19. George Mason had written his objections to the proposed Constitution on the back of his copy of the Committee of Style report. These were allegedly published in Philadelphia as a pamphlet, without his knowledge, on October 4, 1787; however, no existing copy has survived. He began his objections by writing: "There is no Declaration of Rights, and the laws of the general government being paramount to the laws and constitution of the several States, the Declarations of Rights in the separate States are no security." Quoted from George Mason, *The Papers of George Mason: 1725–1792 Volume III: 1787–1792*, ed. Robert A. Rutland, (Chapel Hill: The University of North Carolina Press, 1970), 991. Hereafter cited as Mason, *Papers*.

20. James Wilson, "James Wilson's State House Yard Speech," in *Collected Works of James Wilson*, Vol. 1, Eds. Kermit L. Hall and Mark David Hall. 2 vols. (Indianapolis: Liberty Fund, 2007), 171–77. Hereafter cited as *CWJW*.

21. John P. Kaminski and Gaspare J. Saladino, eds., *The Documentary History of the Ratification of the Constitution, Vol. XIII Commentaries on the Constitution: Public and Private, Vol. 1, 21 February to 7 November 1787*. (Madison: State Historical Society of Wisconsin, 1981), 337. Hereafter cited as *Commentaries Vol. 1*.

22. The editor, Alexander J. Dallas, had immigrated to Philadelphia from the West Indies in 1783. The *Herald* published both literary and political material, including Dallas' account of the debates in the Pennsylvania General Assembly. The *Herald* published pieces from both Federalists and Anti-Federalists, but the paper did not survive to the final ratification of the Constitution. *Commentaries Vol. 1.*, xxxix.

23. Ibid., 344.

24. The *Pennsylvania Gazette* was published by David and William Hall and William Sellers. It was one of the oldest newspapers in America and had been owned by Benjamin Franklin from 1729 to 1766. The *Gazette* was an early supporter of a stronger central government. According to (*Commentaries Vol. 1*, xxxix), "The popularity and prominence of the *Gazette*, in combination with the large quantity of Federalist essays and squibs that it printed, made it the most widely reprinted newspaper in the United States."

25. Ibid., 430. The anthology was entitled: *Addresses to the Citizens of Pennsylvania. Calculated to shew the Safety—Advantages—and Necessity of adopting the proposed Constitution of the United States. In which are included Answers to the*

Objections that have been made to it. The documents contained in the anthology were: two brief excerpts from Washington's circular letter to the states of June 1783; the reply of six Pennsylvania assemblymen to the seceding members of the Pennsylvania General Assembly; the proposed Constitution; James Wilson's speech; "An American Citizen" I–IV; and Washington's letter as President of the Constitutional Convention to the President of Congress. All had previously been printed in Philadelphia, except for "An American Citizen" IV.

26. Ibid., 338.

27. Herbert J. Storing, "The 'Other' Federalist Papers: A Preliminary Sketch," in *Friends of the Constitution: Writings of the "Other" Federalists 1787–88*, Eds. Colleen A. Sheehan and Gary L. McDowell. (Indianapolis: Liberty Fund, 1988), xxii. Hereafter cited as Storing, *"Other" Federalist Papers*.

28. For a comprehensive look at the relative distribution of the arguments see William H. Riker, *The Strategy of Rhetoric: Campaigning for the American Constitution*, (New Haven: Yale University Press, 1996).

29. See Storing, *"Other" Federalist Papers*.

30. Storing, *"Other" Federalist Papers*, xxii.

31. Bernard Bailyn, *The Ideological Origins of the American Revolution*, enlarged edition, (Cambridge: Harvard University Press, 1992), 327. Hereafter Bailyn, *Ideological Origins*.

32. Bailyn, *Ideological Origins*, 327.

33. Ibid., 328.

34. Contemporaries credited Pennsylvania Supreme Court Justice George Bryan, one of the leaders of the Constitutionalist Party, with writing the series, but later, academics have settled upon his son, Samuel Bryan. Both Bryans were political rivals of James Wilson. See *Commentaries Vol. 1*, 326–28.

35. "Centinel" I, *Independent Gazetteer*, 5 October 1787, in *Commentaries Vol. 1*, 329. Hereafter cited as "Centinel" I.

36. "Centinel" I, 329.

37. Ibid., 329.

38. *CWJW*, 171–72. (emphasis mine)

39. The 1776 Pennsylvania Constitution was drafted and put into action by the Pennsylvania legislature itself, without ratification by the people (not an uncommon occurrence in the state constitutions written shortly after the Declaration of Independence). This was one of many problems that James Wilson saw in the document. For discussion on this subject, please consult Paul Leicester Ford, "The Adoption of the Pennsylvania Constitution of 1776," *Political Science Quarterly*, 10, No. 3. (Sep 1895), 426–59; and J. Paul Selsam, *Pennsylvania Constitution of 1776: A Study in Revolutionary Democracy*, 1st ed., Philadelphia: University of Pennsylvania Press, 1936, New Ed., New York: Octagon Books, 1971.

40. *CWJW*, 172. (emphasis mine)

41. Ibid., 172. (emphasis mine)

42. Ibid., 172. (emphasis mine)

43. "Centinel" I, 329.

44. Ibid., 336.

45. *CWJW*, 172.
46. Ibid., 172. (emphasis mine)
47. Ibid., 172. (emphasis mine)
48. Mason, *Papers*, 993.
49. *Address*, 116.
50. This is a direct response to the phrasing of "Centinel" I published the day before, which said "that trial by *jury* in *civil* cases is taken away."
51. *CWJW*, 172–73. (emphasis mine)
52. *Address*, 116.
53. Mason, *Papers*, 991. There is evidence to suggest that the writers of the *Address* had a copy of Mason's then unpublished *Objections* in hand when they wrote their treatise. Therefore, Mason's *Objections* were written first, but had circulated privately before being presented to the public as a pamphlet on October 4, 1787.
54. "Centinel" I, 329.
55. Ibid., 333.
56. *CWJW*, 173.
57. Ibid., 173.
58. *Address*, 116.
59. Mason, *Papers*, 993.
60. "Centinel" I, 332.
61. Jacob E. Cooke, ed., *The Federalist*, (Hanover: Wesleyan University Press, 1961), 162. Hereafter cited as Cooke.
62. *CWJW*, 173. (emphasis mine)
63. "Centinel" I, 336.
64. Ibid., 336.
65. *CWJW*, 173.
66. Ibid., 173–74. (emphasis mine) Wilson's arguments have echoed down through history and found new life in the rhetoric of politicians during the Cold War who advocated a strong national defense, particularly Ronald Reagan's "peace through strength" philosophy.
67. *Address*, 116.
68. Mason, *Papers*, 991.
69. James Madison, *Notes of Debates in the Federal Convention of 1787*. (New York: W.W. Norton and Company, 1987), 87. Hereafter cited as Madison.
70. Mason, *Papers*, 991.
71. "Centinel" I, 335.
72. Ibid., 335.
73. *CWJW*, 174.
74. Ibid., 174.
75. *Address*, 116.
76. Mason, *Papers*, 991.
77. "Centinel" I, 336.
78. *CWJW*, 175.
79. Ibid., 175.
80. Ibid., 175.

81. Ibid., 175.
82. The acknowledged standard on the Pennsylvania Constitution of 1776: J. Paul Selsam, *Pennsylvania Constitution of 1776: A Study in Revolutionary Democracy*, 1st Ed., Philadelphia: University of Pennsylvania Press, 1936, New Ed., New York: Octagon Books, 1971.
83. Section 19 of the 1776 Pennsylvania Constitution.
84. *Address*, 116.
85. "Centinel" I, 333.
86. Ibid., 333.
87. Ibid., 333.
88. *CWJW*, 175.
89. Ibid., 175.
90. Ibid., 176.
91. Ibid., 176. (emphasis mine)
92. Ibid., 176.
93. Ibid., 176.
94. Ibid., 176–77. (emphasis mine)
95. Beatty, Erkuries, "Diary Excerpt for 6 October, 1787," *Pennsylvania Herald*, 26 December 1787, in Jensen, *Pennsylvania*, text-fiche, page 545, (Card 10, Row 1, #4).
96. *CWJW*, 171.
97. Ibid., 177.
98. John C. Fitzpatrick, ed. *The Writings of Washington from the Original Manuscript Sources, 1745–1799*, 39 vols. (Washington, D.C.: Govt. Printing Office, 1931–1944; reprint, New York: Greenwood Press, 1970), xxix, 290.
99. Bushrod Washington assumed James Wilson's seat on the U.S. Supreme Court after Wilson's death.

Chapter Seven

The Anti-Federalists Respond

James Wilson's *State House Yard Speech* of October 6, 1787 garnered much ink and debate over the subsequent weeks and months, especially in the Philadelphia press.[1] The war of words did not end with the convening of the Pennsylvania Ratification Convention on November 20. In fact, the literary blows and counterblows actually accelerated after the ratification of the Constitution by the convention on December 12.[2]

Philadelphia papers were the most active venue for early debate over the merits of the proposed plan for government. Philadelphia was the largest city in the country, and as such was the media capital. In the city the *Pennsylvania Packet* and *Pennsylvania Journal* as well as *Pennsylvania Gazette* were allies of the Federalist cause, while *Freeman's Journal* and *Independent Gazetteer* supported the Anti-Federalists.[3] Another Philadelphia paper, the *Pennsylvania Herald*, tried to steer a course between the two factions by publishing materials from both, but this strategy did not save it from declining subscribers—who did take sides—and the paper ceased publication before the final ratification of the Constitution.[4]

Direct responses to Wilson's speech quickly appeared in the press: "A Democratic Federalist" in the *Pennsylvania Herald* and "An Old Whig II" in the *Independent Gazetteer* on October 17; "An Old Whig III" in the *Independent Gazetteer* again on October 20; "Centinel II" in *Freeman's Journal* on October 24; "Cincinnatus I" in the *New York Journal* on November 1; "An Officer of the Late Continental Army" in the *Independent Gazetteer* on November 6; and "Cincinnatus V" in the *New York Journal* again on November 29 were aimed directly at refuting Wilson's arguments.[5] Until the appearance of *Federalist #1*, written by Alexander Hamilton in *The Independent Journal* (New York) on October 27, the literary debate was dominated by discussion of Wilson's arguments.[6]

Table 7.1. Published Anti-Federalist Responses to Wilson's Speech

Author	City	Paper	Date
"A Democratic Federalist"	Philadelphia	Pennsylvania Herald	October 17, 1787
"An Old Whig" II	Philadelphia	Independent Gazetteer	October 17
"An Old Whig" III	Philadelphia	Independent Gazetteer	October 20
"Centinel" II	Philadelphia	Freeman's Journal	October 24
"A Republican" I	New York	New York Journal	October 25
an unsigned essay	Richmond	Virginia Independent Chronicle	October 31
"Brutus" II	New York	New York Journal	November 1
"Cincinnatus" I	New York	New York Journal	November 1
"Timoleon"	New York	New York Journal	November 1
"An Officer of the Late Continental Army"	Philadelphia	Independent Gazetteer	November 6
"Brutus, Junior"	New York	New York Journal	November 8
"Cincinnatus" II	New York	New York Journal	November 8
"Cincinnatus" III	New York	New York Journal	November 15
"Cincinnatus" IV	New York	New York Journal	November 22
"A Federal Republican"	Philadelphia	pamphlet	November 28
"Cincinnatus" V	New York	New York Journal	November 29
"John DeWitt"	Boston	American Herald	December 3
"Cincinnatus" VI	New York	New York Journal	December 6
"A True Friend"	Richmond	Virginia Independent Chronicle	December 12
"Republican Federalist" II	Boston	Massachusetts Centinel	January 2, 1788
"Republican Federalist" V	Boston	Massachusetts Centinel	January 19
"Junius"	Boston	Massachusetts Gazette	January 22
"Agrippa" XV	Boston	Massachusetts Gazette	January 25
"Hampden"	Boston	Massachusetts Centinel	February 2
"Impartial Examiner"	Richmond	Virginia Independent Chronicle	February 20

A little over a month after James Wilson's *State House Yard Speech*, "A Receipt for an Anti-Federalist Essay" appeared in the *Pennsylvania Gazette*. Attacks on Wilson regularly appeared in the press, conforming to an almost predictable formula.

> WELL-BORN, nine times—*Aristocracy*, eighteen times—*Liberty of the Press*, thirteen times repeated—*Liberty of Conscience*, once—*Negroe slavery*, once mentioned—*Trial by jury*, seven times—*Great Men*, six times repeated—MR. WILSON, forty times—and lastly, GEORGE MASON's *Right Hand in a Cutting-Box*, nineteen times—put them altogether, and dish them up at pleasure. These *words* will bear boiling, roasting, or frying—and, what is remarkable of them, they will bear being served, after being once used, a dozen times to the same table and palate.[7]

THE WAR OF WORDS—OCTOBER 7 TO DECEMBER 20, 1787

James Wilson's explanation of why a bill of rights was not included in the Constitution quickly drew attention from both sides of the debate. On October 12, "A Citizen of Pennsylvania" took the field and defended Wilson. The article appeared in the *Pennsylvania Packet* three days after the first publication of Wilson's speech and the election of the new Pennsylvania Assembly which, when convened on October 22, would yield a 2–1 majority for Wilson's Republican colleagues. "A Citizen" recounted many of the arguments that Wilson utilized, but chose to spend time on what was quickly identified as the weak point of the Constitution—the lack of a bill of rights. "A Citizen" explained, "In articles of agreement *among a number of independent states*, entering into an union, a bill of the rights of individuals is *excluded* of course."[8] The line of argument that "A Citizen" used was quite different from that of James Wilson. "A Citizen" asserted that the Constitution would be an agreement "*among a number of independent states*," a position that was not in line with what Wilson would have agreed.[9]

Wilson believed that the people of the states—through the process of ratification—would bring the Constitution into existence; "A Citizen" fundamentally disagreed with this. "A Citizen" explained his reasoning: "As in the old confederation or compact among the thirteen independent sovereignties of America, no bill of rights of individuals could be or was introduced: so in the proposed compact among the same thirteen independent sovereignties, no bill of the rights of individuals has been or could be introduced."[10] This argument rested on the premise that state constitutions already provided bills of rights and similar protections which would suffice to safeguard the rights of Americans. The argument echoed that made by Connecticut's Roger Sherman at the Constitutional Convention on September 12. Sherman responded to a motion from George Mason for the inclusion of a bill of rights by saying that he "was for securing the rights of the people where requisite. The State Declarations of Rights are not repealed by this Constitution; and being in force are sufficient."[11] A month later, "A Citizen" echoed Sherman's sentiments by writing that by the adoption of a national bill of rights, "this would be to annihilate our state constitutions, by rendering them unnecessary."[12]

An argument that found fertile ground in Anti-Federalist literature was the issue of freedom of the press. "A Citizen," by using the reasoning examined previously of the Constitution being an agreement "*among a number of independent states*," argued that the freedom of the press was actually a *personal* right and one that could only be protected by the states. "The liberty of the press, from an honest republican jealousy, which I highly applaud, has also been a subject of observation; but the right of writing for publication, and of printing, publishing and selling, what may be written are *personal* rights, *are part of the rights of individuals*."[13] By "A Citizen's" logic, the Constitution could not protect rights that were not given to it to protect: "They are the rights of *the people in the states*," he wrote, "and can only be exercised by them. They are not the rights of the thirteen independent sovereignties, therefore could not enter into either the old or new compact among them."[14]

"A Citizen" concluded his discussion of the freedom of the press by reminding readers that this protection had become so interwoven into the fabric of society that "every constitution in the union guards the liberty of the press."[15] He then turned to the issue of who would have the authority to restrict such a treasured right: "But who is to destroy it? Not the people at large, for it is their most invaluable privilege—the palladium of their happiness—Not the state legislatures, for their respective constitutions forbid them to infringe it. Not the foedral government, *for they have never had it transferred into their hands*. It remains among those rights *not conveyed to them*."[16] This was similar to Wilson's contention that the ability to infringe upon the freedom of the press had not been granted to the Constitution, so no such ability existed.

More than a week after James Wilson's *State House Yard Speech*, the first significant response from an Anti-Federalist appeared in the *Pennsylvania Herald* on October 17, penned by "A Democratic Federalist."[17] Wilson's ideas set the terms of the debate that followed. The Baltimore *Maryland Gazette* had previously published Wilson's speech and at the urging of "A Customer" it published "A Democratic Federalist" and included a preface with this statement from "A Customer": "The subject now before the people of America, is of the most important nature, *the happiness of millions* depends on their present determination.—Let them, therefore, enjoy every light a free press can afford, that they may judge for themselves, like rational creatures and freemen—Truth will shine the brighter when brought to the test."[18] Authors engaged in a war of pens over the future of America were very conscious the decisions that their generation made would echo down through the years. Those opposed to the Constitution would at least agree they were fighting to "secure the blessings of liberty to ourselves and our posterity." They just believed there was another way than that proposed by the Constitutional Convention.

From the very first paragraph, "A Democratic Federalist" left no doubt what he thought of Wilson's speech: "The arguments of the Honorable Mr. Wilson . . . although extremely *ingenious* and the best that could be adduced in support of so bad a cause, are yet extremely *futile,* and will not stand the test of investigation."[19] The author then examined the three areas where he had the most disagreement: the need for a bill of rights; trial by jury in civil cases; and a standing army. He concluded with an assessment on the separation of powers, or lack thereof, found in the Constitution.

"A Democratic Federalist" like many Anti-Federalist writers objected to the omission of a bill of rights in the Constitution. When arguing that a bill of rights was unnecessary, James Wilson examined the granting of power by the people in the process of creating constitutions. He found that in the instance of the states *"everything which is not reserved is given"* and in the case of the national government *"everything which is not given is reserved."*[20] "A Democratic Federalist" objected to this reasoning: "If this doctrine is true, and since it is the only security that we are to have for our natural rights, it ought at least to have been clearly expressed in the plan of government."[21] The two sides arrived at their positions from diametrically opposed beliefs. Wilson feared that if rights were written, then the fact that not every single possible right was chronicled would necessarily mean that they weren't protected. "A Democratic Federalist" believed that a listing of rights was the only way that they could be protected.

He then compared the allocation of power under the Articles of Confederation and the proposed Constitution. The Confederation Congress is "merely an executive body; it has no power to raise money, it has no *judicial jurisdiction.*"[22] But, when this is contrasted with the new government, "the federal rulers are vested with each of the three essential powers of government—their laws are to be *paramount* to the laws of the different States, what then will there be to oppose to their encroachments?"[23] "A Democratic Federalist" envisioned a time when "federal rulers" would use a standing army as an instrument of tyranny; although there was no mandate to create a permanent military establishment in the Constitution, crucially, it didn't forbid one. Once the military was used to silence opposition, "Mr. Wilson's distinction will be forgot, denied or explained away, and the liberty of the people will be no more."[24]

The essential thrust of the Anti-Federalist argument on the issue of a bill of rights was this: How can we trust this powerful leviathan holding the potential for all of the evils endured by the people of Europe, without a written protection of rights that the people may appeal to against the encroachments of their new government? The problem, according to "A Democratic Federalist," was that "under the enormous power of the new confederation, which extends to the *individuals* as well as to the *States* of America, a thousand means may be devised to destroy effectually the liberty of the press."[25] To emphasize the lessons of history, "A Democratic Federalist" pointed to recent colonial history and the case of New York's John Peter Zenger.[26] He believed that it "ought still to be present to our minds, to convince us how displeasing the liberty of the press is to men in high power."[27] He cautioned readers, "I lay it down as a general rule, that wherever the powers of a government extend to the lives, the persons, and properties of the subject, all their rights ought to be clearly and expressly defined—otherwise they have but a poor security for their liberties."[28]

Anti-Federalists objected to the scant provisions for jury trials in the Constitution. "The second and most important objection to the federal plan, which Mr. Wilson pretends to be made *in a disingenuous form,* is the entire *abolition of the trial by jury in civil cases,*"[29] wrote "A Democratic Federalist." Anti-Federalists applauded protections provided in the body of the Constitution itself—Article III, Section 2 stated, "The trial of all crimes . . . shall be by jury; and such trial shall be held in the state where the said crimes shall have been committed." However, the absence of any mention of civil cases elicited foreboding thoughts of a sinister plot to deprive Americans access to juries in such cases. Wilson had explained that state regulations governing civil cases were too difficult for the convention to reconcile, without replacing the diverse state guidelines with a uniform federal one. "A Democratic Federalist" dismissed Wilson's logic: "This answer is extremely futile, because a reference might easily have been made to the *common law of England,* which obtains through every State, and cases in the maritime and civil law courts would of course have been excepted."[30] Anti-Federalists featured in their writings warnings of a dominant, unaccountable, federal judiciary that would oppress the people by eclipsing and ultimately replacing the state courts, to the detriment of Americans' interests.

Surveying the body of Anti-Federalist literature, one is struck by the prominence that is given to the fears of a permanent military establishment. The English experience during the Cromwellian period instilled a dread of standing armies in English political literature. Anti-Federalists cited this precedent a century later. Schoolchildren across the country, if they remember one thing about the Anti-Federalists—is that they fought for a bill of rights. This is true, but incomplete, for it neglects a comprehensive appreciation of the alternative vision of the Constitution that they advocated. In the *Address* of the seceding members of the Pennsylvania Assembly, George Mason's *Objections*, and *Centinel I*, the authors shared their fear of potential abuses that a standing army could inflict on the public, and "A Democratic Federalist" allocated the largest portion of his essay to the subject.

For modern readers, the issue of whether or not to authorize a standing army is many times overlooked in Anti-Federalist and Federalist writings of the period. However, the issue featured prominently in Anti-Federalist writings. "But Mr. Wilson . . . has told us that a STANDING ARMY, that *great support of tyrants,* not only was not dangerous, but that it was *absolutely necessary.*"³¹ James Wilson had served in the Continental Congress and worked with John Adams and others to provide George Washington with the money, matériel, but especially men to secure American independence. The military record of the militia in the conflict was less than spectacular and has been blamed by military historians for prolonging the war. Wilson sought to ensure that unreliable state militias would not debilitate the government in time of crisis. "A Democratic Federalist" took a decidedly different view. He pointed to the lessons of history and the "result of the enquiries of the best and most celebrated patriots have taught us to dread a standing army above all earthly evils, are we then to go over all the thread-bare common place arguments that have been used without success by the advocates of tyranny, and which have been for a long time past so gloriously refuted!"³² Lessons gained from studying English/British history and literature should be supplemented with America's own experiences gained during the revolution.

"A Democratic Federalist" dismissed Wilson's contention that "even in times of the most profound tranquility"³³ a military force was useful for all nations. He reminded readers, "Had we a standing army, when the British invaded our peaceful shores? Was it a standing army that gained the battles of Lexington, and Bunker's Hill, and took the ill fated Burgoyne?"³⁴ He continued that even in instances such as Shays' Rebellion, which was an internal disturbance, not an invasion, "Is not a well regulated militia sufficient for every purpose of internal defence? And which of you, my fellow citizens, is afraid of any invasion from foreign powers, that our brave militia would not be able immediately to repel?"³⁵ Much of the Anti-Federalist thought on the subject of standing armies came from Whig opponents of the British government in the early eighteenth century. It was an accepted article of faith that no good could come from a standing army. Reliance upon militias kept the control of military forces locally dispersed, not consolidated in the hands of a few which could lead to tyranny. "A Democratic Federalist" held up the example of Switzerland as the model which America should follow: "Why should we not follow so glorious an example, and are we less able to defend our liberty without an army, than that brave but small nation, which with its militia alone has hitherto defied all Europe?"³⁶

At the close of his section addressing standing armies, "A Democratic Federalist" took issue with the precedent Wilson cited of soldiers sent by the Confederation Congress to guard the frontier from Indians. He refuted Wilson's precedent: "I answer, that *precedent* is not *principle*—Congress have no right to keep up a standing army in time of peace:—If they do, it is an infringement of the liberties of the people—wrong can never be justified by *wrong.*"³⁷ He acknowledged that there was a need to keep troops on the banks of the Ohio; as long as the Indians "remain in our neighbourhood, we are always, with respect to them, in a state of war—as soon as the danger is over, there is no doubt but Congress will disband their handful of soldiers:—it is therefore not true, that Congress keep up a standing army in a time of peace and profound security."[38]

After hammering Wilson on the subjects of a bill of rights, juries for civil cases, and a standing army, "A Democratic Federalist" concluded with a brief swipe against the separation of powers found in the Constitution. He contended that the principle found in the state constitutions was that in which *"the legislative and executive powers ought to be kept forever separate and distinct from each other."*[39] He believed that this principle had been violated in the new constitution with the checks and balances found in the powers of the executive and legislative branches. He warned, "This is an innovation of the most dangerous kind upon every known principle of government, and it will be easy for me to convince my fellow citizens that it will, in the first place, create a *Venetian* aristocracy, and, in the end, produce an *absolute monarchy.*"[40]

The same day, October 17, on which "A Democratic Federalist" was published, "An Old Whig II" was published in Philadelphia's *Independent Gazetteer*.[41] This was another Anti-Federalist response to Wilson's *State House Yard Speech*. The tone of this essay was very different from that of "A Democratic Federalist." The author structured a more academic response to Wilson and before beginning his argument, wrote this observation of Wilson's work: "This speech I find was made for the express purpose of removing objections from the minds of those who doubted, like myself, and wished to be satisfied . . . it bears the marks of more candor than is to be found in most of the production[s], which have been ushered into the world in support of the same measure."[42] After paying Wilson a compliment, he then proceeded to write that he was not convinced and would explain the flaws in Wilson's reasoning. The tone taken by "An Old Whig" is reminiscent of a law brief, not the emotional outbursts found in "A Democratic Federalist."

"An Old Whig" stated that he sought to do James Wilson justice, so when he disagreed with a section of the *State House Yard Speech* he quoted it. The prominent issue that he wanted to dispute was Wilson's position on not including a bill of rights in the Constitution. In creating the Constitution, according to Wilson, the delegates created a plan regarding powers allocated to the national government whereby *"everything which is not given is reserved."*[43] "An Old Whig" responded, "If this be a just representation of the matter, the authority of the several states will be sufficient to protect our liberties from the encroachments of Congress, without any continental bill of rights; *unless* the powers which are *expressly given* to Congress are *too large*."[44] This clearly shifted the debate to the *scope* of power allocated to the new Congress.

The simple black-and-white allocation of powers that Wilson presented in his speech was not so benign for "An Old Whig." He foresaw the possibility—in all likelihood the probability—that the powers of Congress would create a vortex into which all legislative power would be drawn. He believed that *"the future Congress will be fully authorised to assume all such powers as they in their wisdom or wickedness, according as the one or the other may happen to prevail, shall from time to time think proper to assume."*[45]

The author commented on the corruptibility of human nature and that history was littered with cautionary tales. For him, "the new constitution vests Congress with such unlimited powers as ought never to be entrusted to any men or body of men."[46] At the heart of "An Old Whig's" rejection of Wilson's arguments was: "My object is to consider that *undefined, unbounded and immense power* which is comprised in the following clause;—And, to make all laws which shall be necessary and proper for carrying into execution the *foregoing powers and all other powers* vested by this constitution in the government of the United States; or in any department or offices thereof."[47]

Objection to the necessary and proper clause is one which featured prominently in Anti-Federalist writings. "An Old Whig" saw potential for a grant of authority to future legislatures to expand their sphere of action virtually unchecked. The problem was that "Congress are therefore vested with the supreme legislative power, without controul."[48] If this was the case then he asked, "Was there no necessity of a bill of rights to secure to the people their liberties?"[49] Americans needed to place some form of constraint upon Congress at the very outset of the new government, not after it was functioning and exercising its powers. If constraints were not placed now, then "we are left wholly dependent on the wisdom and virtue of the men who shall from time to time be the members of Congress."[50]

After discussing the necessary and proper clause and need for a bill of rights, "An Old Whig" closed with a promise to return in another installment to continue his critique. Three days later, on October 20, "An Old Whig" reappeared in the same paper. He returned to where his last essay concluded and added to his brief against the Constitution a discussion of the freedom of the press. He dismissed Wilson's belief that since no specific power was allocated to Congress to infringe on the freedom of the press then no such ability existed. "An Old Whig" then presented a scenario where Congress could, constitutionally, constrain the press. "What controul!—Suppose that an act of the continental legislature should be passed to restrain the liberty of the press;—to appoint licensers of the press in every town in America;—to limit the number of printers;—and to compel them to give security for their good behaviour, from year to year, as the licenses are renewed: If such a law should be once passed, what is there to prevent the execution of it?"[51] The only course of action was to preclude such a chain of events: "Let us then guard ourselves, as far as we can, against the possibility of being enslaved by wicked men, whilst the power of guarding ourselves is in our own hands."[52] It was vital to add a bill of rights to the Constitution.

A Wilson supporter appeared in the *Carlisle Gazette* on October 24. Carlisle was an area that knew Wilson well; he had become a prosperous lawyer after he moved there in the fall of 1770. Wilson bought a house at the corner of Penn and Hanover Streets to be close to the courthouse, which was only a block away. After a successful courtship, he married Rachel Bird on November 5, 1771, a member of a prominent local family.

Wilson may have been the most notable Federalist in the press at the time, but "A Citizen" came to his defense. His objective was to disparage the writings of "Centinel," whose second installment appeared on the same day in Philadelphia. "A Citizen" warned that "if you reject a good plan of government when proposed to you, and continue in a state of anarchy, or if you adopt a bad plan, the consequences will be ruinous and perhaps equally so."[53] He lamented, "I wished it might have had a fair and unbiassed examination and being left without comment to the native honesty and good sense of the people."[54] But, according to "A Citizen," this was not to be found in the literary works of "Centinel." "I am sorry to find it has met with very different treatment; and that a writer under the signature of centinel, whose performance has been industriously circulated among the people, has abused both that plan and you by setting it in a totally false point of light."[55]

The number of Federalist defenders who rose to Wilson's defense was pitifully small. Federalist writers generally attacked Anti-Federalist authors, rather than defending Wilson. "A Citizen," of course, had nobler motives than those of "Centinel," for "it is purely from a desire to counteract the poison of his performance and to detect his sophistry and misrepresentation, that your minds may be in a condition to examine the plan with candor, and judge of it according to its own merits, that I now address you."[56] "A Citizen" utilized a line of argument similar to that of his fellow supporter of the Constitution, "A Citizen of Pennsylvania," in that he also declared that the Constitution "is a government of states; not of individuals."[57] Building upon this assertion, he wrote, "The constitution of each state has a bill of rights for its own citizens; and the proposed plan guaranties to every state a republican form of government for ever."[58] If indeed, the Constitution would be "a government of states; not of individuals,"[59] then "it would be a novelty indeed to form a bill of rights for *states*."⁶⁰ This line of reasoning was difficult for readers to endorse, especially with the first three words of the Constitution beginning, "We the People," not "We the States." Anti-Federalists continued to hammer away at the lack of a bill of rights. The Federalists quickly abandoned this subject for more productive arguments.⁶¹

"Centinel" returned for another installment attacking the proposed Constitution, but this time he directed his fire against Wilson's *State House Yard Speech*. *Centinel II* was the most comprehensive refutation—in one essay—of Wilson's speech. A lot had happened since "Centinel's" last appearance in the *Independent Gazetteer* on October 5: Wilson's speech on October 6; the election victory by the Republicans on October 9 which rewarded them with a significant majority in the Pennsylvania Assembly; and on October 17 Anti-Federalist responses appeared in the Philadelphia press to Wilson's speech. The next crucial contest would come with the election, on November 6, of delegates to the Pennsylvania Ratification Convention, scheduled to convene two weeks later in Philadelphia. "Centinel" decided it was time to make another appearance refuting Wilson on virtually every point. *Centinel II* was published in Philadelphia's *Freeman's Journal* on October 24 and constituted nearly 2½ times the number of words contained in Wilson's speech.

"Centinel's" opening thrust was aimed against Wilson's stance on a bill of rights. He wrote, "As long as the liberty of the press continues unviolated, and the people have the right of expressing and publishing their sentiments upon every public measure, it is next to impossible to enslave a free nation."⁶² The implication being that if the Constitution was adopted, unamended, the people would no longer enjoy the "liberty of the press" and thus not hear opposing viewpoints, such as those put forth by "Centinel." He explained, "Men of an aspiring and tyrannical disposition, sensible of this truth, have ever been inimical to the press, and have considered the shackling of it, as the first step towards the accomplishment of their hateful domination, and the entire suppression of all liberty of public discussion, as necessary to its support."⁶³ According to "Centinel," Federalists sought to place themselves above the people and rule by restricting the press and to maintain their power through a standing army. However, this bleak future could be thwarted, "for even a standing army, that grand engine of oppression, if it were as numerous as the abilities of any nation could maintain, would not be equal to the purposes of despotism over an enlightened people."⁶⁴ Securing the freedom of the press was essential for the survival of a free people. This echoed arguments made by "A Democratic Federalist" and "An Old Whig" the previous week.

Federalists in Pennsylvania wasted no time embarking upon trying to secure ratification of the proposed Constitution. The swiftness of their efforts took Anti-Federalists by surprise. Forces arrayed for and against the Constitution were synonymous with the Republican (Federalist) and Constitutional (Anti-Federalist) parties in Pennsylvania. Constitutionalists were supporters of the 1776 Pennsylvania Constitution and the Republicans were those who sought to modify the 1776 Constitution to a document more in line with the proposed Federal Constitution. Constitutionalists had been losing electoral strength in the Pennsylvania Assembly and thus could not thwart the early convening of a ratification convention. One of the arguments that they utilized in their writings was that the haste of the Federalists was indicative of sinister motives that could only be brought to light by a slow, deliberate ratification debate. This argument had first been used by the seceding members of the Pennsylvania Assembly in their *Address* published on October 2.

"Centinel" was one of the few Anti-Federalist writers bold enough to impugn the motives of George Washington and Benjamin Franklin participating in the creation of the Constitution. "Centinel" cast doubt on the practice of "name-dropping" by Federalists when he wrote, "The new plan was accordingly ushered to the public with such a splendor of names, as inspired the most unlimited confidence; the people were disposed to receive upon trust, without any examination on their part, what would have proved either a *blessing* or a *curse* to them and their posterity."[65] He warned, "The authors of the new plan, conscious that it would not stand the test of enlightened patriotism, tyrannically endeavoured to preclude all investigation."[66] In other words, Federalists sought to suppress dissent to the Constitution and ratify the document as quickly as possible.

True patriots, "Centinel" among them, seeking to slow down the headlong rush towards ratification, should be celebrated. "The virtuous and spirited exertions of a few patriots, have at length roused the people from their fatal infatuation to a due sense of the importance of the measure before them."[67] Anti-Federalist criticisms began to tarnish the luster of the "splendor of names" endorsing the Constitution. Federalists were alarmed at the results achieved by their opponents, particularly "Centinel." "Centinel" argued, "So serious and general has been the impression of the objections urged against the new plan, on the minds of the people, that its advocates, finding mere declamation and scurrility will no longer avail, are reluctantly driven to defend it on the ground of argument."[68] "Centinel" credited the work of Anti-Federalists for prompting James Wilson to publicly defend the Constitution on October 6. In this assessment he is correct. Federalists *were* concerned that their side of the story was not being told and that a public stand had to be made.

"Centinel" declared the Constitution was not strong enough to defend itself without explanation—the very public debate that "Centinel" said was lacking! "Centinel" concluded Wilson was unsuccessful in his objective: "This able advocate has failed to vindicate it from the objections of its adversaries, must we not consider it is as the production of *frail* and *interested* men?"[69] By casting the Constitution as something less than a divinely inspired document and nothing more than "the production of *frail* and *interested* men," "Centinel" stripped the Constitution of any pretension of being in the best interest of the American people.

One of the lines of argument adopted by Wilson in his defense of the Constitution was to demonstrate how the government itself was predicated upon the continued existence of state governments. "Centinel" attacked this by ridiculing Wilson's assurances "that hence all fears of the several States being melted down into one empire, are groundless and imaginary." "Centinel" replied, "But who is so dull as not to comprehend, that the *semblance* and *forms* of an ancient establishment, may remain, after the *reality* is gone?"[70] To "Centinel's" thinking, the true power would rest with the federal government and the states would be little more than an afterthought.

"Centinel" then assaulted Wilson's stance on the freedom of the press. Wilson declared no power was allocated to Congress restricting liberty of the press, but Anti-Federalists saw this silence as an avenue by which Congress could do just that. In an argument reminiscent of that used by "An Old Whig" four days before in the *Independent Gazetteer*, "Centinel" used the supremacy clause, instead of the necessary and proper clause cited by "An Old Whig." He asked, "Cannot Congress, when possessed of the immense authority proposed to be devolved, restrain the printers, and put them under regulation[?]"[71] After quoting the supremacy clause, "Centinel" wanted to know, "After such a declaration, what security does the *Constitutions* of the several States afford for the *liberty of the press and other invaluable personal rights*, not provided for by the new plan?—Does not this sweeping clause subject every thing to the controul of Congress?"[72] "Centinel" concluded that the Constitution created a unitary government, where all power is held by the central government, through the supremacy clause, for "when such great devolutions of power are proposed, manifests the design of reducing the several States to shadows."[73]

Next, "Centinel" attacked one of James Wilson's phrases which became a favorite target of Anti-Federalist writers. In explaining the scope of powers allocated to the federal government Wilson said that *"everything which is not given is* reserved."[74] "Centinel" rhetorically asked where this principle resided in the Constitution. He contended that the supremacy clause was a window providing insight into the Federalists' true motivation, where the

Constitution "would be *paramount* to all *State* authorities."[75] He denigrated Wilson's reasoning by asserting, "The lust of power is so universal, that a speculative unascertained rule of construction would be a *poor* security for the liberties of the people."[76] "Such a body as the intended Congress, unless particularly inhibited and restrained, must grasp at omnipotence, and before long swallow up the Legislative, the Executive, and the Judicial powers of the several States."[77] Strict safeguards were required on the power of the national government, or the state constitutions and the protections they contained for the rights of the people would be drawn into the sphere of power possessed by the national government. Who or what would protect the people then?

Wilson's stance on excluding a protection of jury trials in civil cases next received "Centinel's" attention. Wilson explained that the diversity of standards and procedures present in the individual states made the establishment of a general rule impractical. "Centinel" dismissed this explanation as disingenuous. He wrote, "Astonishing, that provision could not be made for a jury in civil controversies, of 12 men, whose verdict should be unanimous, *to be taken from the vicinage;* a precaution which is omitted as to trial of crimes, which may be any where in the state within which they have been committed. So that an inhabitant of *Kentucky* may be tried for treason at *Richmond.*"[78] "Centinel" closed his assessment by explaining, "The abolition of jury trial in civil cases, is the more considerable, as at length the courts of Congress will supersede the state courts, when such mode of trial will fall into disuse among the people of the United States."[79]

One of the tenets of Anti-Federalist thought was the fear of a supreme federal judiciary. "Centinel" exemplified this with his reference to residents of Kentucky being brought before a federal tribunal in faraway Richmond to stand trial for treason—far from his peers. This harkened back to abuses detailed in the Declaration of Independence that charged King George III "for depriving us, in many cases, of the benefits of trial by jury; For transporting us beyond seas, to be tried for pretended offenses." Anti-Federalist writers were keen to invoke the "Spirit of '76" in their arguments and to cast their opponents as the latest incarnation of the ministers of George III.

The issue of a standing army in America was close to the top of indictments against the Constitution for Anti-Federalist writers. "Centinel" rebuked Wilson's stance: "Mr. *Wilson* skips very lightly over the danger apprehended from the standing army allowed by the new plan."[80] He pronounced, "This grand machine of power and oppression, may be made a fatal instrument to overturn the public liberties," and this would be accomplished by "a standing army with regular provision of pay and contingencies [that] afford a strong temptation to some ambitious man to step up into the throne, and to seize absolute power."[81] A common Anti-Federalist line of argument was that the sole function of a standing army was to take away people's freedoms and property.

"Centinel" did not forbid the creation of a standing army, but it must only occur "in time of peace" with the approval of two-thirds of Congress. Like "A Democratic Federalist," a week before, "Centinel" rejected Wilson's use of the precedent established by the Confederation Congress of stationing troops on the Western frontier. He mocked Wilson: "Surely Mr. *Wilson* is not serious when he adduces the instance of the troops now stationed on the Ohio, as a proof of the propriety of a standing army."[82] This precedent was invalid because "they are a mere occasional armament for the purpose of restraining divers hostile tribes of savages."[83] Using this as a precedent actually enhanced the Anti-Federalist argument because under the Articles of Confederation "the states severally have [the power] of withholding the supplies necessary to keep these armies on foot, is a sufficient check on the *present* Congress."[84] Wilson based his argument on the assumption that Congress possessed the power to create armies at will, but the ultimate check was held by the states who had to supply the manpower, equipment, and money, a check not present in the proposed Constitution.

"Centinel" proceeded to another favorite target of Anti-Federalist authors—the United States Senate. Anti-Federalists viewed the Senate as the citadel of a new, powerful aristocracy in America. The Senate was not elected directly by the people but selected by state legislatures. This was a component of the Constitution with which even James Wilson was unsatisfied. He had fought hard for a Senate elected by voters but failed to persuade a majority of the Convention's delegates. As a staunch supporter of the Constitution, though not in every detail, Wilson defended the Senate as an example of compromise among the delegates preserving a vital role for the states. Compromise over the Senate should be celebrated, not feared.

In *Centinel I*, the author had disparaged the equal representation of the states that Wilson, who favored proportional representation in the body, would have concurred with. Wilson had urged his audience on October 6 to appreciate the good qualities of the compromise over the Senate and ignore fears generated by words of its opponents. In *Centinel II*, the author vigorously disagreed, "That these fears are not imaginary, a knowledge of the history of other nations, where the powers of government have been injudiciously placed, will fully demonstrate."[85] "Centinel" dismissed Wilson's defense of the Senate's restricted powers within a system of checks and balances. "This I confess is very specious, but experience demonstrates, that checks in government, unless accompanied with *adequate* power and *independently* placed, prove *merely nominal,* and will be *inoperative.*"[86]

It is notable that "Centinel" took this path to criticize James Wilson as Pennsylvania's Constitution of 1776 did not function within a system of effective checks and balances. The Pennsylvania Assembly held the sovereignty of the state, and no effective judicial or independent executive existed. The checks and balances present in the proposed Constitution seemed to be an unwise "mixing" of powers.

"Centinel" believed the president would become a willing accomplice in the desires of the Senate. "It will be his interest to coincide with the views of the senate, and thus become the head of the aristocratic junto."[87] He held little faith that the president would exercise his institutional power of the veto, a check that could be overridden by a two-thirds vote of both chambers. James Wilson had advocated an unrestricted right in the presidential appointment of judges and members of the executive branch, in addition to an unchallengeable veto, both of which he lost—positions that "Centinel" would have approved.

"Centinel" thought little of the check placed upon the Senate by the concurrence of the House of Representatives. Article I, Section 4, Clause 1 of the Constitution states: "The Times, Places and Manner of holding Elections for Senators and Representatives, shall be prescribed in each State by the Legislature thereof; but the Congress may at any time by Law make or alter such Regulations, except as to the Places of choosing Senators." Anti-Federalists viewed the last section of this provision, "but the Congress may at any time by Law make or alter such Regulations," as an avenue for Congress to modify election laws to facilitate their perpetual re-election in office—the establishment of an elected aristocracy. The House of Representatives would not represent the people, but their own personal interest. "Centinel" argued that by controlling the method of election, "the house of representatives may be composed of the *creatures* of the senate. Still the *semblance* of checks, may remain but without *operation*."[88]

One of the primary authorities upon which Anti-Federalists authors drew to buttress their position came from the writings of Montesquieu. "Centinel" warned, "This mixture of the legislative and executive moreover highly tends to corruption."[89] He invoked Montesquieu's authority in his argument for a complete separation of powers among the branches of government. "The chief improvement in government, in modern times, has been the compleat separation of the great distinctions of power; placing the *legislative* in different hands from those which hold the *executive;* and again severing the *judicial* part from the ordinary *administrative*.[90]

James Wilson and other members of the Constitutional Convention were not satisfied with the powers of the Senate and had sought to create a stronger executive. "Centinel" noted Wilson's dissatisfaction with the Senate and applauded the efforts of delegates to create a council, much like that in Pennsylvania, to ratify the actions of the president. He asserted that this would be an effective check upon the unchallenged power of executive pardon granted by the Constitution. This would strengthen the accountability of the president as "such a check upon the chief magistrate would admirably secure the power of pardoning, now proposed to be exercised by the president alone, from abuse."[91] The Anti-Federalist fear was that the president would be able to shield himself and others, such as members of the Senate, from charges of treason after curtailing the liberties of the people.

"Centinel" ridiculed Wilson's stance on the issue of taxation. "But we are cautioned against being alarmed with imaginary evils, for Mr. *Wilson* has predicted that the great revenue of the United States, will be raised by impost. Is there any ground for this?"[92] Anti-Federalists were alarmed by the potential taxing power of Congress. It is a central tenet of politics that money is power. The ability of Congress to levy not just imposts, but internal taxes such as excise taxes which would be laid directly upon the people of the United States, posed a severe threat to Americans' liberties. Further, it would restrict the sphere within which the states themselves could lay taxes. "Centinel" argued the public would not tolerate being taxed by two levels of government and would be inclined to do away with the weaker of the two—the states. This would result from the volume of laws and ordinances necessary for Congress to directly tax the people. This legislative action "would perpetually interfere with the State laws and personal concerns of the people."[93]

"Centinel" disputed Wilson's assurances that the fiscal needs of the federal government would be met by the use of the impost. The federal budget would need to encompass the repayment of debts, the expense of running the new government—including salaries for new federal officials, and the military. The discussion of taxes allowed "Centinel" to warn, once again, of Federalist intentions to create a permanent military establishment. He cautioned that a standing army "will be no trifling establishment, for cantonments of troops in every district of America, will be necessary to compel the submission of the people to the arbitrary dictates of the ruling powers."[94] For "Centinel," if a citizen objectively examined the Constitution, there was no other possible conclusion than that excises and direct taxes, such as land taxes, would become necessary to meet the federal government's fiscal needs. The aristocratic Senate would never enact a progressive land tax, because it would hurt them proportionally more than the lower classes, and so "*poll taxes* will be substituted as provided for in the new plan; for the doctrine then will be, *that slaves ought to pay for wearing their heads.*"[95]

After detailing the expansive grants of power to the new government, "Centinel" concluded "that the general government would necessarily annihilate the particular governments, and that the security of the personal rights of the people by the state constitutions is superseded and destroyed."[96] He determined that the only prudent course of action was to include a federal bill of rights in the Constitution, "for universal experience demonstrates the necessity of the most express declarations and restrictions, to protect the rights and liberties of mankind, from the silent, powerful and ever active conspiracy of those who govern."[97]

"Centinel" conceded that there *were* protections contained in the Constitution, but they were too few. "The new plan, it is true, does propose to secure the people of the benefit of personal liberty by the *habeas corpus;* and trial by jury for all crimes, except in case of impeachment."[98] He then proceeded to list the protections that weren't incorporated in the proposed Constitution—almost all parts of the Bill of Rights eventually adopted in 1791—protections he wanted *before* ratification.

Wilson's stance regarding the ability to amend the Constitution drew disdain from "Centinel." "This is one among the numerous deceptions attempted on this occasion. True, there is a mode prescribed for this purpose. But it is barely possible that amendments may be made."[99] Wilson saw the amendment component of the Constitution as a strength—a great improvement over the Articles of Confederation; it provided for an easier modification of the Constitution, by agreement from three-quarters of the states, than the unanimous consent required by the former document. "Centinel" dismissed the practicality of the amendment process which would not be utilized until "the fascination of power must first cease, the nature of mankind undergo a revolution, that is not to be expected on this side of eternity."[100] "Centinel" believed it was asking too much of members of the new federal legislature to voluntarily limit their powers after they assumed their duties.

The vital step was to obtain amendments *before* the new government began operation. After recounting the amendment process itself, "Centinel" asked, "Does history abound with examples of a voluntary relinquishment of power, however injurious to the community? No; it would require a general and successful rising of the people to effect any thing of this nature.—This provision therefore is mere sound."[101] In response, Wilson could have asked, "The amendment process contained in the Articles of Confederation required unanimity. How was this process better than that contained in the Constitution?"

"Centinel" saw a hint of Wilson's true intentions when he criticized him for attacking those in state government opposed to the Constitution. "He had before denied that the proposed transfer of powers to Congress would annihilate the state governments. But he here lays aside the masque, and avows the fact."[102] By acknowledging that state officials would lose power under the Constitution, Wilson confirmed that the states would in fact lose power under the plan. "For if the state establishments are to remain unimpaired, why should officers peculiarly connected with them, be interested to oppose the adoption of the new plan?"[103] Further, the forces arrayed against the Constitution were "not so partial and interested as Mr. *Wilson* asserts."[104] He explained that opposition not only included members of the Constitutional Convention itself, members of the Confederation Congress, but also "a respectable yeomanry throughout the union, of characters far removed above the reach of his unsupported assertions."[105]

Centinel II closed with an appeal to readers to question Federalist motives and their rush to ratify the Constitution without amendments. He asked, "Is their conduct any recommendation of their plan of government?"[106] Further, "view them preventing investigation and discussion, and in the most despotic manner endeavouring to compel its adoption by the people, with such precipitancy as to preclude the possibility of a due consideration, and then say whether the motives of these men can be pure."[107] The essay ended with a warning and a wish: "My fellow citizens, such false detestable *patriots* in every nation, have led their blind confiding country, shouting their applauses, into the jaws of *despotism* and *ruin*. May the wisdom and virtue of the people of America, save them from the usual fate of nations."[108]

The literary blasts, against the Constitution and James Wilson, launched by Anti-Federalists continued after the comprehensive refutation put forth by Samuel Bryan in *Centinel II*. Bryan wrote another sixteen essays and the last installment did not appear until April 9, 1788. Three other essays, two written by "Cincinnatus" and one by "An Officer of the Late Continental Army," appeared in the New York and Philadelphia press during November 1787. It wasn't until the end of 1787, however, that Wilson's *State House Yard Speech* was critiqued by Thomas Jefferson and Wilson's and other Federalist positions on a bill of rights was memorably refuted.

Eight days after the Pennsylvania Ratification Convention voted to approve the Constitution on December 12, 1787, Thomas Jefferson sat down at his desk in Paris and wrote James Madison his thoughts concerning the proposed Constitution. Jefferson had received a copy of Wilson's October 6 speech and, after identifying components of the Constitution he admired, began his lengthy critique identifying disagreements with the Constitution by first addressing the thrust of Wilson's argument:

> To say, as mr. Wilson does, that a bill of rights was not necessary because all is reserved in the case of the general government which is not given, while in the particular ones all is given which is not reserved, might do for the Audience to whom it was addressed, but is surely a gratis dictum, opposed by strong inferences from the body of the instrument, as well as from the omission of the clause of our present confederation which had declared that in express terms.[109]

Jefferson dismissed Wilson's argument as little more than playing to the assembled crowd. The "omission of the clause" that he refers to is Article II of the Articles of Confederation which stated: "Each state retains its sovereignty, freedom and independence, and every power, jurisdiction and right, which is not by this confederation expressly delegated to the United States in Congress assembled." Jefferson wanted an explicit accounting of the relationship between the states and the national government with regard to powers.

Jefferson next took issue with Wilson's argument that the Constitutional Convention did not provide for guarantees of a trial by jury in civil cases because of the lack of uniformity among the states. He admonished, "It would have been much more just and wise to have concluded the other way that as most of the states had judiciously preserved this palladium, those who had wandered should be brought back to it, and to have established *general right* instead of *general wrong*."[110] In Jefferson's opinion, the Convention had taken the wrong course and trod the easiest path of leaving states to their own practices, rather than making sure that all Americans were guaranteed a basic right to a jury trial for civil as well as criminal cases.

The letter to Madison continued as Jefferson stated a belief that is among his most quoted on the subject of a bill of rights. "Let me add that a bill of rights is what the people are *entitled* to against every government on earth, general or particular, and what no just government should refuse or *rest on inference*."[111] Cutting to the heart of arguments made by James Wilson, Alexander Hamilton, and James Madison that the enumeration of a list of rights would be dangerous, as it would create the belief that the rights not listed were appropriate areas for government to restrict, Jefferson challenged this with one simple and eloquent sentence. Jefferson's letter did not reach Madison until July 1788, after the close of Virginia's Ratification Convention.[112]

IMPACT OF THE STATE HOUSE YARD SPEECH

James Wilson was the first delegate from the Constitutional Convention to publicly defend the document which they created. Philadelphia was the largest city in America and was home to a flourishing publishing industry. It was the publishing hub of the country, with twelve newspapers and the only nationally circulated magazine, at one time or another in 1787 and 1788. Wilson knew that what he said to the crowd assembled on October 6 would be published locally and reprinted around the country. The communications infrastructure of the age, what we would today consider the mass media, existed in the newspapers of the period. The three largest publishing centers were Philadelphia, New York, and Boston. During the ratification debate, the most widely reprinted newspaper in America was the weekly *Pennsylvania Gazette*.[113]

The *State House Yard Speech* first appeared on October 9 in the *Pennsylvania Herald* and in the following twelve weeks was reprinted thirty-four times, in every state except North Carolina. The speech was included in collections of Federalist writings and printed as part of broadsides and pamphlets around the country. For many Americans, it was the arguments put forth by James Wilson in the *State House Yard Speech* which explained the Federalist rationale for ratification. The impact of Wilson's speech can be seen in the large number of essays that Anti-Federalists drafted to challenge his interpretation of the Constitution. Published responses to the speech can be divided into three distinct phases: (1) the first three weeks after October 6 saw essays published in Philadelphia newspapers; (2) the next seven weeks from October 25 through December 12 were dominated by essays appearing in New York newspapers; and (3) the final phase which ran from January 2 to February 2, 1788 brought forth essays in the newspapers of Boston.[114]

The geographic distribution of Anti-Federalist responses to Wilson's speech was what should be expected from the distribution of newspapers in the era. The first essays to reach the public appeared in Philadelphia newspapers. Constitutionalists in Pennsylvania comprised the core of the Anti-Federalist movement and had opposed Wilson and his Republican colleagues since 1776; those who knew Wilson best were the first to publish. Philadelphia's prominence as America's publishing center ensured that Anti-Federalist responses addressing the *State House Yard Speech* would find their way into newspapers outside of Pennsylvania. The two most reprinted Anti-Federalist refutations of Wilson's speech were *Centinel II* published in *Freeman's Journal* on October 24 and the work of "An Officer of the Late Continental Army" published two weeks later on November 6 in the *Independent Gazetteer*.

In 1787, contemporaries generally credited Pennsylvania Supreme Court Justice George Bryan as the author of the "Centinel" series. Bryan was a prominent leader of the Constitutional Party, but subsequently, academics have settled upon his son Samuel Bryan as the true author.[115] In a total of eighteen essays, "Centinel" analyzed the provisions of the Constitution and questioned the motives of delegates who framed the document and those who declared their support for approval. Assessing the collection as a whole, the editors of *The Documentary History of the Ratification of the Constitution* (*DHRC*) characterized "Centinel's" language as "blunt, provocative, and vituperative."[116] In the very first edition of "Centinel," the author charged that the Constitution was "a most daring attempt to establish a despotic aristocracy among freemen, that the world has ever witnessed."[117] A sense of "Centinel's" opinion of the Constitution and of its framers can be found in this passage from *Centinel IV*, published on November 30: "The evil genius of darkness presided at its [the Constitution's] birth, it came forth under the veil of mystery, its true features being carefully concealed, and every deceptive art has been and is practicing to have this spurious brat received as the genuine offspring of heaven-born liberty."[118] This characterization of the Constitution and its supporters appeared during the Pennsylvania Ratification Convention where James Wilson was the Federalist leader.

The impact of "Centinel's" critique of Wilson's *State House Yard Speech* can be seen by the range and influence of its republication. *Centinel II* was reprinted six times outside of Pennsylvania before the close of the Pennsylvania Ratification Convention.[119] In New York, the *New York Journal* and *New York Morning Post* reprinted the essay and in Boston the *American Herald* reprinted "Centinel's" work.[120] *Centinel I* and *II* appeared as broadsides and in pamphlets in Philadelphia, New York, and Richmond.[121] Less than a month after Wilson's speech, during the first week of November, the publisher of the *New York Journal* published *Centinel I* and *II* and "Timoleon" in a two-page broadside which Anti-Federalists circulated across New York state. They also shipped hundreds of copies into Connecticut, where Connecticut Federalists denounced the action.[122] In December, *Centinel I* and *II* were included in the Richmond publication of a pamphlet anthology entitled *Various Extracts on the Foederal Government . . .* , which also included Wilson's speech, and in April 1788, New York Anti-Federalists collected the first nine editions of "Centinel" in a pamphlet anthology entitled *Observation on the Proposed Constitution . . .* and forwarded 225 copies to local county committees around the state.[123]

The number of reprints does not tell the complete story. A staunch Anti-Federalist and member of the Pennsylvania Ratification Convention, John Smilie of Fayette County relied heavily upon the arguments found in *Centinel II* during his speech before the Convention on December 8.[124] On December 12, 1787, Pennsylvania's Convention voted to ratify the Constitution. Returning to the editors of the *DHRC*, they remarked: "In the use of personal invective, "Centinel" was perhaps unequalled among both Antifederalists and Federalists."[125] "Centinel's" critique of James Wilson's October 6 speech received wide distribution in the press, but also by Anti-Federalists themselves; but there was another essay that was reprinted by a still larger number of newspapers.

AN OFFICER OF THE LATE CONTINENTAL ARMY

On September 29, 1787, the Pennsylvania Assembly voted to convene a Ratification Convention in Philadelphia on November 20 with elections to select delegates held on November 6. On election day, the *Independent Gazetteer* published an essay signed by "An Officer of the Late Continental Army," but addressed "To the Citizens of Philadelphia."[126] In an essay only a few hundred words longer than Wilson's October 6 speech, "An Officer" once again refuted many of Wilson's explanations regarding the Constitution. Within nine weeks "An Officer's" essay had been reprinted in eight newspapers, principally in New England. Further, it was republished as a broadside, a pamphlet, and was included in the November issue of the nationally circulated magazine *American Museum*, published in Philadelphia.[127] Paul Leicester Ford believed that the author of "An Officer" was a leading Pennsylvania Anti-Federalist, William Findley, one of the seceding members of the Assembly and a member of the Ratification Convention who cast his vote against ratification. Ford, however, failed to present any substantiating evidence to support his assertion and the true identity of "An Officer" remains an open question.[128]

The two most reprinted refutations of Wilson's speech, *Centinel II* and "An Officer," were published in Philadelphia, but the second phase of Anti-Federalist responses to the speech were found in the papers of New York. Starting with *A Republican I* published in the *New York Journal* on October 25, Wilson was attacked principally in the pages of the *New York Journal*, which featured ten Anti-Federalist essays. On November 1, the *New York Journal* took the extraordinary step of publishing four items on the Constitution—*Brutus II* and *Cincinnatus I* in the regular newspaper edition, and in a special "extraordinary" edition, "Timoleon" and *Centinel II* were published.[129] Collectively, these four essays were a concerted response, by the publisher, to stem any positive impact of Wilson's speech.

The November 1 edition of the *New York Journal* also marked the debut of the first of a series of six essays addressed to "James Wilson, Esquire" from the author "Cincinnatus." The six essays appeared in the *New York Journal* between November 1 and December 6, 1787. The "Cincinnatus" essays were not widely reprinted, although each essay appeared in Philadelphia. The few remaining reprints were scattered among five New England towns.[130] Some contemporaries attributed the essays to Richard Henry Lee, others to his brother, Arthur, but no clear authorship has been established.

The third phase of published responses to Wilson's *State House Yard Speech* occurred in Boston. The Massachusetts Ratification Convention sat from

January 9 to February 7, 1788. The first Anti-Federalist response in Massachusetts came from "John DeWitt" published in Boston's *American Herald* on December 3, 1787, but the bulk of the responses in Boston's papers to Wilson's speech were from January 2 to February 2, coinciding with the sitting of the convention.

Wilson's speech received little coverage in Virginia newspapers—only three responses were published, all in Richmond's *Virginia Independent Chronicle*: October 31 and December 12, 1787; and February 20, 1788. The *State House Yard Speech* was included as part of the previously mentioned *Various Extracts on the Foederal Government* . . . , published in Richmond in December, and in other Federalist pamphlets and broadsides that made their way to Virginia. Virginia's Ratification Convention did not convene until June 2, 1788, and the responses present in the papers of Philadelphia, New York, and Boston prior to the Ratification Conventions convening in their respective states were not to be found in the relatively few papers of the Old Dominion.

There were components of each Anti-Federalist response to James Wilson's speech present in virtually every single essay. Authors placed different emphasis upon which argument made by Wilson was the most objectionable. The top four issues comprising the core of the Anti-Federalist attack against Wilson were: (1) his stance against including a bill of rights in the Constitution; (2) his support for a standing army; (3) his explanation for not providing an explicit protection for the freedom of the press; and (4) the composition and powers of the United States Senate. Similar to "A Receipt for an Anti-Federalist Essay" found at the beginning of this chapter, the standard Anti-Federalist essay refuting Wilson's speech contained each of the four issues listed above, for each author used the same ingredients, but not always in the same proportion.

I have devoted a lot of time examining arguments and counterarguments which flowed between Wilson and his opponents. Other than giving the speech to the assembled crowd in the State House Yard on October 6, were there other avenues through which Wilson defended himself? A popular tactic of authors of the era was to mask their true identity behind a pseudonym.[131] The principal reason for using this tactic was explained by Herbert J. Storing: "But a pseudonym was used not merely or even mainly to enable the author to conceal or to protect himself; it was a convention aimed at directing attention at the arguments rather than at personalities."[132] Authors utilized pseudonyms to ensure that their arguments were considered on their merit, not summarily dismissed if the reader disliked the author.

Wilson had utilized pseudonyms in the past—writing as "the Visitant" in a series of essays with his friend and Anglican minister William White.

The series was a commentary on polite life, gentility, and good feeling that appeared in the *Pennsylvania Chronicle* from February 1 to May 16, 1768.[133] He would again use a pseudonym during various battles against the Constitutionalist forces in the 1780s, but this time, he did not avail himself of the practice during the ratification debate. Wilson utilized public forums, such as the October 6 gathering and particularly his leadership of Federalist delegates in the Pennsylvania Ratification Convention, heavily covered in the press, and his speeches on the floor reprinted around the country, to get his interpretation of the Constitution out.[134]

Very few Federalists publicly defended Wilson. They used his arguments but wouldn't defend him personally. In an examination of the literary debate between Federalists and Anti-Federalists, William Riker examined the first four volumes of the *DHRC* covering the public and private debate on the Constitution from February 21, 1787 to March 31, 1788, to determine what arguments were reprinted the most.[135] Discussing the judgment made by editors of the day in deciding what to publish, Riker wrote that editors "reprinted James Wilson's speeches far more frequently" than those of "Publius."[136] Riker argued that "the combined judgment of the editors tells us what was believed to be rhetorically convincing in 1787."[137]

The Anti-Federalist response to Wilson's October 6 speech represented nearly 6 percent of the total output of the Anti-Federalist campaign examined by Riker, whereas Wilson's speech constituted about 3 percent of the published Federalist campaign.[138] The important fact is that Anti-Federalist responses to Wilson's speech were proportionally "four times as large as Wilson's speech, Antifederal editors must have believed they had a great advantage in attacking him."[139] One subject that anyone who examines the published material of the ratification debate focuses on is the unsatisfactory arguments, for many Americans, of the Federalist position on not including a bill of rights in the Constitution. Very few Federalists utilized Wilson's explanation that he put forth on October 6, in explaining the powers of the national government as *"everything which is not given is reserved."*[140] He declared that "it would have been *superfluous and absurd* to have stipulated with a federal body of our own creation, that we should *enjoy those privileges of which we are not divested*, either by the intention or the act that has brought the body into existence."[141] According to Wilson's thinking, there was no need to protect the public from a government that had no power to constrain rights in the first place. The lack of authority to curb personal rights gave no opportunity for their infringement.

Wilson contended that the Constitution was a positive grant of power; therefore restrictions were unnecessary and even potentially dangerous. In explaining why there was no specific protection for the freedom of the press, he explained, "*that very declaration* might have been construed to imply that *some degree of power* was given, since we undertook to define its extent."[142] The Convention had decided enumerating rights would be dangerous in that some would not be included and thus provide grounds to argue that other rights, such as the right to privacy, were not protected. Enumeration of rights was a slippery slope that delegates—Wilson for one—were not willing to hazard. According to Riker's research, the published weight of Wilson's speech on the issue of a bill of rights constituted more than half of the total Federalist discussion of the topic.[143] For all intents and purposes, James Wilson's stance on a bill of rights became the Federalist position for Americans closely following the ratification debate.

James Wilson *willingly* and *without hesitation* became the "whipping boy" for Anti-Federalists. In the week prior to Wilson's speech the following had happened in Philadelphia: September 29, the Pennsylvania Assembly had created the mechanisms necessary for the convening of a Ratification Convention; on October 2 the *Address* of the seceding Assemblymen had been published denouncing the Assembly and the proposed Constitution; on October 4 the *Objections* of George Mason had been published as a pamphlet in Philadelphia; and just the day after, on October 5, the first "Centinel" essay appeared in the *Independent Gazetteer*. Assaults on the Constitution from Anti-Federalists needed to be countered, and leading figures in Philadelphia went to James Wilson and asked him to make a public stand defending the Constitution. As a leading member of Philadelphia society, a leader of the Republican Party in Pennsylvania, a former member of the Confederation Congress and having served as a delegate in the Constitutional Convention, Wilson was well aware of the exposure that his speech would garner, not just in Pennsylvania, but around the country. Philadelphia was the publishing and media capital of the country and what happened there did not stay there but was reprinted by newspapers far and wide.

Wilson willingly defended the work of the Convention in public and knew the scorn and ridicule which would result. Pennsylvania politics was not an arena for the faint of heart, but for politicians who knew how to survive in a highly contentious political environment. For James Wilson, the ratification debate waged between Federalists and Anti-Federalists was just another stage upon which he could play a substantive role, but this time it would be a national stage.

There is no surviving record of what James Wilson thought when Virginia became the decisive state on December 15, 1791 to ratify the Bill of Rights, but it is very likely that it was similar to a sentiment expressed in a letter by

James Madison, written October 17, 1788 while in New York, to Thomas Jefferson. Madison wrote, "I have never thought the omission a material defect, nor been anxious to supply it even by subsequent amendment, for any other reason than it is anxiously desired by others. I have favored it because I supposed it might be of use, and if properly executed could not be of disservice."[144] Wilson may not have liked acceding to the wishes of Anti-Federalists for a Bill of Rights, but he would have agreed with Madison's desire to bring Anti-Federalists and other opponents of the Constitution into the American polity as co-Founders. The ultimate goal was always to establish a strong, independent federal government and on that point, James Wilson and his colleagues were successful.

NOTES

1. For a discussion of papers published in Pennsylvania and around the country see: John P. Kaminski and Gaspare J. Saladino, eds., *The Documentary History of the Ratification of the Constitution, Vol. XIII Commentaries on the Constitution: Public and Private, Vol. 1, 21 February to 7 November 1787*. Madison: State Historical Society of Wisconsin, 1981), xxx–xxxix. Hereafter cited as *Commentaries Vol. 1*.

2. For a discussion of the battle between Federalists and Anti-Federalists in Pennsylvania see Owen S. Ireland, "The People's Triumph: The Federalist Majority in Pennsylvania, 1787–1788," *Pennsylvania History*, 56, Number 2 (April 1989), 93–113; and Owen S. Ireland, *Religion, Ethnicity, and Politics: Ratifying the Constitution in Pennsylvania*, (University Park, PA: The Pennsylvania State University Press, 1995).

3. Page Smith, *James Wilson: Founding Father, 1742–1798*, (Chapel Hill: University of North Carolina Press, 1956), 262. Hereafter identified as Smith, *James Wilson*.

4. The last known issue was published on February 14, 1788. *Commentaries Vol. 1*, xxxix.

5. Bernard Bailyn, ed. *The Debate on the Constitution: Part One*. (New York: Literary Classics of the United States, Inc., 1993), x–xi.

6. For a complete list of Anti-Federalist responses to Wilson and his ideas see **Table 7.1**.

7. "A Receipt for an Antifederal Essay." *Pennsylvania Gazette*, 9 February 1788, in John P. Kaminski and Gaspare J. Saladino, ed., *The Documentary History of the Ratification of the Constitution, Vol. XIV Commentaries on the Constitution: Public and Private, Vol. 2, 8 November to 17 December 1787*, (Madison: State Historical Society of Wisconsin, 1983), 103.

8. "A Citizen of Pennsylvania." *Pennsylvania Packet*, 12 October 1787, in Jensen, *Pennsylvania*, text-fiche, page 621, (Card 11, Row 1). Hereafter cited as "A Citizen of Pennsylvania."

9. Wilson's position would become clear, six years later, in the opinion that he wrote while on the U.S. Supreme Court as associate justice in the *Chisholm v.*

Georgia case of 1793. Wilson argued that it was the *people of the United States*, **not** the states that ratified the Constitution.

10. "A Citizen of Pennsylvania," 621.

11. James Madison, *Notes of Debates in the Federal Convention of 1787* (New York: W.W. Norton and Company, 1987), 630.

12. "A Citizen of Pennsylvania," 621.

13. Ibid., 621.

14. Ibid., 621.

15. Ibid., 621.

16. Ibid., 622.

17. The piece was reprinted three times in the *New York Morning Post*, 22 October; *Pennsylvania Packet*, 23 October; and Baltimore *Maryland Gazette*, 26 October. *Commentaries Vol. 1*, 386.

18. Ibid., 386.

19. "A Democratic Federalist," *Pennsylvania Herald*, 17 October 1787, in *Commentaries Vol. 1*, 387. Hereafter cited as "A Democratic Federalist."

20. James Wilson, *Collected Works of James Wilson*, ed. Kermit L. Hall and Mark David Hall, (Indianapolis: Liberty Fund, 2007), 172. Hereafter identified as *CWJW*. (emphasis mine)

21. "A Democratic Federalist," 387.

22. Ibid., 387.

23. Ibid., 387.

24. Ibid., 387.

25. Ibid., 388.

26. In November 1734, Zenger, who was the publisher of the *New York Weekly Journal*, was arrested for seditious libel against New York's royal governor, William Cosby. His bail was set at an exorbitant amount that he could not meet and he remained in prison until his acquittal the following summer. His defense was founded upon the freedom of the press and the role of the jury. This served as a landmark case in the development of the concept of the freedom of the press in America. *Commentaries Vol. 1*, 392.

27. "A Democratic Federalist," 388.

28. Ibid., 388.

29. Ibid., 388.

30. Ibid., 388.

31. Ibid., 390.

32. Ibid., 390.

33. *CWJW*, 173.

34. "A Democratic Federalist," 390.

35. Ibid., 390.

36. Ibid., 391.

37. Ibid., 391.

38. Ibid., 391.

39. Ibid., 391.

40. Ibid., 391.

41. "An Old Whig" II, *Independent Gazetteer*, 17 October 1787, in *Commentaries Vol. 1*, 399–403. Hereafter cited as "An Old Whig" II. It was reprinted three times: *Carlisle Gazette*, 31 October; Baltimore *Maryland Gazette*, 2 November; and *New York Journal*, 28 November.

42. "An Old Whig" II, 399.

43. *CWJW*, 172. (emphasis mine)

44. "An Old Whig" II, 400.

45. Ibid., 400–1. (italics in original)

46. Ibid., 401.

47. Ibid., 402.

48. Ibid., 403.

49. Ibid., 403.

50. Ibid., 403.

51. "An Old Whig" III, *Independent Gazetteer*, 20 October 1787, in *Commentaries Vol. 1*, 428. Hereafter cited as "An Old Whig" III. Reprinted in the *New York Journal*, 1 December.

52. "An Old Whig" III, 429.

53. "A Citizen," *Carlisle Gazette*, 24 October 1787, in Jensen, *Pennsylvania*, textfiche, page 808, (Card #14, Row #1 and #2). Hereafter cited as "A Citizen."

54. "A Citizen," 808.

55. Ibid., 808–9.

56. Ibid., 809.

57. Ibid., 820.

58. Ibid., 820.

59. Ibid., 820.

60. Ibid., 820. (emphasis mine)

61. In research conducted by Professor William Riker on publications pertaining to the ratification contained in *The Documentary History of the Ratification of the Constitution, Vol. XIII–XVI Commentaries on the Constitution: Public and Private Vol. 1–IV*, Wilson's position on a Bill of Rights constituted more than half of the total Federalist discussion of the topic. See footnote #7, William H. Riker, *The Strategy of Rhetoric: Campaigning for the American Constitution*, (New Haven: Yale University Press, 1996), 87.

62. "Centinel" II, *Freeman's Journal*, 24 October 1787, in *Commentaries Vol. 1*, 457. Hereafter cited as "Centinel" II. Reprinted 6 times before 13 December: MA (1), RI (1), NY (2), MD (1), VA (1). It was used heavily by John Smilie of Fayette County in the Pennsylvania Ratification Convention in his speech of 8 December.

63. "Centinel" II, 457.

64. Ibid., 457.

65. Ibid., 458.

66. Ibid., 458–59.

67. Ibid., 459.

68. Ibid., 459.

69. Ibid., 459.

70. Ibid., 459.

71. Ibid., 460.
72. Ibid., 460.
73. Ibid., 460.
74. *CWJW*, 172. (emphasis mine)
75. "Centinel" II, 460.
76. Ibid., 460.
77. Ibid., 460.
78. Ibid., 462.
79. Ibid., 462.
80. Ibid., 463.
81. Ibid., 463.
82. Ibid., 463.
83. Ibid., 463.
84. Ibid., 463.
85. Ibid., 464.
86. Ibid., 464.
87. Ibid., 464.
88. Ibid., 464.
89. Ibid., 465.
90. Ibid., 465.
91. Ibid., 465.
92. Ibid., 465.
93. Ibid., 465.
94. Ibid., 465.
95. Ibid., 466.
96. Ibid., 466.
97. Ibid., 466.
98. Ibid., 466.
99. Ibid., 467.
100. Ibid., 467.
101. Ibid., 467.
102. Ibid., 467.
103. Ibid., 467.
104. Ibid., 467.
105. Ibid., 467.
106. Ibid., 468.
107. Ibid., 468.
108. Ibid., 468.
109. Robert A. Rutland and Charles F. Hobson, eds., *The Papers of James Madison: Volume 10, 27 May 1787–3 March 1788*. (Chicago: The University of Chicago Press, 1977), 336. Hereafter cited as *The Papers of James Madison, Volume 10*.
110. *The Papers of James Madison, Volume 10*, 336–37.
111. Ibid., 337. (emphasis mine)
112. Paul Finkelman, "James Madison and the Bill of Rights: A Reluctant Paternity," *The Supreme Court Review*, Vol. 1990. (1990), 328.

113. John P. Kaminski and Gaspare J. Saladino, eds., *The Documentary History of the Ratification of the Constitution, Vol. XIII Commentaries on the Constitution: Public and Private Vol. 1: 21 February to 7 November 1787*, (Madison: State Historical Society of Wisconsin, 1981), xix. Hereafter cited as *Commentaries Vol. 1*.
114. See Table 7.1.
115. See *Commentaries Vol. 1*, 326–28.
116. Ibid., 326.
117. Ibid., 332.
118. John P. Kaminski and Gaspare J. Saladino, eds., *The Documentary History of the Ratification of the Constitution, Vol. XIV Commentaries on the Constitution: Public and Private Vol. 2: 8 November to 17 December 1787*, (Madison: State Historical Society of Wisconsin, 1983), 321. Hereafter cited as *Commentaries Vol. 2*.
119. Massachusetts (1), Rhode Island (1), New York (2), Maryland (1), and Virginia (1). *Commentaries Vol. 1*, 457.
120. Ibid., 327.
121. Ibid., 328.
122. Ibid., 328.
123. Ibid., 328.
124. Ibid., 457.
125. Ibid., 327.
126. Ibid., 564.
127. Ibid., 564. By the opening of the Massachusetts Ratification Convention, "An Officer" had been reprinted four times in Boston newspapers. It was also reprinted once in neighboring Rhode Island and Connecticut.
128. Ibid., 564.
129. Ibid., 524.
130. Ibid., 529.
131. See Eran Shalev, "Ancient Masks, American Fathers: Classical Pseudonyms during the American Revolution and Early Republic," *Journal of the Early Republic*, 23, No. 2 (Summer, 2003): 151–72.
132. Herbert J. Storing, ed., *The Complete Anti-Federalist: Vol. 2—Objections of Non-Signers of the Constitution and Major Series of Essays at the Outset*, (Chicago: The University of Chicago Press, 1981), 222.
133. Smith, *James Wilson*, 32–35.
134. *Commentaries Vol. 2*, 206–7. Wilson's speech on November 24 in the Convention was reprinted even more times than his *State House Yard Speech* of October 6. It also appeared as a pamphlet in two versions.
135. William H. Riker, *The Strategy of Rhetoric: Campaigning for the American Constitution*, New Haven: Yale University Press, 1996. Hereafter cited as Riker. The examination did not include the remaining two volumes that end in September 1788, due to the professor's death.
136. Riker, 27.
137. Ibid., 28.
138. Ibid., 83.
139. Ibid., 84.

140. *CWJW*, 172. (emphasis mine)
141. Ibid., 172. (emphasis mine)
142. Ibid., 172. (emphasis mine)
143. Riker, 87. Footnote #7.
144. Robert A. Rutland and Charles F. Hobson, eds., *The Papers of James Madison: Volume 11, 7 March 1788–1 March 1789*, (Charlottesville: University Press of Virginia, 1977), 297.

Chapter Eight

Twilight

The last decade of James Wilson's life failed to crown him with financial success or national fame—both of which he deeply craved. After the success of his significant contribution at the Constitutional Convention of 1787, the leadership of the Federalist faction at the Pennsylvania Constitutional Ratification Convention, the honor of giving the keynote address at the July 4th, 1788 celebrations in Philadelphia, and his pivotal involvement at the drafting of a new Pennsylvania state constitution in 1790, accomplishments such as these should have augured well for the decade that followed. Sadly, James Wilson's best days were behind him.

His position as an associate justice of the U.S. Supreme Court permitted him time to serve as the first Professor of Law at the College of Philadelphia. He had grand plans—of becoming the American Blackstone, of creating a digest both of the laws of Pennsylvania and another for those of the United States, and of even leading an effort to systematize the mass migration of *millions* of Europeans to the Old Northwest Territory—but as his ambition grew larger, his world began to fracture and crumble around him. Ultimately, it led to his death—on the run from his creditors—in Edenton, North Carolina in 1798.

As a member of the Constitutional Convention of 1787, James Wilson worked closely with James Madison in the creation of the new federal government's judicial branch. Of the three branches of government, it was the judicial branch which was the most conducive to both Wilson's temperament and education.

During the last months of 1788 and into early 1789, elections were held—in those states which had ratified the Constitution—to fill the new Congress established by the Constitution. The first presidential election was also held over a protracted time—from December 15, 1788 to January 10, 1789.¹ Their selection of George Washington to serve as the nation's first chief executive was unanimous. However, a joint session of Congress did not convene until April 6th, more than a month after the scheduled start of the new government on March 4th, to ratify Washington's selection as president and John Adams as vice-president. Washington began his term of office on April 30th when he took the oath of office in New York City on the balcony of Federal Hall on Wall Street.

Before the first meeting of the new Congress, maneuvering for positions in the new federal government had begun in earnest. In Philadelphia's *Federal Gazette*, a piece appeared noting, "The southern states give a President and the eastern states a Vice-President: upon these generous and just principles Pennsylvania humbly puts in her claim to furnish a CHIEF-JUSTICE for the United States."² Two weeks later, on March 9th, the *Federal Gazette* endorsed James Wilson as the best candidate for the job. The piece reported a rumor that Wilson had been selected for the post and heaped praise on the choice. "His hand, his heart, his tongue and his pen, have ever been at the command of his country."³ Wilson would bring "an uncommon share of *legal* and *political* abilities and information" to the position.⁴ Other friends of James Wilson worked behind the scenes as well.

Frederick Muhlenberg wrote to Benjamin Rush, a mutual friend, of his concern that his rumored future election as Speaker of the House of Representatives would damage Wilson's opportunity to be appointed Chief Justice. It was widely believed that positions in the new government would be geographically distributed to bind all sections of the union to the success of the federal government. In praising Wilson, Muhlenberg wrote, "In Point of Abilities I do not know his equal nor any one so well calculated for the Duties of that important Station." Further, "from my personal Regard for him I would sooner forego any Advantage than be in any Manner the Means of injuring him or his Views."⁵ Muhlenberg went on to be elected the first Speaker of the House of Representatives under the Constitution.

Not all commentary appearing in the press praised Wilson's possible selection as Chief Justice. After Congress convened, but before Washington was sworn in, the *New York Journal* published a piece highly critical of Wilson. Responding to the previous praise of Wilson in the *Federal Gazette*, the piece took issue with the *Gazette*'s assertion that "*many thousands* of Federalists" throughout the country desired Wilson's appointment.⁶ On the contrary, the *Journal* declared Wilson was "not the proper person for that high and important office."⁷ Other individuals of worthy character from other states were available, even from Pennsylvania itself. The *Journal* believed that they were "more deserving of it, on account of their abilities, and from their principles and manners being more republican than those of Mr. Wilson."⁸

With public and private discussion of his fitness as Chief Justice swirling around him, James Wilson drafted a letter to president-elect George Washington on April 21st, five days after the critical piece in the *New York Journal*, and dispatched it to New York. By sending the letter, he breached established protocol of the day by writing a personal letter to President Washington putting himself forward as the best candidate for the position of Chief Justice. He explained to Washington that "a Delicacy [*sic*] arising from your Situation and Character as well as my own" had prevented him from broaching the topic before.[9] He would not have contacted Washington if it had not been for "a Regard to the Dignity of the Government, over which you preside, will naturally lead you to take Care that its Honours be in no Event exposed to affected Indifference or Contempt."[10] With that sentiment in mind, Wilson sought to preclude any chance of a possible candidate refusing the honor of an appointment from Washington and then proceeded to put himself forth "without Reserve, and inform you that my Aim rises to the important office of Chief Justice of the United States."[11]

Wilson's friends continued to lobby for his appointment. Benjamin Rush wrote the new Vice President, John Adams, the day after Wilson sent his letter to Washington, asking for help. "Your influence in the Senate over which you have been called to preside, will give you great weight (without a vote) in determining upon the most suitable Characters to fill the first offices in government."[12] He explained to Adams, "Pennsylvania looks up with anxious Solicitude for the commission of Chief Justice for Mr. Wilson," and this was due to "the expectation of this honor being conferred upon him, that he was left out of the Senate, and house of representatives."[13] Opposition to Wilson was due to: "His abilities and knowledge in framing the constitution, and his zeal in promoting its establishment, have exposed him to a most virulent persecution from the antifederalists in this state."[14] Rush pointed to Pennsylvania's current governor, Thomas Mifflin, as a leader of the opposition.

Rush forthrightly addressed concerns about Wilson's financial difficulties. "Much will be said of the deranged state of his Affairs. But where will you find an American landholder free from embarrassments?"[15] He placed the blame on America's weak banking and economy—a principal rationale used by Federalists for adoption of the Constitution. "Our funding System had reduced all our wealthy men to the utmost distress, and has thrown a great part of their property into the hands of quartermasters—Amsterdam Jews, and London brokers."[16] Rush praised Wilson's deportment, for "under all the disappointments which he has met with, he has preserved a fair character, and a dignified line of Conduct."[17] He assured Adams that the two men shared the same political philosophy of vigorous government of three branches.

However, if Wilson was not nominated and "left to sink under this opposition, I shall for ever deplore the ingratitude of republics."[18]

John Adams replied to Rush's letter nearly three weeks later. Unlike Rush's belief, Adams argued that his position as "head of the Senate" held little opportunity to do as Rush requested—"the Influence which you Suppose I may have as President of the Senate will be found to be very little if any at all."[19] He acknowledged, "Mr. Wilson, I have long known esteemed and respected: but, if I had a Vote, I could not promise to give it for him to be Chief Justice."[20] Adams had another in mind: "I feel myself inclined to wish, because I am fully convinced that Services, Hazards, Abilities and Popularity, all properly weighed, the Ballance, is in favour of Mr. Jay."[21] Adams desired Wilson to be a member of the Supreme Court and the difference between being the Chief Justice and an Associate was "not great."[22]

Before closing his letter to Rush, Adams felt obligated to chastise Rush for a paragraph in his April 22nd letter urging him to support Wilson's appointment due to Wilson's support among Pennsylvania's electors of his election as Vice President. "You say I had not a firmer Friend in the late Election. I must protest against this mode of reasoning." Adams angrily replied, "I am not obliged to vote for a Man because he voted for me, had my office been ever so lucrative or ever so important."[23] He concluded his lecture by admonishing, "Never must I again hear a Selfish Motive urged to me, to induce my Vote or Influence in publick affairs."[24]

Writing from America's capital, New York, Virginia's Arthur Lee wrote to his brother, Francis Lightfoot Lee, that gossip circulating in the city indicated that, "Wilson is an avowed Candidate for the Chief Justice ship," but "Jay is the whispered one."[25] Further, he explained that Wilson's friend Robert Morris was vigorously working for his appointment to the Court and that James Madison had given his full support to the effort.[26]

On the same day that Arthur Lee wrote his brother, President Washington returned a frosty letter dashing Wilson's hopes. He wrote, "To you, my dear Sir, and others who know me, I presume it will be unnecessary for me to say that I have entered upon my office without the constraint of a single *engagement*, and that I never wish to depart from that line of conduct which will always leave me at full liberty to act in a manner which is befitting an impartial and disinterested Magistrate."[27] The reason Washington was unwilling to promote Wilson to the top spot was due to his insecure finances. Washington considered Wilson to be the preeminent lawyer of his day, even paying him an exorbitant fee for Bushrod Washington to learn the practice of law from him. Washington was willing to place him on the court but not as Chief Justice.

Wilson's ally Robert Morris acknowledged his failure to convince Washington to make his appointment to the desired post. Morris prepared his friend for the disappointment: "I confirm to you my Idea that you will be nominated to the Bench, but I still doubt not to the first Seat."[28] Three days later, on September 24, 1789, James Wilson was appointed by President George Washington to serve as an associate justice of the first United States Supreme Court. The U.S. Senate confirmed Wilson two days later and he took the oath of office on October 5.

In the early decades of the Supreme Court, justices were required to "ride the circuit" serving as appellate justices in the emerging federal court system.[29] It was here, on the circuit, that James Wilson gained his closest friend on the Court. James Iredell officially joined the U.S. Supreme Court on February 10, 1790, after his nomination by President Washington and approval by the Senate, but he didn't receive his commission until March 3rd.[30] Iredell filled the opening on the bench when Robert Harrison of Maryland resigned his commission on January 21, without ever attending a session.[31]

There were three judicial circuits: the Eastern Circuit (New England and New York); the Middle Circuit (Pennsylvania, New Jersey, Delaware, Maryland and Virginia); and the Southern Circuit (North Carolina, South Carolina, and Georgia). When the Court first convened in February 1790, the justices in attendance (Chief Justice John Jay, John Blair, William Cushing, and James Wilson) decided the circuit court assignments, based on place of residence of each justice.[32] This was both logical and unfair. The justices reasoned that when attorneys put forward their applications for admission to each circuit's bar, they should apply to those justices most likely to be familiar with them. However, this was unfair to the newest justice—who was also not present—James Iredell, since his Southern Circuit was the most arduous (it took nearly 1,900 miles of travel to complete).[33]

CHARGE TO THE GRAND JURY

With the initiation of circuit, riding duty, James Wilson initiated a new practice when he presided. The creation of federal district courts, for many citizens of the United States, was an opportunity for them to experience the workings of the Constitution firsthand. Other than using the services of the national postal service, most Americans had no contact with agents of the federal government on a day-to-day basis. This fact presented a unique opportunity for James Wilson as he gaveled court into session.

Wilson wrote a charge to the grand jury convened in Philadelphia for the first time as a federal court during the Spring 1790 circuit schedule.[34] Since the courts were just getting started, there was very little business for them to conduct. Therefore, James Wilson seized the opportunity to provide civic education to the members of the jury—basically, he assumed the mantle of a law professor and gave them a lecture.

Within a month, Wilson's charge was reprinted in New York (in full) and portions appeared in Boston; Portsmouth, New Hampshire; and Edenton, North Carolina. This April 12th charge formed the basis of future charges to other grand juries, with modifications for local circumstances and business before the court. He explained to the jurors, "Perhaps, therefore, no occasion can be fitter, than the present, to address you on a subject of great, of general, and of lasting importance, and, at the same time, intimately connected with your official character and views.—I mean, the utility, the power, and the duty of Juries."[35]

Wilson acknowledged that "the great movements of the state receive their first force and direction immediately from the people, at elections."[36] At the Constitutional Convention in 1787, James Wilson argued time and again for the widest possible participation of citizens in the federal government they erected—here he again drew power from citizens to energize mechanisms of government. He turned his attention to the work of jurors themselves.

"The administration of justice and the municipal laws is that part of government, which comes most intimately home to the business and bosoms of men."[37] Wilson explained that their jury service was essential to the fairness of and public confidence in the federal judiciary. Their role was so important it was "inferior only to the trust reposed in the Legislature, is that reposed in Grand Juries, in point of national concern," for "[t]hey are entrusted with the custody of the portals of the law, that into the hallowed dome no injustice may be permitted to enter."[38] The crucial job of a grand jury was this: "Facts must be investigated and authenticated: The circumstances attending transactions must be developed and ascertained. In order to make the proper estimates and to discover the true results of things, consideration must be given not only to what is said, but to the character and situation of the witness, who speaks it, and to the character and situation of the person, concerning whom it is spoken."[39]

Jury service, for James Wilson, in many ways superseded the role of voters in a democracy. It was here, in the courtroom, where the laws enacted by the legislators, which voters elect, are put into contact with real people. The jurors bring the law to life and must determine innocence and guilt and provide punishment for those they convict. This was the heart of Wilson's charge to the Philadelphia grand jury in April 1790, but he didn't stop here; he felt it necessary to then provide a legal history of juries to his captive audience.

A year later, in Richmond, Wilson again charged a grand jury with a lecture on their role as jurors. This time, he refocused his argument to draw attention to the linkage of crimes to punishments.[40] He noted, "We are told by some writers, that the number of crimes is unquestionably diminished by the severity of punishment."[41] Wilson directly challenged this belief by criticizing the number of capital crimes under English law and relative lack of success in lowering the crime rate. Instead, Wilson concluded, "on accurate and unbiased examination, however, it will appear to be an opinion unfounded and pernicious, inconsistent with the principles of our nature, and, by a necessary consequence, with those of wise and good government."[42] For Wilson, where juries were not present, the judicial system would become more and more alienated from citizens and less effective in upholding the law.

A judicial system—to earn and retain the trust of citizens—should ensure "that those accused of crimes should be speedily tried, and that those convicted of them should be speedily punished."[43] Punishments should fit the crime, not grossly exceed them. For if they do, "the punishment is procrastinated to a remote period; this connexion is considered as weak and precarious; and the execution of the law is beheld and suffered as a detached instance of severity, warranted by no cogent reason, and springing from no laudable motive."[44]

James Wilson believed that jury duty was an honor, not something to be avoided. Throughout his years on the bench and in the lecture hall, he celebrated the crucial role of jurors which brought the public into the inner workings of the judiciary. It was hoped that jurors who disagreed with certain laws or their punishments would work within the constitutional framework to change them. It was the dual role of voter and juror that held the key to effective and equitable democracy.

RIDING CIRCUIT

When the justices of the Supreme Court gathered in New York for their August session, a majority decided to make the circuit assignments permanent—giving no hope of relief to Iredell from the Southern Circuit. The decision was taken in the belief that rotation of assignments was not provided for under the terms of the Judiciary Act of 1789. Even if it could be construed in a way to provide for rotation, they believed, the business of the circuit courts would be disrupted from term to term if new justices were asked to handle cases that had previously been continued.[45] However, they did agree to draft an appeal to President Washington requesting the practice of circuit riding be stopped on the grounds that it was improper for justices to hear cases on circuit, which may then come before them again, to the Supreme Court, on appeal.

In August of 1790, the U.S. House of Representatives requested a report from Attorney General Edmund Randolph detailing areas needing reform in the judiciary branch. Randolph, with help from at least one of the Supreme Court justices, prepared and submitted a report in December.[46] One of his recommendations supported the justices in their request that circuit riding be discontinued. Connecticut Congressman Roger Sherman—a member of the 1787 Constitutional Convention with James Wilson—commented to Simeon Baldwin in late January 1791 that "the Superiour Judges can acquire a knowledge of the rights of the people of these States much better by riding the circuit, than by Staying at home and reading British and other foreign Laws."[47] Consideration of the report was postponed until the Second Congress, thus allowing it to quietly die—justices would continue to ride circuit.

Frustrated, James Iredell wrote a letter to his colleagues on February 11th asking them to reconsider circuit assignments.[48] The next day, Chief Justice Jay replied, "I have not the least objection to re-examining the Merits of the Question of Rotation."[49] "The inconveniences you mention are doubtless great and unequal; and yet Sir! an adequate Remedy can in my opinion be afforded only by legislative Provisions."[50] Jay urged Iredell to approach James Wilson or John Blair to discuss switching assignments. Apparently, the Judiciary Act of 1789 was no longer a principal concern for the Chief Justice in allocation of assignments—keeping his colleagues happy became paramount. Iredell and Blair agreed to switch their assignments.

Less than two weeks after writing the letter to Jay, James Wilson and James Iredell first rode together on the Middle Circuit in the spring of 1791. Their first court was a special two-day session of the Pennsylvania circuit court, in Philadelphia, on February 21st. From Philadelphia, Wilson and Iredell travelled to Trenton, New Jersey, and opened court there on April 2nd and remained for two weeks.[51] Before the Trenton session was concluded, on April 9th, Wilson left for Philadelphia to hold court.[52] Wilson opened the court on April 11th, with Judge Francis Hopkinson attending, for a two-day session.[53] Iredell arrived back in Philadelphia on the 14th for a few days of rest before setting out with Wilson for their next court date.[54]

Wilson and Iredell were joined by Judge Gunning Bedford, Jr.—another Wilson colleague from the 1787 Constitutional Convention—in New Castle, Delaware where court was convened on April 27th.[55] Their next destination was Annapolis, Maryland, where the two men arrived on May 6th. That evening, Iredell wrote his wife to relate their safe arrival and to give her his first opinion of James Wilson. "I find Mr. Wilson a very agreeable Companion, [our] sentiments in general agree perfectly well."[56] The Annapolis court lasted only a single day, after which the two men dined with Maryland U.S. Senator Charles Carroll of Carrollton, before hiring a private stage for their journey to Alexandria, Virginia. Before leaving Annapolis, Carroll arranged for the two men to ascend to the "very high Cupola on the State House," where Iredell declared, "We saw one of the most delightful prospects I have ever beheld."[57] Wilson and Iredell's stage deposited them in Alexandria on May 9th.[58]

The Middle Circuit next took Wilson and Iredell to Richmond where they opened court on May 23rd for a session lasting three days.[59] This marked the end of the spring session of the Middle Circuit, and the two men were not in court again until a special session of the circuit court was again held in Philadelphia on August 15th for two days.[60] Iredell would, once again, ride the Southern Circuit for the fall 1791 session, this time alone.[61]

In the spring of 1792, James Iredell received the relief that he had been requesting since his letter of February 11, 1791 to his colleagues. His brother-in-law, North Carolina U.S. Senator Samuel Johnston, successfully ushered through Congress the Circuit Court Act of 1792. The act, passed on April 13th, provided that no justice, without his prior consent, could be made to ride the same circuit again until all the other justices had ridden that same circuit.[62] The ramifications of the act were immediate.

THE EASTERN CIRCUIT, FALL 1792

Wilson and Iredell rode the Eastern Circuit, comprised of the states of New York, Connecticut, Massachusetts, New Hampshire, and Rhode Island, together for the first time in the fall of 1792. Neither man had traveled through the region, Wilson, upon coming to America in 1765, had landed in New York, but soon made his way to Philadelphia. The Circuit began on September 5th, when James Wilson held court in New York City for two days.[63] Iredell was travelling to join Wilson but did not arrive until the evening of the 19th. He checked into a room at the City Tavern, where he "awoke quite refreshed from a fine night's sleep," and wrote to his wife early the next morning to ensure that the letter would not miss the post.[64] In his haste to travel north to join Wilson, Iredell had taken the key to the desk in his home's study. He promised to send it home when he could. Iredell's stay in New York would be brief as he and Wilson were scheduled to leave on the next morning's stage to Hartford.[65]

The stage for Hartford left early on Friday morning, "between 3 and 4," and was overcrowded. James Wilson had brought along his daughter Mary (known as Polly) on the journey. The Wilsons and James Iredell were forced to ride in separate stages as there were too many passengers and baggage for just one. As the trip to Hartford began, they had traveled only a few miles before Wilson and Iredell "perceived that some of the Baggage was gone and on examination found it was Mr. Wilson's Trunk and mine."[66] Wilson and Iredell were forced to leave the stage to Hartford and climb aboard the stage to Kingsbridge, where they waited for word of their baggage. Fortunately for the two justices, a young "Boy who had driven a Waggon to Town, had picked the Trunks up, and very honestly deposited them safe near the City."[67] The delay meant that they were unable to reach Hartford that evening and needed to stay in New Haven for the night.

Wilson and Iredell arrived in Hartford to open court on September 25th. The session did not close until October 4th.[68] Writing the evening of the opening of court to his wife, Hannah, James Iredell related that after departing from New Haven on the 23rd, the two justices "stopped at a meeting house, where we heard a very dull Minister, and found not a genteel Congregation. It was a place called Wallingford."[69] Iredell took special note to share with his wife that towards the close of the service, the minister prayed "that they might come better prepared in *body and mind* for public worship in the afternoon."[70]

As the group continued their journey to Hartford, Iredell and Wilson took the time to comment on the scenery as it rolled past their stage. "We dined at a place called Durham, a very small place but with beautiful views from it," and they proceeded through "delightful" Middletown and "a pretty little place called Wethersfield."[71] Summarizing his impressions of their arrival in Hartford, Iredell concluded, "This place in point of beauty is far inferior to almost any I have yet seen in the State, tho' it is the Capital. Had we seen it first it might have passed tolerably well."[72]

Reaching the end of this leg of the Eastern Circuit, Wilson and Iredell checked into their lodgings upon arriving in Hartford. Iredell declared, "We are very well accommodated, though Mr. Wilson and myself have only one room between us."[73] They lodged with Congressman Jeremiah Wadsworth.[74] The Court had not established firm rules for travel by justices; some elected to stay with friends while on circuit, while others accepted invitations from prominent members of the local community, while others, like Iredell and Wilson in Hartford, were forced to share whatever accommodation was available to them.

Before the Hartford court closed on October 4th, James Wilson received news on September 30th that his presence was urgently needed back in Philadelphia to handle business matters. He made plans to leave on the 2nd of October and shared his plans with Iredell, whom he planned on meeting at their next circuit court in Boston. Wilson carried a letter from Iredell to his wife on his hurried trip back to Philadelphia.[75] After Wilson's departure and the night before the end of the court session, Iredell was invited to a ball, before leaving for Boston. He "staid until one. I danced a little, but it was not a remarkably agreeable one."[76]

Iredell left for Boston and arrived there on October 7th.[77] He was joined by Judge John Lowell and opened court on the 12th with the session lasting until the 20th.[78] Wilson's business delayed him and he was unable to arrive in Boston until that evening, rejoining Iredell for the next segment of the Eastern Circuit.[79] During his time in Boston, Iredell shared his impression of the city and state with his wife and Wilson: "It is scarcely possible to meet with a gentleman who is not a man of education. Such are the advantages of schools by public authority!"[80] In contrast to the rest of the nation, "every township is obliged to maintain one or more, to which poor children can have access without any pay."[81] He was impressed with the public spiritedness as well: "From every account I can collect, there is almost as much order and complete obedience among the people, as to all public concerns, as there usually is in other countries in private families."[82] Summarizing his first visit to the region, "I am satisfied so much regularity and decency do not exist in any other country in the world, as in Connecticut and Massachusetts."[83]

Wilson and Iredell continued, on the next leg of the Eastern Circuit, to Exeter, New Hampshire, leaving Boston on the morning of the 22nd. They spent the 23rd "in a very agreeable Manner at a considerable Town called Newbury Port, about 45 miles from Boston."[84] The two men stayed with the town's leading lawyer, Theophilus Parsons, who later became the chief justice of the Supreme Judicial Court of Massachusetts in 1806.[85] Iredell had met Parsons during his time in Boston and had accepted his invitation to lodge with him on the trip to New Hampshire. Their stay in Exeter was brief as the business before the court was slight, requiring only two days.[86] Iredell desired to linger, before returning to Boston and on to Newport, Rhode Island, but "Judge Wilson wishes to press on immediately to Newport as he has some important business which makes him anxious to be as near Philadelphia as he can."[87] They returned to Boston, arriving on October 28th.[88]

The circuit court in Providence was not due to convene until November 7th. Wilson and Iredell parted ways. Wilson immediately made plans to leave for Providence, but Iredell wanted to take advantage of his first visit to New England remained, writing his wife, "I don't think I can leave Boston so soon."[89] Wilson left Boston early on Tuesday morning, October 30th, with Iredell liking "Boston so well that I shall stay till Monday next."[90] With a week in Boston before him, Iredell wanted to experience as much as he could in the time remaining. The very day that Wilson left, Iredell headed to Cambridge to visit Harvard. He "liked extremely well what I saw of the College, and had the honour of dining" with the trustees, among whom was "the famous Sam. Adams [who] tho' an old Man has a great deal of fire yet."[91]

At the time, Adams was serving as Massachusetts' Lieutenant Governor and Iredell was invited to dine with Governor John Hancock a few days later. Before leaving Boston, Hancock held a reception in Iredell's honor to which the Governor "invited a very numerous and genteel company of Ladies and Gentlemen, and some of them danced."[92]

After a week of visits, dinners, and sightseeing, Iredell departed Boston for his rendezvous with Wilson in Providence. His stage arrived the evening of Monday, November 5th, with court not convening until Wednesday.[93] James Wilson wasn't there to greet James Iredell—he was in Newport—but Iredell expected to see Wilson the next evening, the night before court began.[94] Wilson did return the next day and the two justices were joined by Judge Henry Marchant when court opened on Wednesday. Business concluded, and the court adjourned for the term on Monday, November 12th.[95]

In a letter to Rhode Island Congressman Benjamin Bourne, attorney David Leonard Barnes shared impressions of proceedings in the Providence courtroom. "His Honor Judge Wilson gave us a learned dissertation on the first springs of Government, and the trial by jury in general" (this was Wilson's charge to the grand jury), and further, "his manner of conducting the business of the C[ou[r[t] seems to be universally pleasing."[96] Turning to his colleague, "His Honor Judge Iredell puts on his hat, upon the Bench, when his head is cold, and looks as if he was at home. He has won the affections of the Bar at Boston, by his urbanity and politeness, and every one here seems charmed with his civility and frankness."[97]

With the Eastern Circuit complete, Wilson and Iredell returned to Philadelphia, arriving there on Friday, November 23rd.[98] With a change in the allocation of circuits for 1793, the two justices would not be riding together again. Only a single Supreme Court justice would now hold court, with another federal judge, for each session; this would allow each member to ride circuit only once a year.

James Wilson's business problems continued to impede doing his job as a justice riding circuit. For the spring 1793 session, Wilson was, again, allocated the Eastern Circuit. In early May, he wrote, from Hartford, to Justice William Cushing, a colleague on the Supreme Court. They had talked, while both attended the February session of the Supreme Court in Philadelphia, about Wilson's upcoming court sessions in New England and Cushing offered to join Wilson in Boston and Portsmouth. The court in Portsmouth was scheduled to convene on May 27th and Wilson needed Cushing to cover for him. He explained that his "presence will, at that Time, be indispensable at Philadelphia."[99] He assured Cushing that he would be able to return from Philadelphia for the session in Boston. Cushing covered for Wilson in Portsmouth.[100]

James Wilson did indeed make it to Boston in time to convene court on June 7th. Newspaper coverage of Wilson's arrival in Boston was mixed. The *Columbian Centinel* praised his charge to the grand jury. It was "replete with the purest principles of our equal Government, and highly indicative of his legal reputation."[101] Two days later, the *Federal Gazette* replied to this characterization of James Wilson. "It is said that a Charge has been delivered 'replete with the happiness of *equal* government,' This idea comes with an ill grace from a man, who parades our streets with a coach and four horses, when it is known his exorbitant salary enables him to make this *flashy parade*, and the money is taken from the pockets of the industrious part of the community."[102] The paper then asked, "Where is the '*equality*' when an officer of government is enabled by his excessive salary, to live in a stile vastly superior to any member in the society that supports him?"[103]

This was a momentous trip to the city for James Wilson, but not for the business of the court, which only took four days. This is when he first met the very young woman who would become his second wife. On his first Sunday in Boston, Wilson went to the service at the Brattle Street Church to hear the sermon of Dr. Peter Thacher.[104] Seated in an adjacent pew was a lovely young lady, not yet nineteen, who caught Wilson's eye—Miss Hannah Gray. She was younger than Wilson's two oldest children, but the fifty-one-year-old widower was smitten. The relationship quickly became the talk of Boston.

Before leaving the city at the end of the session, Wilson was able to arrange an introduction with Miss Gray. At the conclusion of their meeting, Hannah agreed to allow Wilson to write to her, and he did so after reaching Newport, Rhode Island for his next circuit court session which convened on June 19th. He had promised that he would see her again, in Boston, after his business in Newport was concluded or write to her if his plans changed. He couldn't wait that long. "But why should I delay Writing till the *Conclusion* of the Court? Why should not my Pen sooner take up a Theme so constantly present to my Thoughts?"[105] He apparently had shared his amorous intentions with her at their meeting, and he sought an immediate reply. "Let that Answer be speedy and favourable: Let it authorize me to think and call you mine."[106]

A few days after Wilson dispatched his letter to Boston, John Quincy Adams wrote of the relationship to his youngest brother, Thomas. He shared the latest gossip: "The most extraordinary intelligence, which I have to convey is that the wise and learned Judge and Professor Wilson, has fallen most lamentably in love with a young Lady in this town, under twenty, by the name of Gray." "He came, he saw, and was overcome."[107] He described Wilson as "unable to contain his amorous pain, he breathed his sighs about the Streets; and even when seated on the bench of Justice, he seemed as if teeming with some woful ballad to his mistress eye brow."[108] He claimed to know that Wilson, after the initial introduction, had proposed marriage at their second meeting. The whirlwind nature of the courtship was heightened by Wilson's appearance, "in a very handsome chariot and four."[109] Adams was astonished Hannah Gray "actually has the subject under consideration."[110] For, if she accepted, "and unless the Judge should prove as fickle as he is amorous and repent his precipitate impetuosity so far as to withdraw his proposal, you will no doubt soon behold in the persons of those well assorted lovers a new edition of January and May."[111]

Adams felt it necessary to reassure his youngest brother that this wasn't a joke, but "the plain and simple truth that I tell."[112] He suggested to Thomas that he should inform the daughters of Samuel Breck, a merchant formerly from Boston now living in Philadelphia, "their friend and mine, *Miss Hannah Gray*, has made so profound an impression upon the Heart of judge Wilson, and received in return an impression so profound upon her very own, that in all probability they will soon see her at Philadelphia, the happy consort of the happy judge."[113]

John Quincy Adams did not approve of the potential marriage. He explained to Thomas that "Cupid himself must laugh at his own absurdity, in producing such an Union; but he must sigh to reflect that without the soft persuasion of a deity who has supplanted him in the breast of modern beauty, he could not have succeeded to render the man ridiculous and the woman contemptible."[114]

Not everyone in Boston disapproved. In a letter to Henry Knox, Henry Jackson shared that the marriage would indeed take place. Jackson concluded, "It will be highly flattering to see one of our Boston girls in her *Coach and four* rolling the streets of Philadelphia."[115]

The next time that James Wilson and James Iredell were together was in Philadelphia for a special session of the Circuit Court for the District of Pennsylvania on July 22, which lasted a week. Undoubtedly, the two men discussed Wilson's intent to remarry after returning to Philadelphia upon completing the Eastern Circuit. Wilson arranged with colleague William Paterson to trade his assigned Middle Circuit for Paterson's Eastern Circuit for fall 1793.[116] This would take Wilson back to Boston for his impending marriage.

James Wilson married Hannah Gray on the evening of Thursday, September 19th, 1793. Wilson was due to hold court in Hartford with Justice John Blair on the 25th, and his new bride accompanied him for the remainder of the Eastern Circuit.[117] The *Boston Gazette* carried a brief notice of the ceremony: "MARRIED, In this town . . . the Hon. Judge Wilson, of Philadelphia, to the amiable Miss Hannah Gray, of this town."[118] Conducting the ceremony was the minister Dr. Peter Thacher in whose church they had first met.[119]

The trials and tribulations of life on the road and cramped quarters forged a close bond between James Wilson and James Iredell; during the Eastern Circuit of fall 1792, they had spent more than three months together. Less than a year later, James Wilson married Hannah Gray. Over the coming years, the bond between James Wilson and his young bride, Hannah, became very close with James Iredell and his wife, Hannah. Iredell's wife served as a surrogate mother and the bond between the two wives became nearly as strong as the bond between the two husbands.[120]

ONE LAST SCHEME

The business interests and public life of James Wilson were never distinct arenas, but intertwined, with each influencing the other. Sometime during 1792, Wilson's economic ambitions expanded to encompass a grand and elaborate scheme to bring *millions* of European immigrants to America's shores.[121] Personally, he had received financial help from family members on his journey from Scotland to America in 1765 and upon arrival secured assistance from his cousin Robert Annan. Wilson's vision in the 1790s was much broader in that it would facilitate the movement of immigrants from their ports of embarkation in Europe to their ultimate destination of family farms in the northwest territory.

At the very beginning of the prospectus Wilson drafted for distribution in Europe, he identified the principal assets and deficiencies of both America and Europe: "In the United States there is an immense Quantity of Land, rich, well-situated and in a salubrious Climate. This Land lies useless and unimproved from the Want of Labour and Capital and Stock."[122] However, "in Europe there is an Abundance of Labour and Capital and Stock; but rich and well-situated Land cannot be obtained, unless at a very high Price."[123] Wilson's proposal would join the strengths of both—American land and European labor and capital—to the advantage of both.

In the 1780s, James Wilson had shopped a much smaller immigrant proposal to European investors, but with little success. His friend, Philadelphia physician Benjamin Rush, wrote in an April 1785 letter that he blamed "the decay of the American character in London" for Wilson's failure to secure investors. Less than two years after the formal end of the American Revolution, America faced uncertain and turbulent economic fortunes. Rush added, "War tends to loosen the bonds of morality and government in every country; the effects of it have been greatly increased by the people of America handling for four or five years a depreciating paper currency. The evils produced by both I hope will soon cure themselves."[124] America's economic future brightened after the adoption of the Constitution and the beginning of the new federal government established under it. The time was right for another appeal to European investors.

Wilson identified a further American strength which would benefit European immigrants—America's republican government. "[T]he Nature of our Government is so contrived as to expand in just and accurate Proportion to the Settlement of the Country."[125] The lands of the old Northwest, under the terms of the Northwest Ordinance of 1787, would join the American union as equals to those states which had fought and won the American Revolution—there would be no American colonies with second-class status for Europeans persuaded to hazard the journey across the Atlantic. Further, as immigrants established themselves and became new Americans, "they may be raised to Places of great Dignity and Consequence in the extended and the growing Government of the United States."[126] Their progeny, born in America, could aspire to any office under the Constitution, even that of President of the United States.

America's Constitution created an environment where hard-working immigrants could obtain land, raise a family, and aspire to a better life. This was the heart of Wilson's argument: "If he possesses Skill in Agriculture, and can command sufficient Capital and Labour and Stock; it is, by no Means, an unreasonable Calculation, that, at the End of eight Years, he may, after maintaining his Family in Comfort and Plenty, replace all the Capital, which he has expended and sell his Land at eight Times the Price, which he paid for it."[127] The blend of lawyer and salesman that he was, James Wilson was careful to qualify his statement. IF everything went right for new immigrants and IF no economic difficulties occurred (either national or international), and IF Mother Nature smiled upon immigrants, THEN it just might be possible to accomplish the feat of paying off the expense of coming to America in only eight short years, but Wilson held out the prospect of such an occurrence, a prospect unavailable to prospective immigrants in Europe.

To provide evidence for his thinking, Wilson presented a number of assets which would help immigrant farmers prosper. First, the timber covering much of the lands intended for settlement was a tangible benefit, not a hindrance. Yes, it would take hard work to turn the trees into building materials for homes, buildings, and fencing, but it could be done. Second, once these needs were met, the remaining trees could be reduced to ash to serve as both a ready source of fertilizer and a commodity to obtain other necessary items. He argued that ashes "will reimburse all the Expences of clearing and fencing the Land."[128] The logic Wilson presented of essentially a self-financing enterprise was enticing. This process could be expanded as "What had been said of *one* Settlement, of one Improvement and of one Farm may, with the same Propriety, be said of *Millions* of Settlements and Improvements and Farms."[129] Further, as the stream of immigrants began arriving on America's shores, the process, according to Wilson, would become virtually self-financing. "For every *preceding* Settlement, Improvement and Farm *prepares* the Way for those, which shall *succeed*: And every *subsequent* Settlement, Improvement and Farm bestows an *additional* Value upon those, which have *preceded* it."[130]

Each and every family coming to America would constitute a link in a great endeavor benefiting not only themselves, but all of those around them and those to come. New farms would generate surpluses: "A constant Market will thus be regularly opened and regularly supplied; and the alternate Vicissitudes of Want and excessive Plenty will be equally unknown. Every Thing produced will find a sufficient Demand for its Consumption; and every Demand for Consumption will find Produce in sufficient Quantities to supply it."[131] The vision was breathtaking, but failed to address problems of transportation for this self-perpetuating market. A chronic problem facing farmers, merchants, and travelers of this period was the poor, inefficient, and often non-existent transportation system. This was a glaring weakness of Wilson's proposal.[132]

The middle portion of Wilson's prospectus presented the horror story of the current state of immigration. He lamented the bad food, bad ships, bad treatment, and poor living conditions of the initial Atlantic crossing. Once immigrants stepped ashore, they often had no contacts and little money to continue on to a destination further west. After this litany of woe, Wilson put forth his vision of what could be.

Lands would be purchased by a consortium of investors—which he initially labeled Capitalists, later the Proprietors—where "[t]he *best* Parts of those Tracts should be subdivided into Surveys of one, two or three hundred Acres each."[133] With his hard-earned experience in land speculation and working with surveyors, Wilson declared that surveyors themselves would be unable to have any ability to acquire land they were working so as to remain impartial and would operate under an exclusive contract where they "shall make no Surveys or Locations for others, nor communicate to others Information for making Surveys or Locations."[134] To provide for unforeseen land problems, "every third Survey should be reserved, by Lot, for the Proprietors."[135] This would allow parcels to be exchanged for another of equal size, if issues of suitability or boundary disputes arose—additionally, lots could be held as investments as settlement would inevitably lead to increased land values. The task of providing accurate and reliable descriptions of plots would entail great expense. Wilson determined "it to be essential to the Advantage, to the Success, and to the Reputation of the Plan."[136]

Wilson brazenly declared: "The first Axiom of this Plan is—*never to be in Want of Money.*"[137] For a man whose personal fortunes had rested on a shaky foundation for nearly two decades, this axiom was intended to stabilize his personal financial future, as well as bring about his grand vision for European immigrants. He acknowledged the financial benefit that fellow investors and he himself would realize: "Those, who could devise and execute such a Plan, would perform a most precious Service to Individuals and to Society; and would merit a rich Compensation for their Exertions and Labours."[138] The spark lacking to initiate such a self-supporting program needed to be provided by European investors. The final third of the prospectus spoke to them.

The scale of Wilson's proposal required vast sums of money. Hard currency that could only come from Europeans. He acknowledged the necessity of large up-front expenditures: "All this must be done on *this* Side of the *Atlantic*. But to do all this with Ease and Security, and on a Scale sufficiently large, good Connexions must be formed, and ample Funds must be provided on the *other* Side of the *Atlantic*."[139]

Wilson's prospectus envisioned activities and opportunities on both sides of the Atlantic for investors to participate in and recoup their funds. First, the lands purchased in America would be sold by investors in Europe where they would receive both a "handsome Commission" and "payment in Europe."[140] Receiving payment *before* immigrants embarked for America allayed fears of default by purchasers and fluctuation of international currencies.

Second, the ships required to ferry immigrants across the Atlantic provided opportunities as well. Investors "should also be allowed a Share of the Profits of Passage-Money, arising from Vessels fitted out by them."[141] These ships would need to be "strong and good and sea-worthy in every Respect," "abundantly supplied with every Thing necessary and comfortable," and "under the Command of Officers distinguished by their Humanity as well as by their nautical Abilities."[142] Painting a picture reminiscent of a modern cruise ship, Wilson sought to assure all parties that every facet of the plan had been thoroughly studied from both the perspective of the investors AND that of the European immigrants seeking to begin a new life in America. However, as he stressed time and again, nothing would come cheap.

Third, once ships docked in American ports, immigrants would "be immediately provided with proper Accommodations on Shore." This provided another opportunity for investors to recoup funds as immigrants would then "be conducted in a cheap and convenient Manner, and by easy Stages, to the Place of their Destination."[143] Unlike the actions of William Cooper in the settlement of what became Otsego County in upstate New York, Wilson had no plans of either living among the immigrants or building the infrastructure upon which immigrants would be transported "in a cheap and convenient

Manner."[144] This infrastructure required stages of "about *ten* Miles" where travelers would find "suitable Accommodations."[145]

Finally, upon reaching their final destination, immigrants would first step upon their new homestead—not seeing a dark and heavily forested plot—and see a "House already built, a Garden already made, an Orchard already planted, a Portion of Land already cleared, and Grain already growing or reaped."[146] For all of this preparation, immigrants would "pay at a reasonable Rate."[147] Further, as the new family settled into their ready-made farmhouse, they could purchase livestock "as near as possible to the Place of their Residence," thus ameliorating the "Trouble and Expence of driving them a long Distance."[148] At every step of their journey, from point of embarkation in Europe, to landing in America, to traveling to their new farm, to opening their new front door, to acquiring livestock, immigrants required commodities and services which were to be provided by investors. Investors who would receive a handsome profit from each transaction along the way.

The prospectus rested upon two very important requirements. The first would be to acquire the necessary lands in America, which would then be mortgaged to execute the plan, and the participation of "European Directors in this Plan should be Men of known and established Character as well as Property—such as will attract and deserve the Confidence of those, who propose to emigrate with their Families and nearest Connexions."[149] The sale of American lands in Europe would provide the hard money necessary to retire the mortgages.

Wilson's plan required endorsements from those who received good treatment at every stage of the journey—from Europe to American farms. For the positive, self-financing, aspect of his plan, Wilson pointed to providing a positive experience and good value for the money as vital. "The same inviting Circumstances, which induce *one*, will induce many to embark in the Enterprise."[150] Letters sent to families and friends still in Europe, providing positive testimonials, would entice others to sign on and join those already in America.

"Confidence must be the Soul of a Plan so enlarged and so interesting as this is."[151] Confidence, especially in the accurate survey and evaluation of land, was indeed the pivot upon which everything rested. Like many land speculators, Wilson had no personal knowledge of the prospective homesteads that he intended to sell. He reassured his audience on the qualities of the land, noting: "By every information we are led to believe, that the Severity of Heat in Summer and of Cold in Winter decreases in Proportion as Progress is made to the Westward. This will become the Case more and more, as the Country shall be more and more improved."[152] Immigrants would begin their journey with little knowledge of the true nature of the lands they purchased. Wilson hoped that the "Enterprise" would sell itself.

He admitted, "This Plan, it is obvious, is uncommonly extensive: But the inference should not be made, that it is *therefore*, extravagant."[153] The audacity and scope of the plan should be seen in a different light. "The very *Extent* may sometimes aid the Execution of a System. With Regard to the present one, this, I believe, will, on Reflexion and Experience, be found to be the Case."[154] Wilson closed the prospectus with an appeal to investors' desire for a sizable return on their investments. There existed plenty of opportunities for profit in the many interrelated facets of the plan. Large numbers of surveyors, hospitality workers and lodgings, shipping, and mercantile positions would need filling for the foreseeable future. Europe's population was ever increasing and thus "the Compensation will be not only handsome, but permanent and increasing." If only the plan could be given a chance, everyone could become rich. Such a plan was beyond the means of any one man to bring to fruition—especially James Wilson in the waning years of the 1790s. There is no evidence that Wilson's plan ever made it to a single prospective European investor.[155]

During the summer of 1794, James Wilson wrote a letter to James Iredell requesting that he take his assignment of riding the Southern circuit for the fall term. Iredell was reluctant to deny the request, but he explained that "there are one or more Causes in which will directly come in question the subject as to Interest upon British Debts during the war, a question upon which I expressly declined giving any opinion."[156] Having been born in England, with family still living there, Iredell was reluctant to become embroiled in the cases. Further, Iredell was also an executor "of two Estates that owe large British Debts," something that he believed required him to absent himself from the Southern circuit for the upcoming term. Besides, he had served on the Southern circuit "5 times in 4 years."[157]

The two men were firm friends, and when they were in Philadelphia during sessions of the Supreme Court, Iredell often dined with Wilson and his family at their home in Philadelphia. After returning from trips home to North Carolina, Iredell would "take a family dinner with Judge Wilson."[158] The hospitality would be reciprocated for Wilson, who often took his young wife along while riding circuit. A letter written on November 24, 1794, hand-delivered to Wilson in Wilmington, expressed: "It would give Mrs. I. and myself great pleasure, if you and Mrs. Wilson could spare the time to see this part of the country before you return. In that case we hope you would be so good as to accept during your stay here an apartment under our humble roof, where, with no elegance, you would meet with a most sincere welcome."[159]

In addition to the invitation to spend time at his home in Edenton, Iredell also broached a delicate topic with Wilson—money. The members of the

Supreme Court continually intrigued to keep from riding the Southern circuit. Iredell, living in North Carolina, was extremely sensitive on the issue, especially as it seemed as though the other justices came to expect him to serve exclusively on the most fatiguing, lengthy, and expansive circuit. He had written a letter to Wilson—who either had not received it before leaving Philadelphia or chose to ignore it given the monetary request—inquiring as to whether Wilson knew if he was intended to receive an additional payment for services rendered while riding the Southern circuit in the Spring of 1794. To compensate whoever took the least desirable circuit, each justice would forward one hundred dollars. Iredell proposed that, if this was the case, he and Wilson would now be even as Wilson was now engaged in the fall session of the circuit.[160]

Turning his attention to Wilson's recent involvement with what became known as the Whiskey Rebellion, Iredell wanted to "warmly congratulate you on the great success of the Western expedition."[161] He was convinced that the action "added strength and dignity to the Government."[162] Iredell observed, "We have many discontented people among us, but I think Federalism is in a state of convalescence."[163] He believed a positive turn in foreign affairs would "keep under the little barkings of ill-humor which are now perpetually assailing our ears."[164] President Washington's dispatch of Chief Justice John Jay to Great Britain as a special representative eventually led to the Jay Treaty, but it was not as beneficial to Federalist political fortunes as Iredell hoped.

At the end of the letter, Iredell included a special mention of the individual who delivered the letter to Wilson, a Mr. Collins. Knowing of Wilson's business interests, especially those of land speculation, Iredell endorsed Collins as someone "who has for a great many years been a very respectable and eminent merchant of this place."[165] He believed Collins could provide Wilson with "a great deal of valuable information as to the state of this country, particularly its commercial concerns, andc."[166] Wilson's attention could always be gained when talk turned to potential business opportunities.

The bond between James Wilson and James Iredell was sorely tested early in 1796 when the post of Chief Justice became vacant. Iredell's supporters were urging President Washington to nominate him to the post, but Iredell, mindful of the sensibilities of his friend, did nothing to support the move. Writing to his wife, Iredell confided, "I have this moment read in a newspaper, that Mr. Ellsworth is nominated our Chief Justice, in consequence of which I think it not unlikely that *Wilson* will resign. But this is only my own conjecture."[167] Three weeks later, in another letter to Hannah, Iredell confessed, "The kind expectations of my friends that I might be appointed Chief Justice were too flattering. Whatever other chance I might have had, there could have been no propriety in passing by Judge Wilson to come to me."[168]

James Wilson expected to become the next Chief Justice, after the departure of John Jay. He was the most senior and experienced judge on the bench, but financial difficulties that prevented President Washington from nominating him for the job in 1789 remained a barrier in 1796. Wilson's pride was hurt by the installation of Oliver Ellsworth, but his chaotic financial situation required him to remain on the bench.

The strain of Wilson's finances soon became apparent to his friend. Early in 1797, Iredell wrote Hannah on February 24 that "the misfortunes of Judge Wilson throw an unfortunate gloom over his house, though I have been there two or three times, and have experienced all their former kindness."[169] Wilson's situation worsened and became the subject of another letter to Hannah on August 11: "All the Judges are here but Wilson who unfortunately is in a manner absconding from his creditors—his Wife with him—the rest of the Family here! What a situation! It is supposed his object is to wait until he can make a more favorable adjustment of his affairs than he could in a state of arrest."[170] James Wilson was a man on the run from his creditors. He was convinced that if he was able to broker one more deal, one more extension of payment his situation would improve, but his hourglass was quickly running out.

Wilson left Philadelphia headed south. One of his creditors caught up with him in New Jersey and until his son Bird was able to secure his release, he remained in jail. After his release, Wilson headed for Iredell's home in Edenton, North Carolina. Rumors abounded he was seriously ill and ill-suited to travel, which in part was true; he was sick over his finances and his health suffered. In truth, he was seeking refuge as far away as possible from his liabilities. Another colleague, William Paterson of New Jersey, wrote his wife that "Judge Wilson is in North Carolina, and in such a bad state of health as to render it unsafe for him to travel."[171] But, two weeks later, a relative of his wife wrote that Mrs. Wilson had left Philadelphia "for North Carolina in quest of her unfortunate Husband who is I am told greatly dejected and afraid to make his appearance here. She was accompanied by Judge Iredell."[172] The two friends hurried to Edenton, unsure of what they would find.

Wilson's friends sought news from one another about him. John Rutledge, Jr. wrote to his uncle Edward Rutledge on February 25 about the situation: "His poor wife gives it out that he is sick in Carolina, and I am often asked if my Letters say whether Wilson is getting better—His family, which is large, are supported by the needle work of his wife and daughters, and the practice of his Son which, I understand, is not extensive."[173] The situation had reached its climax, and members of the Adams administration and members of Congress were discussing the possibility of initiating impeachment proceedings against Wilson. He was on the run and unable to perform the duties to which he had been appointed. His Supreme Court seat was for all intents and purposes vacant.

Samuel Johnston, James Iredell's father-in-law, wrote him on July 28 that "I feel very much for Judge Wilson. I hear that he has been ill, what upon earth will become of him and that unfortunate lady who has attached herself to his fortunes, he discovers no disposition to resign his Office, surely, if his feelings are not rendered altogether callous, by his misfortunes, he will not suffer himself to be disgraced by a conviction on an impeachment."[174] The administrative workings of the federal government would not have to perform the duty of the first judicial impeachment—the end of James Wilson's life saw to that.

The end came quickly. After his wife reached him in Edenton, James Wilson was released from the Chowan County Jail and placed on house arrest in a small rented room above the Horniblow's Tavern, where he contracted malaria.[175] James Iredell's younger brother, Thomas, wrote him an urgent message on August 17 that "I am sorry to say Judge Wilson is by no means well."[176] Iredell rushed to Edenton and arrived mere hours before Wilson died. It is doubtful that James Wilson was even aware of his close friend's arrival as his delirium grasped him tightly. After suffering a stroke, Wilson died on August 21, 1798. He was buried in the cemetery of Samuel Johnston's Hayes Plantation with the Iredells, Johnstons, and his wife Hannah Wilson in attendance.[177] There he would remain until November 20, 1906.

On August 25th, Iredell sat at the desk in his study at home and drafted a letter to Secretary of State Timothy Pickering formally notifying him of Wilson's death. He believed "it is of great consequence this vacancy should be supplied as early as it can be found convenient, as the ensuing Southern Circuit was assigned to Judge Wilson, in which business of the utmost consequence is depending."[178] Iredell offered to do what he could but was unwilling to serve as a substitute for the circuit due to pending cases that created a conflict of interest for himself.

President John Adams received a letter from Pickering on September 13th and replied he was "ready to appoint either General Marshall or Bushrod Washington."[179] The same day that Adams wrote Pickering, U.S. Attorney General Charles Lee of Virginia wrote Pickering of his belief that Wilson's seat on the Court should be filled by a Virginian—Bushrod Washington.[180] Having thought a little more on the matter, Adams sent another letter to Pickering on the 14th where he reinforced his determination to appoint a Virginian: "As Virginia has no Judge at present, she is as much intitled as Pennsylvania to Attention."[181] Pickering approached John Marshall, as instructed, who declined.

In the end, it seems fitting that John Adams settled upon the nomination of Bushrod Washington to fill James Wilson's seat on the Supreme Court. In March 1782, George Washington dispatched a letter and Bushrod himself to James Wilson. "The bearer Mr. Bushrod Washington—a nephew of mine—is sent at his own desire to this City to study the Law," he wrote, and "it would give me much pleasure to see him placed under your care."[182] Washington requested a reply from Wilson stating whether he would accept Bushrod as a student and what the fee would be.

Even though George Washington was the commander-in-chief of America's army and the most notable man in the country, James Wilson felt no inclination to discount his fee. Wilson was known to be among the priciest lawyers with which to work and his fee of one hundred guineas reflected that. Washington did not have the necessary funds on hand and was forced to dispatch a promissory note with his return letter of March 22nd. Washington held Wilson in high esteem as a lawyer and did not quibble with the fee. He wrote, "Permit me to recommend my Nephew to you—not only as a student requiring your instruction—but to your attentions as a friend. His youth and inexperience may require it, and I persuade myself his sensibility and gratitude will make you every return which may be in his power."[183] As a contentious uncle, Washington closed by requesting, "If the funds, which his Father has provided for him, should fail, and he stand in need of money, I will see any sum which can be borrowed for his use repaid with Interest."[184] After spending two years in Philadelphia with Wilson, Bushrod Washington returned to Westmoreland County, Virginia, where he was admitted to the Virginia bar and opened a law practice.[185]

With Congress not due to reconvene until December, John Adams used his power to fill James Wilson's seat with a recess appointment on September 29th. The temporary commission was sent to Bushrod Washington on October 6th, which he received in Richmond ten days later. Washington immediately made plans to depart for the Southern circuit and gaveled court into session in Augusta, Georgia on November 9th.[186] President Adams submitted Washington's nomination to the U.S. Senate on December 19th, where his appointment was confirmed the next day.[187] Bushrod Washington would serve on the bench until November 26, 1829.[188]

After Wilson's burial, the Iredells insisted that Hannah Wilson remain with them until she was ready to return to Philadelphia. James Iredell agreed to write a letter to Hannah's sister Sarah explaining what had happened. At Hannah's urging the two had previously exchanged letters. He wrote that he had arrived a few hours before Wilson's death, but that his wife had "with her usual goodness never quitted him, day or night, until his death was plainly approaching; and then she was parted from him with great difficulty." He reassured Sarah that Hannah was in good health and that they were taking good care of her. He told her that though her husband "had been at times in very bad health, evidently occasioned by distress of mind owing to his pecuniary difficulties, yet the Illness of which he died was of short duration, though very sharp: the greater part of the time he was in a state of delirium, during which he would not suffer many things to be done for him which were advised, and might possibly have restored him."[189]

James Iredell continued to serve his departed friend as he secured an escort for Hannah Wilson's return to Philadelphia—a Mr. Wallace who was a member of the city's bar—and bore the burden of both Wilson's burial expenses and his widow's journey. The two families remained close even after Hannah Wilson's return to Philadelphia. Letters between both Hannahs were exchanged over the years. James Iredell did not long survive his friend James Wilson; he joined him in death, a little over a year later, on October 20, 1799.[190]

James Wilson's tenure on the Supreme Court of the United States was far from distinguished. The appellate work of the Court was light, with the bulk of the Justices' time delegated to riding circuit. Members of the Court sought to elevate their importance by lobbying President Washington and Congress to relieve them of their circuit-riding duties, to no avail.

His one notable opinion, in *Chisolm v. Georgia* (1793), was overturned the next year when Congress proposed and the states approved the Eleventh Amendment to the U.S. Constitution. His impact on the bench was while he was riding circuit. It was while riding the Middle Circuit in the spring of 1791 where Wilson first spent quality time with North Carolina's James Iredell. The two men became very close. The members of the Supreme Court in their capacity as federal circuit judges were the face of the federal government in the formative years of the early republic. If citizens encountered a federal official, especially outside of ports, then they were most likely to see a circuit judge.

James Wilson's tenure on the Supreme Court came to an ignominious end as he neglected the duties of his office and fled from his creditors. He was nearly impeached by the U.S. Senate, but saved them the trouble by expiring of a stroke in Edenton, North Carolina. Wilson was no longer an embarrassment to the Court or himself and quickly faded from public memory.

NOTES

1. Electoral votes were not submitted by the two states which had yet to ratify the Constitution—North Carolina and Rhode Island—and also by New York, whose legislature was unable to submit a vote due to a deadlock over doing so.

2. Untitled, *Federal Gazette* (Philadelphia), February 21, 1789, in Maeva Marcus et al., eds., *The Documentary History of the Supreme Court of the United States, 1789–1800 Volume One, Part Two: Commentaries on Appointments and Proceedings*, (New York: Columbia University Press, 1985), 606. Hereafter referenced as DHSC, Volume One, Part Two. [This squib also appeared in the *Massachusetts Centinel* (Boston) on March 7, 1789.]

3. Untitled, *Federal Gazette* (Philadelphia), March 9, 1789, in DHSC, Volume One, Part Two, 609. [This squib also appeared in papers in Vermont, Georgia, New York, and Massachusetts during that spring.]

4. Ibid., 609.

5. Letter from Frederick Muhlenberg to Benjamin Rush, March 21, 1789, in DHSC, Volume One, Part Two, 610.

6. Untitled, *New York Journal* (New York), April 16, 1789 in DHSC, Volume One, Part Two, 611.

7. Ibid., 611.

8. Ibid., 611.

9. From James Wilson to George Washington, April 21, 1789, in Dorothy Twohig, ed., *The Papers of George Washington*, Presidential Series, vol. 2, *1 April 1789–15 June 1789*, (Charlottesville: University Press of Virginia, 1987), 111–12.

10. Ibid.

11. Ibid.

12. From Benjamin Rush to John Adams, April 22, 1789 in DHSC, Volume One, Part Two, 613.

13. Ibid., 613.

14. Ibid., 613.

15. Ibid., 613.

16. Ibid., 613.

17. Ibid., 614.

18. Ibid., 613.

19. Letter from John Adams to Benjamin Rush, May 17, 1789, in DHSC, Volume One, Part Two, 619.

20. Ibid., 619.

21. Ibid., 619.

22. Ibid., 619.

23. Ibid., 619.

24. Ibid., 619.

25. Letter from Arthur Lee to Francis Lightfoot Lee, May 9, 1789 in DHSC, Volume One, Part Two, 617.

26. Maeva Marcus et al., eds., DHSC, Volume One, Part Two, 617.

27. From George Washington to James Wilson, May 9, 1789, in John C. Fitzpatrick, ed., *The Writings of George Washington from the Original Manuscript Sources, 1745–1799, Volume 30: June 20, 1788–January 21, 1790*, (Washington, D.C.: U.S. Government Printing Office, 1939), 314.

28. Letter from Robert Morris to James Wilson, September 21, 1789 in DHSC, Volume One, Part Two, 664.

29. The Judiciary Act of 1801 created separate circuit judgeships and freed the justices from any circuit-riding duties. However, this was reinstated the next year and remained until 1869.

30. Maeva Marcus, James R. Perry, et al., eds., *The Documentary History of the Supreme Court of the United States, 1789–1800 Volume One, Part One: Appointments and Proceedings*, (New York: Columbia University Press, 1985), MISSING. Hereafter referenced as DHSC, Volume One, Part One.

31. Maeva Marcus et al., eds., DHSC, Volume Two, 7.

32. Ibid., 7.

33. Letter from James Iredell to John Jay, William Cushing, and James Wilson, February 11, 1791 in DHSC, Volume Two, 132. [In the letter, Iredell pointed out that he had not been present at the meeting when the circuits were assigned and that it was unfair that any justice, especially himself, should be permanently assigned to the most difficult circuit.]

34. James Wilson, "Charge to the Grand Jury of the Circuit Court for the District of Pennsylvania," *Pennsylvania Gazette*, April 12, 1790 in DHSC, Volume Two, 33–45.

35. Wilson, "Charge," 33.

36. Ibid., 33.

37. Ibid., 34.

38. Ibid., 35.

39. Ibid., 34.

40. James Wilson, "A Charge Delivered to the Grand Jury in the Circuit Court of the United States, for the District of Virginia, in May 1791," in *Works of James Wilson*, 320–45.

41. Wilson, "A Charge," 320.

42. Ibid., 320.

43. Ibid., 323.

44. Ibid., 322.

45. Maeva Marcus et al., eds., DHSC, Volume Two, 7.

46. Ibid., 122.

47. Ibid., 122.

48. Letter from James Iredell to John Jay, William Cushing, and James Wilson, February 11, 1791 in DHSC, Volume Two, 131–35.

49. Letter from John Jay to James Iredell, February 12, 1791 in DHSC, Volume Two, 135.

50. Ibid., 135.

51. Maeva Marcus et al., eds., DHSC, Volume Two, 154.

52. Letter from James Iredell to Hannah Iredell, April 6, 1791 in DHSC, Volume Two, 155.
53. Maeva Marcus et al., eds., DHSC, Volume Two, 158.
54. Letter from James Iredell to John Hay, April 14, 1791, in DHSC, Volume Two, 159.
55. Maeva Marcus et al., eds., DHSC, Volume Two, 160.
56. Letter from James Iredell to Hannah Iredell, May 6, 1791 in DHSC, Volume Two, 161. [The bracketed word was supplied by the editors as the original word was damaged on the document.]
57. Letter from James Iredell to Hannah Iredell, May 9, 1791 in DHSC, Volume Two, 162.
58. Ibid., 162.
59. Maeva Marcus et al., eds., DHSC, Volume Two, 166.
60. Ibid., 197.
61. Letter from James Iredell to Hannah Iredell, August 17, 1791 in DHSC, Volume Two, 204.
62. Maeva Marcus et al., eds., DHSC, Volume Two, 236–37.
63. Ibid., 293.
64. Letter from James Iredell to Hannah Iredell, September 20, 1792 in DHSC, Volume Two, 295.
65. Ibid., 295.
66. Letter from James Iredell to Hannah Iredell, September 23, 1792 in DHSC, Volume Two, 295.
67. Ibid., 295–96.
68. Maeva Marcus et al., eds., DHSC, Volume Two, 298.
69. Letter from James Iredell to Hannah Iredell, September 25, 1792 in DHSC, Volume Two, 298.
70. Ibid., 298.
71. Ibid., 298.
72. Ibid., 298.
73. Ibid., 298.
74. Letter from James Iredell to Hannah Iredell, September 30, 1792 in DHSC, Volume Two, 301.
75. Letter from James Iredell to Hannah Iredell, October 2, 1792 in DHSC, Volume Two, 303.
76. Letter from James Iredell to Hannah Iredell, October 4, 1792 in DHSC, Volume Two, 304.
77. Letter from James Iredell to Hannah Iredell, October 7, 1792 in DHSC, Volume Two, 305.
78. Maeva Marcus et al., eds., DHSC, Volume Two, 308.
79. Letter from James Iredell to Hannah Iredell, October 21, 1792 in DHSC, Volume Two, 318.
80. Ibid., 318.
81. Ibid., 318.
82. Ibid., 318.

83. Ibid., 318.
84. Letter from James Iredell to Hannah Iredell, October 25, 1792 in DHSC, Volume Two, 320.
85. Ibid., 322.
86. Maeva Marcus et al., eds., DHSC, Volume Two, 320.
87. Letter from James Iredell to Hannah Iredell, October 25, 1792, in DHSC, Volume Two, 322.
88. Letter from James Iredell to Hannah Iredell, October 28, 1792 in DHSC, Volume Two, 326.
89. Ibid., 326.
90. Ibid., 326.
91. Ibid., 326.
92. Letter from James Iredell to Hannah Iredell, November 5, 1792 in DHSC, Volume Two, 330.
93. Ibid., 330.
94. Ibid., 330.
95. Maeva Marcus et al., eds., DHSC, Volume Two, 331.
96. Letter from David Leonard Barnes to Benjamin Bourne, November 8, 1792 in DHSC, Volume Two, 332.
97. Ibid., 332.
98. Letter from James Iredell to Arthur Iredell, November 30, 1792 in DHSC, Volume Two, 335.
99. Letter from James Wilson to William Cushing, May 7, 1793 in DHSC, Volume Two, 372.
100. Maeva Marcus et al., eds., DHSC, Volume Two, 393.
101. Untitled, *Columbian Centinel* (Boston), June 8, 1793, in DHSC, Volume Two, 406.
102. Untitled, *Federal Gazette* (Boston), June 10, 1793, in DHSC, Volume Two, 406. Italics in the original.
103. Ibid., 406. Italics in the original.
104. Letter from Henry Jackson to Henry Knox, June 23, 1793 in DHSC, Volume Two, 410.
105. Letter from James Wilson to Hannah Gray, June 20, 1793 in DHSC, Volume Two, 408.
106. Ibid., 408.
107. Letter from John Quincy Adams to Thomas Boylston Adams, June 23, 1793 in DHSC, Volume Two, 408.
108. Ibid., 409.
109. Ibid., 410.
110. Ibid., 410.
111. Ibid., 410.
112. Ibid., 410.
113. Ibid., 410.
114. Ibid., 410.

115. Letter from Henry Jackson to Henry Knox, June 23, 1793 in DHSC, Volume Two, 410.

116. Letter from John Jay to William Cushing, August 6, 1793 in DHSC, Volume Two, 424.

117. Maeva Marcus et al., eds., DHSC, Volume Two, 425.

118. Untitled, *Boston Gazette* (Boston), September 23, 1793, 3, NewsBank/Readex, *America's Historical Newspapers*. Accessed 12:15pm, June 15, 2016.

119. Page Smith, *James Wilson: Founding Father, 1742–1798*, (Chapel Hill: University of North Carolina Press, 1956), 366.

120. For a more in-depth look at the relationships between the four, see a work of historical fiction written by one of the editors of *The Documentary History of the Supreme Court of the United States*, Natalie Wexler, *A More Obedient Wife: A Novel of the Early Supreme Court*, (Washington, D.C.: Kalorama Press, 2007).

121. There are several clues in the document itself, which is undated, that help place it within this time frame. Wilson refers to the ratification of the U.S. Constitution (1788), the initiation of government under the Constitution (1789), and the admittance of Vermont (1791) and Kentucky (1792) as states. It was first published as a Research Bulletin of the Free Library of Philadelphia in 1946 and was included in the *Collected Works of James Wilson* in 2007. Further, in a letter from Rufus King to Robert Southgate, September 30, 1792, King wrote, "Mr. Wilson having it in view to return [to Philadelphia from riding the Eastern Circuit] in order to go to Europe this fall." in DHSC, Volume Two, 303.

122. James Wilson, "On the Improvement and Settlement of Lands in the United States," in *Collected Works of James Wilson*, Eds. Kermit L. Hall and Mark David Hall, 2 vols., (Indianapolis: Liberty Fund, 2007), 372.

123. Wilson, "On the Improvement . . . ," 372.

124. Letter from Benjamin Rush to John Coakley Lettsom, April 8, 1785, in *Letters of Benjamin Rush Volume I: 1761–1792*, L. H. Butterfield, ed., (Princeton: Princeton University Press, 1951), 350.

125. Wilson, "On the Improvement . . . ," 373.

126. Ibid., 373.

127. Ibid., 373–74.

128. Ibid., 374.

129. Ibid., 374. Italics in the original.

130. Ibid., 374–75. Italics in the original.

131. Ibid., 375.

132. To see the problems faced in a similar setting, see Alan Taylor, *William Cooper's Town: Power and Persuasion on the Frontier of the Early American Republic*, (New York: Alfred A. Knopf, 1996), 90–95, and 102–114.

133. Wilson, "On the Improvement . . . ," 378.

134. Ibid., 381.

135. Ibid., 385.

136. Ibid., 381.

137. Ibid., 378.

138. Ibid., 377.

139. Ibid., 378. Italics in the original.
140. Ibid., 378.
141. Ibid., 378.
142. Ibid., 379.
143. Ibid., 379.
144. Ibid., 379.
145. Ibid., 383.
146. Ibid., 379.
147. Ibid., 379.
148. Ibid., 379.
149. Ibid., 378–79.
150. Ibid., 379.
151. Ibid., 380.
152. Ibid., 381–82.
153. Ibid., 383.
154. Ibid., 383.

155. Ibid., 372. [A handwritten copy was found in the papers of Benjamin Rush at the Library Company of Philadelphia and additional copies were found in the Wilson notebooks at the Free Library of Philadelphia.]

156. Letter from James Iredell to James Wilson, August 5, 1794, in DHSC, Volume Two, 477.

157. Ibid., 478.

158. Letter from James Iredell to Hannah Iredell, August 3, 1794, in Griff J. McRee, ed., *Life and Correspondence of James Iredell, One of the Associate Justices of the Supreme Court of the United States*, 1st pub. 1857, (New York: Peter Smith, 1949), 426–27. [Iredell had just arrived the previous day in Philadelphia.]

159. Letter from James Iredell to James Wilson, November 24, 1794, in DHSC, Volume Two, 498.

160. The plan was also mentioned in a letter from John Blair to William Cushing, June 12, 1795, in Maeva Marcus, James R. Perry, et al., eds., *The Documentary History of the Supreme Court of the United States, 1789–1800 Volume Three: The Justices on Circuit 1795–1800*, (New York: Columbia University Press, 1990), 61.

161. Letter from James Iredell to James Wilson, November 24, 1794, in DHSC, Volume Two, 498. [James Wilson had signed a finding that local resources were unable to deal with the uprising, thus providing a legal foundation for the use of military force by the national government.]

162. Ibid., 498.
163. Ibid., 498.
164. Ibid., 498.
165. Ibid., 498.
166. Ibid., 498.

167. Letter from James Iredell to Hannah Iredell, March 4, 1796, in Griff J. McRee, ed., *Life and Correspondence of James Iredell*, 463.

216   *Chapter Eight*

168. Letter from James Iredell to Hannah Iredell, March 25, 1796 in Griff J. McRee, ed., *Life and Correspondence of James Iredell*, 465. Wilson had seniority on the Court in relation to Iredell.

169. Letter from James Iredell to Hannah Iredell, February 24, 1797 in Griff J. McRee, ed., *Life and Correspondence of James Iredell*, 494.

170. Letter from James Iredell to Hannah Iredell, August 11, 1797 in DHSC, Volume One, Part Two, 856–57.

171. Letter from William Paterson to Euphemia Paterson, February 5, 1798 in DHSC, Volume One, Part Two, 857.

172. Letter from Harrison Gray Otis to Sally Otis, February 18, 1798 in DHSC, Volume One, Part Two, 858.

173. Letter from John Rutledge, Jr. to Edward Rutledge, February 25, 1798 in DHSC, Volume One, Part Two, 858–59.

174. Letter from Samuel Johnston to James Iredell, July 28, 1798 in DHSC, Volume One, Part Two, 859.

175. John G. Zehmer, Jr., *Hayes: The Plantation, Its People, and Their Papers*, (Raleigh: North Carolina Office of Archives and History, 2007), 5.

176. Letter from Thomas Iredell to James Iredell, August 17, 1798 in DHSC, Volume One, Part Two, 860. [Thomas had studied law under James and became an attorney in Edenton.]

177. Zehmer, Jr., *Hayes*, 6.

178. Letter from James Iredell to Timothy Pickering, August 25, 1798 in DHSC, Volume One, Part One, 52.

179. Letter from John Adams to Timothy Pickering, September 13, 1798 in DHSC, Volume One, Part One, 126.

180. Letter from Charles Lee to Timothy Pickering, September 13, 1798 in DHSC, Volume One, Part One, 127.

181. Letter from John Adams to Timothy Pickering, September 14, 1798 in DHSC, Volume One, Part One, 127.

182. Letter from George Washington to James Wilson, March 19, 1782, Founders Online, National Archives (http://founders.archives.gov/documents/Washington/99-01-02-08032 [last update: 2015-03-20]). Accessed: 2:18pm, March 23, 2015.

183. Letter from George Washington to James Wilson, March 22, 1782, in John C. Fitzpatrick, ed., *The Writings of George Washington from the Original Manuscript Sources, 1745–1799 Volume 24: February 18, 1782–August 10, 1782*, (Washington, D.C.: U.S. Government Printing Office, 1939), 88.

184. Ibid., 88.

185. Maeva Marcus et al., eds., DHSC, Volume One, Part One, 124.

186. Ibid., 134.

187. Ibid., 134.

188. Ibid., 126.

189. Letter from James Iredell to Sarah Gray, August 25, 1798 in Griff J. McRee, ed., *Life and Correspondence of James Iredell*, 534.

190. See letters from James Iredell to Hannah Iredell, April 11, 1799, p. 571, and another on May 16, 1799, p. 575, in Griff J. McRee, ed., *Life and Correspondence of James Iredell*.

Chapter Nine

Lingering Effects
The Wilson-Roosevelt Doctrine

James Wilson's death brought to a close the difficult last decade of his life. The July 4th celebrations in 1788 was the highlight of Wilson's public life. The next year, he was nominated to and served on the Supreme Court of the United States, his financial affairs became more and more precarious, and it cost him the position he most desired—Chief Justice. The previous chapter covered this time of his life and closed with his death, on the run from creditors in Edenton, North Carolina. Much like the unmarked grave into which he was placed, James Wilson's legacy was quickly overshadowed as Thomas Jefferson and James Madison's Democratic Republican Party came to prominence and dominated national politics over the coming decades.

Wilson's son, Bird, published a selection of his father's writings, but this did not lead to renewed interest in their author. Nearly a century would pass before academic attention was once again directed at James Wilson. The events documented in chapter 1 brought his contributions before the public again. What happened next in late 1906?

The activity of the James Wilson Memorial Committee extended further than just those individuals affiliated with the committee's work. President Theodore Roosevelt reached back into the early days of the republic and put Wilson's ideas to use in his own theory of national government. The theory first appeared in the *North American Review*, written by Philadelphia lawyer and James Wilson Memorial Committee member Lucien H. Alexander. The article, "James Wilson and the Wilson Doctrine," appeared on November 16, 1906, just prior to the beginning of the removal of Wilson's remains from Edenton, NC and their transportation to Philadelphia for reburial.[1] The article was reprinted as a pamphlet which was donated to libraries such as the American Geographical Society by Alexander himself, and additional copies were donated by Andrew Carnegie to libraries he supported such as the Texas Historical Association and the Kansas Academy of Science.[2]

Alexander declared the significance of the doctrine to the nation as "the harbinger, the hope and the salvation for untrammelled [sic] forward progress in the field of destiny."[3] James Wilson, a man of the eighteenth century, provided Progressives an intellectual touchstone with a Founding Father whose words served their purposes in the twentieth century. Industrial America, in Progressive eyes, needed a stronger, more energetic, and effective national government. For Alexander, "the true value of Wilson is not in the glory of past achievement, but in the fact that his doctrine of constitutional interpretation is big with possibilities for the future, and potent to prove the solvent for every constitutional problem involved in the delicate questions resulting from State individuality and National sovereignty."[4] With Wilson's body prominently reinterred on the grounds of Christ Church, the power of his ideas would now reside in "President Roosevelt who embodies the spirit of the Wilson doctrine."[5]

Alexander tried, unsuccessfully, to provide Roosevelt an opportunity to explicitly link Wilson's ideas to those of the Progressives at the Memorial itself in Christ Church. Roosevelt believed it improper to criticize the members of the United States Supreme Court while they were sitting in President George Washington's former pew. Instead, he praised Wilson at the dedication of the new Capitol Building in Harrisburg the previous month. It was in this setting that Roosevelt both praised Wilson and adopted him as an honorary Progressive.

The Supreme Court was not a friend to Roosevelt's efforts to expand regulation of America's industrial economy. It was with this branch that Alexander concluded the Wilson Doctrine would be most useful: "The Constitution marches on; new conditions and new problems are pressing for solution. Eventually, they must be met by the Supreme Court of the United States. The Wilson doctrine presents the key."[6]

Alexander identified the essence of the doctrine, in which "the Constitution should be so construed that there shall be neither vacancies nor interferences between the limits of State and National jurisdictions; both together should compose but one uniform and comprehensive system of government and laws."[7] Simply put, the power of the federal government would be understood to encompass all areas where states were deficient. This would eliminate grey areas where the reality of industrial America, with corporations conducting business in multiple states, challenged the regulatory reach of government. It would fulfill aspirations of Progressives if justices of the Supreme Court embraced Wilson's doctrine, but this wasn't the only avenue of interpretation open for reevaluation.

Lucien Alexander identified another section of the Constitution—the general welfare clause—that needed to be brought to the forefront of arguments before the Supreme Court. He noted, "In recent years the public have heard much of the interstate commerce clause of the Constitution, but very little of the general welfare clause."[8] Contained within this underutilized gem from the Founders was "the blanket provision of the Constitution, and it is a power which, while undoubtedly an inherent national power, the people of the nation have *specifically delegated* to the Federal Government by the Constitution."[9] Alexander believed Progressives could draw upon the inherent power of the general welfare clause to bring about a more just and fair society. This clause would forever close gaps between state and national jurisdictions.

The general welfare clause would cast off constitutional interpretation from any mooring found among the original intent of the Framers. "It is destined in the centuries yet to come to have a vitally important place in our jurisprudence." The power of the clause is that "it is capable of an infinite adaptation to the evolution of our life as a nation." Consequently, the strength was also a potential weakness: "Yet it is a sharp-edged and dangerous tool, like the surgeon's knife which, in skilled hands, deftly wielded, saves life; but misused, takes it."[10] Alexander had faith that Theodore Roosevelt was the correct surgeon for the operation, but what about those who inhabited the White House after him? The Constitution of the United States would truly become a "living document," but what form of life would it take?

At the close of Alexander's article, he took a moment to peer into the future and describe a trip to Washington, D.C. Near the statue of the Great Chief Justice—John Marshall—there would "loom in bronze within the shadow of the Capitol . . . erected by '*the people of the United States*,' the giant form of Wilson . . . and in his hand a quill and scroll with 'Constitution' inscribed thereon."[11] No statue of Wilson would ever be placed, either in Washington or in his adopted state of Pennsylvania. The only life-size representation of Wilson is found in Signers' Hall at the National Constitution Center. Perhaps this is the best Wilson could have hoped for—the site of his greatest achievements was only a short walk away at Independence Hall.

EDITORIAL REACTION TO THE JAMES WILSON MEMORIAL

Not everyone believed that the time, effort, and praise of James Wilson was well spent or even deserved. A few days after the memorial, on November 24th, a little blurb appeared in the *Omaha Daily Bee* commenting on Alton B. Parker's tribute to Wilson.[12] The tribute "made it evident to all that the distinguished jurist had been dead for more than a generation."[13] On the same day in Kentucky, an editorial noted, "There is something characteristically Philadelphian about the demonstration over the remains of James Wilson, a signer of the Declaration of Independence, 108 years after he died."[14] Wilson's role in the creation of the Constitution again went unmentioned. The editorial concluded: "Exhumation in this instance was perfectly safe, but 108 years from now we trust, another generation will have the charity not to dig after corpses in the present stratum of Pennsylvania political affairs."[15] A week later, again in Kentucky, another editorial declared: "They won't let some of the old fellows rest in peace, even in the grave. At Philadelphia the body of James Wilson, a signer of the declaration of Independence, was exhumed after 108 years and placed in another grave, where, let us hope, it will remain till the final trumpet shall sound."[16] The James Wilson Memorial was dismissed as little more than a political stunt of little consequence—an event not to be repeated.

A newspaper in Columbia, South Carolina, *The State*, published an editorial on December 3, 1906, attacking the gift of a copy of Lucien Alexander's pamphlet to a local library.[17] The attack ranged far and wide, encompassing James Wilson, Andrew Carnegie, and even President Theodore Roosevelt.

The editorial criticized Carnegie for "broadcast" distribution of "many things, some of them valuable and stimulating and uplifting, and some that could be left unsown with profit to mankind."[18] Carnegie is chided in his choice of bestowing his gift, for "as in business he often reaped where he had not sowed, so in philanthropy he sows where neither he nor another man will ever reap."[19] The author wondered what the gift was meant to achieve— "With what far-reaching purpose, in his educational campaign, has he sent forth this little pamphlet in such cohorts?"[20]

In answering his own question, the editorial noted that "Wilson was not only a 'patriot' and a very able, learned, and far-sighted thinker, but he was a Scotsman, as Mr. Carnegie also happens to be."[21] Being from the same region in Scotland, Carnegie, "therefore, gladly welcomes him, takes him under his protecting wing, and at once uses him in his wide-flung missionary labors."[22] In the same way that President Roosevelt utilized Wilson's thinking for his own ends, so does Carnegie in gifting Lucien Alexander's "James Wilson and the Wilson Doctrine" as the doctrine itself "strongly supports the view of centralized power that has been held by certain factions ever since the beginnings of this government, and which Mr. Roosevelt holds—at least at the present moment."[23] The editorial proceeded to explain the attraction for Carnegie and Roosevelt to Wilson's ideas due to his purported advocacy of a concentration of power in a national capital. Carnegie and Roosevelt's relationship "is not limited to the subject of simplified spelling."[24]

Wilson's education, training, and theories of government "were all alien, derived from monarchical institutions and traditions."[25] Therefore, the editorial concluded that James Wilson "is not a typical or a representative American, nor is his doctrine native and to the manner born."[26] In the editor's opinion, the use of Wilson as an exemplar of thinking, both among the Founders and supporters of Roosevelt's policies, was "too preposterous."[27]

The editorial's states' rights bias then assumed center stage. It was alleged, "Wilson would have liked to see all State boundaries swept away, or retained merely as marking the bounds of a power a little more extensive than that of a county."[28] The editorial dismissed his theory by reaching the conclusion, "This country would have become a monarchy, perhaps a despotism, under the masquerade of a democracy."[29] These sentiments echoed Anti-Federalist writings from the ratification debates of 1787–88.

The evidence does not support this characterization of James Wilson's belief of the proper role for states within the new constitution established by the Constitutional Convention of 1787. It was Wilson's proposal for an Electoral College that incorporated the states, not Congress, in the selection of a president, even though he was a solitary voice pushing for a direct election by the people. It was true that he argued for a national government stronger than that provided under the Articles of Confederation, but he never argued for the dissolution of the constituent states.

With the indictment of Wilson's ideas as leading to monarchy or despotism, the editorial explained their attraction for Carnegie and Roosevelt. "It is because of these views that Mr. Roosevelt and the Republicans think so much of James Wilson, and that Mr. Carnegie publishes at his own expense and floods the country with thousands of copies of his 'doctrine' unsimplified by the striking out of a single letter."[30] Further evidence of Wilson's dim view of the states was provided by objection to the selection of members of the United States Senate by state legislatures. "He wished them elected by the people, thus seeking to place in the hands of the people all power and taking it from the States as such."[31] Wilson did argue that a new way of sampling the will of the people, citizens of the United States, could be constructed that cut across state boundaries to represent groupings not captured by congressional districts within states. This was seen as a great crime, in the editorial, as U.S. Senators "would not have represented the States."[32] The principal of state sovereignty "would have been lost in the senate and elsewhere, and the smaller States would soon have forfeited their right to equal representation with the larger States."[33] An editorial written, before the Civil War, in the capital of secessionist South Carolina could not have put it better.

The editorial concluded with a determination that James Wilson was not the complete Founding Father which Roosevelt and Carnegie championed.

For "wherever Wilson agrees with the doctrine of centralized power . . . there Mr. Roosevelt approves and Mr. Carnegie begins his propaganda work."[34] Despite their efforts "it is all futile."[35] It is conceded that a more centralized national government may arise, but "we venture to believe, when democracy in America will broaden down still wider, when liberty will be fuller and the individual shall not wither, but be more and more."[36] In the South Carolina of 1906, who did the editorial have in mind for this "broadening" of American democracy? Certainly not the recently disfranchised black male voters or the women of both races advocating for the right to vote.

Two weeks later, on December 18, another editorial picked up themes from the December 3 installment. Instead of an attack on a gift from Andrew Carnegie, this time the target was a speech given before a gathering of the Pennsylvania Society by U.S. Secretary of State Elihu Root. Root's words were not his own, but according to the editorial those of his master Roosevelt, for "whenever there is a 'doctrine' to be announced, the secretary of state is sent forth to fulminate it."[37] Root's speech was "nothing less than the announcement that State rights, State sovereignty, State lines—the State idea, upon which the government was builded [sic] and by virtue of which it persists and prospers—all are obsolete, antiquated."[38] All of South Carolina's history would be for naught, as "the false ideal of the State, which our forefathers upraised with such pride and maintained with such splendors of eloquence and heroism, must now make way for the ideal of 'nationality.' The State is swallowed up, submerged, within the nation."[39]

Root reminded the states, "There is but one way in which the States can maintain their power and authority under the conditions which are now before us. That way is by an awakening to a realization of their own duties to the country at large."[40] He then proceeded to explain that the people themselves would take the issue in hand and seek changes in the Constitution of the United States "to vest the power where it will be exercised, in the national government."[41]

Having determined Root's words to be the sentiments of President Roosevelt himself, the editorial remarked, "Of course they are not original with the President—so few things are."[42] Instead, "they are as old as this government."[43] Here James Wilson makes another appearance, this time with Alexander Hamilton. "Some of the founders of this union, born in other lands and bringing to this domain of liberty, the taint of tyranny, like James Wilson and Alexander Hamilton, enunciated them to perplex and dash maturer counsels and to serve as a perpetual menace and snare for the republic. There has always been a faction in this country that would destroy freedom by leveling its securest fortress, the inviolate bounds of sovereign States."[44] *The State*'s editorial declared President Theodore Roosevelt, Secretary of State Elihu Root, and the Republican Party to be modern-day Federalists.

There could only be one solution to "[t]his drift toward the breakers of despotism"—the Democratic Party. "The Republican party, long entrenched in power, has been gradually usurping the prerogatives of the State governments, and now purposes to seize absolute power."[45] States would shrink into near insignificance as "their ancient honorable boundaries faded to a traditional and shadowy line upon the maps or in the memory of the people."[46] This is what was destined to happen if "popular indifference or lethargy permits it [the Republican party] to remain in power for another quarter of a century."[47]

To preclude this scenario, the editorial urged "the overthrow of the party of centralization."[48] The danger is real, and "[i]t is amazing that the people of the individual States do not recognize the peril that menaces their local governments."[49] When will the public awake to the dangers posed by centralization? "Perhaps some of them will see the danger when the President attempts to 'rough-ride' over the privileges of their State governments, as he threatens to do."[50] What then? "When they reach this point they will see, also, that the only safeguard of the States of the nation as our fathers conceived and founded it and preserved it, is the Democratic party, the defender of the rights of all the States and of all the people." The same questions linger after this editorial, as the previous one—what people? In the view of the author of the editorial, who constitutes the people—just Southern white men?

THE WILSON DOCTRINE IN ACTION

While James Wilson, Theodore Roosevelt, and the Wilson Doctrine were being attacked in the South, editorials appeared in the North and West expressing doubts as well. A little over a week after the conclusion of the memorial services in Philadelphia, a lengthy editorial appeared in the *New York Daily Tribune*.[51] The subject was the introduction of legislation by Republican Albert J. Beveridge of Indiana in the United States Senate. The bill would "forbid common carriers engaged in interstate commerce to distribute the product of any factory or mine the owner of which has not filed with the Department of Commerce and Labor a statement to the effect that he does not employ, and has not for six months employed, any child under fourteen years of age."[52] The Constitutional means to achieve this legislation would be the interstate commerce clause.

The editorial applauded the *objective* of the bill but expressed deep reservations with the *means* used to achieve it. "No doubt the employment of children of tender years in factories is to be deplored, but it is to be hoped that it will be effectually prevented before long in every state in the Union." But, "the attempt to enforce what is practically a federal police regulation in the states, under cover of regulating interstate commerce, should have grave consideration before it is adopted."[53] This was the heart of the objection by the *Daily Tribune*, that the interstate state commerce clause was to be used "not to regulate commerce, but to improve the educational and social conditions of the people in the various states who, possessing ample power to make their own labor laws, have not seen fit to restrict child labor to the extent thought desirable by philanthropists." This was a typically Progressive attempt to address a national issue—child labor—that had previously been a local matter. The editorial warned that the bill went "beyond anything in the way of centralization that this country has yet known."[54]

Supporting the doctrine of implied powers, they "believe that with the integration of our national life the federal government must broaden its activities to deal with matters, formerly delegated to local regulation, which have come to be of national concern."[55] However, this was not all-embracing support of power to nationalize every concern—such as child labor—which they believed to be a local matter for the respective states to regulate. They did support closing loopholes in the law that left "a legal No-Man's Land between the spheres of federal and state jurisdiction in which abuses can intrench [sic] themselves."[56] The intellectual justification for expanding federal power into an area previously left to the states was found in the Wilson Doctrine.

The editorial highlighted a quote attributed to James Wilson as a summary of the doctrine: "Whenever an object occurs to the direction of which no particular state is competent, the management of it must, of necessity, belong to the United States in congress assembled."[57] This quote had most recently appeared in Lucien Alexander's article the previous month. However, the quote was not from anything that James Wilson had said or written while a member of the Supreme Court of the United States. The passage is found in Wilson's argument on behalf of the Bank of North America's attempt to retain a charter from the state of Pennsylvania in 1785.[58]

The interstate commerce clause had been used to establish meat inspections—a power not previously considered federal. This expansion of federal power was deemed, by the editorial, as beneficial to New York as the city and state "was dependent on food prepared in other states, but had no power to see that the food was safely and decently prepared."[59] Meat inspections and other encroachments on state authority had been "in harmony with Wilson's doctrine" because they protected "the states from evils of external origin."[60] But, in the case of child labor, the editorial could not support it.

The *Daily Tribune* viewed goods produced by child labor as unthreatening to other states and thus outside the sphere of federal regulation. "Each state is able to protect its own children, and it would seem as if it should be left to do so, unless, indeed, we have reached the point of subordinating state governments and having a uniform regulation of domestic life throughout the country."[61] The editorial dismissed arguments citing child labor as an unfair competitive advantage for states relying upon it. Their response was to point to unfair use of "cheap water power" in relation to those states that must rely upon the use of coal for power generation. "Much as the protection of children is to be desired and the labor conditions of some states are to be deplored," they could not support expanding federal police power, which they argued would become a "burden [to] commerce with the necessity of inquiring into the origin of every machine, and book, and yard of cloth, when the conditions of their production should be regulated by the state police power."[62]

On December 3rd, President Roosevelt submitted his Sixth Annual Message to Congress. The message, the modern State of the Union Address, surveyed the state of America and identified areas where the president believed federal power should be expanded. One notable area was the interference of local governments with national treaties—specifically, the discrimination of Japanese immigrants by local authorities in San Francisco.

The address contained a number of instances where Roosevelt argued for expansion of federal power, at the expense of the states. He urged the passage of a constitutional amendment to bring "the whole question of marriage and divorce ... [under] ... the authority of the National Congress."[63] He also sought to expand federal involvement in the area of technical education, but recognized, "Under the Constitution the National Legislature can do but little of direct importance for his welfare save where he [the wageworker] is engaged in work which permits it to act under the interstate commerce clause of the Constitution."[64] It was for this reason that Roosevelt "earnestly hope[d] that both the legislative and judicial branches of the Government will construe this clause of the Constitution in the broadest possible manner."[65] In the last third of his address, Roosevelt turned his attention to foreign affairs, with a focus on the relationship with Japan and the status of Japanese citizens in America.

Roosevelt began his discussion of immigrants by declaring: "Not only must we treat all nations fairly, but we must treat with justice and good will all immigrants who come here under the law."[66] This applied to all immigrants, regardless of their nation of origin. It was a solemn obligation to treat everyone with respect and goodwill, if they were in the country lawfully. "It is the sure mark of a low civilization, a low morality, to abuse or discriminate against or in any way humiliate such stranger who has come here lawfully and who is conducting himself properly."⁶⁷ This remark was aimed at every American citizen, but particularly to "every Government official, whether of the nation or of the several States."⁶⁸

The president then turned to the subject of Japanese immigrants. To frame the discussion, Roosevelt gave a history of American and Japanese relations and the progress that the Japanese had experienced since Commodore Perry's visit in 1853. "The Japanese have won in a single generation the right to stand abreast of the foremost and most enlightened peoples of Europe and America; they have won on their own merits and by their own exertions the right to treatment on a basis of full and frank equality."⁶⁹ The Japanese had earned their way into the elite club of white nations that Roosevelt and others considered the natural leaders among nations. Local officials barred Japanese children from attending public schools. Instead, they were segregated, along with Korean and Chinese immigrant children, into the Oriental Public School.⁷⁰ In a letter to his son, Kermit, Roosevelt wrote he was "horribly bothered about the Japanese business," and, further, "The infernal fools in California, and especially in San Francisco, insult the Japanese recklessly."⁷¹ Roosevelt dispatched Secretary of Commerce Victor H. Metcalf to negotiate with the San Francisco school board over the status of Japanese students. On November 26, 1906, Secretary Metcalf submitted a report to Roosevelt on the matter. An agreement was reached where the students were permitted to attend public schools if Japan stopped issuing passports to laborers to come to the United States.⁷²

Conscious of possible diplomatic repercussions in Japanese-American relations, Roosevelt argued, in his message to Congress, that anti-Japanese sentiment was "sporadic and is limited to a very few places. Nevertheless, it is most discreditable to us as a people, and it may be fraught with the gravest consequences to the nation."⁷³ He reminded Americans they were well treated in Japan and to not do likewise in our own country was a "confession of inferiority in our civilization."⁷⁴ He urged everyone involved, local officials, state officials, and representatives of the federal government, to ensure the fair treatment of Japanese citizens in America.

Roosevelt went further and urged Congress to pass an act establishing procedures for the naturalization of those Japanese who desired to become American citizens. He asked Congress to revisit federal statutes relating to treatment of foreign nationals. "They fail to give to the National Government sufficiently ample power, thru United States courts and by the use of the Army and Navy, to protect aliens in the rights secured to them under solemn treaties which are the law of the land."⁷⁵ His proposal would expand the powers of the Executive to enforce the rights of aliens under treaties.

Two days later, on December 5th, an editorial appeared in *The Minneapolis Journal*, and the subject was again the Wilson Doctrine and President Roosevelt's embrace of it. The editorial warned: "The anti-Japanese feeling in San Francisco seems to presage a recrudescence of the old states rights doctrine, which played so prominent a part in the causation of the civil war."[76] The solution? The Wilson Doctrine.

Echoing sentiments from the *New York Daily Tribune* editorial, *The Minneapolis Journal* acknowledged the necessity for "the growth of our constitution to fit modern needs." The concept of a "living Constitution" could be realized through: "The application of the Wilson doctrine, now much discussed, and designed to bridge the hiatus, wherever one develops, between the powers of the federal government and those of the state governments, is likely to cure many evils."[77]

Two weeks later, a lengthy editorial appeared in the *Albuquerque Evening Citizen*, surveying the state of politics in America since Theodore Roosevelt's speech in Harrisburg, Pennsylvania in October.[78] The editorial pointedly asked: "Are we on the eve of another great congressional debate on the doctrine of states rights?" Though still a territory, New Mexico was on the path to becoming a state in 1912. Like the *Minneapolis* editorial, the topic of most concern was Roosevelt's discussion of San Francisco and Japanese immigrants.

The editorial hinted at a larger objective—a grand master plan—shaping the remainder of Theodore Roosevelt's time in office. "Is the president's message on admitting the Japs to the public schools of San Francisco and the threat to use all the power he has as president to enforce the rights of aliens under treaties, merely a lubrication of the ways preparatory to launching the Wilson doctrine?"[79] If taken to a logical conclusion, the doctrine would "so broadly interpret the powers of the national government that congress may go beyond constitutional limitations and exercise general rights and powers not derived from the particular states but resulting from the union of the whole?"[80] This was indeed the intent of utilizing the Wilson Doctrine—to rely upon an interpretation of the Constitution's inherent powers that would allow federal powers to expand into areas of concern to the nation as a whole. Before addressing the wisdom of such a constitutional interpretation, the editorial asked a pointed question: "Who was James Wilson and what is the Wilson doctrine?"[81]

The discussion began with taking a new look at Roosevelt's October speech in Harrisburg at the dedication of the state's new capitol building. Roosevelt's praise of James Wilson and how his view of the Constitution could benefit certain problems found in twentieth-century industrial America was highlighted. Roosevelt thundered that recent judicial decisions had "left vacancies, left blanks between the limits of possible state jurisdiction and the limits of actual national jurisdiction over the control of the great business corporations. It is the narrow construction of the powers of the national government which in our democracy has proved the chief means of limiting the national power to cut out abuses, and which is now the chief bulwark of those great moneyed interests, which oppose and dread any attempt to place them under efficient governmental control."[82] The editorial argued that Roosevelt was exploiting the Wilson Doctrine to justify expansion of federal powers to "exercise . . . a far more complete control than at present over these great corporations."[83]

Attention was given to Lucien Alexander's article, which appeared in print just prior to the James Wilson Memorial. The author went unmentioned, but Andrew Carnegie's participation in the distribution of the article as a pamphlet and subsequent donation to libraries around the country was prominently noted. A little over a week after the conclusion of the events of the Memorial, Roosevelt's Annual Message appeared. Reading the message through the lens of the Wilson Doctrine, "may throw light also on his reference to the Japanese situation in the message."[84] Roosevelt deplored the situation of Japanese citizens in California, particularly San Francisco, and urged Congress to expand the powers of the president to ensure the protection of rights of foreign nationals.

For the *Albuquerque Evening Citizen*, the "Wilson doctrine means a nation with a big capital N and that's what President Roosevelt stands for."[85] An assertion with which Roosevelt himself would have concurred. "The resurrection and exploitation of the Wilson doctrine at this time plainly means a movement to have the constitution so broadly interpreted that congress will not be confined within constitutional limitations." The result of this expansion of power would be considerable as Congress and the president would "have power to do whatever [they] think is necessary for the general interests of the United States as a whole—all of the people."[86]

The following week saw the publication of another editorial by the *Albuquerque Evening Citizen*, and this time it was a more cutting treatment of Roosevelt's embrace of the Wilson Doctrine. His "admiration for a strong centralized government led him to resuscitate Judge James Wilson, of Pennsylvania. . . . Few in his own state had any recollection of him, and outside of that state he had been forgotten."[87] The editorial questioned Roosevelt's use of Wilson since "he had advocated doctrines that were rejected then, and have since been rejected by the supreme court." The remaining lines consist of a summary of Wilson's speculation in the Yazoo lands and his financial collapse.

On December 18th, President Roosevelt sent a special message to Congress, accompanied by a report on the Japanese schoolchildren situation in San Francisco.[88] He had authorized Secretary Metcalf to relay to the authorities in San Francisco his determination—in the event of violence against Japanese immigrants—that "the entire power of the Federal Government within the limits of the Constitution would be used promptly and vigorously to enforce the observance of our treaty, the supreme law of the land, which treaty guaranteed to Japanese residents everywhere in the Union full and perfect protection for their persons and property; and to this end everything in my power would be done, and all the forces of the United States, both civil and military, which I could lawfully employ, would be employed."[89]

Theodore Roosevelt had not found the works of James Wilson and taken them to heart on his own. He was introduced to him by his Attorney General, William Moody, and convinced of his importance by the work of Lucien Alexander and the events surrounding the James Wilson Memorial. Roosevelt was a shrewd politician and quickly realized that Wilson's interpretation of the Constitution was extremely useful in his own attempts to expand federal power.

THE WILSON DOCTRINE AND THE U.S. SUPREME COURT

Just a few short weeks after the conclusion of the James Wilson Memorial, one of Wilson's most notable supporters and a principal speaker at the event in Christ Church became a member of the United States Supreme Court. William H. Moody first served as Theodore Roosevelt's Secretary of the Navy (1902–1904) and then took over as Attorney General (1904–1906) before being nominated by Roosevelt on December 12, 1906 and confirmed by the U.S. Senate on December 17th as an associate justice.

One of the last cases that Moody worked on, as Attorney General, was *Kansas v. Colorado* (1907).[90] Oral arguments were held from December 17–20, 1906 and a decision was handed down on May 13, 1907. Justice Moody recused himself from participation in the case. However, as Attorney General he helped prepare the petition submitted by the Justice Department on behalf of the United States.

The case was brought before the Supreme Court as an original suit by Kansas against Colorado—and certain corporations operating under Colorado law—who were diverting water from the Arkansas River to irrigate land in Colorado. Kansas alleged it was being harmed by the irrigation, leaving the state with a marked decrease in water available for use in Kansas. The U.S. Department of Justice filed an intervening petition, which claimed a right to control the waters of the Arkansas River to aid in the irrigation of land owned by the United States. The petition did not claim that "the diversion of the waters tended to diminish the navigability of the river." The overarching logic of the case relied upon the Wilson Doctrine.

In a lengthy commentary in the July 6, 1907 edition of *The New York Sun*, the paper took an in-depth look at *Kansas v. Colorado* and how it fit within the larger context of President Roosevelt and his administration's view of the Constitution. The article wanted to know where "[t]he source of the novel and therefore unknown legislative powers the exercise of which President Roosevelt, members of his administration and his political admirers have within the last half dozen years advocated as residing in Congress," came from.[91] After an intensive investigation, *The Sun* concluded, "The mystery has at last been revealed by those who represented the Administration in its intervention in the controversy in the Supreme Court between Kansas and Colorado."[92]

The Roosevelt administration became involved in the case on March 14, 1904, when then Attorney General Philander C. Knox requested the Supreme Court for leave to intervene in the case on behalf of the United States. The Court granted the petition and a week later a brief was filed. It argued that "if the court upheld all the contention of either of the litigants irreparable damage would be caused to the nation, and its policy in respect to its own arid lands would be jeopardized if not entirely defeated."[93] Before oral arguments were heard, Knox resigned in June to accept the appointment of Governor Samuel W. Pennypacker of Pennsylvania to fill the unexpired term of the late Matthew S. Quay in the United States Senate—both men subsequently played prominent roles in the James Wilson Memorial in 1906, with Knox a founding member of the James Wilson Memorial Committee and Pennypacker serving as the master of ceremonies at the Memorial itself in Philadelphia.

Oral arguments in *Kansas v. Colorado* were set for October 9, 1906, but were delayed until December 17, when newly sworn-in Justice William Moody joined the Court. Previously, on September 5th, lawyers at the Justice Department filed a brief of more than 200 printed pages.[94] Special Assistant to the Attorney General A. C. Campbell had barely begun his presentation when Justices began peppering him with questions asking for the relevance of his argument to the case before them. Justice Edward White—who had given the address at the James Wilson Memorial on behalf of the Supreme Court and the federal judiciary—asked if "a hundred acres of public land in a State gave to Congress power to destroy the law of the State."[95] Later, Justice Oliver Wendell Holmes asked: "What rule do you say should be entered?"[96] Mr. Campbell replied "that the rule should be an application of the doctrine of Mr. Justice Wilson, which was, he said, 'that the inherent power of the nation exists, outside of the enumerated powers of the Constitution, in cases where the object is beyond the power of the State and was a power originally exercised, or ordinarily exercised, by sovereign nations.'"[97] Justice White wanted to know where the quote came from. White was correct in challenging the citation as it came from a passage found in Wilson's argument on behalf of the Bank of North America in 1785—before Wilson's work at the Constitutional Convention, the adoption of the Constitution, and his joining the newly established U.S. Supreme Court.[98]

Mr. Campbell closed his time by stating that the "Department of Justice took issue with Colorado over her treatment of the waters and the Federal statutes, but only as to her claim of sovereignty over the waters of the river."[99] In *The Sun*'s opinion, "Whenever throughout the oral arguments by the representatives of the Administration the reserved rights of a State were under consideration they were treated with intolerance."[100] The expansion of federal power that the Justice Department argued for was far beyond that thought wise by the paper.[101]

Supporting the line of argument put forth in the December 15 editorial in the *Albuquerque Evening Citizen*, *The New York Sun*'s July 6, 1907 editorial also placed the arguments used by the Justice Department in *Kansas v. Colorado* in a broader—Roosevelt administration wide—context. The period under examination included Secretary of State Root's December 12th speech, Roosevelt's Annual Message on December 18th, and a letter written to Mrs. Frederick Nathan, President of the New York Consumers' League in New York on January 20, 1907, all occurred after the events of the James Wilson Memorial and before the decision on *Kansas v. Colorado* was handed down in March 1907.[102]

In the letter to Mrs. Nathan, Roosevelt was "particularly interested in your efforts to improve the conditions under which working girls do their work in the great shops; and I have, of course, an interest in your effort to combat the evils of child labor."[103] The owners of the businesses who employed child labor and their political allies were "against interference by the national Government with work which should be done by the State Governments."[104] Roosevelt, on numerous occasions, argued that the regulation of elimination of child labor was a power properly executed by local authorities, but "if the State authorities do not do as they should in matters of such vital importance to the whole nation as this of child labor, then there will be no choice but for the national Government to interfere."[105] He assured Mrs. Nathan that he was "striving to secure either final action, or else a full and thoro investigation of the matter by the authority of Congress at the present time."[106] *The New York Sun* dubbed the letter "startling" as it "threaten[ed] astounding interference by the nation with reserved rights of the States."[107] If this letter represented the true path the Roosevelt administration sought to take during its remaining time in office, the decision of the U.S. Supreme Court in *Kansas v. Colorado* took on even greater significance for the *Sun*'s editors.

The *Sun*'s editors believed that the purpose of the Justice Department's participation in the case was to validate the use of the Wilson Doctrine as a source of "an 'inherent' power imparted by the Constitution beyond the recognized 'delegated' and 'implied' powers."[108] They noted that "the Solicitor-General did not cite any judgment by the Supreme Court upholding the strange doctrine and rule that he wished the court to apply."[109] They criticized the logic used by the Justice Department in promoting the Wilson Doctrine and applauded the opinion handed down by the Court on May 13, 1907.

In a unanimous decision, the Court "quickly squelched and stamped out with absolute certainty the doctrine and the logic by these three sentences: 'But the proposition that there are legislative powers affecting the nation as a whole which belong to, although not expressed in, the grant of powers is in direct conflict with the doctrine that this is a Government of enumerated powers. That this is such a Government clearly appears from the Constitution, independently of the amendments, for otherwise there would be an instrument granting certain specified things made operative to grant other and distinct things. This natural construction of the original body of the Constitution is made absolutely certain by the Tenth Amendment.'"[110] In 1936, the Supreme Court returned to the issue of inherent powers. In the case of *Carter v. Carter Coal Co.* it again rejected the theory that the Federal Government possessed inherent powers in the field of internal affairs.

The Supreme Court, however, exhibited no qualms in applying the Wilson Doctrine in the realm of foreign affairs. In the decision written by Justice George Sutherland in *United States v. Curtiss-Wright Export Corp.* (1936), the Court found, in a 7 to 1 ruling, that "the powers of the federal government in respect of foreign or external affairs and those in respect of domestic or internal affairs [are different] . . . both in respect of their origin and their nature. The broad statement that the federal government can exercise no powers except those specifically enumerated in the Constitution, and such implied powers as are necessary and proper to carry into effect the enumerated powers, is categorically true only in respect of our internal affairs."[111] Sutherland argued that powers over foreign affairs never resided with the individual states, but were transferred from the British Empire to the Continental Congress upon the adoption of the Declaration of Independence. Before joining the Court in September 1922, Sutherland had written approvingly of Wilson's stance on inherent powers.[112] The Wilson Doctrine, as a means to justify the expansion of federal power domestically, retreated from the halls of power in Washington, but found an extended life in textbooks of the era.

THE WILSON DOCTRINE AND THE ACADEMY

Westel W. Willoughby helped establish political science as a distinct discipline and wrote several of the core texts found in early political science courses.[113] *The Constitutional Law of the United States* appeared in 1910 and contained an entry entitled "The Wilson-Roosevelt Doctrine of Construction." Willoughby declared this doctrine of construction to be "radically different" and one that "has never been accepted by the Supreme Court ... and in recent years [was] urged by President Roosevelt."[114] He then presented a concise summary of the doctrine: "That when a subject has been neither expressly excluded from the regulating power of the Federal Government, nor expressly placed within the exclusive control of the States, it may be regulated by Congress if it be, or become, a matter the regulation of which is of general importance to the whole nation, and at the same time a matter over which the States are, in practical fact, unable to exercise the necessary controlling power."[115]

James Wilson's argument from 1785, explaining his theory of inherent powers, is quoted in full and Willoughby noted that "President Roosevelt has expressly adopted the foregoing doctrine as sound."[116] He then quoted extensively from Roosevelt's Harrisburg speech. To put the Wilson-Roosevelt Doctrine in context, Willoughby remarked that "[t]he foregoing doctrine is one quite different from the established doctrine of implied powers as developed by [John] Marshall."[117] The key difference between the two interpretations was that "[t]he Wilson-Roosevelt doctrine ... asserts that a given subject not originally within the sphere of federal control, may, by mere change of circumstances, be brought within the federal field."[118] No other constitutional support—such as the commerce clause, the necessary and proper clause, or any other expressly provided for power—is required for the expansion of federal power.

The Wilson-Roosevelt Doctrine could thus fulfill Progressive desires for a "living Constitution," one that expanded to fit the situation as required. The presumption of constitutionality is flipped to where the power is available, unless it has been expressly denied by the Constitution. The sphere of federal power would continue to expand over time as issues arose where regulation by individual states was deemed insufficient.

Willoughby closed his discussion of the Wilson-Roosevelt Doctrine by examining the case of *Kansas v. Colorado* where the doctrine met the Supreme Court. He quoted heavily from the opinion and left the reader with the conclusion that the doctrine had been soundly rejected by the Court and would have little influence on future constitutional development.[119]

LAST CONTRIBUTION

In the years following the work of the James Wilson Memorial Committee, Burton Alva Konkle continued to collect research on Wilson with the intent of publishing a comprehensive biography. With the construction of a permanent home for the United States Supreme Court in Washington, D.C., scheduled for completion in 1935, Konkle was adamant portraits of both James Wilson and his good friend James Iredell grace the new building. He contacted members of the Iredell family and owners of Wilson portraits to secure copies. In mid-1934, Konkle contacted L. Merle Iredell seeking help. She replied that she did not know of a suitable image but considered the goal as very worthy. Commenting on the two justices for the Iredell family, she wrote, "Some-how [sic] we always associate the names of Wilson and Iredell very closely, as they became such staunch friends."[120] Martha Iredell, writing to Konkle on August 21, 1934, provided the only piece of evidence of the feelings of the Iredell family towards Konkle's successful effort to disinter Wilson. She wrote:

> You are very bold to tell a North Carolinian you engineered the removal of the remains of James Wilson from North Carolina to Philadelphia, aren't you? I am a Virginian but Mother is from N.C. Virginians have a huge time teasing the Carolinians. Of course, Wilson should probably be buried in Philadelphia, but little Edenton, N.C. is proud. I daresay Edenton would have preferred to have had Wilson's remains to simply remain as placed so many years ago. No. I don't think you are bold. I am only jesting. As a matter of fact, I think we have some newspaper clippings regarding Wilson's remains being removed.[121]

Portraits of both justices were eventually presented to the court.

Burton Alva Konkle's years of research on James Wilson were never published as one publisher after another turned the project down due to a concern over likely modest sales. Despite efforts of the James Wilson Memorial Committee, and Konkle in particular, James Wilson's historical reputation failed to attain renewed luster.

NOTES

1. Lucien H. Alexander, "James Wilson and the Wilson Doctrine," *North American Review*, Vol. 183, No. 8 (Nov. 16, 1906), 971–89.

2. _____, "Accessions to the Library: October–December 1906," *Bulletin of the American Geographical Society*, Vol. 39, No. 1 (1907), 47–59; _____, "Affairs of the Association," *The Quarterly of the Texas State Historical Association*,

Vol. 11, No. 1 (Jul. 1907), 77; and _____, "Accessions to the Library," *Transactions of the Kansas Academy of Science* (1903–), Vol. 20 (Dec 1906), 301.
   3. Alexander, "James Wilson and the Wilson Doctrine," 971.
   4. Ibid., 983.
   5. Ibid., 983.
   6. Ibid., 986.
   7. Ibid., 986.
   8. Ibid., 988.
   9. Ibid., 988.
  10. Ibid., 988.
  11. Ibid., 989.
  12. Parker, a Democrat, had lost his bid to become president to Theodore Roosevelt in 1904. He was then serving as president of the American Bar Association.
  13. _____, "Untitled," *Omaha Daily Bee*, (Nov. 24, 1906), 10.
  14. _____, "Untitled," *The Paducah Evening Sun*, (Nov. 24, 1906), 4.
  15. Ibid.
  16. _____, "Untitled," *The Interior Journal*, (Nov. 30, 1906), 2.
  17. _____, "Compliments of Andrew Carnegie." *The State*, (Dec. 3, 1906), 4. The gift was accompanied by a note that said the pamphlet was from Andrew Carnegie, but in reality, it had been sent with money provided for reprints by Carnegie, and the pamphlets were to have been distributed without acknowledging Carnegie's involvement.
  18. Ibid.
  19. Ibid.
  20. Ibid.
  21. Ibid.
  22. Ibid.
  23. Ibid.
  24. Ibid.
  25. Ibid.
  26. Ibid.
  27. Ibid.
  28. Ibid.
  29. Ibid.
  30. Ibid.
  31. Ibid.
  32. Ibid.
  33. Ibid.
  34. Ibid.
  35. Ibid.
  36. Ibid.
  37. _____, "The Drift Toward Centralization" *The State*, (Dec. 18, 1906), 4.
  38. Ibid.
  39. Ibid.
  40. Ibid.

41. Ibid.
42. Ibid.
43. Ibid.
44. Ibid.
45. Ibid.
46. Ibid.
47. Ibid.
48. Ibid.
49. Ibid.
50. Ibid.
51. _____, "National Child Labor Legislation," *New York Daily Tribune*, (Dec. 2, 1906), 8.
52. Ibid.
53. Ibid.
54. Ibid.
55. Ibid.
56. Ibid.
57. Ibid.
58. James Wilson, "Considerations on the Bank of North America," in *Collected Works of James Wilson*, Vol. I., Eds. Kermit L. Hall and Mark David Hall, 2 vols., (Indianapolis: Liberty Fund, 2007), 66.
59. "National Child Labor Legislation," 8.
60. Ibid.
61. Ibid.
62. Ibid.
63. Theodore Roosevelt, "Sixth Annual Message to Congress," (Dec. 3, 1906), online by Gerhard Peters and John T. Wooley, *The American Presidency Project*, http://www.presidency.ucsb.edu/ws/?pid=29547. Accessed 1:45pm, March 8, 2016.
64. Ibid.
65. Ibid.
66. Ibid.
67. Ibid.
68. Ibid.
69. Ibid.
70. H. W. Brands, *T.R.: The Last Romantic*, (New York: Basic Books, 1997), 579.
71. Ibid, 580.
72. For further information see: H. W. Brands, *T.R.: The Last Romantic*, (New York: Basic Books, 1997), 578–83.
73. Ibid.
74. Ibid.
75. Ibid.
76. _____, "The Constitutional Blank Wall," *The Minneapolis Journal*, (Dec. 5, 1906), 14.
77. Ibid.

78. _____, "President's Demand for Greater National Power," *Albuquerque Evening Citizen*, (Dec. 15, 1906), 4.
79. Ibid.
80. Ibid.
81. Ibid.
82. Ibid.
83. Ibid.
84. Ibid.
85. Ibid.
86. Ibid.
87. _____, "Recalling Some History," *Albuquerque Evening Citizen*, (Dec. 22, 1906), 4.
88. Theodore Roosevelt, "Special Message," (Dec. 18, 1906), online by Gerhard Peters and John T. Wooley, *The American Presidency Project*, http://www.presidency.ucsb.edu/ws/?pid=69683. Accessed 10:09pm, March 12, 2016.
89. Ibid.
90. 206 U.S. 46 *Kansas v. Colorado* (1907), HeinOnline, (Accessed 3:45pm, March 9, 2015).
91. _____, "A Great Opinion," *The Sun*, (July 6, 1907), 6.
92. Ibid.
93. Ibid.
94. Ibid.
95. Ibid.
96. Ibid.
97. Ibid.
98. James Wilson, "Considerations on the Bank of North America," in *Collected Works of James Wilson*, Vol. I., Eds. Kermit L. Hall and Mark David Hall, 2 vols., (Indianapolis: Liberty Fund, 2007), 66.
99. _____, "A Great Opinion," *The Sun*, (July 6, 1907), 6.
100. Ibid.
101. In a note on the presentation by the Justice Department, *The Sun* wrote: "A note in the printed publication of a stenographic report of all the oral arguments that was filed on February 7, 1907, seventeen days after the conclusion of those arguments, mentions that as the Solicitor-General had filed 'a printed abstract' of his oral argument a shorthand report of it is omitted. Therefore the public cannot know precisely what he uttered, nor the questions put by members of the court and his replies."
102. Letter from Theodore Roosevelt to Mrs. Frederick Nathan, January 20, 1907, in *The Papers of Theodore Roosevelt*.
103. Ibid.
104. Ibid.
105. Ibid.
106. Ibid.
107. _____, "A Great Opinion," *The Sun*, (July 6, 1907), 6.
108. Ibid.
109. Ibid.

110. Ibid.

111. 299 U.S. 304 *United States v. Curtiss-Wright Export Corp.* (1936), 315–16.

112. See George Sutherland, *The External and Internal Powers of the National Government*, 61st Congress, 2nd Sess., 1910, Senate Doc. No. 417, 1; and George Sutherland, *Constitutional Power and World Affairs* (New York, 1919), especially chapters 1 and 6.

113. Michael C. Tolley, "Willoughby, Westel Woodbury," *American National Biography Online*, Feb. 2000, http://www.anb.org/articles/14/14-00708.html. Accessed 4:29pm, March 14, 2015. Willoughby received his Ph.D. in 1891 from Johns Hopkins University. At Johns Hopkins in 1903, he created the graduate department of political science. In the same year, he also played a leading role in founding the American Political Science Association (APSA) and is credited with helping to establish political science as an independent field of study. He served as APSA president in 1913 and edited its journal *American Political Science Review* during its first ten years of publication (1906–1916).

114. Westel Woodbury Willoughby, *The Constitutional Law of the United States*, (New York: Baker, Voorhis and Company), 1910, 47.

115. Ibid., 47.

116. Ibid, 47–48.

117. Ibid, 49.

118. Ibid, 49.

119. The 1929 edition of the book contained the section on the Wilson-Roosevelt doctrine unchanged. The only difference was that the section was now entitled: "The James Wilson-Roosevelt Doctrine of Construction." This more clearly marked the correct Wilson, after the presidency of Woodrow Wilson. In 1912, Willoughby published *Principles of the Constitutional Law of the United States*, another textbook, which contained a section on the Wilson-Roosevelt doctrine virtually identical to that found in *The Constitutional Law of the United States*.

120. Letter from L. Merle Iredell to Burton Alva Konkle, August 16, 1934, in the Burton Alva Konkle Papers, #2428-z, Southern Historical Collection, The Wilson Library, University of North Carolina at Chapel Hill.

121. Letter from Martha Iredell to Burton Alva Konkle, August 21, 1934, in the Burton Alva Konkle Papers, #2428-z, Southern Historical Collection, The Wilson Library, University of North Carolina at Chapel Hill.

Concluding Thoughts
James Wilson's Contribution

With the 200th anniversary of the Constitutional Convention in 1987, James Wilson began appearing more prominently in narratives of the Convention's work. This can be attributed to the work of the massive *Documentary History of the Ratification of the Constitution*, cited by Pauline Maier as the most valuable resource on the subject. Wilson's ideas, first adopted by turn-of-the-century Progressives, received a second look and appear very modern indeed.

In 2007, Wilson benefitted from the republication of a collection of his writings by Liberty Fund.[1] The *Collected Works of James Wilson* republished his law lectures at the University of Pennsylvania and a number of his other writings. The *Collected Works* superseded the 1967 edition of Wilson's writings edited by Robert McCloskey.[2] The heart of historical writing is access to sources and as Wilson's work has become available, his relative standing among the Founders has risen.

James Wilson achieved many of his goals in life but failed miserably at others. Americans have been accused of mythologizing many of the individuals responsible for the establishment of the United States and adoption of her Constitution. Wilson wanted the respect of his peers, which he achieved through his legal practice; work in the Second Continental and Confederation Congresses federal Constitutional Convention, and Pennsylvania Ratification Convention; and participation in the framing of a new state constitution for Pennsylvania in 1790. However, the national acclaim garnered by figures like James Madison, Thomas Jefferson, Alexander Hamilton, Benjamin Franklin, and George Washington eluded him.

Wilson worked best in venues similar to courtrooms, places with rules, order, and a place where his blazing intellect and broad Scottish Enlightenment learning could be utilized to their fullest. He never truly suppressed the ambitions of that bright Scottish student who yearned for more than a life devoted to the church, which his parents fervently prayed for. His future lay across the Atlantic in the British colonies of North America—playing a substantial role in guiding the newly independent United States to nationhood.

Two years stand out prominently in his life—1768 and 1787. Having finished his legal training with John Dickinson and embarking on a legal career in Reading, Pennsylvania, Wilson and his best friend, William White, wrote *The Visitant*, a commentary on colonial life in Pennsylvania. Like many men throughout the ages, Wilson and White were anxious about their future careers in the law and church, but also worrying about how they were to relate to the opposite sex in the search for a wife. Wilson's horizon in the first half of the year was limited to domestic life and that of the city, but the second half of the year was dominated by thoughts of Pennsylvania and British America's place within the Empire.

James Wilson used his legal training to research and prepare a brief on his findings. *Considerations on the Nature and Extent of the Legislative Authority of the British Parliament* surveyed arguments of authors from the previous three years, on both sides of the Atlantic, covering the dispute between the North American colonies and Great Britain over the passage of the Stamp Act. Wilson was surprised at his conclusion that the British Parliament had no authority whatsoever over the colonies. In 1768 this was truly radical, but he delayed publication after friends and colleagues urged him to wait until the public mood was ripe. Wilson did as they advised, waiting until 1774 to publish, making him one among many putting forth similar arguments. Anxiety over potential harm to his young legal practice harmed the historical reputation of his work.

As the events of what became the American Revolution unfolded, James Wilson became an active participant through election first to provincial committees in Pennsylvania and then to the Second Continental Congress and its successor the Confederation Congress. Even at this date, he held back from full-throated support for American independence. Not until the eve of the final vote on July 2, 1776, did James Wilson defy his friend and mentor John Dickinson and switch his support in favor of the Declaration of Independence. With an eye to his potential future political career, Wilson refused to defy the instructions given to the Pennsylvania delegation—written by Dickinson himself!—until the Pennsylvania legislature rescinded those instructions to permit the delegation to support independence. In many ways James Wilson was a conservative politician, but a revolutionary political thinker.

The other momentous year of Wilson's life was 1787. The Constitutional Convention was an environment in which he thrived. His working relationship with James Madison was established before the Convention convened in a series of dinners between the Pennsylvania and Virginia delegations. The men agreed on much, but Wilson's thinking on the executive branch was far more developed than that of Madison. The Convention adopted much of the Virginia Plan in early debates, until more small state delegations appeared who looked to John Dickinson for leadership.

James Wilson was unsuccessful in shaping a Constitution that he could have supported in every detail, but like any good politician, he secured what he could and for that he deserves our thanks and remembrance. James Wilson's vision came to be realized more closely than even that of Madison. As much as we live in a world envisioned by James Madison, we very much live in the world that James Wilson anticipated.

When colleagues approached James Wilson to prepare a defense of the Constitution for the assembled crowd gathered in the Pennsylvania State House Yard on October 6, 1787, he didn't fail to grasp the opportunity to explain the work of the Constitutional Convention. Wilson was a very direct and confident man. He was a ball of energy—someone who had his hand in dozens of financial, political, and personal ventures at the same time. The time that he spent on his education growing up in Scotland, studying for the bar with John Dickinson after his arrival in America in 1765, and the decade that he spent practicing law before the American Revolution, all prepared him for his historic contribution in the creation and ratification of the Constitution of the United States.

For good or ill, James Wilson become the visible face of the Federalist effort to secure ratification of the Constitution. He willingly stepped forth on October 6, 1787 and defended the work that he and his fellow delegates had given to craft a new blueprint of government, on which the public was now asked to pass judgment. Wilson's speech spread around the country—given only a few short steps from where the convention had sat—but few of his fellow Federalists rose to his defense or did so under their own names. James Wilson was the figure Anti-Federalists relished to criticize.

Wilson's "State House Yard Speech" and the response from Anti-Federalist writers was a wonderful virtual debate, for all to read, over the nation's political future. While the debate raged in the press, Wilson was busy leading pro-ratification forces at the Pennsylvania Ratification Convention in Philadelphia. The work of the Pennsylvania Ratification Convention received wide coverage in the press, but it was the "State House Yard Speech" that effectively spread Wilson's views on the Constitution.

Federalists, including Benjamin Franklin, desired to have the honor of being the first state to ratify the Constitution and secure Philadelphia as the new capital of the United States. Alas, neither of these objectives were achieved. Pennsylvania was indeed the first large state to ratify, but only the third overall. Philadelphia did serve as the temporary capital for a decade while Washington, D.C. was under construction.

James Wilson helped create the Constitution and like many of his colleagues at the Convention, desired to hold a prominent place in the new federal government. He and his friends let it be known that he sought the post of Chief Justice of the new U.S. Supreme Court. Benjamin Rush lobbied Vice President John Adams, but it was Wilson himself who took the unprecedented step of dispatching a letter to President George Washington offering to accept the post. Washington's reply was extremely frosty, due in part to Wilson's well-known financial difficulties, and his nomination as an associate justice was subsequently made and confirmed.

Wilson's tenure as a U.S. Supreme Court justice was undistinguished, given a man of his talents. The newness of the Constitution, the scarcity of notable cases, the debilitating experience of circuit riding, and his increasingly tenuous financial situation tainted his time on the bench. However, even here, Wilson sought to strengthen the institutions of the new Constitution by educating grand juries while riding circuit.

We must situate the man and his ideas within his own time and on his own terms. If there is one overarching lesson to be taken from the events surrounding the James Wilson Memorial Committee, it is this: James Wilson and his ideas are from a time and place in eighteenth-century America. He should have never been used by Progressives as an advocate for policies which did not exist when he was alive. James Wilson was a man with a multi-faceted personality and a penetrating intellect. He sought to build the best world that he could imagine, but the modern world is more alien than he could have foreseen.

NOTES

1. Kermit L. Hall and Mark David Hall, eds., *Collected Works of James Wilson*. 2 vols. Indianapolis: Liberty Fund, 2007.

2. Robert G. McCloskey, ed., *The Works of James Wilson*. 2 vols. Cambridge: Harvard University Press, 1967.

References

206 U.S. 46 *Kansas v. Colorado* (1907). HeinOnline. Accessed 3:45pm, March 9, 2015.

298 U.S. 238 *Carter v. Carter Coal Co.* (1936).

299 U.S. 304 *United States v. Curtiss-Wright Export Corp.* (1936).

———, "President's Demand for Greater National Power." *Albuquerque Evening Citizen* (Albuquerque, NM), Dec. 15, 1906, pp. 4.

———, "Recalling Some History." *Albuquerque Evening Citizen* (Albuquerque, NM), Dec. 22, 1906, pp. 4.

———, "After Hundred Years." *The Bamberg Herald* (Bamberg, SC), Nov. 29, 1906, pp. 3.

———, "Funeral of a Patriot" *Barton County Democrat* (Great Bend, KS), Nov. 23, 1906, pp. 5.

———, "Reinterred at Philadelphia." *The Bemidji Daily Pioneer* (Bemidji, MN), Nov. 23, 1906, pp. 4.

———, "A Virginia Tribute to Judge James Wilson." *Bisbee Daily Review* (Bisbee, AZ), Dec. 05, 1906, p. 5.

———, "Reinterred at Philadelphia." *Bismarck Daily Tribune* (Bismarck, ND), Nov. 23, 1906, pp. 1.

———, "Beside His Beloved." *Bryan Morning Eagle* (Bryan, TX), Nov. 24, 1906, pp. 1.

———, "Body of Signer of Declaration is Removed." *The Butler Weekly Times* (Butler, MO), Nov. 29, 1906, pp. 3.

———, "Wilson's Body Exhumed." *The Caucasian* (Clinton, NC), Nov. 29, 1906, pp. 1.

———, "To Rest Near Independence Hall." *The Citizen* (Berea, KY), Nov. 22, 1906, pp. 6.

———, "Untitled." *The Clayton Citizen* (Clayton, NM), Nov. 30, 1906, pp. 7.

———, "Dug Up an Old Timer." *Daily Capital Journal* (Salem, OR), Nov. 20, 1906, pp. 1.

———, "After Many Years." *Daily Capital Journal* (Salem, OR), Nov. 22, 1906, pp. 1.
———, "Patriot's Body Reburied." *Daily Press* (Newport News, VA), Nov. 23, 1906, pp. 1.
———, "Marking Graves of Signers of Declaration of Independence." *Evening Star* (Washington, D.C.), Nov. 18, 1906, pp. 9.
———, "Wilson Disinterred." *Evening Star* (Washington, D.C.), Nov. 20, 1906, pp. 1.
———, "Wilson Lay in State." *Evening Star* (Washington, D.C.), Nov. 22, 1906, pp. 9.
———, "Justice to Wilson." *Evening Star* (Washington, D.C.), Dec. 15, 1906, pp. 5.
———, "Remembering a Patriot." *The Evening Statesman* (Walla Walla, WA), Nov. 27, 1906, pp. 4.
———, "Body Removed." *The Evening Times* (Grand Forks, ND), Nov. 23, 1906, pp. 1.
———, "Pennsylvania Honors James Wilson." *The Forest Republican* (Tionesta, PA), Nov. 28, 1906, p. 1.
———, "Patriot's Body Re-Interred." *Free Press* (Hays, KS), Dec. 01, 1906, pp. 3.
———, "Body of Wilson Exhumed." *The French Broad Hustler* (Hendersonville, NC), Nov. 29, 1906, pp. 2.
———, "Untitled." *The French Broad Hustler* (Hendersonville, NC), Nov. 29, 1906, pp. 3.
———, "(Editorial Squib), untitled." *The Interior Journal* (Stanford, KY), Nov. 30, 1906, pp. 2.
———, "Untitled." *Lexington Gazette* (Lexington, VA), Nov. 28, 1906, pp. 1.
———, "Reinter Body Buried More than a Century." *Los Angeles Herald*, Nov. 23, 1906, pp. 12.
———, "Disinter Patriot's Remains." *The McCook Tribune* (McCook, NE), Nov. 23, 1906, pp. 2.
———, "A Patriot's Body Re-Interred." *Meade County News* (Meade, KS), Nov. 29, 1906, pp. 3.
———, "James Wilson is Honored." *The Minneapolis Journal*, Nov. 22, 1906, pp. 8.
———, "A Great Man Mislaid." *The Minneapolis Journal*, Nov. 23, 1906, pp. 20.
———, "The Constitutional Blank Wall." *The Minneapolis Journal*, Dec. 5, 1906, pp. 14.
———, "Graves of the Signers." *New York Daily Tribune*, Nov. 18, 1906, pp. 2.
———, "James Wilson Honored." *New York Daily Tribune*, Nov. 23, 1906, pp. 1 and 7.
———, "Mr. Bryce's Tribute to Wilson." *New York Daily Tribune*, Nov. 26, 1906, pp. 7.
———, "National Child Labor Legislation." *New York Daily Tribune*, Dec. 2, 1906, pp. 8.
———, "To Rest Near Independence Hall." *The News-Herald* (Hillsboro, OH), Nov. 29, 1906, pp. 2.

———, "Revolutionary Patriot's Reburial." *The Ocala Evening Star* (Ocala, FL), Nov. 24, 1906, pp. 1.
———, "Wilson's Body is at Rest." *Omaha Daily Bee* (Omaha, NE), Nov. 23, 1906, pp. 1.
———, "(Editorial Squib), untitled." *Omaha Daily Bee* (Omaha, NE), Nov. 24, 1906, pp. 10.
———, "High Honor Comes Long After Death." *Omaha Daily Bee* (Omaha, NE), Dec. 2, 1906, pp. 10.
———, "After 108 Years." *The Paducah Evening Sun* (Paducah, KY), Nov. 23, 1906, pp. 1.
———, "(Editorial Squib), untitled." *The Paducah Evening Sun* (Paducah, KY), Nov. 24, 1906, pp. 4.
———, "James Wilson." *Palestine Daily Herald* (Palestine, TX), Nov. 22, 1906, pp. 1.
———, "Pyrotechnic Display the Crowning Feature." *Patriot* (Harrisburg, PA), Oct. 4, 1906, pp. 1.
———, "The Program." *Patriot* (Harrisburg, PA), Oct. 4, 1906, pp. 1.
———, "Thousands Flock to The Dedication." *Patriot* (Harrisburg, PA), Oct. 4, 1906, pp. 1.
———, "Ovation tor President Throughout His Visit." *Patriot* (Harrisburg, PA), Oct. 5, 1906, pp. 1–2.
———, "Great Figure of Revolution." *The Pensacola Journal* (Pensacola, FL), Nov. 23, 1906, pp. 1.
———, "Untitled." *Perrysburg Journal* (Perrysburg OH), Nov. 30, 1906, pp. 2.
———, "Roosevelt, Rain-Soaked and Exposed to Storm, Gets Splendid Ovation at Capitol's Dedication." *The Philadelphia Inquirer* (Philadelphia, PA), Oct. 5, 1906, pp. 1–3.
———, "Never Such a Tie-Up, Mariners Declare." *Public Ledger* (Philadelphia, PA), Nov. 22, 1906, pp. 9.
———, "From Edenton Grave to Lie Beneath Sod of his Native State." *Raleigh Evening Times* (Raleigh, NC), Nov. 20, 1906, pp. 1.
———, "A Patriot's Body Re-Interred." *The Rich Hill Tribune* (Rich Hill, MO), Nov. 29, 1906, pp. 2.
———, "Patriot's Body is Taken from Earth." *Rock Island Argus* (Rock Island, IL), Nov. 20, 1906, pp. 1.
———, "Body in State at Philadelphia." *Rock Island Argus* (Rock Island, IL), Nov. 22, 1906, pp. 1.
———, "Rests Beside His Wife." *The Salt Lake Herald* (Salt Lake City, UT), Nov. 23, 1906, pp. 8.
———, "Patriot's Remains are Reinterred." *The San Francisco Call*, Nov. 23, 1906, pp. 5.
———,"Honors to the Dead." *The Semi-Weekly Messenger* (Wilmington, NC), Oct. 30, 1906, pp. 1.
———,"To Remove Body of Jas. Wilson." *The Semi-Weekly Messenger* (Wilmington, NC), Nov. 23, 1906, pp. 7.

———,"Remains of Wilson." *The Semi-Weekly Messenger* (Wilmington, NC), Nov. 27, 1906, pp. 2.
———,"Tributes to Dead." *The Semi-Weekly Messenger* (Wilmington, NC), Nov. 27, 1906, pp. 7.
———, "Untitled." *The Spanish American* (Roy, NM), Dec. 1, 1906, pp. 7.
———, "Honor American Immortal." *The Spokane Press*, Nov. 20, 1906, pp. 1.
———, "Debt of Honor Paid." *The Spokane Press*, Nov. 22, 1906, pp. 4.
———, "Compliments of Andrew Carnegie." *The State*, Dec. 3, 1906, pp. 4.
———, "The Drift Toward Centralization." *The State*, Dec. 18, 1906, pp. 4.
———, "Revival of State Rights." *The State*, Feb. 27, 1907, pp. 4.
———, "Bringing Patriot's Body Home." *The Sun* (New York, NY), Nov. 21, 1906, pp. 10.
———, "A Great Opinion." *The Sun* (New York, NY), Jul. 6, 1907, pp. 6.
———, "Untitled." *The Taney County Republican* (Forsyth, MO), Nov. 29, 1906, pp. 4.
———, "Bryce Praises James Wilson." *The Times Dispatch* (Richmond, VA), Nov. 26, 1906, pp. 1.
———, "Wilson's Body Disinterred." *Valentine Democrat* (Valentine, NE), Dec. 6, 1906, p. 3.
———, "James Wilson's Remains Pass Through Norfolk Enroute to Philadelphia." *Virginian Pilot* (Norfolk, VA), November 21, 1906, p. 4.
———, "Signer's Ashes Removed." *The Washington Herald* (Washington, D.C.), Nov. 21, 1906, pp. 3.
———, "Hero is Reinterred." *The Washington Herald* (Washington, D.C.), Nov. 23, 1906, pp. 11.
———, "Honor to a Forgotten Patriot." *The Washington Post* (1877–1922), Mar. 31, 1906, pp. 6.
———, "Tardy Honors for Wilson." *The Washington Post* (1877–1922), Nov. 20, 1906, pp. 5.
———, "Cenotaph to Wilson." *The Washington Post* (1877–1922), Nov. 21, 1906, pp. 4.
———, "Tributes to Wilson." *The Washington Post* (1877–1922), Nov. 23, 1906, pp. 4.
———, "Moody's Panegyric on James Wilson at Philadelphia." *The Washington Times* (Washington, D.C.), Nov. 22, 1906, pp. 8.
———, "Library Notes." *Willmar Tribune* (Willmar, MN), Dec. 12, 1906, pp. 1.
———, "To Remove Body of Jas. Wilson." *The Wilmington Messenger* (Wilmington, NC), Nov. 23, 1906, pp. 7.
———, "Remains of Wilson." *The Wilmington Messenger* (Wilmington, NC), Nov. 27, 1906, pp. 2.
———, "Tributes to Dead." *The Wilmington Messenger* (Wilmington, NC), Nov. 27, 1906, pp. 7.
St. Andrew's Society of Philadelphia. *An Historical Catalogue of The St. Andrew's Society of Philadelphia: With Biographical Sketches of Deceased Members 1749–1907*. Printed for the Society, 1907.

---. "Accessions to the Library: October-December 1906." *Bulletin of the American Geographical Society*, Vol. 39, No. 1 (1907), pp. 47–59.

---. "Affairs of the Association." *The Quarterly of the Texas State Historical Association*, Vol. 11, No. 1 (Jul. 1907), pp. 76–83.

---. "The Nation Supreme." *The Congregationalist and Christian World* (1901–1906), Vol. 91, No. 41 (Oct. 13, 1906), p. 463.

---. "Accessions to the Library." *Transactions of the Kansas Academy of Science* (1903–), Vol. 20 (Dec 1906), pp. 295–310.

"A Plain Dealing Whig." "To JAMES WILSON, Esquire, Attorney at Law." Philadelphia: *The Pennsylvania Packet*, October 10, 1780.

Ackerman, Bruce. *The Failure of the Founding Fathers: Jefferson, Marshall, and the Rise of Presidential Democracy*. Cambridge: Harvard University Press, 2005.

Alexander, John K. *The Selling of the Constitutional Convention: A History of News Coverage*. Madison, WI: Madison House, 1990.

Alexander, Lucien H. "In re JAMES WILSON MEMORANDA PREPARED FROM VARIOUS SOURCES FOR ATTORNEY-GENERAL MOODY." July 14, 1906, in the *Lucien H. Alexander Papers*, Historical Society of Pennsylvania. Unpublished.

---. "James Wilson, Patriot, and the Wilson Doctrine." *North American Review*, Vol. 183, No. 8 (Nov. 16, 1906), pp. 971–89.

---. "The James Wilson Memorial." *The Albany Law Journal: A Weekly Record of the Law and the Lawyers* (1870–1908), (Dec. 1906), pp. 380–2.

---. *James Wilson, Nation-Builder*. (Reprint of articles appearing in *The Green Bag* from January, February, March, and May 1907, vol. XIX, Nos. 1, 2, 3, and 5.) Boston: The Boston Book Co., 1907.

---. "Memorandum *in re Corpus Juris*." *The Green Bag*, Vol. 22, No. 2 (Feb. 1910), pp. 59–90.

Allan, David. *Scotland in the Eighteenth Century: Union and Enlightenment*. London: Pearson Education, 2002.

"An Address of the Subscribers Members of the late House of Representatives of the Commonwealth of Pennsylvania to their Constituents," October 2, 1787, in Merrill Jensen, ed., *The Documentary History of the Ratification of the Constitution, Vol. II Ratification of the Constitution by the States: Pennsylvania*. (Madison: State Historical Society of Wisconsin, 1976), 112–17.

Andrew Carnegie Papers, LOC.

Bailyn, Bernard, ed. *Pamphlets of the American Revolution 1750–1776*. Cambridge: Harvard University Press, 1965.

---. *The Ideological Origins of the American Revolution*. Cambridge: Harvard University Press, 1992.

---, ed. *The Debate on the Constitution: Part One*. New York: Literary Classics of the United States, Inc., 1993.

Bailyn, Bernard, and Philip D. Morgan, eds. *Strangers within the Realm: Cultural Margins of the First British Empire*. Chapel Hill: The University of North Carolina Press, 1991.

Beard, Charles. *An Economic Interpretation of the Constitution of the United States*, 1st pub. 1913. New York: Macmillan Company, 1941.

Beeman, Richard. *Plain, Honest Men: The Making of the American Constitution*. New York: Random House, 2009.

Bennett, Walter H. "Twentieth-Century Theories of the Nature of the Union." *The Journal of Politics*, Vol. 8, No. 2 (May 1946), pp. 160–173.

Berkin, Carol. *A Brilliant Solution: Inventing the American Constitution*. New York: Harcourt, Inc., 2002.

Bilder, Mary Sarah. *Madison's Hand: Revising the Constitutional Convention*. Cambridge: Harvard University Press, 2015.

Bowen, Catherine Drinker. *Miracle at Philadelphia: The Story of the Constitutional Convention May to September 1787*. Boston: Little, Brown and Company, 1966.

Brands, H. W. *T.R.: The Last Romantic*. New York: Basic Books, 1997.

Brant, Irving. *The Fourth President: A Life of James Madison*. New York: The Bobbs-Merrill Company, 1970.

Brigham, Clarence S. *History and Bibliography of American Newspapers 1690–1820 Volume Two*. Worcester, MA: American Antiquarian Society, 1947.

Brunhouse, Robert L. *The Counter-Revolution in Pennsylvania: 1776–1790*. 1st ed. 1942. Harrisburg: The Pennsylvania Historical and Museum Commission, 1971.

Bryce, James. *The American Commonwealth*. New York: Macmillan and Co., 1888.

———. "Bryce Praises Wilson." *The Washington Post* (1877–1922), Nov. 26, 1906, pp. 4.

———. "James Wilson: An Appreciation by James Bryce." *Pennsylvania Magazine of History and Biography*, Vol. 60, No. 4 (Oct 1936), pp. 358–61.

Buchan, James. *Crowded with Genius: Edinburgh, 1745–1789*. New York: HarperCollins, 2003.

Bueltmann, Tanja, Andrew Hinson, and Graeme Morton. *The Scottish Diaspora*. Edinburgh: Edinburgh University Press, 2013.

Burns, Eric. *Infamous Scribblers: The Founding Fathers and the Rowdy Beginnings of American Journalism*. New York: PublicAffairs, 2006.

Burton, David H. "Theodore Roosevelt's Harrisburg Speech, A Progressive Appeal to James Wilson." *Pennsylvania Magazine of History and Biography*, Vol. 93, No. 4 (Oct. 1969), pp. 527–42.

Burton Alva Konkle Papers, HSP.

Burton Alva Konkle Papers, SHC.

Butterfield, L. H., ed. *Letters of Benjamin Rush Volume I: 1761–1792*. Princeton: Princeton University Press, 1951.

———. *Letters of Benjamin Rush Volume II: 1793–1813*. Princeton: Princeton University Press, 1951.

Calloway, Colin G. *White People, Indians, and Highlanders: Tribal Peoples and Colonial Encounters in Scotland and America*. New York: Oxford University Press, 2008.

Carson, Hampton L. "The Works of James Wilson." *The American Law Register and Review*, Vol. 44, No. 10, Volume 35 New Series (Oct 1896), pp. 633–41.

———. "Oration." *The American Law Register* (1898–1907), Vol. 55, No. 1, Volume 46 New Series. (Jan 1907), pp. 35–46.

———. "James Wilson and James Iredell: A Parallel and a Contrast." *Pennsylvania Magazine of History and Biography*, Vol. 45, No. 1 (Jan 1921), pp. 1–33.

Cerami, Charles. *Young Patriots: The Remarkable Story of Two Men, Their Impossible Plan, and the Revolution That Created the Constitution*. Naperville, IL: Sourcebooks, Inc., 2005.

Christie, I.R. *Crisis of Empire: Great Britain and the American Colonies 1754–1783*. New York: W.W. Norton & Company, 1966.

Clagett, Martin. "James Wilson—His Scottish Background: Corrections and Additions," *Pennsylvania History: A Journal of Mid-Atlantic Studies,* Vol. 79, No. 2 (Spring 2012), pp. 154–176.

Collier, Christopher, and James Lincoln Collier. *Decision in Philadelphia: The Constitutional Convention of 1787*. New York: Ballantine Books, 2007.

Cook, Frank G. "James Wilson." *Atlantic Monthly* 64, September 1889, pp. 316–330.

Cooke, Jacob E., ed. *The Federalist*. Hanover: Wesleyan University Press, 1961.

Cornell, Saul. *The Other Founders*. Chapel Hill: The University of North Carolina Press, 1999.

Cushman, Robert Eugene. "The National Police Power Under the Commerce Clause of the Constitution," *Minnesota Law Review*, Vol. 3, No. 5 (Apr. 1919), pp. 289–319.

Davidson, Philip. *Propaganda and the American Revolution 1763–1783*. 1st pub. 1941. New York: W.W. Norton & Company, 1973.

Devine, T. M. *Scottish Emigration and Scottish Society*. Edinburgh: John Donald Publishers, LTD, 1992.

Dobson, David. *The Original Scots Colonists of Early America 1612–1783*. Baltimore: Geneaological Publishing Co., Inc., 1989.

Dougherty, Keith, Jac Heckleman, Paul Carlsen, and David Gelman. "A New Dataset of Delegate Positions on All Substantive Roll Calls at the U.S. Constitutional Convention." *Historical Methods*, Vol. 45, No. 3, pp. 135–141.

Ewald, William. "James Wilson and the Drafting of the Constitution." *Journal of Constitutional Law*, Vol. 10, No. 5 (June 2008), pp. 901–1009.

———. "James Wilson and the Scottish Enlightenment," *Journal of Constitutional Law*, Vol. 12, No. 4 (Apr. 2010), pp. 1053–1114.

Farrand, Max. *The Framing of the Constitution of the United States*. New Haven: Yale University Press, 1913.

———, ed. *The Records of the Federal Convention of 1787*. 3 vols. Rev. ed. in 4 vols. New Haven: Yale University Press, 1966.

Finkelman, Paul. "James Madison and the Bill of Rights: A Reluctant Paternity." *The Supreme Court Review*, Vol. 1990. (1990), pp. 301–47.

Fitzpatrick, John C., ed. *The Writings of Washington from the Original Manuscript Sources, 1745–1799*. 39 vols. Washington, D.C.: Govt. Printing Office, 1931–1944.

Ford, Paul Leicester, ed. *The Political Writings of John Dickinson 1764–1774*. 1st pub. 1895. New York: Da Capo Press, 1970.

Gienapp, Jonathan. *The Second Creation: Fixing the American Constitution in the Founding Era*. Cambridge, MA: The Belknap Press of Harvard University Press, 2018.

Good, Cassandra A. *Founding Friendships: Friendships between Men and Women in the Early American Republic*. New York: Oxford University Press, 2015.

Goodman, Dena. *The Republic of Letters: A Cultural History of the French Enlightenment*. Ithaca, NY: Cornell University Press, 1994.

Green, Jack P. *Peripheries and Center: Constitutional Development in the Extended Polities of the British Empire and the United States 1607–1788*. New York: W.W. Norton and Company, 1990.

Hall, Mark David. *The Political and Legal Philosophy of James Wilson, 1742–1798*. Columbia: The University of Missouri Press, 1997.

Harlan, John Marshall. "James Wilson and the Formation of the Constitution," *The American Law Review*, Vol. 34. (Jul–Aug 1900), pp. 481–504.

Himmelfarb, Gertrude. *The Roads to Modernity: The British, French, and American Enlightenments*. New York: Alfred A. Knopf, 2004.

Hoffer, Peter Charles, Williamjames Hull Hoffer, and N. E. H. Hull. *The Supreme Court: An Essential History*. Lawrence, KS: University Press of Kansas, 2007.

———. *The Federal Courts: An Essential History*. New York: Oxford University Press, 2016.

Hogeland, William. *The Whiskey Rebellion*. New York: Scribner, 2006.

HSP. Historical Society of Pennsylvania.

Hutson, James H., ed. *Supplement to Max Farrand's "The Records of the Federal Convention of 1787."* New Haven: Yale University Press, 1987.

Ireland, Owen S. "The People's Triumph: The Federalist Majority in Pennsylvania, 1787–1788." *Pennsylvania History*, Vol. 56, No. 2 (Apr. 1989), pp. 93–113.

———. *Religion, Ethnicity, and Politics: Ratifying the Constitution in Pennsylvania*. University Park, PA: The Pennsylvania State University Press, 1995.

———. "The Invention of American Democracy: The Pennsylvania Federalists and the New Republic." *Pennsylvania History*, Volume 67, Number 1 (Winter 2000), pp. 161–71.

Jensen, Merrill, ed. *Tracts of the American Revolution, 1763–1776*. New York: The Bobbs-Merrill Company, Inc., 1967.

———, ed. *The Documentary History of the Ratification of the Constitution, Vol. II Ratification of the Constitution by the States: Pennsylvania*. Madison: State Historical Society of Wisconsin, 1976.

LOC. Library of Congress.

Logbook, *U.S.S. Dubuque*, November 1906.

Lucien H. Alexander Papers, HSP.

Kamen, Michael. *Digging Up the Dead: A History of Notable American Reburials*. Chicago: University of Chicago Press, 2010.

Kaminski, John P. and Gaspare J. Saladino, ed. *The Documentary History of the Ratification of the Constitution, Vol. XIII Commentaries on the Constitution: Public and Private Vol. 1: 21 February to 7 November 1787*. Madison: State Historical Society of Wisconsin, 1981.

Keasbey, Edward Q. "The Honors Done to James Wilson." *The American Lawyer* (1893–1908), Dec. 1906; Vol. 14, No. 12, pp. 550–54.

Ketcham, Ralph. *James Madison: A Biography*. Charlottesville: University Press of Virginia, 1971.

Klarman, Michael J. *The Framers' Coup: The Making of the United States Constitution*. New York: Oxford University Press, 2016.

Klepp, Susan E. *"The Swift Progress of Population: A Documentary and Bibliographic Study of Philadelphia's Growth, 1642–1859*. Philadelphia: American Philosophical Society, 1991.

Konkle, Burton Alva. *James Wilson and The Constitution*. Philadelphia: Published by Order of the Law Academy, 1907.

———. "The James Wilson Memorial." *The American Law Register* (1898–1907), Vol. 55, No. 1, Volume 46 New Series. (Jan 1907), pp. 1–11.

———. "The Life and Writings of James Wilson, 1742–1798." Unpublished. 4 vols. Miscellaneous Manuscripts Collection, Friends Historical Library of Swarthmore College.

Leffler, Richard, John P. Kaminski, and Samuel K. Fore, eds. *William Pierce on The Constitutional Convention and the Constitution*. Dallas: Harlan Crow Library, 2012.

Letter from George Washington to James Wilson, March 19, 1782, Founders Online, National Archives (http://founders.archives.gov/documents/Washington/99-01-02-08032 [last update: 2015-03-20]). Accessed: 2:18pm, March 23, 2015.

Lindsey, Edward. "Wilson versus the 'Wilson Doctrine.'" *The American Law Review*, Vol. 44 (Sept–Oct 1910), pp. 641–62.

Lipscomb, Terry W., ed. *The Letters of Pierce Butler 1790–1794: National Building and Enterprise in the New American Republic*. Columbia: The University of South Carolina Press, 2007.

Madison, James. *Notes of Debates in the Federal Convention of 1787*. New York: W.W. Norton & Company, 1987.

Maier, Pauline. *Ratification: The People Debate the Constitution, 1787–1788*. New York: Simon and Schuster, 2010.

Main, Jackson Turner. *The Anti-Federalists: Critics of the Constitution, 1781–1788*. Chapel Hill: University of North Carolina Press, 1961.

Marcus, Maeva, James R. Perry, et al., eds. *The Documentary History of the Supreme Court of the United States, 1789–1800 Volume One, Part One: Appointments and Proceedings*. New York: Columbia University Press, 1985.

———, eds. *The Documentary History of the Supreme Court of the United States, 1789–1800 Volume One, Part Two: Commentaries on Appointments and Proceedings*. New York: Columbia University Press, 1985.

———, eds. *The Documentary History of the Supreme Court of the United States, 1789–1800 Volume Two: The Justices on Circuit 1790–1794*. New York: Columbia University Press, 1988.

———, eds. *The Documentary History of the Supreme Court of the United States, 1789–1800 Volume Three: The Justices on Circuit 1795–1800*. New York: Columbia University Press, 1990.

Mason, George. *The Papers of George Mason: 1725–1792 Volume III: 1787–1792*. Ed. Robert A. Rutland. Chapel Hill: The University of North Carolina Press, 1970.

Maxey, David W. "The Translation of James Wilson," in *Supreme Court Historical Society 1990 Yearbook*. Washington, D.C.: Supreme Court Historical Society, 1990, pp. 29–43.

McAlister, Sandie, "No. 5, The Supreme Court." *The Labor World* (Duluth, MN), Nov. 28, 1906, p. 2.

McDonald, Forrest. *We the People: The Economic Origins of the Constitution*. Chicago: University of Chicago Press, 1958.

McGerr, Michael. *A Fierce Discontent: The Rise and Fall of the Progressive Movement in America, 1870–1920*. New York: Free Press, 2003.

McLaughlin, Andrew C. *James Wilson in the Philadelphia Convention*. Boston: Ginn & Co., 1897.

McLean, Iain. "Adam Smith, James Wilson, and the US Constitution," in *The Adam Smith Review*, Vol. 8. London: Routledge, 2014.

McMaster, John B., and Frederick D. Stone., eds. *Pennsylvania and the Federal Constitution, 1787–1788*. 2 vols. 1888. Reprint in 1 vol. Indianapolis: Liberty Fund, 2011.

McRee, Griffith J. *Life and Correspondence of James Iredell, One of the Associate Justices of the Supreme Court of the United States*. 1st pub. 1857. New York: Peter Smith, 1949.

Merrell, James H. *Into the American Woods: Negotiators on the Pennsylvania Frontier*. New York: W. W. Norton & Company, 1999.

Miller, William Lee. *The Business of May Next: James Madison & the Founding*. Charlottesville: University Press of Virginia, 1992.

Minutes of The St. Andrew's Society of Philadelphia for 1767 and 1906.

Montgomery, Morton L. *History of Reading, Pennsylvania and the Anniversary Proceedings of the Sesqui-Centennial June 5–12, 1898*. Reading, PA: Times Book Print, 1898.

Morgan, Edmund S, and Helen M. Morgan. *The Stamp Act Crisis: Prologue to Revolution*. 1st ed. 1953. Chapel Hill: The University of North Carolina Press, 1995.

Morgan, Edmund S., ed. *Prologue to Revolution: Sources and Documents on the Stamp Act Crisis, 1764–1766*. Chapel Hill: The University of North Carolina Press, 1959.

Nash, Gary B. *First City: Philadelphia and the Forging of Historical Memory*. Philadelphia: University of Pennsylvania Press, 2002.

Nelson, Eric. *The Royalist Revolution: Monarchy and the American Founding*. Cambridge, MA: The Belknap Press of Harvard University Press, 2014.

Ousterhout, Anne M. *The Most Learned Woman in America: A Life of Elizabeth Graeme Fergusson*. University Park, PA: The Pennsylvania State University Press, 2004.

Padover, Saul K., ed. *To Secure These Blessings: The Great Debates of the Constitutional Convention of 1787, Arranged According to Topics*. New York: Washington Square Press/Ridge Press, 1962.

Pennsylvania History Club. *Publications of the Pennsylvania History Club. Vol. I.: A Contribution of Pennsylvania Historical Bibliography*. Philadelphia: Pennsylvania History Club, 1909.
Pennypacker, Samuel W., et al. "Tributes Delivered at the Memorial Services." *The American Law Register* (1898–1907), Vol. 55, No. 1, Volume 46 New Series. (Jan 1907), pp. 12–34.
Purvis, Thomas L. *Almanacs of American Life: Revolutionary America 1763 to 1800*. New York: Facts on File, Inc., 1995.
Rakove, Jack N. *Original Meanings: Politics and Ideas in the Making of the Constitution*. New York: Alfred A. Knopf, 1996.
———, ed. *Madison: Writings*. New York: Library of America, 1999.
Rappaport, George David. *Stability and Change in Revolutionary Pennsylvania: Banking, Politics, and Social Structure*. University Park: The Pennsylvania State University Press, 1996.
Read, James H. *Power versus Liberty: Madison, Hamilton, Wilson, and Jefferson*. Charlottesville: University Press of Virginia, 2000.
Ridner, Judith. *A Town In-Between: Carlisle, Pennsylvania, and the Early Mid-Atlantic Interior*. Philadelphia: University of Pennsylvania Press, 2010.
Riker, William H. *The Strategy of Rhetoric: Campaigning for the American Constitution*. New Haven: Yale University Press, 1996.
Rodell, Fred. *Fifty-Five Men*. 1st Pub. 1936. Birmingham, AL: Palladium Press, 2005.
Roosevelt, Theodore. "Address of President Roosevelt at the Dedication Ceremonies of the new State Capitol Building at Harrisburg, Pennsylvania, October 4, 1906." Washington, D.C.: Government Printing Office, 1906.
———. "Sixth Annual Message to Congress." December 3, 1906. Online by Gerhard Peters and John T. Wooley. *The American Presidency Project*. http://www.presidency.ucsb.edu/ws/?pid=29547. Accessed 1:45pm, March 8, 2016.
———. "Special Message." December 18, 1906. Online by Gerhard Peters and John T. Wooley. *The American Presidency Project*. http://www.presidency. ucsb.edu/ws/?pid=69683. Accessed 10:09pm, March 12, 2016.
Rosenberg, Morton M. "In Search of James Wilson." *Pennsylvania History*, 55 (Jul. 1988), pp. 107–17.
Rossiter, Clinton. *1787: The Grand Convention*. New York: The Macmillan Company, 1966.
Rothschild, Emma. *The Inner Life of Empires: An Eighteenth-Century History*. Princeton: Princeton University Press, 2011.
Rush, Benjamin. "Account of the Life and Character of Mrs. Elizabeth Ferguson." *Port Folio*, 3rd series, 1 (1809), pp. 520-7.
Rutland, Robert Allen. *The Birth of the Bill of Rights, 1776–1791*. Chapel Hill: University of North Carolina Press, 1955.
——— and Charles F. Hobson, eds. *The Papers of James Madison: Volume 10: 27 May 1787–3 March 1788*. Chicago: The University of Chicago Press, 1977.

St. Andrew's Society of Philadelphia. *An Historical Catalogue of The St. Andrew's Society of Philadelphia: With Biographical Sketches of Deceased Members 1749–1907.* Philadelphia: Printed for the Society, 1907.

Seed, Geoffrey. *James Wilson.* Millwood, NY: KTO Press, 1978.

Selsam, J. Paul. *Pennsylvania Constitution of 1776: A Study in Revolutionary Democracy.* 1st Ed., Philadelphia: University of Pennsylvania Press, 1936, New Ed., New York: Octagon Books, 1971.

Shalev, Eran. "Ancient Masks, American Fathers: Classical Pseudonyms during the American Revolution and Early Republic." *Journal of the Early Republic*, Vol. 23, No. 2 (Summer, 2003), pp. 151–72.

SHC. Southern Historical Collection, The Wilson Library, University of North Carolina at Chapel Hill.

Sheehan, Colleen A. and Gary L. McDowell. *Friends of the Constitution: Writings of the "Other" Federalists 1787–88.* Indianapolis: Liberty Fund, 1988.

Sherow, James E. "The Contest for the 'Nile of America': Kansas V. Colorado (1907)" (1990). *Great Plains Quarterly*, Paper 504, http://digitalcommons.unl.edu/greatplainsquarterly/504. Accessed 1:00pm, May 15, 2016.

Sidbury, James, and Jorge Cañizares-Esguerra. "Mapping Ethnogenesis in the Early Modern Atlantic." *The William and Mary Quarterly,* Vol. 68, No. 2 (April 1, 2011), pp. 181–208.

Sikes, Lewright B. *The Public Life of Pierce Butler*. Washington, D.C.: University Press of America, 1979.

Slaughter, Thomas P. *The Whiskey Rebellion*. New York: Oxford University Press, 1986.

Smith, Page. *James Wilson: Founding Father, 1742–1798*. Chapel Hill: University of North Carolina Press, 1956.

Stewart, David O. *The Summer of 1787: The Men Who Invented the Constitution.* New York: Simon & Schuster, 2007.

———. *Madison's Gift: Five Partnerships That Built America*. New York: Simon & Schuster, 2015.

Storing, Herbert J., ed. *The Complete Anti-Federalist,* 6 vols. Chicago: The University of Chicago Press, 1981.

———. "The 'Other' Federalist Papers: A Preliminary Sketch," in *Friends of the Constitution: Writings of the "Other" Federalists 1787–88*, Eds. Colleen A. Sheehan and Gary L. McDowell. (Indianapolis: Liberty Fund, 1988), pp. xxi-l.

Sutherland, George. *Constitutional Power and World Affairs*. 1st pub. 1919. New York: Johnson Reprint Corporation, 1970.

Taylor, Alan. *William Cooper's Town: Power and Persuasion on the Frontier of the Early American Republic*. New York: A.A. Knopf, 1995.

Taylor, Michael H., and Kevin Hardwick. "The Presidency of James Wilson." *White House Studies,* Vol. 9, No. 4 (Winter 2010), pp. 331–46.

Theodore Roosevelt Papers, LOC.

Tolley, Michael C. "Willoughby, Westel Woodbury." *American National Biography Online*, Feb. 2000, http://www.anb.org/articles/14/14-00708.html. Accessed 4:29pm, March 14, 2015.

Treasurer's Book of The St. Andrew's Society of Philadelphia for 1906.
Untitled. *Boston Gazette*, 23 September 1793. NewsBank/Readex, *America's Historical Newspapers*. Accessed 12:15pm, June 15, 2016.
U.S. Army Center of Military History. *Pierce Butler*. Washington, D.C.: U.S. Army Center of Military History, 1986.
Van Doren, Carol. *The Great Rehearsal*. New York: The Viking Press, 1948.
Vile, John R. *The Constitutional Convention of 1787: A Comprehensive Encyclopedia of America's Founding*. 2 vols. Santa Barbara: ABC-CLIO, 2005.
———. *The Writing and Ratification of the U.S. Constitution*. New York: Rowman & Littlefield Publishers, Inc., 2012.
———. *The Men Who Made the Constitution: Lives of the Delegates to the Constitutional Convention*. Lanham, MD: The Scarecrow Press, Inc., 2013.
Warner, Jessica. *John the Painter: Terrorist of the American Revolution*. London: Profile Books, 2004.
Warren, Charles. *The Making of the Constitution*. Boston: Little, Brown, and Company, 1928.
Wexler, Natalie. *A More Obedient Wife: A Novel of the Early Supreme Court*. Washington, D.C.: Kalorama Press, 2007.
Wharton, Anne Hollingsworth. *Salons Colonial and Republican*. 1st pub. 1900. New York: Benjamin Blom, Inc., 1971.
Whichard, Willis P. *Justice James Iredell*. Durham: Carolina Academic Press, 2000.
White, William. "The Visitant - No. II" *Pennsylvania Chronicle*. 8 February 1768.
———. "The Visitant - No. IV" *Pennsylvania Chronicle*. 22 February 1768.
———. "The Visitant - No. VI" *Pennsylvania Chronicle*. 7 March 1768.
———. "The Visitant - No. VIII" *Pennsylvania Chronicle*. 21 March 1768.
———. "The Visitant - No. X" *Pennsylvania Chronicle*. 4 April 1768.
———. "The Visitant - No. XII" *Pennsylvania Chronicle*. 18 April 1768.
———. "The Visitant - No. XVI" *Pennsylvania Chronicle*. 16 May 1768.
William Moody Papers, LOC.
Willoughby, Westel Woodbury. *The Constitutional Law of the United States*. New York: Baker, Voorhis & Company, 1910.
Wills, Helen DeBerniere H. "Grave of a Signer Unmarked." *The Washington Post* (1877–1954), Mar. 7, 1904, pp. 9.
Wilson, Bird. *Memoir of the Life of the Right Reverend William White, D.D., Bishop of the Protestant Episcopal Church in the State of Pennsylvania*. Philadelphia: James Kay, Jun. & Brother, 1839.
Wilson, James. "The Visitant - No. I" *Pennsylvania Chronicle*. 1 February 1768.
———. "The Visitant - No. III" *Pennsylvania Chronicle*. 15 February 1768.
———. "The Visitant - No. V" *Pennsylvania Chronicle*. 29 February 1768.
———. "The Visitant - No. VII" *Pennsylvania Chronicle*. 14 March 1768.
———. "The Visitant - No. IX" *Pennsylvania Chronicle*. 28 March 1768.
———. "The Visitant - No. XI" *Pennsylvania Chronicle*. 11 April 1768.
———. "The Visitant - No. XIII" *Pennsylvania Chronicle*. 25 April 1768.
———. "The Visitant - No. XIV" *Pennsylvania Chronicle*. 2 May 1768.
———. "The Visitant - No. XV" *Pennsylvania Chronicle*. 9 May 1768.

———. *The Works of the Honourable James Wilson, L.L.D.* Ed. Bird Wilson. 2 vols. Philadelphia: Lorenzo Press, 1804.

———. "On the Improvements and Settlement of Lands in the United States." A Research Bulletin of The Free Library of Philadelphia, 1946.

———. *The Works of James Wilson.* Ed. Robert G. McCloskey. 2 vols. Cambridge: Harvard University Press, 1967.

———. *Collected Works of James Wilson.* Eds. Kermit L. Hall and Mark David Hall. 2 vols. Indianapolis: Liberty Fund, 2007.

———. "Considerations on the Bank of North America" in *Collected Works of James Wilson, Vol. 1.* Eds. Kermit L. Hall and Mark David Hall. 2 vols. Indianapolis: Liberty Fund, 2007, pp. 60–79.

———. "Considerations on the Nature and Extent of the Legislative Authority of the British Parliament" in *Collected Works of James Wilson, Vol. 1.* Eds. Kermit L. Hall and Mark David Hall. 2 vols. Indianapolis: Liberty Fund, 2007, pp. 3–31.

———. "James Wilson's State House Yard Speech" in *Collected Works of James Wilson, Vol. 1.* Eds. Kermit L. Hall and Mark David Hall. 2 vols. Indianapolis: Liberty Fund, 2007, pp. 171–177.

———. "Speech Delivered in the Convention for the Province of Pennsylvania, Held at Philadelphia, in January 1775," in *Collected Works of James Wilson, Vol. 1.* Eds. Kermit L. Hall and Mark David Hall. 2 vols. Indianapolis: Liberty Fund, 2007, pp. 32–45.

Wood, Gordon, ed. *The American Revolution: Writings from the Pamphlet Debate 1764–1772.* New York: Library of America, 2015.

———. *The American Revolution: Writings from the Pamphlet Debate 1773–1776.* New York: Library of America, 2015.

Zehmer, John G Jr. *Hayes: The Plantation, Its People, and Their Papers.* Raleigh: North Carolina Office of Archives and History, 2007.

Zimmerman, John J. "Benjamin Franklin and the Pennsylvania Chronicle," *The Pennsylvania Magazine of History and Biography*, Vol. 81, No. 4 (Oct 1957), pp. 351–364.

Index

1776, xi

A
Adams, John Quincy:
  mocks James Wilson and Hannah Gray's relationship, 197–198
Albuquerque Evening Citizen:
  editorials on Wilson Doctrine, 229–230
Alexander, Lucien H., 5, 7, 13
  first letter to Theodore Roosevelt, 10
  invitation to Andrew Carnegie, 14
  "James Wilson and the Wilson Doctrine," 12, 219–221
  memorial draft, 8
  publicity, 8
  second letter to Theodore Roosevelt, 13
  Washington meeting with Roosevelt and Moody, 11
Annan, Robert, 36, 37, 45
Anti-Federalist publications before *State House Yard Speech*, 136
An Address of the Subscribers Members of the late House of Representatives of the Commonwealth of Pennsylvania to their Constituents, 132, 137, 139, 140, 142–143, 145

"Centinel I," 137–143, 145
  Objections to this Constitution of Government, 138, 140, 142–143
Aspasia, 58, 63, 64

B
Bailyn, Bernard:
  places Wilson's *State House Yard Speech* in context, 135–136
Bland, Richard:
  An Inquiry into the Rights of the British Colonies, 79–80
Boyd, Peter:
  President of the St. Andrew's Society of Philadelphia, 7
Bryce, James, 12
  invitation to participate in memorial, 14
Butler, Pierce, xiv
  brief biography, 102
  delegate to Constitutional Convention—compensation of senators, 113
  delegate to Constitutional Convention—does not support absolute executive veto, 106
  delegate to Constitutional Convention—support of a unitary executive, 106

260 Index

delegate to Constitutional Convention—view on representation in House of Representatives, 112
delegate to Constitutional Convention—view on residency requirement for senators, 119
delegate to Constitutional Convention—view on Electoral College, 108
delegate to Constitutional Convention—view on legislative branch, 110
delegate to Constitutional Convention—view on the executive, 108

C

Carlisle Gazette:
"A Citizen," 162–163
Carnegie, Andrew, 5, 15
James Wilson Memorial speech, 25
request to participate in memorial from Alexander, 14
Carskerdo:
Wilson birthplace, 36
Carson, Hampton L., 6
James Wilson Memorial speech, 26–27
Christ Church, Philadelphia:
permission for reburial, 9
College of Philadelphia:
Wilson hired as a Latin tutor, 39
Considerations on the Nature and Extent of the Legislative Authority of the British Parliament, 14, 85–88
publication delay, 1768, 88–89
published, 1774, 91
Constitutional Convention of 1787, 1
debate on citizenship, 119–121
debate on executive branch, 103–110
debate on legislative branch, 110–119
delegates, Table 5.1, 98
delegates born outside of the United States, Table 5.2, 100

D

Dickinson, John, 11, 15
delegate to Constitutional Convention—removal of executive by states, 105
delegate to Constitutional Convention— view on congressional qualifications, 118
delegate to Constitutional Convention— view on election of senators, 111
delegate to Constitutional Convention— view on legislative branch, 110
delegate to Constitutional Convention— view on representation in House of Representatives, 113
delegate to Constitutional Convention— view on the executive, 108
The Late Regulations Respecting the British Colonies on the Continent of American Considered, in a letter from a gentleman in Philadelphia to his friend in London, 76
"Letter I," 81
"Letter II," 81
"Letter III," 82
"Letter IV," 83
"Letter VII," 83, 86
"Letter XII," 84
Letters from a Farmer in Pennsylvania to the Inhabitants of the British Colonies, 50, 80
Wilson law teacher, 17, 39
Dickson, Samuel, 5, 7
James Wilson Memorial speech, 23–24
Duché, Rev. Jacob:
sponsors William White, 47
Dulany, Daniel:
Considerations on the Propriety of Imposing Taxes in the British Colonies, For the Purpose of Raising

Index 261

a Revenue, by Act of Parliament, 75–76

F
Farrand, Max, xiii
Franklin, Benjamin, 2, 117, 119, 129–130
Freeman's Journal:
  "Centinel II," 153, 163–171

G
Gerry, Elbridge, 1
Graeme, Elizabeth, 63–64
  Philadelphia salon, 63
  travels to Great Britain, 63
Gray, Hannah
  meets James Wilson, first husband, 197

H
Hamilton, Alexander, 1, 14
  brief biography, 102
  Confederation Congress, 101
  delegate to Constitutional Convention— absolute veto by executive, 106
  delegate to Constitutional Convention— congressional compensation, 115
  delegate to Constitutional Convention— proposed constitution, 106
  delegate to Constitutional Convention— view on holding state and national office, 116
  delegate to Constitutional Convention— view on residency qualification for Representatives, 120
Historical Society of Pennsylvania:
  James Wilson Memorial reception, 27
Hopkins, Stephen:
  The Rights of Colonies Examined, 74–75
Howard, Martin, Jr.:

A Letter from a Gentleman at Halifax to his Friend in Rhode Island, 75

I
Independent Gazetteer:
  "An Officer of the Late Continental Army," 153, 175
  "An Old Whig II," 153, 160–1
  "An Old Whig III," 153, 161–162
  "Centinel I," 136–143, 145
Iredell, James:
  does not seek to be SCOTUS Chief Justice, 1796, 206
  Eastern Circuit, 1792, 193
  grave, 2
  joins SCOTUS, 189
  Middle Circuit, 1791, 192
  officially notifies Adams Administration of Wilson's death, 1798, 207
  requests rotation in circuit riding, 192

J
James Wilson Memorial, 5
  Christ Church activities, 23
  disinterment in Edenton, NC, 20
  draft of activites, 9
  first act, 8
  procession to Christ Church, 22
  procession to Independence Hall, 22
  schedule of events, 19
  Wilson lies in state in Independence Hall, 22
Jefferson, Thomas:
  letter to James Madison on Wilson's *State House Yard Speech*, 171–172

K
Kansas v. Colorado:
  editorial on Wilson Doctrine, 232
  Wilson Doctrine in SCOTUS, 231
Knox, Philander C., 6
  memorial request, 10
  Roosevelt Harrisburg Speech, 15
Konkle, Burton Alva, 13, 5

"James Wilson and the
    Constitution," 11
James Wilson biography, 12
portraits of Wilson and Iredell for new
    SCOTUS building, 236
secretary of the James Wilson
    Memorial, 6
Washington meeting with Roosevelt
    and Moody, 11
Wilson research sent to Moody, 12

L
Lewis, William Draper, 4, 7
James Wilson Memorial speech, 24

M
Madison, James, 1
    Confederation Congress—working
        with James Wilson, 101
    delegate to Constitutional
        Convention—joins Wilson to oppose
        a compromise committee on the
        issue of representation, 117
    delegate to Constitutional
        Convention—view on election of
        Executive, 105
    delegate to Constitutional
        Convention—view on residency
        qualification for Representatives, 120
    delegate to Constitutional
        Convention—view on Senate
        approval for treaties, 109
    delegate to Constitutional
        Convention—working with James
        Wilson, 103
Maryland Gazette:
    "A Democratic Federalist," 156
Mason, George, 1
    delegate to Constitutional
        Convention—age qualifications for
        congress, 115
    delegate to Constitutional
        Convention—view on residency
        qualifications for office, 119

evolving view on the Senate, 142
    *Objections to this Constitution of
        Government*, 138, 140, 142–143
Mitchell, S. Weir, 3, 7
    James Wilson Memorial speech,
        24–25
Moody, William H., 5
    James Wilson Memorial speech,
        25–26
    Washington meeting with Alexander
        and Konkle, 11
    Wilson research received from
        Alexander, 12
Morris, Gouverneur, 2
    delegate to Constitutional
        Convention—view on residency
        requirement for senators, 119

N
National Constitution Center, 1
    Signers' Hall, 1
New York Daily Tribune:
    negative editorial on use of Wilson
        Doctrine, 225
New York Journal:
    "Cincinnatus I," 153
    "Cincinnatus V," 153
North American Review:
    "James Wilson and the Wilson
        Doctrine," 12, 219–221

O
Omaha Daily Bee:
    negative editorial on James Wilson
        Memorial, 221–222
Otis, James, Jr.:
    *The Rights of the British Colonies
        Asserted and Proved*, 72–74

P
Parker, Alton B.:
    James Wilson Memorial speech, 25
Pennsylvania Assembly:

An Address of the Subscribers Members of the late House of Representatives of the Commonwealth of Pennsylvania to their Constituents, 132, 137, 139, 140, 142–143, 145
creation of ratification convention, 131
Federalist response to the Pennsylvania Assembly *Address*, 133
opposition to Constitution, 132
Pennsylvania Chronicle, 14
Dickinson's *Letters from a Farmer* series, 80
publishing *The Visitant*, 48
Pennsylvania Gazette:
"1776 vs. 1787," 97
"A Receipt for an Anti-Federalist Essay," 154
Pennsylvania Herald:
"A Democratic Federalist," 153, 156–160
"An Overheard Conversation," 129–130
first publication of Wilson's *State House Yard Speech*, 173
publishes special edition of Wilson's *State House Yard Speech*, 134
Pennsylvania History Club, 5, 6
James Wilson Memorial members, 27
Pennsylvania Packet:
Federalist response to the Pennsylvania Assembly *Address*, 133
Pro-Wilson *State House Yard Speech* article, 155–156
Pennypacker, Samuel W., 6
James Wilson Memorial master of ceremonies, 23
Roosevelt Harrisburg Speech, 15
Penrose, Boies, 6
Roosevelt Harrisburg Speech, 15
Peters, Dr. Richard:
escorts Elizabeth Graeme, 63
sponsors William White, 47
Pinckney, Charles Cotesworth, 15

delegate to Constitutional Convention—view on holding state and federal office, 116
delegate to Constitutional Convention—view on length of senator term, 116
delegate to Constitutional Convention—view on legislative branch, 111
delegate to Constitutional Convention—view on senator compensation, 117

R
Randolph, Edmund, 1, 99
delegate to Constitutional Convention—introduces Virginia Plan, 103
delegate to Constitutional Convention—proposed three-person executive, 104
delegate to Constitutional Convention—residency requirement for office, 119
Reading, PA:
Wilson moves there in 1767, 71
Rodney, Caesar, xi
Roosevelt, Theodore, 5, 15
response to Alexander letter, 10
response to second letter from Alexander, 13
Roosevelt Harrisburg Speech, 13, 15–18
third letter to Alexander, 13
Washington meeting with Alexander and Konkle, 11
Rossiter, Clinton, xiii
Rutledge, John, 15
delegate to Constitutional Convention—compensation of senators, 113
delegate to Constitutional Convention—executive elected by Congress, 107

delegate to Constitutional Convention—executive elected by Senate, 105
delegate to Constitutional Convention—unitary executive, 104
delegate to Constitutional Convention—view on Electoral College, 109
delegate to Constitutional Convention—view on representation in House of Representatives, 112
delegate to Constitutional Convention—view on residency qualifications for office, 119

S
SCOTUS justices riding circuit
  circuits, composition, 189
Second Continental Congress, xi, 3–4, 91–92
Sherman, Roger
  delegate to Constitutional Convention—compromise on representation, 112–113
  delegate to Constitutional Convention—moves election of Executive from Senate to House in Electoral College, 109
  delegate to Constitutional Convention—view on election of Executive, 115
  delegate to Constitutional Convention—view on multiple office holding, 116
Shiras, George, Jr., 7
St. Andrew's Society of Philadelphia, 2
  new casket for Wilson, 14
  participation in memorial activities, 18
  Wilson joins the Philadelphia chapter, 40
State House Yard Speech, 15, 134–147
  publication history, 173
State House Yard Speech Responses, Anti-Federalist
  "A Democratic Federalist," 156–160

"An Officer of the Late Continental Army," 175
"An Officer of the Late Continental Army," reprints, 175
"An Old Whig II," 160–161
"An Old Whig III," 161–162
"Centinel II," 163–171
"Centinel's" identity, 173–174
impact of "Centinel" series, 173–174
publication phases, 173, 175–176
Thomas Jefferson letter to James Madison, 171–172
State House Yard Speech Responses, Federalist
"A Citizen," 162–163
"A Citizen of Pennsylvania," 155–156

T
The Minneapolis Journal:
  editorial on Wilson Doctrine, 229
The New York Sun:
  editorial on Wilson Doctrine in SCOTUS, 232
The Philadelphia Inquirer:
  coverage of Roosevelt Harrisburg Speech, 15
The State:
  negative editorial on James Wilson Memorial, 222
"The Visitant," 14
  begins publication, 48
  No. I, 49
  No. II, 52
  No. III, 53
  No. IX, 57
  No. VII, the virtual salon begins, 56
  No. XII, 60
  No. XVI, 62
  publication history, Table 3.1, 51
  speculation on authorship, 50
  why a pseudonym?, 48
The Washington Post:
  editorial in support of James Wilson Memorial, 11

U

U.S.S. *Dubuque*, 2
  arrival in Philadelphia, 22
  departure for Philadelphia, 21
  leaves for Edenton, NC, 19
University of St. Andrews:
  Wilson's college education begins, 36

V

virtual salon, 14
  American adapation, 51

W

Washington, Bushrod:
  recess appointment to SCOTUS by John Adams, 1798, 208
Washington, George, 1
  letter to James Wilson, on appointment as SCOTUS chief justice, 188
  secures James Wilson to train Bushrod Washington as a lawyer, 1782, 208
White, Justice Edward D.:
  James Wilson memorial speech, 25
White, William, 14
  background, 47–48
  Wilson and White become friends, 46
Willoughby, Westel W.:
  Wilson-Roosevelt Doctrine, 235
Wilson, James:
  Anti-Federalist Responses to *State House Yard Speech*, 153
  Anti-Federalist Responses to *State House Yard Speech*, Table 7.1, 154
  business prospectus for European immigrants, 199–204
  Confederation Congress, 92, 101
  Considerations on the Nature and Extent of the Legislative Authority of the British Parliament, 14, 85–88
  Considerations publication delay, 88
  Considerations published, 1774, 91
  continues flight from debtors to Edenton, NC, 1797, 206
  delegate to Constitutional Convention— age qualifications for congress, 115
  delegate to Constitutional Convention— congressional compensation, 115
  delegate to Constitutional Convention— direct election of executive, 105
  delegate to Constitutional Convention— Electoral College, 105
  delegate to Constitutional Convention—unitary executive, 104
  delegate to Constitutional Convention— view of election of senators, 111
  delegate to Constitutional Convention— view on congressional qualifications, 118
  delegate to Constitutional Convention— view on election of House of Representatives, 115, 117
  delegate to Constitutional Convention— view on election of senators, 116
  delegate to Constitutional Convention— view on Electoral College, 109
  delegate to Constitutional Convention— view on holding state and national office, 116
  delegate to Constitutional Convention— view on legisaltive branch, 110, 111, 114
  delegate to Constitutional Convention— view on length of senator term, 116
  delegate to Constitutional Convention— view on residency qualification for congress, 119–120
  delegate to Constitutional Convention— view on residency qualification for Representatives, 120
  departs Scotland for America, 1765, 37

Dickinson sponsors admission to practice before PA Supreme Court, 90
dies in Edenton, NC, 1798, 207
Eastern Circuit, 1792, 193
elected to Provincial Convention, 1774 and 1775, 91
first charge to a grand jury, circulation, 190
flees debtors, jailed in New Jersey, 1796, 206
grave, 2
Hannah Gray, second wife, 197–198
how representative of fellow Scottish immigrants, 38
letter to George Washington, SCOTUS Chief Justice nomination, 187
Middle Circuit, 1791, 192
passed over for SCOTUS Chief Justice, 1796, 205
practicing law in Reading, 90
Rachel Bird, first wife, 90
Second Continental Congress, 91
serves as president of The St. Andrew's Society of Philadelphia, 41
State House Yard Speech, 134–147
State House Yard Speech, publication history, 173
State House Yard Speech, reprints, 134
Wilson, Rachel:
Wilson's mother's letters, 40
Wilson/Roosevelt Doctrine of Construction, 15
appearance in textbooks, 235
Roosevelt Harrisburg Speech, 18

About the Author

Michael H. Taylor, Ph.D. earned his doctorate at the University of Georgia. Prior to this he was a social studies teacher at Turner Ashby High School in Bridgewater, Virginia. He then served as a staff member at the Center for the Constitution at James Madison's Montpelier in Orange, Virginia. His first encounter with James Wilson came through a research assignment for a presentation at the Center for the Constitution, which turned into his master's thesis at James Madison University. He currently teaches at Kennesaw State University in Kennesaw, Georgia. He is working on a new book examining the role of James Wilson at the Pennsylvania Ratification Convention of 1787.

www.ingramcontent.com/pod-product-compliance
Lightning Source LLC
Chambersburg PA
CBHW020112010526
44115CB00008B/793